THE STARR REPORT

THE STARR REPORT

THE FINDINGS OF
INDEPENDENT COUNSEL
KENNETH W. STARR
ON PRESIDENT CLINTON
AND THE LEWINSKY AFFAIR

WITH ANALYSIS BY THE STAFF OF

The Washington Post

PUBLICAFFAIRS
New York

This edition of *The Starr Report* is based on the Referral to
the United States House of Representatives pursuant to
Title 28, United States Code, § 595 (c) released by the U.S.
Congress on September 11, 1998.
The independent counsel neither authorized nor approved
its publication. Any errors it may contain
will be corrected in future editions.

Analysis copyright © *The Washington Post*.

Published by PublicAffairs™,
a member of the Perseus Books Group.

For information, address PublicAffairs,
250 West 57th Street, Suite 1825, New York, NY 10107.

ISBN: 1–891620–24–x

Contents

ANALYSIS

Starr Alleges 'Abundant' Lies; President Denies Impeachability

By Peter Baker and Susan Schmidt

President Clinton betrayed his "constitutional duty to faithfully execute the laws" by engaging in a pattern of "abundant and calculating" lies regarding his relationship with Monica S. Lewinsky, prosecutors charged in an impeachment report overflowing with graphic accounts of sexual escapades in the Oval Office suite.

The extraordinary 453-page document prepared by independent counsel Kenneth W. Starr and made public by the House of Representatives accused Clinton of becoming sexually involved with "a young subordinate employee" and then orchestrating a cover-up campaign using aides, friends and the resources of the White House. In all, it listed 11 possible grounds for impeachment, including perjury, witness tampering, obstruction of justice and abuse of power.

"In view of the enormous trust and responsibility attendant to his high Office, the President has a manifest duty to ensure that his conduct at all times complies with the law of the land, " Starr wrote in the report. Perjury and obstruction "are profoundly serious matters. When such acts are committed by the President of the United States, we believe those acts 'may constitute grounds for an impeachment. ' "

Clinton has admitted publicly that he carried on an inappropriate relationship with Lewinsky and "misled people, including even my wife, " but he has adamantly denied committing any illegal acts. While making no comment on the devastating report cataloguing his activities on Friday, September 11, Clinton at a prayer breakfast issued a new and more emotional public apology for his dalliances, saying "I have sinned" and vowing to repent.

Although he agreed that "legal language must not obscure the fact that I have done wrong," Clinton said he had ordered his lawyers to mount a "vigorous defense" and they quickly did just that. Hours before the Starr report was even released, Clinton's lawyers attacked it as an illegitimate excavation of the president's personal life that has nothing to do with his performance in office.

"This private mistake does not amount to an impeachable action," they wrote in a 78-page rebuttal report. In the end, the lawyers wrote, the independent counsel chose to highlight salacious sexual material because he had no genuine case of legal wrongdoing by Clinton. The Starr report, they said, "is left with nothing but the details of a private sexual relationship told in graphic details with the intent to embarrass."

Culminating an eight-month national spectacle that has held Washington up to ridicule on the world stage, Starr's findings were made public following an emotional debate on the House floor about the propriety of releasing a document that none of its members, let alone Clinton or his lawyers, had even read. Within minutes after it was posted on the Internet, millions of Americans jammed Web sites where it was posted, along with lawmakers and presidential aides who found themselves stunned by the breathtaking amount of detail included about Clinton's sexual adventures with Lewinsky.

Never before in American history has a legal document of this sort made its way into public view and never before have a president's sexual habits been so thoroughly exposed to scrutiny. Even the Paula Jones sexual harassment lawsuit, which spawned the Lewinsky investigation, never yielded court papers with this level of crude and unvarnished detail.

With the voluminous document just being absorbed by the members of Congress who ultimately have to determine whether the alleged offenses amount to the "high crimes and misdemeanors" required for impeachment by the Constitution, lawmakers said their initial impression was that the report amounts to a further damage blow to a president whose public standing has already been severely damaged.

The Starr report depicted a president who engaged in sex acts in the Oval Office suite even as aides or Secret Service guards stood just outside the door and sometimes came close to catching him. All told, it recounted 10 sexual encounters between Clinton and Lewinsky, all in the White House.

On one occasion, it said, they got together on Easter Sunday, at a time that news accounts show he had just returned from church services with Hillary Rodham Clinton. On other occasions, it said, Lewinsky performed oral sex on him while he simultaneously conducted telephone conversationsóonce with a political adviser and three other times with different members of Congress. While they never had intercourse, it said, he once used a cigar to sexually satisfy her. Even after they broke up, it said, he stole a quick kiss before rushing off to a state dinner for visiting Mexican President Ernesto Zedillo.

"What in the heck are we doing, making this kind of near-pornographic material available on the Internet with the imprimatur of the U.S. Congress?" Rep. James P. Moran Jr. (D-Va.), who voted against disclosure, said after reviewing the report.

Starr said he had no choice but to include the blunt descriptions of sexual acts because Clinton, even while acknowledging a physical relationship during his grand jury testimony last month, continued to deny that he had "sexual relations" with Lewinsky as defined during his deposition in the Jones case.

Republican leaders signaled that they would resist attempts by the White House to characterize the case as merely an intrusion into private affairs.

"Some will try to make this just a purely sexual matter," said Senate Judiciary Committee Chairman Orrin G. Hatch (R-Utah). "But I don't see anything that I've read so far that indicates that Judge Starr is saying that he should be impeached because of a sexual relationship. It's because of other matters that are very significant."

The other matters are the 11 counts of Starr claims may be impeachable offensesófour allegations of perjury in his January 17 deposition in the Jones case, one charge of perjury in his August 17 grand jury testimony in the Starr investigation, four counts of obstructing justice, one of witness tampering and one of abuse of his office.

To back those up, prosecutors included significant new information and assertions about the affair and the investigation. Among new revelations:

Clinton himself informed Lewinsky that she would be called as a witness during the Jones case during a 2 a.m. telephone call to her Watergate apartment on December 17. She had appeared on a witness list provided to Clinton's lawyer on December 5 and she would not be served with a subpoena until December 19.

Clinton met with his personal secretary, Betty Currie, on a second, previously undisclosed occasion after his Jones deposition in which prosecutors said he appeared to be coaching her to agree with his false characterization of his relationship with Lewinsky. Clinton testified he did not recall that meeting.

Clinton asked White House Chief of Staff Erskine B. Bowles to help provide a job reference for Lewinsky as late as January, shortly before the Starr investigation was launched.

Clinton was told two weeks before he admitted the affair that the stain on a navy blue Gap dress that Lewinsky provided authorities had in fact tested positive for semen. Investigators took a sample of Clinton's blood on August 3 and it later matched the DNA on the dress. Starr contends in the report that Clinton's knowledge that prosecutors possessed the DNA evidence spurred his decision to confess on August 17.

FBI investigators found that some of Linda R. Tripp's 27 secret tapes of her conversations with Lewinsky may have been doctored and Starr said he is investigating whether that happened. Starr said he did not rely on any tapes that appeared to be duplicated for his report.

A Secret Service officer wanted to put Lewinsky on a watch list of people to be banned from the White House because he was concerned about Clinton's reputation, but a commander overruled him, saying it was none of their business.

While the report focused exclusively on the Lewinsky matter, Starr did provide information about other issues under investigation. He said he is still actively looking into possible perjury and obstruction of justice related to former White House volunteer Kathleen E. Willey, who accused Clinton of groping her against her will in the Oval Office suite, and into possible misuse of personnel records regarding Tripp, whose file was described to a journalist in part by a Pentagon official.

Starr wrote that he wanted to wait to send Congress a single report summarizing all of his findings but decided to proceed just on Lewinsky because of the urgency. Other phases of his 4 1/2-year investigation, including the Whitewater land deal, the travel office firings and the improper handling of FBI files, "are now nearing completion."

The report provides the first extensive account of the 18-month, on-and-off affair, from its unusual beginning through several rocky periods and to its eventual end, based largely on Lewinsky's account and with corroboration from White House records and contemporaneous conversations and calendar entries:

As she recalled it, Lewinsky and the president began flirting in the months after she arrived at the White House as an unpaid intern in July 1995; she tried to put herself in positions to come across him and made eye contact when she could. On November 15, during the federal government shutdown when most regular employees were furloughed and much of the White House was being operated by interns, Lewinsky finally had a chance to approach Clinton.

While they were alone at one point, she flirted, raised her jacket to show him the straps of her thong underwear and later told him she had a crush on him. He invited the 22-year-old woman to the study adjacent to the Oval Office, where they kissed. Hours later, he found her in the chief of staff's office and suggested she come back to the private enclave and she performed oral sex on him. During their encounter, he took telephone calls from Reps. Jim Chapman (D-Tex.) and John S. Tanner (D-Tenn.), according to her testimony and phone logs.

They had another encounter two days later this time he had a phone call from Rep. Sonny Callahan (R-Ala.) but soon afterward, the government reopened and it was not until New Year's Eve that she got close to him again. She introduced herself in case he forgot her name, but he said he remembered and they went into the study for sex.

After that, most of their rendezvous were on weekends; the president called her to set them up. She carried a folder with her and told aides or Secret Service officers that she was there to deliver papers. It was not until after their sixth encounter, she said, that Clinton spent significant time talking with her and getting to know her. But over the course of their affair, they engaged in telephone sex 10 to 15 times and exchanged gifts she gave him 30, including six neckties, and he gave her 18, including a hat pin, two brooches and a special edition of Walt Whitman's "Leaves of Grass."

Although she had gotten a job as a correspondence clerk, too many people began to worry about her attentions on the president and then-deputy chief of staff Evelyn S. Lieberman banished her to a Pentagon job in April 1996. Clinton had tried breaking off their relationship in February, only to resume it weeks later, but her transfer effectively ended their liaisons until after the election.

According to Lewinsky, they had two more encounters in early 1997, though. It was the first of these get-togethers, on February 28, that she was wearing the dress.

He ended the relationship for good on May 24, three days before the Supreme Court ruled unanimously that Jones's case could go to trial.

Clinton's account of their affair is far sketchier because he would not answer specific questions during his testimony. As described by Starr, the president testified that their first sexual encounters did not take place until early 1996 when she was no longer an intern and he remembered only the first of the two 1997 episodes Lewinsky described.

Even after they broke up, though, Lewinsky was convinced their affair would eventually resume. "I just knew he was in love with me," she testified. And she interpreted comments he made to believe that he might divorce Hillary Clinton after leaving the White House and marry her.

To prove Starr's contention that the president perjured himself both in his Jones deposition and his grand jury testimony, the report details many instances when the president fondled Lewinsky's breasts and genitalia, even though Clinton denied such touching in his August 17 testimony and implicitly admitted only receiving oral sex.

Clinton has said he did not believe that he committed perjury in the Jones case because he did not think the definition of "sexual relations" used by the Jones lawyers included oral sex performed on him. Clinton further said in his grand jury testimony that he thought the language used by the Jones lawyers about whether he "caused contact" between him and Lewinsky "implies forcing" and "forcible abusive behavior."

The evidence supporting Lewinsky's account of the trysts included White House logs showing she was in the building on eight of the 10 occasions and telephone records of phone calls. Lewinsky kept detailed calendars noting when she had visited the president.

In addition to the DNA evidence on the dress, Lewinsky told 11 people about the affair, mostly as it happened, including a host of friends, family members and two therapists who provided corroborating testimony. The president, said one of the therapists who urged her to break it off, "became Lewinsky's life."

Clinton also lied when he said in the deposition that he did not recall ever being alone with Lewinsky except when she came to drop off papers briefly, the report argued, and the president acknowledged he had in fact been alone with Lewinsky when asked again about it during his grand jury testimony. Currie, his secretary, testified he was alone with her on at least three occasions and six current or former Secret Service officers guarding the Oval Office said they had observed the two alone together.

The report cast Currie in a more ambiguous light than she has previously been portrayed, a facilitator who testified that she would "sneak" in Lewinsky to see the president, sometimes returning to the White House in the evening solely for that purpose. Currie testified that she would lead Lewinsky to the Oval Office by unusual routes to avoid other aides who she believed would disapprove. Currie used an alias when she paged Lewinsky, and she told the grand jury that she suspected an affair but told Lewinsky she didn't "want to hear it."

Prosecutors argued that the president also lied in his deposition when he said he could not recall any specific gifts he gave Lewinsky, even though he acknowledged last month giving her several just three weeks before the deposition. Lewinsky also testified that they discussed how to handle the gifts at that December 28 meeting because they had been subpoenaed by Jones's lawyers.

Beyond perjury, Starr outlined a variety of instances where he maintained Clinton committed obstruction of justice in the Jones case and the subsequent criminal investigation, such as coaching one potential witness, lying to others, helping to hide the subpoenaed gifts and arranging for job interviews for Lewinsky to encourage her allegiance.

Much attention in the report focuses on the December 28 White House meeting between Clinton and Lewinsky. In her handwritten, 10-page proffer given to Starr's office on February 1, Lewinsky said she talked to Clinton that day about whether she should hide the gifts and he said he did not know. Shortly afterward, she said, Currie called her at home and said "the president had told her Ms. Lewinsky wanted her to hold on to something for her." Currie later showed up at the Watergate and took a box of gifts.

Currie, the report said, testified she could not remember whether Clinton told her he wanted her to hold on to the gifts. Clinton has denied he instructed Currie to retrieve the gifts.

Starr further contended that when Clinton made his late-night call to Lewinsky to tell her she would be subpoenaed in the Jones case, he urged her to resist testifying by preparing a written affidavit, which she later did. The January 7 affidavit denied any sexual relationship with the president.

That affidavit was then submitted as evidence during Clinton's Jones deposition by his own lawyer, Robert S. Bennett, to try to curtail questioning about Lewinsky. With Clinton listening, Bennett told the federal judge supervising the deposition that Lewinsky had asserted "there is absolutely no sex of any kind in any manner, shape or form" with the president.

Clinton was questioned sharply during his grand jury testimony about how the president, as a lawyer himself, could knowingly have allowed his lawyer to submit the false statement. Clinton responded that Bennett was speaking only in the present tense and, therefore, had made a true statement. "It depends on what the meaning of the word 'is' is,' said Clinton, and "actually, in the present tense, that is an accurate statement."

The prosecutor questioning him, Solomon L. Wisenberg, responded, "Do you mean today that because you were not engaging in sexual activity with Ms. Lewinsky during the deposition that the statement of Mr. Bennett might literally be true?"

Clinton responded: "No, sir. I mean that at the time of the deposition, it had been that was well beyond any point of the improper contact between me and Ms. Lewinsky."

The report focuses heavily on Clinton's discussions with Currie in the days after his Jones deposition. After returning to the White House that night, he called Currie at home and asked her to come to work the next day, when he compared his recollections with hers. He told the grand jury he was trying to "refresh my memory"; Starr argued that "he was attempting to enlist a witness to back up his false testimony from the day before."

Currie told the grand jury that the president offered her a series of leading questions. "You were always there when she was there, right? We were never really alone." And, "You could see and hear everything." And, "Monica came on to me, and I never touched her, right?" Currie said she took those to be "more like statements than questions."

In the next two days, the report documents frantic efforts by Currie to contact Lewinsky, including the new information that Currie unsuccessfully paged Lewinsky seven times on January 19, using the alias "Kay" or "Kate."

The report discloses a second, previously unknown meeting

between the president and Currie on January 20 or 21 in which he appeared to be urging her to agree with his false testimony about Lewinsky. Currie described it as a "recapitulation of what we had talked about on Sunday you know, 'I was never alone with her' that sort of thing."

In his grand jury testimony, Clinton argued that in talking to Currie he meant to deny that he had any contact with Lewinsky in 1997 only although he never mentioned that time frame to her and it is unclear why he would think the Jones deposition would cover only that year. He also testified to the grand jury that "he did not remember having a second conversation with her along these lines."

His discussions with Currie, the president testified, were spurred by his concern that Lewinsky's name would become public as a result of the Jones deposition. "I was trying to get the facts and try to think of the best defense we could construct in the face of what I thought was going to be a media onslaught."

In another obstruction count, Starr accused the president of seeking to obstruct justice by lying to his senior aides knowing that they would then repeat his lie to the grand jury. Specifically, the report documented Clinton's denials to four top advisers in the days immediately after the Lewinsky story broke: Bowles, deputy chief of staff John D. Podesta, special assistant Sidney Blumenthal and then-deputy chief of staff Harold M. Ickes.

The report hinted at the speed with which Clinton moved to personally make his denials to the top aides as the political storm grew in the first days of the scandal. On January 21, the day the news broke, Clinton told Bowles in an Oval Office meeting, "Erskine, I want you to know that this story is not true," according to Podesta. Two days later, Podesta said Clinton told him in another meeting that he did not have sex of any "kind, shape or manner" with Lewinsky.

Starr argued these denials by Clinton to his closest advisers "had the effect of presenting a false view of events to the grand jury" and the president knew what he was doing in lying to potential grand jury witnesses.

In several instances, the Starr report detailed what it claims is the White House's lack of full compliance with its subpoenas in the Lewinsky probe. For example, it noted that Lewinsky gave the president a copy of Nicholson Baker's novel about phone sex, "Vox," which was found on an inventory of the books Clinton kept on the shelf in his private study. But it was never turned over to Starr.

Clinton, the report contended, tried to obstruct justice by helping Lewinsky get a private-sector job in New York "at a time when she would have been a witness against him were she able to tell the truth during the Jones case."

The presidential assistance began after Lewinsky sent him a letter by courier expressing frustration about her job search last October. Two days later, on October 9, Lewinsky got a late-night call from Clinton, who told her he would help her find a job in New York, according to her testimony. She met with Clinton for over an hour two days later. Clinton agreed to get her a White House reference, enlisting Bowles in the effort, and at Lewinsky's suggestion he called Vernon E. Jordan Jr. to garner his aid.

Lewinsky told Tripp in a taped conversation that she had concerns about involving Bowles in her job search: "Somebody could construe or say, 'Well, they gave her a job to shut her up. . . . And [Bowles] works for the government and shouldn't have done that.' And with the other one [Jordan] you can't say that."

Lewinsky met with Jordan November 5, but the well-connected presidential confidant did not step up efforts on her behalf until December, after the Jones lawyers identified her as a potential witness, the report said. During their second meeting December 11, Lewinsky told Jordan she became upset when Clinton did not "call me enough or see me enough." Lewinsky told the grand jury Jordan replied, "You're in love, that's what your problem is."

Jordan kept Clinton closely apprised of his substantial efforts on Lewinsky's behalf, and when she landed an offer in early January notified Clinton with the news: "Mission accomplished." Clinton testified in his Jones deposition that he knew only vaguely through his secretary that Jordan was helping Lewinsky look for a job.

"The question . . . is whether the president's efforts in obtaining a job for Ms. Lewinsky were to influence her testimony or simply to help an ex-intimate without concern for her testimony," said the report. The president was motivated to help Lewinsky at least in part, the report said, to "keep her on the team" in the Jones litigation.

Kendall, Clinton's lawyer, told reporters the president "never, never advised her to testify falsely. He has admitted a wrongful relation. And the fact is that in all such wrongful, improper relations, there is a concomitant concealment by its very nature. That's all that is involved here. The independent counsel has extravagantly exaggerated that to try and make allegations of obstruction of justice."

For Clinton, a Day to Atone but Not Retreat
At Prayer Breakfast, President Apologizes and Pledges Legal Defense White House Issues Apologies, Gets Defensive

By John F. Harris

President Clinton said the time had come to speak "rock-bottom truth," and he stayed up until 4 a.m. laboring on the words to express it. Five hours later, a man who a few weeks ago would not utter the words "I am sorry" stood before men and women of the cloth and vaulted the history of presidential apologies into a new realm.

"I don't think there is a fancy way to say that I have sinned," said Clinton, his eyes glistening and his voice thick with emotion, as he addressed the ministers gathered Friday, September 11, in the East Room for the White House's annual prayer breakfast.

But even as Clinton seemed to be giving up any effort to deny or defend his behavior on moral grounds, he served notice that he was not done fighting: "I will instruct my lawyers to mount a vigorous defense, using all available appropriate arguments."

The meaning of that statement became clear seven hours later.

His personal attorney, David E. Kendall, sat before reporters in the Roosevelt Room—the very place where Clinton eight months ago declared that "I did not have sexual relations with that woman"— and made plain that Clinton's defense against impeachment will rely heavily upon legalistic distinctions between lying and misleading, and between concealment and coverup.

"If answers are literally truthful but misleading, there is no perjury, as a matter of law, no matter how misleading the testimony is or is intended to be," said a report that Kendall and White House Counsel Charles F.C. Ruff prepared to rebut independent counsel Kenneth W. Starr's report to Congress on possible impeachable offenses Clinton allegedly committed while trying to hide his affair with Lewinsky.

That sharp contrast—between Clinton's abject apology and Kendall's lawyerly legerdemain—highlighted the dual tracks the White House was following on perhaps the most remarkable day of the Clinton presidency, when the release of the Starr report made his survival in office an open question.

Clinton's East Room mea culpa was a gripping moment, but it turned out to be just one scene in a kaleidoscopic day of astonishing moments. There was a 50-foot line of reporters waiting at the White House press office like teenagers trying to buy tickets to a rock concert, eager for copies of the defense memo that was made public even before Starr's report—a "prebuttal," as aides dubbed it.

There was White House press secretary Michael McCurry, live on national television, denying that the president was receiving psychological treatment but declining to say what counseling he might be receiving. That question was inspired by Clinton's morning reference to the fact that as he continues on the "path to redemption," he will seek "pastoral support and that of other caring people so that they can hold me accountable for my own commitment."

There were other indelicate questions. One reporter asked whether Clinton suffered from "satyriasis," a term for sexual addiction. No, McCurry said.

It was a day of low moments at the White House, the place abuzz with ceaseless chatter among senior aides and reporters alike of what Kendall called "salacious allegations—intended to humiliate, embarrass and politically damage the president."

It was part of Clinton's defense to move the drama to a higher plane. Not a morning person under the best of circumstances, Clinton looked tired and subdued as he took to the lectern, after a brief introduction by Vice President Gore, to talk to the 106 religious leaders. First lady Hillary Rodham Clinton looked on as he spoke, her face calm and betraying no particular mood.

Clinton, reading from a handwritten script, gave the speech that many of his aides wished he had given eight months ago, when the scandal first broke, or at the very least after his August 17 grand jury testimony. The president himself said he had not been contrite enough in his defiant first address to the nation.

And while he had once lashed out angrily at Starr for invading his privacy, the president said the investigation into his extramarital affair may actually have been "a blessing" because it forced him to confront his failings. For the first time, he said he was asking for Monica S. Lewinksy's forgiveness.

And he said he was hoping that something positive could come out of personal disaster.

"If my repentance is genuine and sustained, and if I can maintain both a broken spirit and a strong heart, then good can come of this for our country as well as for me and my family," Clinton said, as applause rose from the audience. "The children of this country can learn in a profound way that integrity is important and selfishness is wrong, but God can change us and make us strong at the broken places."

Some in the White House cracked that Clinton had delivered a "full Swaggart," referring to the flamboyant, sobbing confession that televangelist Jimmy Swaggart gave in 1988 when his sexual transgressions were exposed.

The president read a passage from a Jewish text called the "Gates of Repentance" that had been given to him by Miami lawyer Ira Leesfield, whose home Clinton visited for dessert after a Democratic fund-raiser Wednesday night.

The East Room gathering plainly loved the message. "Yes, sir!" a group of African American ministers shouted as he spoke. Afterward, Jesse L. Jackson rose to shake Clinton's hand. The Rev. Joan Brown Campbell, general secretary of the National Council of Churches, described the atmosphere as "subdued" and "deeply spiritual."

"Nobody sitting in that room wasn't moved by his humility," she said. "He called forth some of who we all are."

As a political matter, however, it was far from clear that the speech would accomplish its apparent goal of winning sympathy for Clinton and convincing the public that he has held himself fully accountable for wrongdoing.

"What do his words mean? Do they reflect his sentiment or do they reflect his predicament?" asked Martha Joynt Kumar, a fellow at Harvard University's Kennedy School of Government who has studied the Clinton presidency. If it had been delivered earlier, Clinton's speech "would have had the power to answer some questions and prevent others from being delivered," Kumar said. As it is, she added, his fate will be determined much more by Congress's reading of the facts in the Starr report than by Clinton's ability to strike emotional chords in a confession.

Inside the White House, the disconsolate mood of recent days began to lift a bit on Friday. Many senior aides said they believed that Starr's lurid presentation of sexual episodes would rebound to the president's advantage, underscoring their case that the investigation was a prurient exercise that was more about titillation than law-breaking.

For all the fears among some senior White House officials that they would not be able to present an effective response yesterday, aides said Friday night they were satisfied that Clinton's side had not been swamped by Starr's allegations.

The months-long tension between senior political aides and the president's legal team has lessened in recent days, as lawyers have begun to share information and coordinate more closely with other advisers. The political team pressed the lawyers to have a written document ready to go by the afternoon; lawyers, cautious by instinct, said they wanted to wait until they had read Starr's report. But the lawyers eventually yielded, with several staying up all night to prepare the rebuttal, based on news leaks of what Starr would allege.

The prayer breakfast was just the first event in a busy public day for both the president and first lady. A few hours later, they appeared together at Washington National Cathedral for a memorial service for people killed in last month's East Africa terrorist bombings. And, later still, they appeared together at a South Lawn ceremony honoring Irish Americans.

The Irish American crowd that gathered for a reception on the South Lawn showered the Clintons with sustained applause and throaty cheers. They stood in ovation as soon as the president and first lady were announced and continued clapping, despite the president's attempts to quiet them with an aw-shucks wave of both arms. Finally Clinton sat down, and when the hollers continued he stood to take a bow, a la Mark McGwire, which prompted more applause.

Hillary Clinton, who has yet to speak publicly on the Lewinsky matter since her husband acknowledged his extramarital affair, was among those leading the extended applause, as she gazed beamingly at the president.

Earlier in the day, she appeared separately in the Maryland suburbs to promote foster care programs. She spoke in personal terms about her own mother's difficult childhood, in which she spent time as a teenager working in another family's home. "She got to see a real family," Hillary Clinton said. "She got to watch what happens inside the home where parents and children went through all that you go through as a family because she had never had that before."

"I think there's a lot you can help teach Americans about resilience, hope, grit and determination," she said.

Staff writer Kevin Merida contributed to this report.

'I Will Continue on the Path of Repentance'

Following are President Clinton's remarks on Friday, September 11, 1998 at a prayer breakfast:

Welcome to the White House and to this day to which Hillary and the vice president and I look forward so much every year.

This is always an important day for our country for the reasons that the vice president said. It is an unusual and I think unusually important day today.

I may not be quite as easy with my words today as I have been in years past, and I was up rather late last night thinking about and praying about what I ought to say today.

And rather unusually for me, I actually tried to write it down. So if you will forgive me, I will do my best to say what it is I want to say to you. And I may have to take my glasses out to read my own writing.

First, I want to say to all of you that, as you might imagine, I have been on quite a journey these last few weeks to get to the end of this, to the rock bottom truth of where I am and where we all are.

I agree with those who have said that, in my first statement after I testified, I was not contrite enough.

I don't think there is a fancy way to say that I have sinned. It is important to me that everybody who has been hurt know that the sorrow I feel is genuine: first and most important, my family, also my friends, my staff, my Cabinet, Monica Lewinsky and her family, and the American people.

I have asked all for their forgiveness. But I believe that to be forgiven, more than sorrow is required. At least two more things: first, genuine repentance, a determination to change and to repair breaches of my own making. I have repented.

Second, what my Bible calls a broken spirit. An understanding that I must have God's help to be the person that I want to be. A willingness to give the very forgiveness I seek.

A renunciation of the pride and the anger, which cloud judgment, lead people to excuse and compare and to blame and complain. Now, what does all this mean for me and for us?

First, I will instruct my lawyers to mount a vigorous defense using all available, appropriate arguments. But legal language must not obscure the fact that I have done wrong.

Second, I will continue on the path of repentance seeking pastoral support and . . . that of other caring people so that they can hold me accountable for my own commitment.

Third, I will intensify my efforts to lead our country and the world toward peace and freedom, prosperity and harmony. And in the hope that with a broken spirit and a still strong heart, I can be used for greater good, for we have many blessings and many challenges and so much work to do.

In this, I ask for your prayers and for your help in healing our nation. And though I cannot move beyond or forget this, indeed I must always keep it as a caution light in my life. It is very important that our nation move forward.

I am very grateful for the many, many people clergy and ordinary citizens alike who have written me with wise counsel. I am profoundly grateful for the support of so many Americans who somehow, through it all, seem to still know that I care about them a great deal, that I care about their problems and their dreams.

I am grateful for those who have stood by me and who say that, in this case and many others, the bounds of privacy have been excessively and unwisely invaded. That may be. Nevertheless, in this case, it may be a blessing because I still sinned. And if my repentance is genuine and sustained, and if I can then maintain both a broken spirit and a strong heart, then good can come of this for our country, as well as for me and my family.

The children of this country can learn in a profound way that integrity is important and selfishness is wrong. But God can change us and make us strong at the broken places.

I want to embody those lessons for the children of this country; for that little boy in Florida who came up to me and said that he wanted to grow up and be president and to be just like me. I want the parents of all the children in America to be able to say that to their children.

A couple of days ago when I was in Florida, a Jewish friend of mine gave me this liturgy book called "Gates of Repentance." And there was this incredible passage from a Yom Kippur liturgy, and I would like to read it to you:

"Now is the time for turning. The leaves are beginning to turn from green to red to orange. The birds are beginning to turn and are heading once more toward the south. The animals are beginning to turn to storing their food for the winter. For leaves, birds and animals, turning comes instinctively.

"But for us, turning does not come so easily. It takes an act of will for us to make a turn. It means breaking old habits. It means admitting that we have been wrong, and this is never easy. It means losing face. It means starting all over again. And this is always painful. It means saying I am sorry. It means recognizing that we have the ability to change. These things are terribly hard to do.

"But unless we turn, we will be trapped forever in yesterday's ways. Lord help us to turn from callousness to sensitivity, from hostility to love, from pettiness to purpose, from envy to contentment, from carelessness to discipline, from fear to faith. Turn us around, oh, Lord, and bring us back toward you. Revive our lives as at the beginning. And turn us toward each other, Lord, for in isolation, there is no life."

I thank my friend for that and I thank you for being here. I ask you to share my prayer that God will search me and know my heart, try me and know my anxious thoughts, see if there is any hurtfulness in me and lead me toward a life everlasting. I ask that God give me a clean heart, let me walk by faith and not sight.

I ask once again to be able to love my neighbor all my neighbors as myself, to be an instrument of God's peace, to let the words of my mouth and the meditations of my heart, and in the end, the work of my hands, be pleasing.

This is what I wanted to say to you today. Thank you, God bless you. . . .

Report's Details On Sexual Acts Prompt Regrets

By Michael Grunwald

The remarkably explicit sexual details throughout independent counsel Kenneth W. Starr's impeachment report astonished the nation, fueling intense criticism of the special prosecutor among some legal and cultural commentators and prompting some House members to second-guess their hasty decision to release the report over the Internet.

Starr's report had been expected to include graphic material about President Clinton's relationship with Monica S. Lewinsky, but few realized that wire service stories about it would require warnings that the contents "may be OFFENSIVE to some readers." The report includes hundreds of sordid details about which sexual acts Clinton and Lewinsky performed, where they performed them, what they said about them and how they felt about them.

By Friday afternoon, some of Clinton's harshest critics were regretting their votes that morning to publicize the report, wondering aloud whether they had helped release pornography over the Internet. And as congressional switchboards lit up with outraged callers, some of Clinton's defenders were predicting that the titillating details would spark an anti-Starr backlash.

"I've probably never read anything this graphic before," said Rep. Mark Edward Souder (R-Ind.), a staunch conservative who has called for Clinton's resignation. "I don't think anyone in this country is comfortable with such detailed probing of someone's sex life."

"These graphic details should be taken off the Internet," said Rep. E. Clay Shaw Jr. (R-Fla.), who had voted a few hours earlier to put the report on the Internet. "We shouldn't have it all out there for kids to read."

The report describes the inclusion of sexually explicit material as "unfortunate, but essential," contending that the precise details of the president's 10 sexual encounters with Lewinsky were necessary to demonstrate that he lied under oath. But some legal experts said that Starr easily could have described what Clinton did without including so many lurid specifics. In a normal case, they said, some of those details might have been ruled inadmissible in court, but there is no way to strike them from the Internet.

"You don't have to show the severed head of a victim to show that a victim died, and you don't have to show all these graphic details about sex to show that sex took place," said Lawrence Fox, a Philadelphia trial lawyer and former chair of the American Bar Association's ethics committee. "It's fun to read, but it just isn't necessary."

Then again, Starr was not just trying to show that sex took place; he was trying to show that it took place in ways that Clinton has denied. The president testified in the Paula Jones case that he never engaged in "sexual relations" or "sexual contact" with Lewinsky, and then testified to Starr's grand jury that he still thought that was true under the Jones case's specific definition of "sexual relations." Clinton explained to the grand jury that while Lewinsky had performed oral sex on him, he had never performed any sex acts on her.

The Starr report goes to extreme lengths to refute that testimony. It provides a full description of 10 sexual encounters, portraying Clinton as an enthusiastic participant, not a passive recipient of sexual favors.

"The president said he never performed any sexual acts on Lewinsky, so it was important for Starr to show who touched whom and where," said Georgetown University law professor Paul Rothstein. "But it's horrible that it's come to this. The report is absolutely unprecedented in its raunchy details."

To many critics, the report included far more explicit detail than Starr needed to make a perjury case, and far more information than the American people needed to know. It even cited 15 instances of phone sex between Clinton and Lewinsky, contending that "while phone sex may not itself constitute a 'sexual relationship,' it adds detail to Ms. Lewinsky's testimony and underscores the sexual and intimate nature of the relationship between the President and Ms. Lewinsky."

In their rebuttal to the report, Clinton's attorneys accused Starr of including those details for the sole purpose of embarrassing the president. After all, they pointed out, Clinton has already admitted that he had a sexual relationship with Lewinsky.

Many members of Congress said they were deluged with calls from constituents who made similar arguments. Rep. Porter J. Goss (R-Fla.) said his grown son had called him to complain about the sexual details, and to ask what he should tell his own young sons. House Judiciary Chairman Henry J. Hyde (R-Ill.) had raised this issue in a GOP caucus before the vote to release the report, but the House still voted overwhelmingly to release the report immediately.

"We have just made this country into a nation of voyeurs," said Rep. James P. Moran Jr. (D-Va.), one of only 63 members to vote against release.

At a House Commerce Committee hearing Friday on several bills designed to protect children from smut on the Internet, civil libertarians warned that some of the legislation might make it illegal to distribute the Starr report. "Look, it's pretty strong stuff," said Jerry Berman, executive director of the Center for Democracy and Technology.

Debra Haffner is president of the Sexuality Information and Education Council of the United States, an advocacy group that promotes open discussion of sexuality, but even she was appalled by the explicit nature of the report. For a while, she said, the Lewinsky matter had provided "teachable moments" for parents to talk to their children about sex, and offered opportunities for spouses to talk to each other about fidelity. But before discussing the Starr report with a reporter yesterday, she sent her 13-year-old daughter out of the room.

"I never do that, but this stuff just crosses the line," Haffner said. "The level of detail is just indefensible. There are some things about people we don't need to know."

Staff Writers Judith Havemann, Eric Pianin and Barbara Vobejda contributed to this report.

Public Reacts To Details With Anger, Amusement

By Marc Fisher and David Montgomery

The oddest mass political act in the history of American democracy began with an electronic storm, a blizzard of attempts to find the Starr report on the Internet. By late afternoon, the details, the explicit stuff-the sex-was everywhere: in solemn readings on television, in breathless recitations on talk radio, in gossip that sizzled across workplaces, shopping malls and neighborhood gatherings.

Within an hour of the report's release, thanks to the Internet, the nation began history's first simultaneous reading of smut. In coffee shops and exercise gyms, at soccer practices and cybercafes, Americans expressed exasperation, amusement, sorrow and anger as they scanned the voluminous text, stunned by its explicit recitation of the president's alleged sexual behavior.

Office mates traded juicy bits by e-mail; instead of the usual jokes, there were verbatim quotations from the report by the Office of the Independent Counsel. It was an afternoon of giggles, whistles, and sighs of disgust. But was this the nervous laughter of a nation writhing under an avalanche of sexual detail, or a first, emotional exhalation at the beginning of a constitutional crisis?

"I'm embarrassed just looking at these words," said Cindy Kelly, a New York receptionist who, like nearly everyone else in her office on a lazy Friday afternoon, read the report and immediately copied choice phrases to send her friends.

"Lying under oath is a big deal," said Paul Terpak, 42, a Fairfax lawyer who interrupted his workout at Gold's Gym to watch TV accounts of the prosecution's case against the president. Terpak wasn't sure whether President Clinton should be removed from office or punished some other way. "If you can't believe someone under oath, the whole system will fail. Whatever deal he had with Hillary, he didn't have with the American people. I know that my wife wouldn't make a deal like that with me."

For most of this year, Americans confounded the pundits by insisting that their support of the president was undiminished by increasingly persuasive accounts of his sexual misdeeds. Yet many Washington insiders, Republicans and Democrats alike, persisted in their belief that when finally confronted with what Clinton had done, the American public would turn on their president with a vengeance.

But the first reactions to the report and its startlingly graphic descriptions of the relationship between Clinton and former White House intern Monica S. Lewinsky were of a different sort of revulsion, a visceral feeling that, while hardly anyone could stop reading, this was a body of material that citizens simply weren't supposed to see.

The Barber Shop

The explicit details were cascading from the TV set blaring at Preston's Barber Shop on Georgia Avenue NW in the District.

". . . the president's DNA . . ." said the announcer.

"Oh no!" shuddered barber Melvin Edler, 75, completing a trim in the chair on the right.

". . . sex while on the telephone with three U.S. congressmen . . ."

"Come on!" said barber Jason Lewis, 30, at the center chair, who had shaken hands with Clinton and wished him luck when he visited the neighborhood shortly after he won election in 1992.

"I don't believe that," chimed in Edler, wincing and shaking his head.

This stuff was over the top even for these barbers, men who thought that everything a person could ever hear had been said at some time in their 36-year-old shop. But this—about the president! — well, it shocked even them.

They absorbed the shock, but just as quickly shrugged it off.

To them, and to a dozen other people interviewed along the avenue, Clinton was still an admirable president who ought not be driven out of office over the Lewinsky affair. They pointed to a strong economy, successful foreign policy, the generally solid America in the late 1990s, and they credited Clinton.

The barbers referred frequently to biblical themes. Lewis said Americans, before judging Clinton, should look in the mirror and question whether they are qualified to cast the first stone.

The Senior Center

At the Miami Beach Senior Center, the Friday Singalong had just concluded with "Goody Goody." The center's director, who doesn't usually tolerate TV watching, turned on the big set in the activity room so the seniors could follow the unfolding events in Washington. The volume was way up, but those with strong opinions made their voices heard over the din.

"It's a dirty trick, a dirty little political trick," said Winnie Spintig, who wouldn't give her age. "Somebody is behind it, someone wants to get him out of office. He is a good president. I had tears in my eyes when he spoke this morning of having his spirit broken. He has a good heart." She gave her white pageboy a flip before leaving in disgust.

On ordinary Fridays, her friend, Juliet Rothenberg, plays the piano while Winnie sings. "How many others have done the same thing?" Rothenberg wondered. "This Ken Starr—he is doing too much. Now the president, his defenses are down, he has nothing else to do but apologize. But there is no cause for impeachment. If he could, I would bet that he would be reelected."

Anna Kuferschmidt, 95, disagreed loudly. Sure, she said, "it isn't nice to impeach a president. But Clinton should have resigned when this started." The others tried to shush her, but she would not be silenced. "If Hillary hadn't stuck by him at the start then he would have resigned. She knew the marriage was on the rocks for a long time."

Gertrude Lunenfeld, 90, shook her head as the details trickled out. "In other countries, the leaders have girlfriends and mistresses and even in this country-look at Kennedy. Nobody cared as long as they run the country right. What is Ken Starr's job? Does he think this is some feather in his cap? And Lewinsky, she is going to write a book? Everyone is disgusted with her."

"If they were to look this hard at other people, the people in Congress or in public, if they were to dig like they've done, they'd find a lot worse about them," said a Jamaican nurse at the center, Yvonne Bogle, 55. "And who is suppose to cast the first stone? If God can forgive him, who are we? Only God can pull him down."

The Cybercafe

At 2:55 p.m., Georgetown University freshman John Ferris hit pay dirt.

After more than half an hour of error messages and endless hourglasses dancing across his computer screen, Ferris finally pulled up the Starr report on his terminal at the Atomic Grounds cybercafe in Rosslyn.

"I don't want this part," Ferris, 19, complained as he paged through a long list of chapter headings. "This is the part about Monica Lewinsky. That's not my business. I'm interested in the legal part."

But as he scrolled through, the details soon entranced Ferris. His cursor halted at passages that described Lewinsky's garments and her account of Clinton's advances. The finance and business law major read aloud from one of the report's most explicit sections, then exclaimed, "Oh, way to go, Mr. President."

"November 17, the second date," Ferris said as he read, raising his eyebrows and turning slightly red as the report grew more and more graphic. "Usually it's the second date you get the most out of."

After a few minutes, he had had enough. "That's a little more than I wanted to know about my president," he said. "I don't want to be here any more." He signed off and returned to work behind the cafe's counter.

Across the river on the College Park campus of the University of Maryland, computer labs teemed with students, but their screens were filled mostly with personal e-mail or martial arts computer games. Few bothered to search for the Starr report.

"I'm so tired with the Clinton sex scandal," said Kelly Lavin, 18, a freshman who was checking her e-mail for her academic assignments. "It'll be interesting to see what Starr has to say, but I'm not obsessed with the report."

But graduate student Katherine Kerr, 24, was wearing down the Enter key on her computer as she repeatedly tried to call up the report.

"Reload reload reload reload," she moaned, running into one of the Internet's largest traffic jams to date. Kerr, a former intern for Sen. Pete V. Domenici (R-N.M.), was especially eager to see if Starr had found evidence of any other presidential extramarital relationships.

Despite her interest in more dirt, she said she was irritated "that it all had to come to this. If he had told the truth in the beginning, we wouldn't have to go through this now. People are badmouthing Ken Starr. But that's unfair, he's just doing his job."

Readers looked for support for their partisan views-evidence that Starr had gone too far, or proof that Clinton ought to be bounced from office. But the pro and anti camps were united in one emotion: sadness.

"This is the man I voted for," Meg Smith, 21, a journalism senior, said as she unsuccessfully sought to download the report. "I am Monica's age when she was in that position. For people my age, this is our coming of age. We missed the Vietnam War and Watergate and gas lines... It's the worst political disaster I've ever been in. It's so disgusting and sickening and it's all happening 10 miles away. I'm afraid to look."

Nonetheless, she kept trying.

"Oh, this is so useless," she said as she downloaded the White House's rebuttal to the Starr report. "I want the real thing."

The Gymnasium

Glancing back and forth between *Time* magazine and the scrolling captions on an overhead television, Victor Johnson shook his head slowly. He pedaled his exercycle over a virtual hill. Sweat dripped from Johnson's hair and a look of disgust covered his face. As the details poured out of the television, Johnson and other folks working out at Gold's Gym in Fairfax craned their necks to see the latest.

"It's just that he was so stupid about it, like it was a funny, stupid game," said Johnson, 45, a medical assistant at Inova Fairfax Hospital. "I don't know if I can believe that he's sorry, but he shouldn't have to be dealing with any of this in the first place. He's just a human, and he made a mistake. Or a few mistakes."

Stepping off a treadmill, Misook Lee, 35, of Fairfax, looked content. A theological seminary student, Lee wasn't interested in the Starr report's details.

"I appreciate that he said he was sorry to Monica Lewinsky and her family," Lee said. "He has repented. When we repent, God really forgives us. If God can forgive him, I think we can forgive him, and that is all that matters."

But on religious radio, another theology reigned. "This is not a good day for America," talk host Janet Parshal said on her syndicated program. "But it is a good day to learn that there is a transcendent right and wrong, and that there are consequences for our behavior."

The Delicatessen

At the Stage Deli in Century City shopping mall in Los Angeles, a popular lunch spot for lawyers and entertainment industry employees, an empty room suddenly filled as a waiter flipped on CNN.

As the litany of allegations was read for the first time, a waiter muttered, "Aw, dude, he's going down so hard."

Immediately, waiters and waitresses quit lining up ketchup bottles and stacking pies in the rotating dessert case. They watched, then debated.

"Who cares?" said Linda Sindon, 51. Several other waitresses standing behind her joined in a chorus of approval.

Waiter Kenny Koch couldn't believe what he was hearing. "That's an emotional response," he said of his colleagues' view. Dismissively, he added, "They are so forgiving."

While the salacious reports drew a crowd and sparked several rounds of cigar jokes, there was at the Stage and in other places beyond the Beltway a far more powerful sense of detachment from the goings-on in Washington, a clear belief that the president's travails had little if anything to do with daily life in the country he governs.

"It's just a good distraction from work, but most people don't really care," said waiter Andy Sankus, 27. "What does this have to do with everyday life?" He doesn't watch much television or read the papers, but Sankus nevertheless ripped a ticket out of his order pad to jot down an Internet address so he could look up the report later.

As the TV news droned on, with reporters brandishing individual pages from the Starr narrative, the lunch crowd got back to the business of eating. Within an hour, the bartender asked whether anyone would mind if he switched over to coverage of the U.S. Open. There was no objection.

Staff writers Desson Howe, Josh White, Brooke A. Masters and Dana Hull in Washington, and special correspondents Cassandra Stern in Los Angeles, Kari Lydersen in Chicago and Catherine Skipp in Miami contributed to this report.

Democrats Brace for Public's Reaction to Report

By David S. Broder and Ceci Connolly

As members of Congress headed home after the release of independent counsel Kenneth W. Starr's report on the White House scandal, many of their political consultants agreed privately with the judgment of former senator Paul Simon (D-Ill.): "Things are starting to unravel for the administration."

Republican reaction was summarized by GOP consultant Michael Murphy. "He's in huge trouble," Murphy said. "He's lost his ability to lead and set the national debate."

Whatever the potential political damage to Clinton and his party, most members of Congress and political operatives said the odds against his impeachment and conviction remained high.

"There's a very high standard for impeachment," said Rep. Mark Edward Souder (R-Ind.), a leader of arguably the most conservative faction of House Republicans. "You really need to have a compelling case, not just a partisan case."

Many of those interviewed in the first hours after Starr's 453-page report was released cautioned that it might be days before the full public reaction to the detailed description of Clinton's affair with former White House intern Monica S. Lewinsky can be gauged. But the first impression was that, even though the report had been expected for months, it was a further blow to a president whose personal approval ratings had already been on the skids.

"The more that the dialogue moves from the general and speculative to specific and factual, the slipperier the hill gets for Bill Clinton," said Democratic pollster Alan Secrest.

Some of the president's supporters expressed personal outrage at the explicit descriptions of sexual encounters in the Starr report and predicted there would be a public backlash against what one House member called the "vendetta" by the independent counsel.

"It's a weak case at best for impeachment," said Rep. Chakah Fattah (D-Pa.) "It really raises the question of Starr's motives." Another House Democrat, who declined to be quoted by name, said, "If he gets through this week and there's a backlash and people resent Starr for bringing all this crap into their living room, then maybe he could level out."

The release of the massive, sexually explicit report barely more than seven weeks before the midterm election created an unprecedented political environment. Few in either party were ready to bet heavily on how the public will react.

"It all depends on what seeing this in print does to the American people. There's nothing new in here. There's no smoking gun," said Rep. John Linder (R-Ga.), chairman of the National Republican Congressional Committee. "But I think the stark, written word will have an impact, and if the American people are totally shocked, it will register in Congress."

Jeff Eller, a White House spokesman during Clinton's first term and now a Texas-based political consultant, agreed that the situation is volatile. "The American people are going to have a full, unadulterated, head-on dose of some of the most personal and graphic descriptions of things about their president," he said. "That is going to take some time to absorb and some time for them to analyze."

Some veterans of past political wars, however, were ready to venture predictions.

Former Senate majority leader Howard H. Baker Jr. (R-Tenn.) said, "I think the House will report bills of impeachment. . . . . I've not heard anyone really stand up to defend him. But I'm not certain what the Senate will do. It takes a lot to move that body."

Even if Clinton remains in office, many said he would never overcome the damage that has been inflicted by his admission that he lied in an effort to conceal his relationship with Lewinsky.

Sen. Robert F. Bennett (R-Utah) said, "He may cling to office the way Lyndon Johnson did in his last year, but he will not be able to claim any respect anywhere—sympathy perhaps, but not respect."

Stephen Wayne, a Georgetown University expert on the presidency, said the combination of Clinton's initial lies and belated apologies has destroyed his credibility. "When it comes to personal things, he has operated for so long in a self-interested, self-aggrandizing manner, we are less apt to believe him."

Simon, now teaching at Southern Illinois University, said he had been in Washington for several days visiting with old colleagues in the Capitol. "There is more and more talk about resignation. We

should not be hasty," he said. "I'm sure there will be political fall-
out. It simply adds to public cynicism, but the greater damage will
be on the Democratic side."

Simon's point was bolstered by a variety of public and private
polls conducted in recent days. Although Clinton's job approval rating has remained strong, analysts found other troubling indicators
for Democrats. Specifically, the surveys found a sharp drop in the
president's personal approval rating, renewed interest in moral
issues and gains for the GOP in congressional races.

Steve Mitchell, an independent Michigan pollster, said three surveys taken in his state in late August "all showed his [Clinton's]
favorables dropping, and that means his job approval ultimately
will fall, too."

GOP pollster Bill McInturff said, "Generally, this week we're seeing a net 6- or 8-point movement to Republican candidates. The
environment is shifting very precariously against Democrats."

A new poll by the nonpartisan Pew Research Center found senior
citizens shifting allegiance rapidly from Clinton and his Democratic
Party to the Republicans. "Now, older people are solidly on the side
of the GOP," the survey found, noting that 55 percent of elderly
view the Republican Party favorably and only 36 percent view it
unfavorably.

The erosion in grass-roots support could ultimately affect Clinton's chances of surviving an impeachment move. But middle-
ground lawmakers of both parties said they were still reluctant to
contemplate that step.

Rep. Michael N. Castle (R-Del.), a moderate, said of Clinton,
"He's probably at his lowest ebb right now. We have to focus on the
question, 'Did he abuse the powers of his office?' He'll have a
chance to answer the Starr report. I'm quite undecided now."

Rep. Ray LaHood (R-Ill.), another moderate, said, "I want to
read the report to see if in fact he is accused of lying or getting members of his staff to lie. . . . Those are impeachable offenses."

Another moderate Republican, speaking on background, said if
the charges against Clinton stem solely from his sexual affair, he

seriously doubts he will be impeached. But this lawmaker voiced sympathy for those on the Democratic side of the aisle: "This guy has cost the Democrats three friggin' elections and now he's asking them to stand up for him."

Staff writers Helen Dewar and Eric Pianin and staff researcher Ben White contributed to this report.

Congress Faces Two Starkly Different Legal Arguments

By Ruth Marcus and Roberto Suro

Independent counsel Kenneth W. Starr's report confronts members of Congress with the daunting task of analyzing difficult questions of criminal law, vaguely defined constitutional standards for impeachment and the largely uncharted interplay between the two realms.

Were President Clinton an ordinary target in a run-of-the-mill criminal investigation, it is highly unlikely, many legal experts agree, that the evidence upon which Starr bases his impeachment argument that Clinton lied under oath, obstructed justice, and tampered with a witness ever would have resulted in criminal charges.

But Starr's report depicts the president's alleged offenses as conduct that not only is unlawful, but goes to the heart of his constitutional duties.

Invoking "the enormous trust and responsibility attendant to his high office," the report argues that Clinton, perhaps more than any other citizen, has "a manifest duty to ensure that his conduct at all times complies with the law of the land."

As a result, the coming congressional debate—much as the initial round of arguments between Starr and Clinton's lawyers—is likely to center both on the specific question of whether any of the president's actions constituted criminal violations and the broader constitutional issue of whether his misdeeds were so egregious as to warrant his removal from office, regardless of what verdict they might produce in a courtroom.

Starr's 11 grounds for possible impeachment of the president break down into three categories:

- Perjury—that Clinton lied under oath about his relationship with Monica S. Lewinsky and related matters, both during his deposition in the Paula Jones sexual harassment lawsuit, and, more ominously, in his grand jury testimony.

- Obstruction of justice—in trying to cover up the relationship, encouraging Lewinsky to lie about it, helping her get a job, trying to influence the testimony of his secretary, Betty Currie, and thwarting the subsequent grand jury investigation of his actions.

- Official misconduct—including lying to the public and Congress about his relationship with Lewinsky, balking at testifying before the grand jury, and invoking executive privilegeóthat "constitute[s] an abuse of authority inconsistent with the president's constitutional duty to faithfully execute the laws."

Legal experts said that Starr's strongest evidence and clearest arguments appear to lie in the allegations of perjury, and particularly the charge that Clinton lied about the nature of his sexual encounters with Lewinsky. They said that the independent counsel's evidence on the questions of obstruction and witness-tampering are, as the report acknowledges, largely circumstantial; the report offers no "smoking gun" of a Watergate-style conspiracy to thwart investigators.

The weakest part of Starr's case, they said, is the attempt to transform some of the president's actions, particularly his court battles on executive privilege, into violations of his constitutional duties.

"There is substantial and credible information that the President's lies about his relationship with Ms. Lewinsky were abundant and calculating," the Starr report alleges, and that claim of perjury forms the core of the case against Clinton. Four of the 11 grounds for impeachment cited by Starr are allegations of perjury in Clinton's deposition in the Jones case and a fifth accuses Clinton of perjury in his grand jury testimony last month.

Perjury is generally a difficult crime to prove, because prosecutors must show that a defendant not only made false statements but knowingly lied. Clinton's lawyers yesterday set the stage for arguing that the president's statements were merely "narrow answers to ambiguous questions."

But as the Starr report set out, some of the alleged false statements—for example, whether Clinton ever remembered being alone with Lewinsky—did not involve possible misinterpretations of badly phrased questions. "The president's denials, semantic and factual, do not withstand scrutiny," the report said.

In addition, the issue of whether the president lied to the grand jury—a potentially far more serious matter for congressional inquiry—appears likely to come down to a contest between the sworn statements of Lewinsky and the president, who has already admitted making statements about his relationship with the intern that were misleading at best.

Clinton said in his grand jury testimony that he did not engage in any conduct with Lewinsky covered by the definition of "sexual relations" used by Jones's lawyers; Lewinsky related 10 incidents in which she described conduct by the president that is clearly within the Jones definition. The report says her testimony is corroborated by Lewinsky's contemporaneous descriptions of the encounters to 10 friends and family members. "Given that his credibility has been shattered, Monica Lewinsky would seem more credible than Bill Clinton on this point, unless the defense can present evidence that Lewinsky had reason to exaggerate their sexual contact or a had a history of such exaggerations," said UCLA law professor Peter Arenella.

As the debate over Clinton's actions has proceeded during the last eight months, most members of Congress have said that the biggest areas of jeopardy for the president concern possible obstruction of justice—in allegedly coaching Lewinsky or Currie to lie, in ensuring that Lewinsky did not turn over to the Jones lawyers the gifts from the president that they had subpoenaed, or in helping secure a job for Lewinsky during the period when the Jones lawyers were seeking her testimony.

On that score, the Starr report provided extensive new evidence about Clinton's intense personal involvement in helping Lewinsky obtain a job. For example, the report says that immediately after Clinton learned that Lewinsky was on the witness list for the Jones case, his efforts to help her find a job intensified.

The report also details testimony from Currie about Clinton's conversations with her just after his deposition in the Jones case, episodes that prosecutors say show the president was trying to coach Currie to cover up his relationship with Lewinsky.

Although Clinton during his grand jury testimony said he was merely "trying to determine whether my recollection was right" and "get the facts down," Starr contends that Clinton's statements, and his insistent tone, as related by Currie, show that he feared Currie might become a witness in the case and "sought improperly to influence" her testimony.

The Currie allegations are "one of the more damning things," in the Starr report, said William & Mary law school professor Michael Gerhardt. But, he said, "It's going to be practically impossible to try to prove he had specific intent to tamper with a witness. But it's going to again reflect on his basic truthfulness and credibility."

Some legal experts said they thought Starr's report went further afield when it accused Clinton of obstructing justice by lying to potential grand jury witnesses.

Starr's final set of allegations, involving Clinton's alleged abuse of office, sought to bring Clinton's conduct out of the arena of criminal law and into that constitutional framework, but it also seemed the most subject to accusations of overreaching, some experts said.

"I just find that to be incredibly thin," said Gerhardt, author of a book on impeachment.

Still, scholars said the ultimate judgment for Congress will not be so much whether Clinton is guilty of specific crimes as whether his conduct calls into question his fitness to serve as chief executive.

"It is not a technical statute book question but whether this is worthy of undoing a national election," said Yale Law School professor Akhil Reed Amar. "That's what the debate should be about. Looking the American people in the eye and lying to them, looking your Cabinet in the eye and lying to them, is potentially far more serious, high political misconduct, than technical perjury in a civil deposition, even thought that one might be more technically criminal."

Said Harvard Law School professor Laurence H. Tribe, "The lines that we draw in the criminal law are not always particularly relevant to this question of whether there was a grave abuse of presidential power that makes someone unfit to serve and makes it appropriate to undo the results of an election. . . . I do think this is in a gray area where it's entirely appropriate and unavoidable to be thinking about whether impeachment is right."

Dreary Prose, Silly Plot. Can't Put It Down

By Joel Achenbach

The discerning reader should be aware that the Starr Report is a challenging piece of literature. It does not fit precisely into any of the familiar genres. It is certainly not a romance in the traditional sense. At moments it can be read as farce, other times as tragedy. But probably the genre into which the report fits best would be "pornography."

Quite frankly this is smut, an incredibly offensive and numbingly repetitive tale of sex and its consequences. The main characters, "The President" and "Ms. Lewinsky," are repulsive. But so, gradually, is the narrator himself. There are portions early in his work that are compelling. But his story is punishingly long, humorless, with an almost crazed zeal. It is not enough to show that The President lied about sex. It must be shown again and again, literally piling on, page after page.

There has been some commentary bandied about that this is not a story "about sex," but if that is so, then the same can be said of "Valley of the Dolls."

To an astonishing degree, the material, for all its sexual exertions, is not at all titillating. The sex is pathetic. One senses that the two principals are engaged not only in the most scandalous sexual relationship in history but also the least satisfying.

The parties to the affair have brief, fleeting semi-sex in a hallway with the door slightly ajar so that they can hear if someone comes. The President has a tendency to talk on the phone while enjoying sexual gratification, a sly commentary on the modern fanaticism for "multi-tasking." They have a "Christmas kiss," but the man has his eyes wide open, scanning for witnesses. Nothing goes right for this pair. They argue. They tell lies. They get scared. They get exposed. He denies their love. She is hurt. Eventually an Independent Counsel writes a 445-page report with 2,600 pages of appendixes to prove that they did, in fact, have this long, stupid relationship.

One longs for the comparative pith of Tolstoy.

The reader gasps in reading certain details. If The President is telling the truth-that, for him, sexual gratification had nothing to do with pleasing his partner-then his monstrous selfishness is surely the impeachable offense that the Independent Counsel tries so feverishly to discover.

There are other moments when the reader is unsure how to react. Do we laugh when an aide tells Ms. Lewinsky that she is getting a lot of "face time" with The President?

A few telling moments reward the patience of the reader. At one point, The President summons his political consultant to ask for an instant poll on whether he could survive the revelation of an adulterous affair. The consultant says he can't. "Well, we just have to

win, then," The President says. For a moment the text becomes genuine literature, if not quite at the level of Robert Penn Warren.

But then there is a bizarre, implausible event involving a cigar. It
is simply too incredible to be taken seriously. Dickens is known for
phenomenal plot twists, but not even he would stretch the reader's
credulity so!

Roughly around the 47th mention of the cigar-the report actually
uses the shorthand "the cigar incident"-it has become a bore. The
reader thinks, tell me something I don't know. That is coupled with
a feeling of extreme guilt and shame, a sense of invasiveness. The
reader realizes that this is not exactly "Profiles in Courage."

The perverse reader may actually begin to root for the despicable
President as he seeks to elude the clutches of the prosecuting team.
The Starr Report declares:

"The chance that the semen is not the President's is one in 7.87
trillion."

And the reader thinks: Good, at least it's not an absolute certainty.

A note about the writing style. It is certainly postmodern in its stead-
fast inelegance, its rejection of "readability." The tone is so lawyerly
it almost reads like an indictment. The clever reader may wonder:
Could this really be a subtle satire of an absurdly legalistic society?

A typical passage, in the Introduction to the Grounds for
Impeachment section, reads:

"10. President Clinton endeavored to obstruct justice during the
grand jury investigation by refusing to testify for seven months and
lying to senior White House aides with knowledge that they would
relay the President's false statements to the grand jury-and did
thereby deceive, obstruct, and impede the grand jury."

One wishes for something more vernacular, perhaps as Erskine
Caldwell might have rendered it:

"Bubba tole his people: Cover my butt."

Argumentative, parsing, persnickety, the Starr Report spends a
brutal amount of its energy discussing what is and what is not sex.

"The President refused to say whether he had oral sex. Instead, the President said (i) that the undefined terms 'sexual affair,' 'sexual relationship,' and 'sexual relations' necessarily require sexual intercourse, (ii) that he had not engaged in intercourse with Ms. Lewinsky, and (iii) that he therefore had not committed perjury in denying a sexual relationship, sexual affair, or sexual relations."

And so on. Droning and tedious. The report violates the standard narrative arc, showing no interest in foreshadowing or the gradual development of character and conflict.

Some readers may find that the tale suffers from a fatal obviousness. The story involves a powerful man who is having an affair. He seeks to keep it a secret. The reader expects a plot twist at this point. Perhaps the man will do something unusual, like remain true to his secret love and resign his office, as did the King of England with Wallis Warfield Simpson.

But no, instead he tries to weasel and squirm his way out of it. A stock character acts in a predictable fashion. No one evolves. No one has a spiritual transformation. No one dies. This is a story? This is a yarn for the ages?

Perhaps the sequel will be more edifying.

Worries About Nation's Morals Test a Reluctance to Judge

By Richard Morin and David S. Broder

For many Americans, the White House scandal is just the latest symptom of broad and deep moral decline. Everywhere they look—in the newspaper, on television, in their own neighborhoods and even within their own families—they see eroding values.

An in-depth study of the values Americans espouse suggests why President Clinton's extramarital dalliance with Monica S. Lewinsky angers and upsets so many people—and why the country has been so reluctant to punish him politically for behavior it considers wrong.

On one hand, Clinton has confronted the country with a sample of what three out of four of his constituents see as a dangerous decline in the values on display in the national culture. They link the White House escapade to their broader worries about the lack of respect for tradition and authority, to the coarse content of the movies, television and music, to personal dishonesty and sexual promiscuity.

At the same time, Clinton has become a test case of whether this generation of Americans wants to sit in judgment on each other or be willing to live and let live.

More than seven in 10 said adultery was unacceptable and "should not be tolerated." Yet when it comes to Clinton, what the public says and what it means are two different things: Fewer than half of those who said adultery "should not be tolerated" said Clinton's affair with Lewinsky was an important matter. Twice as many said it was important whether he had lied about it or encouraged Lewinsky to lie.

The survey, conducted by The Post in collaboration with Harvard University and the Henry J. Kaiser Family Foundation, was virtually complete before the president's August 17 speech acknowledging the widely suspected relationship with Lewinsky. The public judgment may shift with the release of the report from independent counsel Kenneth W. Starr.

Clinton's actions are not viewed in isolation. They come at a time when many Americans are also upset by what they regard as other threatening social trends, from alcoholism to sexual harassment to homosexuality to homelessness.

Coming to judgment on Clinton requires resolving a complex of considerations.

The survey found that nine out of 10 Americans said an affair by a married person is unacceptable. The condemnation for that behavior was far stronger than for other controversial actions, including bearing a child out of wedlock, marijuana smoking or same-sex marriage.

The poll also showed that only one American in five thought Clinton shared most of that person's values, with twice as many saying he embodied hardly any or none of them. Vice President Gore and first lady Hillary Rodham Clinton fared better; House Speaker Newt Gingrich (R-Ga.), worse. But Clinton's low rating apparently has pulled down the Democratic Party. Its rating on upholding moral standards has slumped.

At a deeper level, the survey showed Americans sharply divided on what to expect from a political leader. Half of those interviewed—49 percent—say it is performance alone that counts in a president, agreeing that "as long as he does a good job running the country, whatever he does in his personal life is not important." But just as many disagree: They say the president has a "greater responsibility" to set "an example with his personal life."

When asked to say in their own words what worries them most about the country's values and morals, nearly as many mentioned Clinton or some aspect of the Lewinsky sub scandal as specified declining family values.

Edward Krutulis, 34, a Plainfield, Ill., pharmaceutical sales representative, after lamenting the country's moral condition, said, "Obviously, President Clinton's not much of a role model for us."

That might not be so worrisome if people were not concerned about the trends they see in American society. Three in four said the country's values and morals are in serious decline. Nearly two in three said they were dissatisfied with the "honesty and standards of behavior of the people in this country."

Large majorities of men and women, Democrats and Republicans, liberals and conservatives, blacks and whites, young people and old, the wealthy and the poor sense something has gone terribly wrong with the country's moral compass.

"Our values are in very, very poor shape and society is dropping at a dramatic rate," said Richard Easton Jr., 28, a shipping clerk in a plastics factory in Turner's Falls, Mass. His short list of examples that illustrate America's moral decline is revealing: Just behind crime but ahead of the erosion of family life, he cites politics.

"I am tired of politics," Easton admits. "The political system needs to be revamped. There's too few honest people in politics."

Easton, who voted for Clinton in 1996, said the president's troubles "confirmed for me even more that in politics, values and morals and honesty and truth don't go together."

The survey revealed a growing "morality gap" in the perception of the two parties. The percentage of Americans who say they trust the Democratic Party to encourage "high moral standards and values" has never been lower, dropping from 33 percent in July to 26 percent last month.

But the poll also found that Republicans have not greatly improved their reputation: 41 percent of those surveyed said the GOP was the party of values and morals, unchanged from July but up slightly from a year ago.

The proportion that said they trusted neither party to set the moral and ethical tone for the country increased from 13 percent in July to 20 percent barely a month later.

The surging importance of values and moral issues may dramatically affect vote choices this November. Among the 21 percent of Americans who believe the country's values are strong, 62 percent say they plan to vote for a Democratic candidate for Congress. But among those who think the country's values are headed in the wrong direction—a much larger number—Republicans enjoy a 46 percent to 40 percent advantage, according to the Post/ Harvard/ Kaiser survey.

A majority of Americans—55 percent—believe their values are losing influence, while 35 percent say their morals and values are on the rise, views that are correlated with candidate preferences.

Among those who think their values are gaining influence, 50 percent plan to vote for a Democratic congressional candidate while 38 percent support a Republican. But among those who say their values are losing, Republicans held a 46 percent to 42 percent advantage.

The poll found that one in four Americans are "values voters" — casting their ballot primarily on the basis of a candidate's personal values and morals, rather than on issues, ideology or experience. Republican House candidates were the choice of 57 percent of these voters, while 30 percent supported a Democrat.

One other consequence of the White House scandal is rising dissatisfaction with the government generally: 41 percent of those interviewed said they were satisfied with the way the federal government is working, down from 46 percent in a Post survey conducted immediately before the scandal broke.

At the same time, the proportion indicating they were dissatisfied with the federal government increased, from 53 percent in January to 57 percent in the Post/Harvard/Kaiser poll.

While modest, these changes reversed an encouraging trend: Immediately before the Lewinsky scandal broke, public confidence in the government was on the sub rise. The latest results suggest that even the good economy and America's superpower status may not be good enough to prevent an increase in public mistrust of government, which had never been higher when Clinton took office six years ago.

"I teach children," said Donald Jackson, 36, of Easton, Pa. "They look up to me. I see children imitating what I do. Whether or not I like that role, or accept that role, it is there. Many kids look up to the president and say, sub 'I want to be president.' Look at the presidency now," he said. "Is this what they want to be like?"

Other conflicts complicate the values debate, contributing to this sense of division and confusion symbolized by public reaction to the White House scandal.

Nine in 10 Americans agree that the country "would have many fewer problems if there were more emphasis on traditional family values." At the same time, nearly as many—70 percent—agree that "we should be more tolerant of people who choose to live according to their own moral standards even if we think they are wrong."

Delia Mohlie, 44, a married mother of two who works part time as an assistant librarian, says she knows her attitudes toward the issues involved in the Clinton scandal seem "very inconsistent." The Waldoboro, Maine, resident is strongly against adultery, but at the same time does not believe Clinton's marital infidelity is an important issue.

Mohlie, a Democrat and 1996 Clinton voter, said, "Number one, it doesn't matter to other parts of his presidency. And number two, no longer do Americans expect leaders to be lily white in their behavioral patterns. . . . I can't expect perfection. It's not realistic."

Another Democrat, Alice May Pugh, 42, who runs a group home for the mentally retarded and serves as mayor of Dillonvale, Ohio, said she worries that "so many young people seem to have no values and a lot of the people who are leading have no morals. I'm more or less disgusted with the whole political situation and I'm very disgusted with all the media attention to all the wrong issues."

But Pugh declines to pass critical judgment on Clinton. "I think he's done a good job as president," she said. "His private life is between him and his wife. It's been blown out of proportion by the media."

Yet such tolerance for unacceptable behavior clearly disturbs many Americans and contributes to the sense that the country's morals and ethics will only get worse, not better.

Two in three said they worried that the country would become "too tolerant of behaviors that are bad for society"; fewer than a third said their greatest fear for the future was that we would become "too intolerant of behaviors that don't do any real harm."

"There are very few values left," said Patrice Weston, a 31-year-old teacher who lives in Hudson, N.C. "There's not even small-town values anymore. I feel that nowadays no one stands up for what they believe in . . . for things they would have stood up for 20 years ago. You will be berated if you do."

Assistant director of polling Claudia Deane contributed to this report.

Publisher's Note:

PublicAffairs and the *Washington Post* recognize that the independent counsel's report contains extensive sexually explicit material that normally would be unacceptable for publication in the *Post*. However, we have decided not to edit the text of the report because of the unique circumstances of its release by the U.S. Congress, on government Internet sites and by other means, in the midst of public controversy over whether the president has committed impeachable offenses. Because these documents are central to public and political debate over the conduct of both Clinton and Starr that is now underway, we have decided to provide the full text of the Starr report and the White House response issued on Friday, September 11, 1998. It should be noted that the White House and President Clinton's lawyers were unable to review the Starr report before writing their response. It should also be noted that some material in these unedited texts is inappropriate for children and younger readers, and some of the material will be offensive to some adults.

THE STARR REPORT

Table of Contents

Referral

Key Dates

November 1992	William Jefferson Clinton elected President of the United States
May 1994	Paula Jones files lawsuit against President Clinton
July 1995	Monica S. Lewinsky begins White House internship
November 15, 1995	President begins sexual relationship with Lewinsky
April 5, 1996	Lewinsky transferred from White House to Pentagon
November 1996	President Clinton reelected
March 29, 1997	Last intimate contact between President and Monica Lewinsky
December 5, 1997	Lewinsky appears on *Jones* Witness List
December 19, 1997	Lewinsky served with subpoena to appear at deposition and produce gifts from President Clinton
December 24, 1998	Lewinsky's last day of work at the Pentagon
December 28, 1997	Lewinsky meets with the President and receives gifts; later gives box of gifts from the President to Betty Currie.
January 7, 1998	Lewinsky signs affidavit intended for filing in *Jones* case.

January 13, 1998	Lewinsky accepts job offer at Revlon in New York.
January 16, 1998	Special Division appoints Independent Counsel Kenneth W. Starr to investigate Lewinsky matter
January 17, 1998	President deposed in *Jones* case
January 18, 1998	President meets with Betty Currie to discuss President's deposition
January 21, 1998	Lewinsky matter reported in press; President denies allegations of a sexual relationship and of suborning perjury
April 1, 1998	Judge Wright grants summary judgment for President Clinton in the *Jones* litigation
July 17, 1998	President served with grand jury subpoena, later withdrawn in return for testimony
July 28, 1998	Immunity/Cooperation Agreement reached between Lewinsky and OIC
August 17, 1998	President testifies before the grand jury; later he publicly acknowledges improper relationship
September 9, 1998	OIC submits Referral to Congress pursuant to 28 U.S.C. § 595(c)

Table of Names

The Principals

William Jefferson Clinton	President of the United States
Paula Corbin Jones	Plaintiff in a civil suit against President Clinton
Monica Lewinsky	Former White House Intern and Employee
Betty Currie	Personal Secretary to the President
Vernon Jordan	Friend of President Clinton, and Partner at Law Firm of Akin, Gump, Strauss, Hauer & Feld

The First Family

Hillary Rodham Clinton	First Lady of the United States
Chelsea Clinton	Daughter of the President and First Lady

Presidential Aides/Advisors/Assistants

Madeline Albright	Secretary of State
Sidney Blumenthal	Assistant to the President
Erskine Bowles	White House Chief of Staff
Lanny Bruer	Special Counsel to the President
Stephen Goodin	Aide to President Clinton
Nancy Hernreich	Deputy Assistant to the President and Director of Oval Office Operations

John Hilley	Assistant to the President and Director of Legislative Affairs; Monica Lewinsky's Supervisor
Harold Ickes	Former Deputy Chief of Staff
Janis Kearney	Special Assistant to the President and Records Manager
Timothy Keating	Special Assistant to the President and Staff Director for Legislative Affairs; Monica Lewinsky's Immediate Supervisor
Ann Lewis	Director, White House Communications
Evelyn Lieberman	Former Deputy Chief of Staff
Bruce Lindsey	Deputy White House Counsel
Sylvia Mathews	Deputy White House Chief of Staff
Thomas "Mack" McLarty	Former White House Chief of Staff
Cheryl Mills	Deputy White House Counsel
Dick Morris	Former Advisor to President Clinton
Bob Nash	Assistant to the President and Director of Presidential Personnel
Leon Panetta	Former White House Chief of Staff
John Podesta	Deputy White House Chief of Staff
Hon. Bill Richardson	U.S. Ambassador to the United Nations

Charles Ruff	White House Counsel
Marsha Scott	Deputy Director of Personnel
George Stephanopoulous	Former Senior Advisor for Policy and Strategy
Barry Toiv	Deputy White House Press Secretary

Other White House Personnel

Karin Joyce Abramson	Former Director of the White House Intern Program
Caroline Badinelli	Former White House Intern
Douglas Band	Former White House Intern
Tracy Anne Bobowick	Former White House Employee, Correspondence Office
Laura Capps	Former White House Intern
Jay Footlik	Former Employee of the Office of Presidential Personnel
Patrick Griffin	Former Assistant to the President and Director of Legislative Affairs
George Hannie	White House Butler
Jocelyn Jolley	Former Director of Congressional Correspondence in the White House
Maureen Lewis	Former White House Employee, Correspondence Office
Glen Maes	White House Steward to President Clinton

Bayani Nelvis	White House Steward to President Clinton
Charles O'Malley	White House Operations Deputy Chief
Jennifer Palmieri	Former Special Assistant to the Chief of Staff
Debra Schiff	Receptionist, West Wing Lobby
Jamie Beth Schwartz	Former Special Assistant to the Social Secretary in the White House Social Office
Patsy Thomasson	Director of the Office of Administration, Executive Office of the President
Kathleen Willey	Former White House Volunteer
Michael Williams	Former White House Intern

Department of Defense Employees

Kenneth Bacon	Assistant Secretary of Defense for Public Affairs; Monica Lewinsky's Pentagon Supervisor
Elizabeth Bailey	Special Assistant to the Secretary of Defense for White House Liaison
Clifford Bernath	Former Deputy to Assistant Secretary of Defense for Public Affairs
Donna Boltz	Assistant in the Office of the Assistant Secretary of Defense for Public Affairs

Jeremy "Mike" Boorda	Admiral, United States Navy (deceased)
Richard Bridges	Colonel, Director for Defense Information
Rebecca Cooper	Chief of Staff, United States Mission to the United Nations
Monica Ramirez Cranick	Sergeant, Broadcast Engineer, Office of the Secretary of Defense for Public Affairs
Marsha Dimel	Administrative Support Specialist for Personnel and Administration in the National Security Council
Charles Duncan	Former Special Assistant to the Secretary of Defense for Public Affairs
Kate Friedrich	Special Assistant, National Security Advisor
Jeff Gradick	Commander, Military Assistant to the Deputy Assistant to the Assistant Secretary of Defense for Public Affairs
James Graybeal	Lt. Commander, Military Assistant to the Deputy Assistant to the Assistant Secretary of Defense for Public Affairs
Mark Huffman	Office Manager, Office of Public Affairs, United States Department of Defense
Jodi Kessinger	Former Administrative Assistant, Office of the National Security Advisor, National Security Council

Janet Reno	Attorney General of the United States
Darby Ellen Stott	Special Assistant, White House Press Secretary
Mona Sutphen	Special Assistant to the United States Ambassador to the United Nations
Robert Tyrer	Chief of Staff for the Secretary of Defense
Isabelle Watkins	Executive Assistant to Bill Richardson

Monica Lewinsky's Friends/Family/Acquaintances

Andrew Bleiler	Former Boyfriend of Monica Lewinsky
Catherine Allday Davis	Friend of Monica Lewinky
Kelly Lynn Davis	Friend of Monica Lewinsky
Neysa Erbland	Friend of Monica Lewinsky
Kathleen Estep	Counselor to Monica Lewinsky
Deborah Finerman	Aunt of Monica Lewinsky
David Grobanie	Owner of Briarwood Bookstore
Dr. Irene Kassorla	Therapist to Monica Lewinsky
Walter Kaye	Family friend of Monica Lewinsky
Marcia Lewis	Mother of Monica Lewinsky
Ashley Raines	Friend of Monica Lewinsky and White House Director of Office and Policy Development Operations and Special Liaison

Peter Strauss	Husband of Marcia Lewis
Linda Tripp	Friend of Monica Lewinsky
Natalie Rose Ungvari	Friend of Monica Lewinsky
Dale Young	Family friend of Monica Lewinsky

Monica Lewinsky's New York Employment Contacts

Celia Berk	Managing Director of Human Resources at Burson-Marstellar
Ursula Fairbairn	Executive Vice President, Human Resources and Quality of American Express
Peter Georgescu	Chairman and Chief Executive Officer at Young & Rubicam
Richard Halerpin	Executive Vice President and Special Counsel to the President of Revlon
Barbara Naismith	Secretary at American Express
Ronald Perelman	Chairman of the Board of McAndrews & Forbes Holding Incorporated
Thomas Schick	Executive Vice President, Corporate Affairs and Communications at American Express
Douglas S. Willey	Vice President, Hecht-Spencer

Secret Service

| William C. Bordley | Secret Service Uniformed Officer |
| Gary Byrne | Secret Service Uniformed Officer |

Daniel Carbonetti	Secret Service Uniformed Officer
Brent Chinery	Secret Service Uniformed Officer
Larry Cockell	Special Agent In Charge, Secret Service Presidential Protective Division
Douglas Dragotta	Secret Service Uniformed Officer
Robert C. Ferguson	Secret Service Uniformed Officer
Lewis Fox	Retired Secret Service Uniformed Officer
Mathew Fitsch	Lt., Secret Service Uniformed Division
Nelson Garabito	Secret Service Uniformed Officer
Bryan Hall	Secret Service Uniformed Officer
Brian Henderson	Secret Service Uniformed Officer
Reginald Hightower	Secret Service Uniformed Officer
Oliver Janney	Secret Service Uniformed Officer
Greg LaDow	Secret Service Uniformed Officer
William Ludtke III	Secret Service Uniformed Officer
Tim Lynn	Secret Service Uniformed Officer
Lewis Merletti	Director, Secret Service
John Muskett	Secret Service Uniformed Officer
Fremon Myles, Jr.	Secret Service Uniformed Officer
Robert Myrick	Secret Service Uniformed Officer
Gary Niedzwieki	Secret Service Uniformed Officer
Joe Overstreet	Secret Service Uniformed Officer
Steven Pape	Secret Service Uniformed Officer

Stacy Porter	Secret Service Uniformed Officer
Geoffrey Purdie	Secret Service Uniformed Officer, Captain
William Clair Shegogue	Secret Service Uniformed Officer
Barry Smith	Secret Service Uniformed Officer
William Tyler	Secret Service Uniformed Officer
Sandra Verna	Secret Service Uniformed Officer
Keith Williams	Secret Service Uniformed Officer, Sergeant
Michael Wilson	Secret Service Uniformed Officer
Bryant Withrow	Lt., Secret Service Uniformed Office Division

Lawyers and Judges

Kirbe Behre	Linda Tripp's former attorney
Robert Bennett	Attorney for President Clinton
Robert Bittman	Deputy Independent Counsel
Plato Cacheris	Attorney for Monica Lewinsky
Frank Carter	Monica Lewinsky's former attorney
Lloyd Cutler	Former White House Counsel
Mitchell Ettinger	Attorney for President Clinton
Vince Foster	Former Deputy White House Counsel
Hon. Norma Holloway Johnson	Chief Judge, U.S. District Court for the District of Columbia
David Kendall	Attorney for President Clinton

Karl Metzner	Attorney for Betty Currie
Kathy Sexton	Attorney for President Clinton
Hon. Susan Webber Wright	U.S. District Judge presiding over Jones v. Clinton civil suit
Hon. David Tatel	Judge, U.S. Court of Appeals for the D.C. Circuit

Media

Matt Drudge	Drudge Report
Kristen Ganong	Manager of Publications, The Heritage Foundation
Lucianne Goldberg	Literary Agent
Michael Isikoff	Reporter, Newsweek Magazine
Jim Lehrer	Television Journalist
Eleanor Mondale	Reporter, CBS News
Susan Schmidt	Correspondent, Washington Post

Foreign Dignitaries

Yitzak Rabin	Former Prime Minister of Israel
Ernesto Zedillo	President of Mexico

Other

Ron Brown	Former Commerce Secretary
Patrick Fallon	Special Agent, Federal Bureau of Investigation
Webster L. Hubbell	Former Associate Attorney General, Friend of the Clinton Family

Introduction

As required by Section 595(c) of Title 28 of the United States Code, the Office of the Independent Counsel ("OIC" or "Office") hereby submits substantial and credible information that President William Jefferson Clinton committed acts that may constitute grounds for an impeachment.[1]

The information reveals that President Clinton:

- lied under oath at a civil deposition while he was a defendant in a sexual harassment lawsuit;

- lied under oath to a grand jury;

- attempted to influence the testimony of a potential witness who had direct knowledge of facts that would reveal the falsity of his deposition testimony;

- attempted to obstruct justice by facilitating a witness's plan to refuse to comply with a subpoena;

- attempted to obstruct justice by encouraging a witness to file an affidavit that the President knew would be false, and then by making use of that false affidavit at his own deposition;

- lied to potential grand jury witnesses, knowing that they would repeat those lies before the grand jury; and

• engaged in a pattern of conduct that was inconsistent with his constitutional duty to faithfully execute the laws.

The evidence shows that these acts, and others, were part of a pattern that began as an effort to prevent the disclosure of information about the President's relationship with a former White House intern and employee, Monica S. Lewinsky, and continued as an effort to prevent the information from being disclosed in an ongoing criminal investigation.

FACTUAL BACKGROUND

In May 1994, Paula Corbin Jones filed a lawsuit against William Jefferson Clinton in the United States District Court for the Eastern District of Arkansas.[2] Ms. Jones alleged that while he was the Governor of Arkansas, President Clinton sexually harassed her during an incident in a Little Rock hotel room.[3] President Clinton denied the allegations. He also challenged the ability of a private litigant to pursue a lawsuit against a sitting President. In May 1997, the Supreme Court unanimously rejected the President's legal argument. The Court concluded that Ms. Jones, "[l]ike every other citizen who properly invokes [the District Court's] jurisdiction . . . has a right to an orderly disposition of her claims," and that therefore Ms. Jones was entitled to pursue her claims while the President was in office.[4] A few months later, the pretrial discovery process began.[5]

One sharply disputed issue in the *Jones* litigation was the extent to which the President would be required to disclose information about sexual relationships he may have had with "other women." Ms. Jones's attorneys sought disclosure of this information, arguing that it was relevant to proving that the President had propositioned Ms. Jones. The President resisted the discovery requests, arguing that evidence of relationships with other women (if any) was irrelevant.

In late 1997, the issue was presented to United States District Judge Susan Webber Wright for resolution. Judge Wright's decision was unambiguous. For purposes of pretrial discovery, President Clinton was required to provide certain information about his alleged relationships with other women. In an order dated December 11, 1997, for example, Judge Wright said: "The Court finds, therefore, that the plaintiff is entitled to information regarding any individuals with whom the President had sexual relations or proposed or sought to have sexual relations and who were during the relevant time frame state or federal employees."[6] Judge Wright left for another day the issue whether any information of this type would be admissible were the case to go to trial. But for purposes of answering the written questions served on the President, and for purposes of answering questions at a deposition, the District Court ruled that the President must respond.

In mid-December 1997, the President answered one of the written discovery questions posed by Ms. Jones on this issue. When asked to identify all women who were state or federal employees and with whom he had had "sexual relations" since 1986,[7] the President answered under oath: "None."[8] For purposes of this interrogatory, the term "sexual relations" was not defined.

On January 17, 1998, President Clinton was questioned under oath about his relationships with other women in the workplace, this time at a deposition. Judge Wright presided over the deposition. The President was asked numerous questions about his relationship with Monica Lewinsky, by then a 24-year-old former White House intern, White House employee, and Pentagon employee. Under oath and in the presence of Judge Wright, the President denied that he had engaged in a "sexual affair," a "sexual relationship," or "sexual relations" with Ms. Lewinsky. The President also stated that he had no specific memory of having been alone with Ms. Lewinsky, that he remembered few details of any gifts they might have exchanged, and indicated that no one except his attorneys had kept him informed of Ms. Lewinsky's status as a potential witness in the *Jones* case.

THE INVESTIGATION

On January 12, 1998, this Office received information that Monica Lewinsky was attempting to influence the testimony of one of the witnesses in the *Jones* litigation, and that Ms. Lewinsky herself was prepared to provide false information under oath in that lawsuit. The OIC was also informed that Ms. Lewinsky had spoken to the President and the President's close friend Vernon Jordan about being subpoenaed to testify in the *Jones* suit, and that Vernon Jordan and others were helping her find a job. The allegations with respect to Mr. Jordan and the job search were similar to ones already under review in the ongoing Whitewater investigation.[9]

After gathering preliminary evidence to test the information's reliability, the OIC presented the evidence to Attorney General Janet Reno. Based on her review of the information, the Attorney General determined that a further investigation by the Independent Counsel was required.

On the following day, Attorney General Reno petitioned the Special Division of the United States Court of Appeals for the District of Columbia Circuit, on an expedited basis, to expand the jurisdiction of Independent Counsel Kenneth W. Starr. On January 16, 1998, in response to the Attorney General's request, the Special Division issued an order that provides in pertinent part:

The Independent Counsel shall have jurisdiction and authority to investigate to the maximum extent authorized by the Independent Counsel Reauthorization Act of 1994 whether Monica Lewinsky or others suborned perjury, obstructed justice, intimidated witnesses, or otherwise violated federal law other than a Class B or C misdemeanor or infraction in dealing with witnesses, potential witnesses, attorneys, or others concerning the civil case *Jones v. Clinton*.[10]

On January 28, 1998, after the allegations about the President's relationship with Ms. Lewinsky became public, the OIC filed a Motion for Limited Intervention and a Stay of Discovery in *Jones v. Clinton*. The OIC argued that the civil discovery process should be halted because it was having a negative effect on the criminal investigation. The OIC represented to the Court that numerous individuals then under subpoena in *Jones*, including Monica Lewinsky, were integral to the OIC's investigation, and that courts routinely stayed discovery in such circumstances.[11]

The next day Judge Wright responded to the OIC's motion. The Court ruled that discovery would be permitted to continue, except to the extent that it sought information about Monica Lewinsky. The Court acknowledged that "evidence concerning Monica Lewinsky might be relevant to the issues in [the *Jones*] case."[12] It concluded, however, that this evidence was not "essential to the core issues in this case," and that some of that evidence "might even be inadmissible."[13] The Court found that the potential value of this evidence was outweighed by the potential delay to the *Jones* case in continuing to seek discovery about Ms. Lewinsky.[14] The Court also was concerned that the OIC's investigation "could be impaired and prejudiced were the Court to permit inquiry into the Lewinsky matter by the parties in this civil case."[15]

On March 9, 1998, Judge Wright denied Ms. Jones's motion for reconsideration of the decision regarding Monica Lewinsky. The order states:

The Court readily acknowledges that evidence of the Lewinsky matter might have been relevant to plaintiff's case and, as she argues, that such evidence might possibly have helped her establish, among other things, intent, absence of mistake, motive, and habit on the part of the President. . . . Nevertheless, whatever relevance such evidence may otherwise have . . . it simply is not essential to the core issues in this case . . . .[16]

On April 1, 1998, Judge Wright granted President Clinton's motion for summary judgment, concluding that even if the facts alleged by Paula Jones were true, her claims failed as a matter of law.[17] Ms. Jones has filed an appeal, and as of the date of this Referral, the matter remains under consideration by the United States Court of Appeals for the Eighth Circuit.

After the dismissal of Ms. Jones's lawsuit, the criminal investigation continued. It was (and is) the view of this Office that any attempt to obstruct the proper functioning of the judicial system, regardless of the perceived merits of the underlying case, is a serious matter that warrants further inquiry. After careful consideration of all the evidence, the OIC has concluded that the evidence of wrong-doing is substantial and credible, and that the wrongdoing is of suf-ficient gravity that it warrants referral to Congress.[18]

THE SIGNIFICANCE OF THE EVIDENCE OF WRONGDOING

It is not the role of this Office to determine whether the Presi-dent's actions warrant impeachment by the House and removal by the Senate; those judgments are, of course, constitutionally entrusted to the legislative branch.[19] This Office is authorized, rather, to conduct criminal investigations and to seek criminal pros-ecutions for matters within its jurisdiction.[20] In carrying out its investigation, however, this Office also has a statutory duty to dis-close to Congress information that "may constitute grounds for an impeachment," a task that inevitably requires judgment about the seriousness of the acts revealed by the evidence.

From the beginning, this phase of the OIC's investigation has been criticized as an improper inquiry into the President's personal behavior; indeed, the President himself suggested that specific inquiries into his conduct were part of an effort to "criminalize my private life."[21] The regrettable fact that the investigation has often required witnesses to discuss sensitive personal matters has fueled this perception.

All Americans, including the President, are entitled to enjoy a pri-vate family life, free from public or governmental scrutiny. But the privacy concerns raised in this case are subject to limits, three of which we briefly set forth here.

First. The first limit was imposed when the President was sued in federal court for alleged sexual harassment. The evidence in such lit-igation is often personal. At times, that evidence is highly embar-rassing for both plaintiff and defendant. As Judge Wright noted at the President's January 1998 deposition, "I have never had a sexual harassment case where there was not some embarrassment."[22] Nevertheless, Congress and the Supreme Court have concluded that embarrassment-related concerns must give way to the greater interest in allowing aggrieved parties to pursue their claims. Courts have long recognized the difficulties of proving sexual harassment in the workplace, inasmuch as improper or unlawful behavior often takes place in private.[23] To excuse a party who lied or concealed evidence on the ground that the evidence covered only "personal" or "private" behavior would frustrate the goals that Congress and the courts have sought to achieve in enacting and interpreting the Nation's sexual harassment laws. That is particularly true when the conduct that is being concealed—sexual relations in the workplace between a high official and a young subordinate employee—itself conflicts with those goals.

Second. The second limit was imposed when Judge Wright required disclosure of the precise information that is in part the subject of this Referral. A federal judge specifically ordered the President, on more than one occasion, to provide the requested information about relationships with other women, including Monica Lewinsky. The fact that Judge Wright later determined that the evidence would not be admissible at trial, and still later granted judgment in the President's favor, does not change the President's legal duty at the time he testified. Like every litigant, the President was entitled to object to the discovery questions, and to seek guidance from the court if he thought those questions were improper. But having failed to convince the court that his objections were well founded, the President was duty bound to testify truthfully and fully. Perjury and attempts to obstruct the gathering of evidence can never be an acceptable response to a court order, regardless of the eventual course or outcome of the litigation.

The Supreme Court has spoken forcefully about perjury and other forms of obstruction of justice:

In this constitutional process of securing a witness' testimony, perjury simply has no place whatever. Perjured testimony is an obvious and flagrant affront to the basic concepts of judicial proceedings. Effective restraints against this type of egregious offense are therefore imperative.[24]

The insidious effects of perjury occur whether the case is civil or criminal. Only a few years ago, the Supreme Court considered a false statement made in a civil administrative proceeding: "False testimony in a formal proceeding is intolerable. We must neither reward nor condone such a 'flagrant affront' to the truth-seeking function of adversary proceedings. . . . Perjury should be severely sanctioned in appropriate cases."[25] Stated more simply, "[p]erjury is an obstruction of justice."[26]

Third. The third limit is unique to the President. "The Presidency is more than an executive responsibility. It is the inspiring symbol of all that is highest in American purpose and ideals."[27] When he took the Oath of Office in 1993 and again in 1997, President Clinton swore that he would "faithfully execute the Office of President."[28] As the head of the Executive Branch, the President has the constitutional duty to "take Care that the Laws be faithfully executed."[29] The President gave his testimony in the *Jones* case under oath and in the presence of a federal judge, a member of a co-equal branch of government; he then testified before a federal grand jury, a body of citizens who had themselves taken an oath to seek the truth. In view of the enormous trust and responsibility attendant to his high Office, the President has a manifest duty to ensure that his conduct at all times complies with the law of the land.

In sum, perjury and acts that obstruct justice by any citizen—whether in a criminal case, a grand jury investigation, a congressional hearing, a civil trial, or civil discovery—are profoundly serious matters. When such acts are committed by the President of the United States, we believe those acts "may constitute grounds for an impeachment."

THE SCOPE OF THE REFERRAL

1. Background of the Investigation.

The link between the OIC's jurisdiction—as it existed at the end of 1997—and the matters set forth in this Referral is complex but direct. In January 1998, Linda Tripp, a witness in three ongoing

OIC investigations, came forward with allegations that: (i) Monica Lewinsky was planning to commit perjury in *Jones v. Clinton*, and (ii) she had asked Ms. Tripp to do the same. Ms. Tripp also stated that: (i) Vernon Jordan had counseled Ms. Lewinsky and helped her obtain legal representation in the *Jones* case, and (ii) at the same time, Mr. Jordan was helping Ms. Lewinsky obtain employment in the private sector.

OIC investigators and prosecutors recognized parallels between Mr. Jordan's relationship with Ms. Lewinsky and his earlier relationship with a pivotal Whitewater-Madison figure, Webster L. Hubbell. Prior to January 1998, the OIC possessed evidence that Vernon Jordan—along with other high-level associates of the President and First Lady—helped Mr. Hubbell obtain lucrative consulting contracts while he was a potential witness and/or subject in the OIC's ongoing investigation. This assistance took place, moreover, while Mr. Hubbell was a target of a separate criminal investigation into his own conduct. The OIC also possessed evidence that the President and the First Lady knew and approved of the Hubbell-focused assistance.

Specifically, in the wake of his April 1994 resignation from the Justice Department, Mr. Hubbell launched a private consulting practice in Washington, D.C. In the startup process, Mr. Hubbell received substantial aid from important public and private figures. On the day prior to Mr. Hubbell announcing his resignation, White House Chief of Staff Thomas "Mack" McLarty attended a meeting at the White House with the President, First Lady, and others, where Mr. Hubbell's resignation was a topic of discussion.

At some point after the White House meeting, Mr. McLarty spoke with Vernon Jordan about Mr. Jordan's assistance to Mr. Hubbell. Mr. Jordan introduced Mr. Hubbell to senior executives at New York-based MacAndrews & Forbes Holding Co. Mr. Jordan is a director of Revlon, Inc., a company controlled by MacAndrews & Forbes. The introduction was successful; MacAndrews & Forbes retained Mr. Hubbell at a rate of $25,000 per quarter. Vernon Jordan informed President Clinton that he was helping Mr. Hubbell.[31]

By late 1997, this Office was investigating whether a relationship existed between consulting payments to Mr. Hubbell and his lack of cooperation (specifically, his incomplete testimony) with the OIC's investigation.[32] In particular, the OIC was investigating whether Mr. Hubbell concealed information about certain core Arkansas matters, namely, the much-publicized Castle Grande real estate project and related legal work by the Rose Law Firm, including the First Lady.

Against this background, the OIC considered the January 1998 allegations that: (i) Ms. Lewinsky was prepared to lie in order to benefit the President, and (ii) Vernon Jordan was assisting Ms. Lewinsky in the *Jones* litigation, while simultaneously helping her apply for a private-sector job with, among others, Revlon, Inc.

Based in part on these similarities, the OIC undertook a preliminary investigation. On January 15, 1998, this Office informed the Justice Department of the results of our inquiry. The Attorney General immediately applied to the Special Division of the Court of Appeals for the District of Columbia Circuit for an expansion of the OIC's jurisdiction. The Special Division granted this request and authorized the OIC to determine whether Monica Lewinsky or others had violated federal law in connection with the *Jones v. Clinton* case.

2. Current Status of the Investigation.

When the OIC's jurisdiction was expanded to cover the Lewinsky matter in January 1998, several matters remained under active investigation by this Office. Evidence was being gathered and evaluated on, among other things, events related to the Rose Law Firm's representation of Madison Guaranty Savings & Loan Association; events related to the firings in the White House Travel Office; and events related to the use of FBI files. Since the current phase of the investigation began, additional events arising from the Lewinsky matter have also come under scrutiny, including possible perjury and obstruction of justice related to former White House volunteer Kathleen Willey, and the possible misuse of the personnel records of Pentagon employee Linda Tripp.

From the outset, it was our strong desire to complete all phases of the investigation before deciding whether to submit to Congress information—if any—that may constitute grounds for an impeachment. But events and the statutory command of Section 595(c) have dictated otherwise. As the investigation into the President's actions with respect to Ms. Lewinsky and the *Jones* litigation progressed, it became apparent that there was a significant body of substantial and credible information that met the Section 595(c) threshold. As that phase of the investigation neared completion, it also became apparent that a delay of this Referral until the evidence from all phases of the investigation had been evaluated would be unwise. Although Section 595(c) does not specify when information must be submitted, its text strongly suggests that information of this type belongs in the hands of Congress as soon as the Independent Counsel determines that the information is reliable and substantially complete.

All phases of the investigation are now nearing completion. This Office will soon make final decisions about what steps to take, if any, with respect to the other information it has gathered. Those decisions will be made at the earliest practical time, consistent with our statutory and ethical obligations.

THE CONTENTS OF THE REFERRAL

The Referral consists of several parts. Part One is a Narrative. It begins with an overview of the information relevant to this investigation, then sets forth that information in chronological sequence. A large part of the Narrative is devoted to a description of the President's relationship with Monica Lewinsky. The nature of the relationship was the subject of many of the President's false statements, and his desire to keep the relationship secret provides a motive for many of his actions that apparently were designed to obstruct justice.

The Narrative is lengthy and detailed. It is the view of this Office that the details are crucial to an informed evaluation of the testimony, the credibility of witnesses, and the reliability of other evidence. Many of the details reveal highly personal information; many are sexually explicit. This is unfortunate, but it is essential. The President's defense to many of the allegations is based on a close parsing of the definitions that were used to describe his conduct. We have, after careful review, identified no manner of providing the information that reveals the falsity of the President's statements other than to describe his conduct with precision.

Part Two of the Referral is entitled "Information that May Constitute Grounds for An Impeachment." This "Grounds" portion of the Referral summarizes the specific evidence that the President lied under oath and attempted to obstruct justice. This Part is designed to be understandable if read without the Narrative, although the full context in which the potential grounds for impeachment arise can best be understood if considered against the backdrop of information set forth in Part One.

Several volumes accompany the Referral. The Appendix contains relevant court orders, tables, a discussion of legal and evidentiary issues, background information on the *Jones* litigation, a diagram of the Oval Office, and other reference material. We next set forth a series of "Document Supplements," which attempt to provide some of the most important support material in an accessible format. Document Supplement A contains transcripts of the President's deposition testimony and grand jury testimony; Document Supplement B contains transcripts of Monica Lewinsky's testimony and interview statements. Document Supplements C, D, and E set forth the full text of the documents cited in the Referral. Although every effort has been made to provide full and accurate quotations of witnesses in their proper context, we urge review of the full transcripts of the testimony cited below.

Narrative

I. NATURE OF PRESIDENT CLINTON'S RELATIONSHIP WITH MONICA LEWINSKY

A. INTRODUCTION

This Referral presents substantial and credible information that President Clinton criminally obstructed the judicial process, first in a sexual harassment lawsuit in which he was the defendant and then in a grand jury investigation. The opening section of the Narrative provides an overview of the object of the President's cover-up, the sexual relationship between the President and Ms. Lewinsky. Subsequent sections recount the evolution of the relationship chronologically, including the sexual contacts, the President's efforts to get Ms. Lewinsky a job, Ms. Lewinsky's subpoena in *Jones v. Clinton,* the role of Vernon Jordan, the President's discussions with Ms. Lewinsky about her affidavit and deposition, the President's deposition testimony in Jones, the President's attempts to coach a potential witness in the harassment case, the President's false and misleading statements to aides and to the American public after the Lewinsky story became public, and, finally, the President's testimony before a federal grand jury.

B. EVIDENCE ESTABLISHING NATURE OF RELATIONSHIP

1. PHYSICAL EVIDENCE

Physical evidence conclusively establishes that the President and Ms. Lewinsky had a sexual relationship. After reaching an immunity and cooperation agreement with the Office of the Independent Counsel on July 28, 1998, Ms. Lewinsky turned over a navy blue dress that she said she had worn during a sexual encounter with the President on February 28, 1997. According to Ms. Lewinsky, she noticed stains on the garment the next time she took it from her closet. From their location, she surmised that the stains were the President's semen.[1]

Initial tests revealed that the stains are in fact semen.[2] Based on that result, the OIC asked the President for a blood sample.[3] After requesting and being given assurances that the OIC had an evidentiary basis for making the request, the President agreed.[4] In the White House Map Room on August 3, 1998, the White House Physician drew a vial of blood from the President in the presence of an FBI agent and an OIC attorney.[5] By conducting the two standard DNA comparison tests, the FBI Laboratory concluded that the President was the source of the DNA obtained from the dress.[6] According to the more sensitive RFLP test, the genetic markers on the semen, which match the President's DNA, are characteristic of one out of 7.87 trillion Caucasians.[7]

In addition to the dress, Ms. Lewinsky provided what she said were answering machine tapes containing brief messages from the President, as well as several gifts that the President had given her.

2. MS. LEWINSKY'S STATEMENTS

Ms. Lewinsky was extensively debriefed about her relationship with the President. For the initial evaluation of her credibility, she submitted to a detailed "proffer" interview on July 27, 1998.[8] After entering into a cooperation agreement, she was questioned over the course of approximately 15 days. She also provided testimony under oath on three occasions: twice before the grand jury, and, because of the personal and sensitive nature of particular topics, once in a deposition. In addition, Ms. Lewinsky worked with prosecutors and investigators to create an 11-page chart that chronologically lists her contacts with President Clinton, including meetings, phone calls, gifts, and messages.[9] Ms. Lewinsky twice verified the accuracy of the chart under oath.[10]

In the evaluation of experienced prosecutors and investigators, Ms. Lewinsky has provided truthful information. She has not falsely inculpated the President. Harming him, she has testified, is "the last thing in the world I want to do."[11]

Moreover, the OIC's immunity and cooperation agreement with Ms. Lewinsky includes safeguards crafted to ensure that she tells the truth. Court-ordered immunity and written immunity agreements often provide that the witness can be prosecuted only for false statements made during the period of cooperation, and not for the underlying offense. The OIC's agreement goes further, providing that Ms. Lewinsky will lose her immunity altogether if the government can prove to a federal district judge—by a preponderance of the evidence, not the higher standard of beyond a reasonable doubt—that she lied. Moreover, the agreement provides that, in the course of such a prosecution, the United States could introduce into evidence the statements made by Ms. Lewinsky during her cooperation. Since Ms. Lewinsky acknowledged in her proffer interview and in debriefings that she violated the law, she has a strong incentive to tell the truth: If she did not, it would be relatively straightforward to void the immunity agreement and prosecute her, using her own admissions against her.

3. MS. LEWINSKY'S CONFIDANTS

Between 1995 and 1998, Ms. Lewinsky confided in 11 people about her relationship with the President. All have been questioned by the OIC, most before a federal grand jury: Andrew Bleiler,

Catherine Allday Davis, Neysa Erbland, Kathleen Estep, Deborah Finerman, Dr. Irene Kassorla, Marcia Lewis, Ashley Raines, Linda Tripp, Natalie Ungvari, and Dale Young.[12] Ms. Lewinsky told most of these confidants about events in her relationship with the President as they occurred, sometimes in considerable detail.

Some of Ms. Lewinsky's statements about the relationship were contemporaneously memorialized. These include deleted email recovered from her home computer and her Pentagon computer, email messages retained by two of the recipients, tape recordings of some of Ms. Lewinsky's conversations with Ms. Tripp, and notes taken by Ms. Tripp during some of their conversations. The Tripp notes, which have been extensively corroborated, refer specifically to places, dates, and times of physical contacts between the President and Ms. Lewinsky.[13]

Everyone in whom Ms. Lewinsky confided in detail believed she was telling the truth about her relationship with the President. Ms. Lewinsky told her psychologist, Dr. Irene Kassorla, about the affair shortly after it began. Thereafter, she related details of sexual encounters soon after they occurred (sometimes calling from her White House office).[14] Ms. Lewinsky showed no indications of delusional thinking, according to Dr. Kassorla, and Dr. Kassorla had no doubts whatsoever about the truth of what Ms. Lewinsky told her.[15] Ms. Lewinsky's friend Catherine Allday Davis testified that she believed Ms. Lewinsky's accounts of the sexual relationship with the President because "I trusted in the way she had confided in me on other things in her life. . . . I just trusted the relationship, so I trusted her."[16] Dale Young, a friend in whom Ms. Lewinsky confided starting in mid-1996, testified:

> [I]f she was going to lie to me, she would have said to me, "Oh, he calls me all the time. He does wonderful things. He can't wait to see me." . . . [S]he would have embellished the story. You know, she wouldn't be telling me, "He told me he'd call me, I waited home all weekend and I didn't do anything and he didn't call and then he didn't call for two weeks."[17]

4. DOCUMENTS

In addition to her remarks and email to friends, Ms. Lewinsky wrote a number of documents, including letters and draft letters to the President. Among these documents are (i) papers found in a consensual search of her apartment; (ii) papers that Ms. Lewinsky turned over pursuant to her cooperation agreement, including a calendar with dates circled when she met or talked by telephone with the President in 1996 and 1997; and (iii) files recovered from Ms. Lewinsky's computers at home and at the Pentagon.

5. CONSISTENCY AND CORROBORATION

The details of Ms. Lewinsky's many statements have been checked, cross-checked, and corroborated. When negotiations with Ms. Lewinsky in January and February 1998 did not culminate in an agreement, the OIC proceeded with a comprehensive investigation, which generated a great deal of probative evidence.

In July and August 1998, circumstances brought more direct and compelling evidence to the investigation. After the courts rejected a novel privilege claim, Secret Service officers and agents testified about their observations of the President and Ms. Lewinsky in the White House. Ms. Lewinsky agreed to submit to a proffer interview (previous negotiations had deadlocked over her refusal to do so), and, after assessing her credibility in that session, the OIC entered into a cooperation agreement with her. Pursuant to the cooperation agreement, Ms. Lewinsky turned over the dress that proved to bear traces of the President's semen. And the President, who had spurned six invitations to testify, finally agreed to provide his account to the grand jury. In that sworn testimony, he acknowledged "inappropriate intimate contact" with Ms. Lewinsky.

Because of the fashion in which the investigation had unfolded, in sum, a massive quantity of evidence was available to test and verify Ms. Lewinsky's statements during her proffer interview and her later cooperation. Consequently, Ms. Lewinsky's statements have been corroborated to a remarkable degree. Her detailed statements

to the grand jury and the OIC in 1998 are consistent with statements to her confidants dating back to 1995, documents that she
created, and physical evidence.[18] Moreover, her accounts generally
match the testimony of White House staff members; the testimony
of Secret Service agents and officers; and White House records
showing Ms. Lewinsky's entries and exits, the President's where-
abouts, and the President's telephone calls.

C. SEXUAL CONTACTS

1. THE PRESIDENT'S ACCOUNTS

A. JONES TESTIMONY

In the Jones deposition on January 17, 1998, the President
denied having had "a sexual affair," "sexual relations," or "a sexual relationship" with Ms. Lewinsky.[19] He noted that "[t]here are
no curtains on the Oval Office, there are no curtains on my private
office, there are no curtains or blinds that can close [on] the windows in my private dining room," and added: "I have done everything I could to avoid the kind of questions you are asking me here
today. . . ."[20]

During the deposition, the President's attorney, Robert Bennett,
sought to limit questioning about Ms. Lewinsky. Mr. Bennett told
Judge Susan Webber Wright that Ms. Lewinsky had executed "an
affidavit which [Ms. Jones's lawyers] are in possession of saying
that there is absolutely no sex of any kind in any manner, shape or
form, with President Clinton." In a subsequent colloquy with
Judge Wright, Mr. Bennett declared that as a result of "preparation of [President Clinton] for this deposition, the witness is fully
aware of Ms. Lewinsky's affidavit."[21] The President did not dispute
his legal representative's assertion that the President and Ms.
Lewinsky had had "absolutely no sex of any kind in any manner,
shape or form," nor did he dispute the implication that Ms.
Lewinsky's affidavit, in denying "a sexual relationship," meant
that there was "absolutely no sex of any kind in any manner,

shape or form." In subsequent questioning by his attorney, President Clinton testified under oath that Ms. Lewinsky's affidavit was "absolutely true."[22]

B. GRAND JURY TESTIMONY

Testifying before the grand jury on August 17, 1998, seven months after his Jones deposition, the President acknowledged "inappropriate intimate contact" with Ms. Lewinsky but maintained that his January deposition testimony was accurate.[23] In his account, "what began as a friendship [with Ms. Lewinsky] came to include this conduct."[24] He said he remembered "meeting her, or having my first real conversation with her during the government shutdown in November of '95." According to the President, the inappropriate contact occurred later (after Ms. Lewinsky's internship had ended), "in early 1996 and once in early 1997."[25]

The President refused to answer questions about the precise nature of his intimate contacts with Ms. Lewinsky, but he did explain his earlier denials.[26] As to his denial in the Jones deposition that he and Ms. Lewinsky had had a "sexual relationship," the President maintained that there can be no sexual relationship without sexual intercourse, regardless of what other sexual activities may transpire. He stated that "most ordinary Americans" would embrace this distinction.[27]

The President also maintained that none of his sexual contacts with Ms. Lewinsky constituted "sexual relations" within a specific definition used in the Jones deposition.[28] Under that definition:

> [A] person engages in "sexual relations" when the person knowingly engages in or causes—(1) contact with the genitalia, anus, groin, breast, inner thigh, or buttocks of any person with an intent to arouse or gratify the sexual desire of any person . . . . "Contact" means intentional touching, either directly or through clothing.[29]

According to what the President testified was his understanding, this definition "covers contact by the person being deposed with the enumerated areas, if the contact is done with an intent to arouse or gratify," but it does not cover oral sex performed on the person being deposed.[30] He testified:

> [I]f the deponent is the person who has oral sex performed on him, then the contact is with—not with anything on that list, but with the lips of another person. It seems to be self-evident that that's what it is. . . . Let me remind you, sir, I read this carefully.[31]

In the President's view, "any person, reasonable person" would recognize that oral sex performed on the deponent falls outside the definition.[32]

If Ms. Lewinsky performed oral sex on the President, then—under this interpretation—she engaged in sexual relations but he did not. The President refused to answer whether Ms. Lewinsky in fact had performed oral sex on him.[33] He did testify that direct contact with Ms. Lewinsky's breasts or genitalia would fall within the definition, and he denied having had any such contact.[34]

2. MS. LEWINSKY'S ACCOUNT

In his grand jury testimony, the President relied heavily on a particular interpretation of "sexual relations" as defined in the Jones deposition. Beyond insisting that his conduct did not fall within the Jones definition, he refused to answer questions about the nature of his physical contact with Ms. Lewinsky, thus placing the grand jury in the position of having to accept his conclusion without being able to explore the underlying facts. This strategy—evidently an effort to account for possible traces of the President's semen on Ms. Lewinsky's clothing without undermining his position that he did not lie in the Jones deposition—mandates that this Referral set forth evidence of an explicit nature that otherwise would be omitted.

In light of the President's testimony, Ms. Lewinsky's accounts of their sexual encounters are indispensable for two reasons. First, the detail and consistency of these accounts tend to bolster Ms. Lewinsky's credibility. Second, and particularly important, Ms. Lewinsky contradicts the President on a key issue. According to Ms. Lewinsky, the President touched her breasts and genitalia—which means that his conduct met the Jones definition of sexual relations even under his theory. On these matters, the evidence of the President's perjury cannot be presented without specific, explicit, and possibly offensive descriptions of sexual encounters.

According to Ms. Lewinsky, she and the President had ten sexual encounters, eight while she worked at the White House and two thereafter.[35] The sexual encounters generally occurred in or near the private study off the Oval Office—most often in the windowless hallway outside the study.[36] During many of their sexual encounters, the President stood leaning against the doorway of the bathroom across from the study, which, he told Ms. Lewinsky, eased his sore back.[37]

Ms. Lewinsky testified that her physical relationship with the President included oral sex but not sexual intercourse.[38] According to Ms. Lewinsky, she performed oral sex on the President; he never performed oral sex on her.[39] Initially, according to Ms. Lewinsky, the President would not let her perform oral sex to completion. In Ms. Lewinsky's understanding, his refusal was related to "trust and not knowing me well enough."[40] During their last two sexual encounters, both in 1997, he did ejaculate.[41]

According to Ms. Lewinsky, she performed oral sex on the President on nine occasions. On all nine of those occasions, the President fondled and kissed her bare breasts. He touched her genitals, both through her underwear and directly, bringing her to orgasm on two occasions. On one occasion, the President inserted a cigar into her vagina. On another occasion, she and the President had brief genital-to-genital contact.[42]

Whereas the President testified that "what began as a friendship came to include [intimate contact]," Ms. Lewinsky explained that the relationship moved in the opposite direction: "[T]he emotional and friendship aspects . . . developed after the beginning of our sexual relationship."[43]

D. Emotional Attachment

As the relationship developed over time, Ms. Lewinsky grew emotionally attached to President Clinton. She testified: "I never expected to fall in love with the President. I was surprised that I did."[44] Ms. Lewinsky told him of her feelings.[45] At times, she believed that he loved her too.[46] They were physically affectionate: "A lot of hugging, holding hands sometimes. He always used to push the hair out of my face."[47] She called him "Handsome"; on occasion, he called her "Sweetie," "Baby," or sometimes "Dear."[48] He told her that he enjoyed talking to her—she recalled his saying that the two of them were "emotive and full of fire," and she made him feel young.[49] He said he wished he could spend more time with her.[50]

Ms. Lewinsky told confidants of the emotional underpinnings of the relationship as it evolved. According to her mother, Marcia Lewis, the President once told Ms. Lewinsky that she "had been hurt a lot or something by different men and that he would be her friend or he would help her, not hurt her."[51] According to Ms. Lewinsky's friend Neysa Erbland, President Clinton once confided in Ms. Lewinsky that he was uncertain whether he would remain married after he left the White House. He said in essence, "[W]ho knows what will happen four years from now when I am out of office?" Ms. Lewinsky thought, according to Ms. Erbland, that "maybe she will be his wife."[52]

E. CONVERSATIONS AND PHONE MESSAGES

Ms. Lewinsky testified that she and the President "enjoyed talking to each other and being with each other." In her recollection, "We would tell jokes. We would talk about our childhoods. Talk about current events. I was always giving him my stupid ideas about what I thought should be done in the administration or different views on things."[53] One of Ms. Lewinsky's friends testified that, in her understanding, "[The President] would talk about his childhood and growing up, and [Ms. Lewinsky] would relay stories about her childhood and growing up. I guess normal conversations that you would have with someone that you're getting to know."[54]

The longer conversations often occurred after their sexual contact. Ms. Lewinsky testified: "[W]hen I was working there [at the White House] . . . we'd start in the back [in or near the private study] and we'd talk and that was where we were physically inti-mate, and we'd usually end up, kind of the pillow talk of it, I guess, . . . sitting in the Oval Office . . . ."[55] During several meetings when they were not sexually intimate, they talked in the Oval Office or in the area of the study.[56]

Along with face-to-face meetings, according to Ms. Lewinsky, she spoke on the telephone with the President approximately 50 times, often after 10 p.m. and sometimes well after midnight.[57] The President placed the calls himself or, during working hours, had his secretary, Betty Currie, do so; Ms. Lewinsky could not telephone him directly, though she sometimes reached him through Ms. Cur-rie.[58] Ms. Lewinsky testified: "[W]e spent hours on the phone talk-ing."[59] Their telephone conversations were "[s]imilar to what we discussed in person, just how we were doing. A lot of discussions about my job, when I was trying to come back to the White House and then once I decided to move to New York. . . . We talked about everything under the sun."[60] On 10 to 15 occasions, she and the President had phone sex.[61] After phone sex late one night, the Presi-dent fell asleep mid-conversation.[62]

On four occasions, the President left very brief messages on Ms. Lewinsky's answering machine, though he told her that he did not like doing so because (in her recollection) he "felt it was a little unsafe."[63] She saved his messages and played the tapes for several confidants, who said they believed that the voice was the Presi-dent's.[64]

By phone and in person, according to Ms. Lewinsky, she and the President sometimes had arguments. On a number of occasions in 1997, she complained that he had not brought her back from the Pentagon to work in the White House, as he had promised to do after the election.[65] In a face-to-face meeting on July 4, 1997, the President reprimanded her for a letter she had sent him that obliquely threatened to disclose their relationship.[66] During an argu-ment on December 6, 1997, according to Ms. Lewinsky, the Presi-dent said that "he had never been treated as poorly by anyone else as I treated him," and added that "he spent more time with me than anyone else in the world, aside from his family, friends and staff, which I don't know exactly which category that put me in."[67]

Testifying before the grand jury, the President confirmed that he and Ms. Lewinsky had had personal conversations, and he acknowledged that their telephone conversations sometimes included "inappropriate sexual banter."[68] The President said that Ms. Lewinsky told him about "her personal life," "her upbringing," and "her job ambitions."[69] After terminating their intimate relationship in 1997, he said, he tried "to be a friend to Ms. Lewinsky, to be a counselor to her, to give her good advice, and to help her."[70]

F. GIFTS

Ms. Lewinsky and the President exchanged numerous gifts. By her estimate, she gave him about 30 items, and he gave her about 18.[71] Ms. Lewinsky's first gift to him was a matted poem given by her and other White House interns to commemorate "National Boss Day," October 24, 1995.[72] This was the only item reflected in White House records that Ms. Lewinsky gave the President before (in her account) the sexual relationship began, and the only item that he sent to the archives instead of keeping.[73] On November 20—five days after the intimate relationship began, according to Ms. Lewinsky—she gave him a necktie, which he chose to keep rather than send to the archives.[74] According to Ms. Lewinsky, the President telephoned the night she gave him the tie, then sent her a photo of himself wearing it.[75] The tie was logged pursuant to White House procedures for gifts to the President.[76]

In a draft note to the President in December 1997, Ms. Lewinsky wrote that she was "very particular about presents and could never give them to anyone else—they were all bought with you in mind."[77] Many of the 30 or so gifts that she gave the President reflected his interests in history, antiques, cigars, and frogs. Ms. Lewinsky gave him, among other things, six neckties, an antique paperweight showing the White House, a silver tabletop holder for cigars or cigarettes, a pair of sunglasses, a casual shirt, a mug emblazoned

"Santa Monica," a frog figurine, a letter opener depicting a frog, several novels, a humorous book of quotations, and several antique books.[78] He gave her, among other things, a hat pin, two brooches, a blanket, a marble bear figurine, and a special edition of Walt Whitman's *Leaves of Grass*.[79]

Ms. Lewinsky construed it as a sign of affection when the President wore a necktie or other item of clothing she had given him. She testified: "I used to say to him that 'I like it when you wear my ties because then I know I'm close to your heart.' So—literally and figuratively."[80] The President was aware of her reaction, according to Ms. Lewinsky, and he would sometimes wear one of the items to reassure her—occasionally on the day they were scheduled to meet or the day after they had met in person or talked by telephone.[81] The President would sometimes say to her, "Did you see I wore your tie the other day?"[82]

In his grand jury testimony, the President acknowledged that he had exchanged a number of gifts with Ms. Lewinsky. After their intimate relationship ended in 1997, he testified, "[S]he continued to give me gifts. And I felt that it was a right thing to do to give her gifts back."[83]

G. MESSAGES

According to Ms. Lewinsky, she sent the President a number of cards and letters. In some, she expressed anger that he was "not paying enough attention to me"; in others, she said she missed him; in still others, she just sent "a funny card that I saw."[84] In early January 1998, she sent him, along with an antique book about American presidents, "[a]n embarrassing mushy note."[85] She testified that the President never sent her any cards or notes other than formal thank-you letters.[86]

Testifying before the grand jury, the President acknowledged having received cards and notes from Ms. Lewinsky that were "somewhat intimate" and "quite affectionate," even after the intimate relationship ended.[87]

H. SECRECY

1. MUTUAL UNDERSTANDING

Both Ms. Lewinsky and the President testified that they took steps to maintain the secrecy of the relationship. According to Ms. Lewinsky, the President from the outset stressed the importance of keeping the relationship secret. In her handwritten statement to this Office, Ms. Lewinsky wrote that "the President told Ms. L to deny a relationship, if ever asked about it. He also said something to the effect of if the two people who are involved say it didn't happen—it didn't happen."[88] According to Ms. Lewinsky, the President sometimes asked if she had told anyone about their sexual relationship or about the gifts they had exchanged; she (falsely) assured him that she had not.[89] She told him that "I would always deny it, I would always protect him," and he responded approvingly.[90] The two of them had, in her words, "a mutual understanding" that they would "keep this private, so that meant deny it and . . . take whatever appropriate steps needed to be taken."[91] When she and the President both were subpoenaed to testify in the Jones case, Ms. Lewinsky anticipated that "as we had on every other occasion and every other instance of this relationship, we would deny it."[92]

In his grand jury testimony, the President confirmed his efforts to keep their liaisons secret.[93] He said he did not want the facts of their relationship to be disclosed "in any context," and added: "I certainly didn't want this to come out, if I could help it. And I was concerned about that. I was embarrassed about it. I knew it was wrong."[94] Asked if he wanted to avoid having the facts come out through Ms. Lewinsky's testimony in Jones, he said: "Well, I did not want her to have to testify and go through that. And, of course, I didn't want her to do that, of course not."[95]

2. COVER STORIES

For her visits to see the President, according to Ms. Lewinsky, "[T]here was always some sort of a cover."[96] When visiting the President while she worked at the White House, she generally planned to tell anyone who asked (including Secret Service officers and agents) that she was delivering papers to the President.[97] Ms. Lewinsky explained that this artifice may have originated when "I got there kind of saying, 'Oh, gee, here are your letters,' wink, wink, wink, and him saying, 'Okay, that's good.'"[98] To back up her stories, she generally carried a folder on these visits.[99] (In truth, according to Ms. Lewinsky, her job never required her to deliver papers to the President.[100]) On a few occasions during her White House employment, Ms. Lewinsky and the President arranged to bump into each other in the hallway; he then would invite her to accompany him to the Oval Office.[101] Later, after she left the White House and started working at the Pentagon, Ms. Lewinsky relied on Ms. Currie to arrange times when she could see the President. The cover story for those visits was that Ms. Lewinsky was coming to see Ms. Currie, not the President.[102]

While the President did not expressly instruct her to lie, according to Ms. Lewinsky, he did suggest misleading cover stories.[103] And, when she assured him that she planned to lie about the relationship, he responded approvingly. On the frequent occasions when Ms. Lewinsky promised that she would "always deny" the relationship and "always protect him," for example, the President responded, in her recollection, "'That's good,' or—something affirmative. . . . [N]ot—'Don't deny it.'"[104]

Once she was named as a possible witness in the *Jones* case, according to Ms. Lewinsky, the President reminded her of the cover stories. After telling her that she was a potential witness, the President suggested that, if she were subpoenaed, she could file an affidavit to avoid being deposed. He also told her she could say that, when working at the White House, she had sometimes delivered letters to him, and, after leaving her White House job, she had sometimes returned to visit Ms. Currie.[105] (The President's own testimony in the Jones case mirrors the recommendations he made to Ms. Lewinsky for her testimony. In his deposition, the President testified that he saw Ms. Lewinsky "on two or three occasions" during the

November 1995 government furlough, "one or two other times when she brought some documents to me," and "sometime before Christmas" when Ms. Lewinsky "came by to see Betty."[106])

In his grand jury testimony, the President acknowledged that he and Ms. Lewinsky "might have talked about what to do in a nonlegal context" to hide their relationship, and that he "might well have said" that Ms. Lewinsky should tell people that she was bringing letters to him or coming to visit Ms. Currie.[107] But he also stated that "I never asked Ms. Lewinsky to lie."[108]

3. STEPS TO AVOID BEING SEEN OR HEARD

After their first two sexual encounters during the November 1995 government shutdown, according to Ms. Lewinsky, her encounters with the President generally occurred on weekends, when fewer people were in the West Wing.[109] Ms. Lewinsky testified:

> He had told me . . . that he was usually around on the weekends and that it was okay to come see him on the weekends. So he would call and we would arrange either to bump into each other in the hall or that I would bring papers to the office.[110]

From some of the President's comments, Ms. Lewinsky gathered that she should try to avoid being seen by several White House employees, including Nancy Hernreich, Deputy Assistant to the President and Director of Oval Office Operations, and Stephen Goodin, the President's personal aide.[111]

Out of concern about being seen, the sexual encounters most often occurred in the windowless hallway outside the study.[112] According to Ms. Lewinsky, the President was concerned that the two of them might be spotted through a White House window. When they were in the study together in the evenings, he sometimes turned out the light.[113] Once, when she spotted a gardener outside the study window, they left the room.[114] Ms. Lewinsky testified that, on December 28, 1997, "when I was getting my Christmas kiss" in the doorway to the study, the President was "looking out the window with his eyes wide open while he was kissing me and then I got mad because it wasn't very romantic." He responded, "Well, I was just looking to see to make sure no one was out there."[115]

Fear of discovery constrained their sexual encounters in several respects, according to Ms. Lewinsky. The President ordinarily kept the door between the private hallway and the Oval Office several inches ajar during their encounters, both so that he could hear if anyone approached and so that anyone who did approach would be less likely to suspect impropriety.[116] During their sexual encounters, Ms. Lewinsky testified, "[W]e were both aware of the volume and sometimes . . . I bit my hand—so that I wouldn't make any noise."[117] On one occasion, according to Ms. Lewinsky, the President put his hand over her mouth during a sexual encounter to keep her quiet.[118] Concerned that they might be interrupted abruptly, according to Ms. Lewinsky, the two of them never fully undressed.[119]

While noting that "the door to the hallway was always somewhat open," the President testified that he did try to keep the intimate relationship secret: "I did what people do when they do the wrong thing. I tried to do it where nobody else was looking at it."[120]

4. Ms. LEWINSKY'S NOTES AND LETTERS

The President expressed concern about documents that might hint at an improper relationship between them, according to Ms. Lewinsky. He cautioned her about messages she sent:

> There were . . . some occasions when I sent him cards or notes that I wrote things that he deemed too personal to put on paper just in case something ever happened, if it got lost getting there or someone else opened it. So there were several times when he remarked to me, you know, you shouldn't put that on paper.[121]

She said that the President made this point to her in their last conversation, on January 5, 1998, in reference to what she characterized as "[a]n embarrassing mushy note" she had sent him.[122] In addition, according to Ms. Lewinsky, the President expressed concerns about official records that could establish aspects of their relationship. She said that on two occasions she asked the President if she could go upstairs to the Residence with him. No, he said, because a record is kept of everyone who accompanies him there.[123]

The President testified before the grand jury: "I remember telling her she should be careful what she wrote, because a lot of it was clearly inappropriate and would be embarrassing if somebody else read it."[124]

5. MS. LEWINSKY'S EVALUATION OF THEIR SECRECY EFFORTS

In two conversations recorded after she was subpoenaed in the Jones case, Ms. Lewinsky expressed confidence that her relationship with the President would never be discovered.[126] She believed that no records showed her and the President alone in the area of the study.[127] Regardless of the evidence, in any event, she would continue denying the relationship. "If someone looked in the study window, it's not me," she said.[128] If someone produced tapes of her telephone calls with the President, she would say they were fakes.[129]

In another recorded conversation, Ms. Lewinsky said she was especially comforted by the fact that the President, like her, would be swearing under oath that "nothing happened."[130] She said:

> [T]o tell you the truth, I'm not concerned all that much any-more because I know I'm not going to get in trouble. I will not get in trouble because you know what? The story I've signed under— under oath is what someone else is saying under oath.[131]

II. 1995: INITIAL SEXUAL ENCOUNTERS

Monica Lewinsky began her White House employment as an intern in the Chief of Staff's office in July 1995. At White House functions in the following months, she made eye contact with the President. During the November 1995 government shutdown, the President invited her to his private study, where they kissed. Later that evening, they had a more intimate sexual encounter. They had another sexual encounter two days later, and a third one on New Year's Eve.

A. OVERVIEW OF MONICA LEWINSKY'S WHITE HOUSE EMPLOYMENT

Monica Lewinsky worked at the White House, first as an intern and then as an employee, from July 1995 to April 1996. With the assistance of family friend Walter Kaye, a prominent contributor to political causes, she obtained an internship starting in early July, when she was 21 years old.[132] She was assigned to work on correspondence in the office of Chief of Staff Leon Panetta in the Old Executive Office Building.[132]

As her internship was winding down, Ms. Lewinsky applied for a paying job on the White House staff. She interviewed with Timothy Keating, Special Assistant to the President and Staff Director for Legislative Affairs.[133] Ms. Lewinsky accepted a position dealing with correspondence in the Office of Legislative Affairs on November 13, 1995, but did not start the job (and, thus, continued her internship) until November 26.[134] She remained a White House employee until April 1996, when—in her view, because of her intimate relationship with the President—she was dismissed from the White House and transferred to the Pentagon.[135]

B. FIRST MEETINGS WITH THE PRESIDENT

The month after her White House internship began, Ms. Lewinsky and the President began what she characterized as "intense flirting."[136] At departure ceremonies and other events, she made eye contact with him, shook hands, and introduced herself.[137] When she ran into the President in the West Wing basement and introduced herself again, according to Ms. Lewinsky, he responded that he already knew who she was.[138*] Ms. Lewinsky told her aunt that the President "seemed attracted to her or interested in her or something," and told a visiting friend that "she was attracted to [President Clinton], she had a big crush on him, and I think she told me she at some point had gotten his attention, that there was some mutual eye contact and recognition, mutual acknowledgment."[139]

In the autumn of 1995, an impasse over the budget forced the federal government to shut down for one week, from Tuesday, November 14, to Monday, November 20.[140] Only essential federal employees were permitted to work during the furlough, and the White House staff of 430 shrank to about 90 people for the week. White House interns could continue working because of their unpaid status, and they took on a wide range of additional duties.[141]

During the shutdown, Ms. Lewinsky worked in Chief of Staff Panetta's West Wing office, where she answered phones and ran errands.[142] The President came to Mr. Panetta's office frequently because of the shutdown, and he sometimes talked with Ms. Lewinsky.[143] She characterized these encounters as "continued flirtation."[144] According to Ms. Lewinsky, a Senior Adviser to the Chief of Staff, Barry Toiv, remarked to her that she was getting a great deal of "face time" with the President.[145]

C. NOVEMBER 15 SEXUAL ENCOUNTER

Ms. Lewinsky testified that Wednesday, November 15, 1995— the second day of the government shutdown—marked the beginning of her sexual relationship with the President.[146] On that date, she entered the White House at 1:30 p.m., left sometime thereafter (White House records do not show the time), reentered at 5:07 p.m., and departed at 12:18 a.m. on November 16.[147] The President was in the Oval Office or the Chief of Staff's office (where Ms. Lewinsky worked during the furlough) for almost the identical period that Ms. Lewinsky was in the White House that evening, from 5:01 p.m. on November 15 to 12:35 a.m. on November 16.[148]

According to Ms. Lewinsky, she and the President made eye contact when he came to the West Wing to see Mr. Panetta and Deputy Chief of Staff Harold Ickes, then again later at an informal birthday party for Jennifer Palmieri, Special Assistant to the Chief of Staff.[149] At one point, Ms. Lewinsky and the President talked alone in the Chief of Staff's office. In the course of flirting with him, she raised her jacket in the back and showed him the straps of her thong underwear, which extended above her pants.[150]

En route to the restroom at about 8 p.m., she passed George

Stephanopoulos's office. The President was inside alone, and he beckoned her to enter.[151] She told him that she had a crush on him. He laughed, then asked if she would like to see his private office.[152] Through a connecting door in Mr. Stephanopoulos's office, they went through the President's private dining room toward the study off the Oval Office. Ms. Lewinsky testified: "We talked briefly and sort of acknowledged that there had been a chemistry that was there before and that we were both attracted to each other and then he asked me if he could kiss me." Ms. Lewinsky said yes. In the windowless hallway adjacent to the study, they kissed.[153] Before returning to her desk, Ms. Lewinsky wrote down her name and telephone number for the President.[154]

At about 10 p.m., in Ms. Lewinsky's recollection, she was alone in the Chief of Staff's office and the President approached.[155] He invited her to rendezvous again in Mr. Stephanopoulos's office in a few minutes, and she agreed.[156] (Asked if she knew why the President wanted to meet with her, Ms. Lewinsky testified: "I had an idea."[157]) They met in Mr. Stephanopoulos's office and went again to the area of the private study.[158] This time the lights in the study were off.[159]

According to Ms. Lewinsky, she and the President kissed. She unbuttoned her jacket; either she unhooked her bra or he lifted her bra up; and he touched her breasts with his hands and mouth.[160] Ms. Lewinsky testified: "I believe he took a phone call . . . and so we moved from the hallway into the back office . . . . [H]e put his hand down my pants and stimulated me manually in the genital area."[161] While the President continued talking on the phone (Ms. Lewinsky understood that the caller was a Member of Congress or a Senator), she performed oral sex on him.[162] He finished his call, and, a moment later, told Ms. Lewinsky to stop. In her recollection: "I told him that I wanted . . . to complete that. And he said . . . that he needed to wait until he trusted me more. And then I think he made a joke . . . that he hadn't had that in a long time."[163]

Both before and after their sexual contact during that encounter, Ms. Lewinsky and the President talked.[164] At one point during the conversation, the President tugged on the pink intern pass hanging from her neck and said that it might be a problem. Ms. Lewinsky thought that he was talking about access—interns were not supposed to be in the West Wing without an escort—and, in addition, that he might have discerned some "impropriety" in a sexual relationship with a White House intern.[165]

White House records corroborate details of Ms. Lewinsky's account. She testified that her November 15 encounters with the President occurred at about 8 p.m. and 10 p.m., and that in each case the two of them went from the Chief of Staff's office to the Oval Office area.[166] Records show that the President visited the Chief of Staff's office for one minute at 8:12 p.m. and for two minutes at 9:23 p.m., in each case returning to the Oval Office.[167] She recalled that the President took a telephone call during their sexual encounter, and she believed that the caller was a Member of Congress or a Senator.[168] White House records show that after returning to the Oval Office from the Chief of Staff's office, the President talked to two Members of Congress: Rep. Jim Chapman from 9:25 p.m. to 9:30 p.m., and Rep. John Tanner from 9:31 p.m. to 9:35 p.m.[169]

D. NOVEMBER 17 SEXUAL ENCOUNTER

According to Ms. Lewinsky, she and the President had a second sexual encounter two days later (still during the government furlough), on Friday, November 17. She was at the White House until 8:56 p.m., then returned from 9:38 to 10:39 p.m.[170] At 9:45 p.m., a few minutes after Ms. Lewinsky's reentry, the President went from the Oval Office to the Chief of Staff's office (where Ms. Lewinsky worked during the furlough) for one minute, then returned to the Oval Office for 30 minutes. From there, he went back to the Chief of Staff's office until 10:34 p.m. (approximately when Ms. Lewinsky left the White House), then went by the Oval Office and the Ground Floor before retiring to the Residence at 10:40 p.m.[171]

Ms. Lewinsky testified:

We were again working late because it was during the furlough and Jennifer Palmieri . . . had ordered pizza along with Ms. Currie and Ms. Hernreich. And when the pizza came, I went down to let them know that the pizza was there and it was at that point when I walked into Ms. Currie's office that the President was standing there with some other people discussing something.

And they all came back to the office and Mr.—I think it was Mr. Toiv, somebody accidentally knocked pizza on my jacket, so I went to go use the restroom to wash it off and as I was coming out of the restroom, the President was standing in Ms. Currie's doorway and said, "You can come out this way."[172]

Ms. Lewinsky and the President went into the area of the private study, according to Ms. Lewinsky. There, either in the hallway or the bathroom, she and the President kissed. After a few minutes, in Ms. Lewinsky's recollection, she told him that she needed to get back to her desk. The President suggested that she bring him some slices of pizza.[173]

A few minutes later, she returned to the Oval Office area with pizza and told Ms. Currie that the President had requested it. Ms. Lewinsky testified: "[Ms. Currie] opened the door and said, 'Sir, the girl's here with the pizza.' He told me to come in. Ms. Currie went back into her office and then we went into the back study area again."[174] Several witnesses confirm that when Ms. Lewinsky delivered pizza to the President that night, the two of them were briefly alone.[175]

Ms. Lewinsky testified that she and the President had a sexual encounter during this visit.[176] They kissed, and the President touched Ms. Lewinsky's bare breasts with his hands and mouth.[177] At some point, Ms. Currie approached the door leading to the hallway, which was ajar, and said that the President had a telephone call.[178] Ms. Lewinsky recalled that the caller was a Member of Congress with a nickname.[179] While the President was on the telephone, according to Ms. Lewinsky, "he unzipped his pants and exposed himself," and she performed oral sex.[180] Again, he stopped her before he ejaculated.[181]

During this visit, according to Ms. Lewinsky, the President told her that he liked her smile and her energy. He also said: "I'm usually around on weekends, no one else is around, and you can come and see me."[182]

Records corroborate Ms. Lewinsky's recollection that the President took a call from a Member of Congress with a nickname. While Ms. Lewinsky was at the White House that evening (9:38 to 10:39 p.m.), the President had one telephone conversation with a Member of Congress: From 9:53 to 10:14 p.m., he spoke with Rep. H.L. "Sonny" Callahan.[183]

In his Jones deposition on January 17, 1998, President Clinton— who said he was unable to recall most of his encounters with Ms. Lewinsky—did remember her "back there with a pizza" during the government shutdown. He said, however, that he did not believe that the two of them were alone.[184] Testifying before the grand jury on August 17, 1998, the President said that his first "real conversation" with Ms. Lewinsky occurred during the November 1995 furlough. He testified: "One night she brought me some pizza. We had some remarks."[185]

E. DECEMBER 31 SEXUAL ENCOUNTER

According to Ms. Lewinsky, she and the President had their third sexual encounter on New Year's Eve. Ms. Lewinsky—by then a member of the staff of the Office of Legislative Affairs— was at the White House on Sunday, December 31, 1995, until 1:16 p.m.; her time of arrival is not shown.[186] The President was in the Oval Office area from 12:11 p.m. until about the time that Ms. Lewinsky left, 1:15 p.m., when he went to the Residence.[187]

Sometime between noon and 1 p.m., in Ms. Lewinsky's recollection, she was in the pantry area of the President's private dining room talking with a White House steward, Bayani Nelvis. She told Mr. Nelvis that she had recently smoked her first cigar, and he offered to give her one of the President's cigars. Just then, the President came down the hallway from the Oval Office and saw Ms. Lewinsky. The President dispatched Mr. Nelvis to deliver something to Mr. Panetta.[188]

According to Ms. Lewinsky, she told the President that Mr. Nelvis had promised her a cigar, and the President gave her one.[189] She told him her name—she had the impression that he had forgotten it in the six weeks since their furlough encounters because, when passing her in the hallway, he had called her "Kiddo."[190] The President replied that he knew her name; in fact, he added, having lost the phone number she had given him, he had tried to find her in the phonebook.[191]

According to Ms. Lewinsky, they moved to the study. "And then . . . we were kissing and he lifted my sweater and exposed my breasts and was fondling them with his hands and with his mouth."[192] She performed oral sex.[193] Once again, he stopped her before he ejaculated because, Ms. Lewinsky testified, "he didn't know me well enough or he didn't trust me yet."[194]

According to Ms. Lewinsky, a Secret Service officer named Sandy was on duty in the West Wing that day.[195] Records show that Sandra Verna was on duty outside the Oval Office from 7 a.m. to 2 p.m.[196]

F. PRESIDENT'S ACCOUNT OF 1995 RELATIONSHIP

As noted, the President testified before the grand jury that on November 17, 1995, Ms. Lewinsky delivered pizza and exchanged "some remarks" with him, but he never indicated that anything sexual occurred then or at any other point in 1995.[197] Testifying under oath before the grand jury, the President said that he engaged in "conduct that was wrong" involving "inappropriate intimate contact" with Ms. Lewinsky "on certain occasions in early 1996 and once in early 1997."[198] By implicitly denying any sexual contact in 1995, the President indicated that he and Ms. Lewinsky had no sexual involvement while she was an intern.[199] In the President's testimony, his relationship with Ms. Lewinsky "began as a friendship," then later "came to include this conduct."[200]

III. JANUARY-MARCH 1996: CONTINUED SEXUAL ENCOUNTERS

President Clinton and Ms. Lewinsky had additional sexual encounters near the Oval Office in 1996. After their sixth sexual encounter, the President and Ms. Lewinsky had their first lengthy conversation. On President's Day, February 19, the President terminated their sexual relationship, then revived it on March 31.

A. JANUARY 7 SEXUAL ENCOUNTER

According to Ms. Lewinsky, she and the President had another sexual encounter on Sunday, January 7, 1996. Although White House records do not indicate that Ms. Lewinsky was at the White House that day, her testimony and other evidence indicate that she was there.[201] The President, according to White House records, was in the Oval Office most of the afternoon, from 2:13 to 5:49 p.m.[202]

According to Ms. Lewinsky, the President telephoned her early that afternoon. It was the first time he had called her at home.[203] In her recollection: "I asked him what he was doing and he said he was going to be going into the office soon. I said, oh, do you want some company? And he said, oh, that would be great."[204] Ms. Lewinsky went to her office, and the President called to arrange their rendezvous:

> [W]e made an arrangement that . . . he would have the door to his office open, and I would pass by the office with some papers and then . . . he would sort of stop me and invite me in. So, that was exactly what happened. I passed by and that was actually when I saw [Secret Service Uniformed Officer] Lew Fox who was on duty outside the Oval Office, and stopped and spoke with Lew for a few minutes, and then the President came out and said, oh, hey, Monica . . . come on in . . . . And so we spoke for about 10 minutes in the [Oval] office. We sat on the sofas. Then we went into the back study and we were intimate in the bathroom.[205]

Ms. Lewinsky testified that during this bathroom encounter, she and the President kissed, and he touched her bare breasts with his hands and his mouth.[206] The President "was talking about performing oral sex on me," according to Ms. Lewinsky.[207] But she stopped him because she was menstruating and he did not.[208] Ms. Lewinsky did perform oral sex on him.[209]

Afterward, she and the President moved to the Oval Office and talked. According to Ms. Lewinsky: "[H]e was chewing on a cigar. And then he had the cigar in his hand and he was kind of looking at the cigar in . . . sort of a naughty way. And so . . . I looked at the cigar and I looked at him and I said, we can do that, too, some time."[210]

Corroborating aspects of Ms. Lewinsky's recollection, records show that Officer Fox was posted outside the Oval Office the afternoon of January 7.[211] Officer Fox (who is now retired) testified that he recalled an incident with Ms. Lewinsky one weekend afternoon when he was on duty by the Oval Office:[212]

> [T]he President of the United States came out, and he asked me, he says, "Have you seen any young congressional staff members here today?" I said, "No, sir." He said, "Well, I'm expecting one." He says, "Would you please let me know when they show up?" And I said, "Yes, sir."[213]

Officer Fox construed the reference to "congressional staff members" to mean White House staff who worked with Congress—i.e., staff of the Legislative Affairs Office, where Ms. Lewinsky worked.[214]

Talking with a Secret Service agent posted in the hallway, Officer Fox speculated on whom the President was expecting: "I described Ms. Lewinsky, without mentioning the name, in detail, dark hair— you know, I gave a general description of what she looked like."[215] Officer Fox had gotten to know Ms. Lewinsky during her tenure at the White House, and other agents had told him that she often spent time with the President.[216]

A short time later, Ms. Lewinsky approached, greeted Officer Fox, and said, "I have some papers for the President." Officer Fox admitted her to the Oval Office. The President said: "You can close the door. She'll be here for a while."[217]

B. JANUARY 21 SEXUAL ENCOUNTER

On Sunday, January 21, 1996, according to Ms. Lewinsky, she and the President had another sexual encounter. Her time of White House entry is not reflected in records. She left at 3:56 p.m.[218] The President moved from the Residence to the Oval Office at 3:33 p.m. and remained there until 7:40 p.m.[219]

On that day, according to Ms. Lewinsky, she saw the President in a hallway by an elevator, and he invited her to the Oval Office.[220] According to Ms. Lewinsky:

> We had . . . had phone sex for the first time the week prior, and I was feeling a little bit insecure about whether he had liked it or did-n't like it . . . . I didn't know if this was sort of developing into some kind of a longer-term relationship than what I thought it ini-tially might have been, that maybe he had some regular girlfriend who was furloughed. . . .[221]

According to Ms. Lewinsky, she questioned the President about his interest in her. "I asked him why he doesn't ask me any questions about myself, and . . . is this just about sex . . . or do you have some interest in trying to get to know me as a person?"[222] The President laughed and said, according to Ms. Lewinsky, that "he cherishes the time that he had with me."[223] She considered it "a little bit odd" for him to speak of cherishing their time together "when I felt like he didn't really even know me yet."[224]

They continued talking as they went to the hallway by the study. Then, with Ms. Lewinsky in mid-sentence, "he just started kissing me."[225] He lifted her top and touched her breasts with his hands and mouth.[226] According to Ms. Lewinsky, the President "unzipped his pants and sort of exposed himself," and she performed oral sex.[227]

At one point during the encounter, someone entered the Oval Office. In Ms. Lewinsky's recollection, "[The President] zipped up real quickly and went out and came back in . . . . I just remember laughing because he had walked out there and he was visibly aroused, and I just thought it was funny."[228]

A short time later, the President got word that his next appointment, a friend from Arkansas, had arrived.[229] He took Ms. Lewinsky out through the Oval Office into Ms. Hernreich's office, where he kissed her goodbye.[230]

C. FEBRUARY 4 SEXUAL ENCOUNTER AND SUBSEQUENT PHONE CALLS

On Sunday, February 4, according to Ms. Lewinsky, she and the President had their sixth sexual encounter and their first lengthy and personal conversation. The President was in the Oval Office from 3:36 to 7:05 p.m.[231] He had no telephone calls in the Oval Office before 4:45 p.m.[232] Records do not show Ms. Lewinsky's entry or exit.

According to Ms. Lewinsky, the President telephoned her at her desk and they planned their rendezvous. At her suggestion, they bumped into each other in the hallway, "because when it happened accidentally, that seemed to work really well," then walked together to the area of the private study.[233]

There, according to Ms. Lewinsky, they kissed. She was wearing a long dress that buttoned from the neck to the ankles. "And he unbuttoned my dress and he unhooked my bra, and sort of took the dress off my shoulders and . . . moved the bra . . . . [H]e was looking at me and touching me and telling me how beautiful I was."[234] He touched her breasts with his hands and his mouth, and touched her genitals, first through underwear and then directly.[235] She performed oral sex on him.[236]

After their sexual encounter, the President and Ms. Lewinsky sat and talked in the Oval Office for about 45 minutes. Ms. Lewinsky thought the President might be responding to her suggestion during their previous meeting about "trying to get to know me."[237] It was during that conversation on February 4, according to Ms. Lewinsky, that their friendship started to blossom.[238]

When she prepared to depart, according to Ms. Lewinsky, the President "kissed my arm and told me he'd call me, and then I said, yeah, well, what's my phone number? And so he recited both my home number and my office number off the top of his head."[239] The President called her at her desk later that afternoon and said he had enjoyed their time together.[240]

D. PRESIDENT'S DAY (FEBRUARY 19) BREAK-UP

According to Ms. Lewinsky, the President terminated their relationship (only temporarily, as it happened), on Monday, February 19, 1996—President's Day. The President was in the Oval Office from 11 a.m. to 2:01 p.m. that day.[241] He had no telephone calls between 12:19 and 12:42 p.m.[242] Records do not reflect Ms. Lewinsky's presence at the White House.

In Ms. Lewinsky's recollection, the President telephoned her at her Watergate apartment that day. From the tone of his voice, she could tell something was wrong. She asked to come see him, but he said he did not know how long he would be there.[243] Ms. Lewinsky went to the White House, then walked to the Oval Office sometime between noon and 2 p.m. (the only time she ever went to the Oval Office uninvited).[244] Ms. Lewinsky recalled that she was admitted by a tall, slender, Hispanic plainclothes agent on duty near the door.[245]

The President told her that he no longer felt right about their intimate relationship, and he had to put a stop to it.[246] Ms. Lewinsky was welcome to continue coming to visit him, but only as a friend. He hugged her but would not kiss her.[247] At one point during their conversation, the President had a call from a sugar grower in Florida whose name, according to Ms. Lewinsky, was something like "Fanuli." In Ms. Lewinsky's recollection, the President may have taken or returned the call just as she was leaving.[248]

Ms. Lewinsky's account is corroborated in two respects. First, Nelson U. Garabito, a plainclothes Secret Service agent, testified that, on a weekend or holiday while Ms. Lewinsky worked at the White House (most likely in the early spring of 1996), Ms. Lewinsky appeared in the area of the Oval Office carrying a folder and said, "I have these papers for the President."[249] After knocking, Agent Garabito opened the Oval Office door, told the President he had a visitor, ushered Ms. Lewinsky in, and closed the door behind her.[250] When Agent Garabito's shift ended a few minutes later, Ms. Lewinsky was still in the Oval Office.[251]

Second, concerning Ms. Lewinsky's recollection of a call from a sugar grower named "Fanuli," the President talked with Alfonso Fanjul of Palm Beach, Florida, from 12:42 to 1:04 p.m.[252] Mr. Fanjul had telephoned a few minutes earlier, at 12:24 p.m.[253] The Fanjuls are prominent sugar growers in Florida.[254]

E. CONTINUING CONTACTS

After the break-up on February 19, 1996, according to Ms. Lewinsky, "there continued to sort of be this flirtation . . . when we'd see each other."[255] After passing Ms. Lewinsky in a hallway one night in late February or March, the President telephoned her at home and said he was disappointed that, because she had already left the White House for the evening, they could not get together. Ms. Lewinsky testified that the call "sort of implied to me that he was interested in starting up again."[256] On March 10, 1996, Ms. Lewinsky took a visiting friend, Natalie Ungvari, to the White House. They bumped into the President, who said to Ms. Ungvari when Ms. Lewinsky introduced them: "You must be her friend from California."[257] Ms. Ungvari was "shocked" that the President knew where she was from.[258]

Ms. Lewinsky testified that on Friday, March 29, 1996, she was walking down a hallway when she passed the President, who was wearing the first necktie she had given him. She asked where he had gotten the tie, and he replied: "Some girl with style gave it to me."[259] Later, he telephoned her at her desk and asked if she would like to see a movie. His plan was that she would position herself in the hallway by the White House Theater at a certain time, and he would invite her to join him and a group of guests as they entered. Ms. Lewinsky responded that she did not want people to think she was lurking around the West Wing uninvited.[260] She asked if they could arrange a rendezvous over the weekend instead, and he said he would try.[261] Records confirm that the President spent the evening of March 29 in the White House Theater.[262] Mrs. Clinton was in Athens, Greece.[263]

F. MARCH 31 SEXUAL ENCOUNTER

On Sunday, March 31, 1996, according to Ms. Lewinsky, she and the President resumed their sexual contact.[264] Ms. Lewinsky was at the White House from 10:21 a.m. to 4:27 p.m. on that day.[265] The President was in the Oval Office from 3:00 to 5:46 p.m.[266] His only call while in the Oval Office was from 3:06 to 3:07 p.m.[267] Mrs. Clinton was in Ireland.[268]

According to Ms. Lewinsky, the President telephoned her at her desk and suggested that she come to the Oval Office on the pretext of delivering papers to him.[269] She went to the Oval Office and was admitted by a plainclothes Secret Service agent.[270] In her folder was a gift for the President, a Hugo Boss necktie.[271]

In the hallway by the study, the President and Ms. Lewinsky kissed. On this occasion, according to Ms. Lewinsky, "he focused on me pretty exclusively," kissing her bare breasts and fondling her genitals.[272] At one point, the President inserted a cigar into Ms. Lewinsky's vagina, then put the cigar in his mouth and said: "It tastes good."[273] After they were finished, Ms. Lewinsky left the Oval Office and walked through the Rose Garden.[274]

IV. APRIL 1996: MS. LEWINSKY'S TRANSFER TO THE PENTAGON

With White House and Secret Service employees remarking on Ms. Lewinsky's frequent presence in the West Wing, a deputy chief of staff ordered Ms. Lewinsky transferred from the White House to the Pentagon. On April 7—Easter Sunday—Ms. Lewinsky told the President of her dismissal. He promised to bring her back after the election, and they had a sexual encounter.

A. EARLIER OBSERVATIONS OF MS. LEWINSKY IN THE WEST WING

Ms. Lewinsky's visits to the Oval Office area had not gone unnoticed. Officer Fox testified that "it was pretty commonly known that she did frequent the West Wing on the weekends."[275] Another Secret Service uniformed officer, William Ludtke III, once saw her exit from the pantry near the Oval Office; she seemed startled and possibly embarrassed to be spotted.[276] Officer John Muskett testified that "if the President was known to be coming into the Diplomatic Reception Room, a lot of times [Ms. Lewinsky] just happened to be walking down the corridor, you know, maybe just to see the President."[277] Ms. Lewinsky acknowledged that she tried to position herself to see the President.[278]

Although they could not date them precisely, Secret Service officers and agents testified about several occasions when Ms. Lewinsky and the President were alone in the Oval Office. William C. Bordley, a former member of the Presidential Protective Detail, testified that in late 1995 or early 1996, he stopped Ms. Lewinsky outside the Oval Office because she did not have her pass.[279] The President opened the Oval Office door, indicated to Agent Bordley that Ms. Lewinsky's presence was all right, and ushered Ms. Lewinsky into the Oval Office.[280] Agent Bordley saw Ms. Lewinsky leave about half an hour later.[281]

Another former member of the Presidential Protective Detail, Robert C. Ferguson, testified that one Saturday in winter, the President told him that he was expecting "some staffers."[282] A short time later, Ms. Lewinsky arrived and said that "[t]he President needs me."[283] Agent Ferguson announced Ms. Lewinsky and admitted her to the Oval Office.[284] About 10 or 15 minutes later, Agent Ferguson rotated to a post on the Colonnade outside the Oval Office.[285] He glanced through the window into the Oval Office and saw the President and Ms. Lewinsky go through the door leading toward the private study.[286]

Deeming her frequent visits to the Oval Office area a "nuisance," one Secret Service Officer complained to Evelyn Lieberman, the Deputy Chief of Staff for Operations.[287] Ms. Lieberman was already aware of Ms. Lewinsky. In December 1995, according to Ms. Lewinsky, Ms. Lieberman chided her for being in the West Wing and told her that interns are not permitted around the Oval Office.

Ms. Lewinsky (who had begun her Office of Legislative Affairs job) told Ms. Lieberman that she was not an intern anymore. After expressing surprise that Ms. Lewinsky had been hired, Ms. Lieberman said she must have Ms. Lewinsky confused with someone else.[288] Ms. Lieberman confirmed that she reprimanded Ms. Lewinsky, whom she considered "what we used to call a 'clutch' . . . always someplace she shouldn't be."[289]

In Ms. Lewinsky's view, some White House staff members seemed to think that she was to blame for the President's evident interest in her:

> [P]eople were wary of his weaknesses, maybe, and . . . they didn't want to look at him and think that he could be responsible for anything, so it had to all be my fault . . . I was stalking him or I was making advances towards him.[290]

B. DECISION TO TRANSFER MS. LEWINSKY

Ms. Lieberman testified that, because Ms. Lewinsky was so persistent in her efforts to be near the President, "I decided to get rid of her."[291] First she consulted Chief of Staff Panetta. According to Mr. Panetta, Ms. Lieberman told him about a woman on the staff who was "spending too much time around the West Wing." Because of "the appearance that it was creating," Ms. Lieberman proposed to move her out of the White House. Mr. Panetta—who testified that he valued Ms. Lieberman's role as "a tough disciplinarian" and "trusted her judgment"—replied, "Fine."[292]

Although Ms. Lieberman said she could not recall having heard any rumors linking the President and Ms. Lewinsky, she acknowledged that "the President was vulnerable to these kind of rumors . . . yes, yes, that was one of the reasons" for moving Ms. Lewinsky out of the White House.[293] Later, in September 1997, Marcia Lewis (Ms. Lewinsky's mother) complained about her daughter's dismissal to Ms. Lieberman, whom she met at a Voice of America ceremony. Ms. Lieberman, according to Ms. Lewis, responded by "saying something about Monica being cursed because she's beautiful." Ms. Lewis gathered from the remark that Ms. Lieberman, as part of her effort to protect the President, "would want to have pretty women moved out."[294]

Most people understood that the principal reason for Ms. Lewinsky's transfer was her habit of hanging around the Oval Office and the West Wing.[295] In a memo in October 1996, John Hilley, Assistant to the President and Director of Legislative Affairs, reported that Ms. Lewinsky had been "got[ten] rid of" in part "because of 'extracurricular activities'" (a phrase, he maintained in the grand jury, that meant only that Ms. Lewinsky was often absent from her work station).[296]

White House officials arranged for Ms. Lewinsky to get another job in the Administration.[297] "Our direction is to make sure she has a job in an Agency," Patsy Thomasson wrote in an email message on April 9, 1996.[298] Ms. Thomasson's office (Presidential Personnel) sent Ms. Lewinsky's resume to Charles Duncan, Special Assistant to the Secretary of Defense and White House Liaison, and asked him to find a Pentagon opening for her.[299] Mr. Duncan was told that, though Ms. Lewinsky had performed her duties capably, she was being dismissed for hanging around the Oval Office too much.[300] According to Mr. Duncan—who had received as many as 40 job referrals per day from the White House—the White House had never given such an explanation for a transfer.[301]

C. Ms. Lewinsky's Notification of Her Transfer

On Friday, April 5, 1996, Timothy Keating, Staff Director for Legislative Affairs, informed Ms. Lewinsky that she would have to leave her White House job.[302] According to Mr. Keating, he told her that she was not being fired, merely "being given a different opportunity." In fact, she could tell people it was a promotion if she cared to do so.[303] Upon hearing of her dismissal, Ms. Lewinsky burst into tears and asked if there was any way for her to stay in the White House, even without pay.[304] No, Mr. Keating said. According to Ms. Lewinsky, "He told me I was too sexy to be working in the East Wing and that this job at the Pentagon where I'd be writing press releases was a sexier job."[305]

Ms. Lewinsky was devastated. She felt that she was being transferred simply because of her relationship with the President.[306] And she feared that with the loss of her White House job, "I was never going to see the President again. I mean, my relationship with him would be over."[307]

D. CONVERSATIONS WITH THE PRESIDENT ABOUT HER TRANSFER

1. EASTER TELEPHONE CONVERSATIONS AND SEXUAL ENCOUNTER

On Easter Sunday, April 7, 1996, Ms. Lewinsky told the President of her dismissal and they had a sexual encounter. Ms. Lewinsky entered the White House at 4:56 and left at 5:28 p.m.[308] The President was in the Oval Office all afternoon, from 2:21 to 7:48 p.m.[309]

According to Ms. Lewinsky, the President telephoned her at home that day. After they spoke of the death of the Commerce Secretary the previous week, she told him of her dismissal:

> I had asked him . . . if he was doing okay with Ron Brown's death, and then after we talked about that for a little bit I told him that my last day was Monday. And . . . he seemed really upset and sort of asked me to tell him what had happened. So I did and I was crying and I asked him if I could come see him, and he said that that was fine.[310]

At the White House, according to Ms. Lewinsky, she told Secret Service Officer Muskett that she needed to deliver papers to the President.[311] Officer Muskett admitted her to the Oval Office, and she and the President proceeded to the private study.[312]

According to Ms. Lewinsky, the President seemed troubled about her upcoming departure from the White House:

> He told me that he thought that my being transferred had something to do with him and that he was upset. He said, "Why do they have to take you away from me? I trust you." And then he told

me—he looked at me and he said, "I promise you if I win in November I'll bring you back like that."[313]

He also indicated that she could have any job she wanted after the election.[314] In addition, the President said he would find out why Ms. Lewinsky was transferred and report back to her.[315]

When asked if he had promised to get Ms. Lewinsky another White House job, the President told the grand jury:

> What I told Ms. Lewinsky was that . . . I would do what I could to see, if she had a good record at the Pentagon, and she assured me she was doing a good job and working hard, that I would do my best to see that the fact that she had been sent away from the Legislative Affairs section did not keep her from getting a job in the White House, and that is, in fact, what I tried to do. . . . But I did not tell her I would order someone to hire her, and I never did, and I wouldn't do that. It wouldn't be right.[316]

Ms. Lewinsky, when asked if the President had said that he would bring her back to the White House only if she did a good job at the Pentagon, responded: "No."[317]

After this Easter Sunday conversation, the President and Ms. Lewinsky had a sexual encounter in the hallway, according to Ms. Lewinsky.[318] She testified that the President touched her breasts with his mouth and hands.[319] According to Ms. Lewinsky: "I think he unzipped [his pants] . . . because it was sort of this running joke that I could never unbutton his pants, that I just had trouble with it."[320] Ms. Lewinsky performed oral sex. The President did not ejaculate in her presence.[321]

During this encounter, someone called out from the Oval Office that the President had a phone call.[322] He went back to the Oval Office for a moment, then took the call in the study. The President indicated that Ms. Lewinsky should perform oral sex while he talked on the phone, and she obliged.[323] The telephone conversation was about politics, and Ms. Lewinsky thought the caller might be Dick Morris.[324] White House records confirm that the President had one telephone call during Ms. Lewinsky's visit: from "Mr. Richard Morris," to whom he talked from 5:11 to 5:20 p.m.[325]

A second interruption occurred a few minutes later, according to Ms. Lewinsky. She and the President were in the study.[326] Ms. Lewinsky testified:

> Harold Ickes has a very distinct voice and . . . I heard him holler "Mr. President," and the President looked at me and I looked at him and he jetted out into the Oval Office and I panicked and . . . thought that maybe because Harold was so close with the President that they might just wander back there and the President would assume that I knew to leave.[327]

Ms. Lewinsky testified that she exited hurriedly through the dining room door.[328] That evening, the President called and asked Ms. Lewinsky why she had run off. "I told him that I didn't know if he was going to be coming back . . . . [H]e was a little upset with me that I left."[329]

In addition to the record of the Dick Morris phone call, the testimony of Secret Service Officer Muskett corroborates Ms. Lewinsky's account. Officer Muskett was posted near the door to the Oval Office on Easter Sunday.[330] He testified that Ms. Lewinsky (whom he knew) arrived at about 4:45 p.m. carrying a manila folder and seeming "a little upset."[331] She told Officer Muskett that she needed to deliver documents to the President.[332] Officer Muskett or the plainclothes agent on duty with him opened the door, and Ms. Lewinsky entered.[333]

About 20 to 25 minutes later, according to Officer Muskett, the telephone outside the Oval Office rang. The White House operator said that the President had an important call but he was not picking up.[334] The agent working alongside Officer Muskett knocked on the door to the Oval Office. When the President did not respond, the agent entered. The Oval Office was empty, and the door leading to the study was slightly ajar.[335] (Ms. Lewinsky testified that the President left the door ajar during their sexual encounters.[336]) The agent called out, "Mr. President?" There was no response. The agent stepped into the Oval Office and called out more loudly, "Mr. President?" This time there was a response from the study area, according to Officer Muskett: "Huh?" The agent called out that the President had a phone call, and the President said he would take it.[337]

A few minutes later, according to Officer Muskett, Mr. Ickes approached and said he needed to see President Clinton. Officer Muskett admitted him through Ms. Currie's office.[338] Less than a minute after Mr. Ickes entered Ms. Currie's reception area, according to Officer Muskett, the pantry or dining room door closed audibly. Officer Muskett stepped down the hall to check and saw Ms. Lewinsky walking away briskly.[339]

At 5:30 p.m., two minutes after Ms. Lewinsky left the White House, the President called the office of the person who had decided to transfer Ms. Lewinsky, Evelyn Lieberman.[340]

2. APRIL 12-13: TELEPHONE CONVERSATIONS

Ms. Lewinsky testified that the President telephoned her the following Friday, April 12, 1996, at home. They talked for about 20 minutes. According to Ms. Lewinsky, the President said he had checked on the reason for her transfer:

> [H]e had come to learn . . . that Evelyn Lieberman had sort of spearheaded the transfer, and that she thought he was paying too much attention to me and I was paying too much attention to him and that she didn't necessarily care what happened after the election but everyone needed to be careful before the election.[341]

According to Ms. Lewinsky, the President told her to give the Pentagon a try, and, if she did not like it, he would get her a job on the campaign.[342]

In the grand jury, Ms. Lieberman testified that the President asked her directly about Ms. Lewinsky's transfer:

> After I had gotten rid of her, when I was in there, during the course of a conversation, [President Clinton] said, "I got a call about —"
> I don't know if he said her name. He said maybe "— an intern you

fired." And she was evidently very upset about it. He said, "Do you know anything about this?" I said, "Yes." He said, "Who fired her?" I said, "I did." And he said, "Oh, okay."[343]

According to Ms. Lieberman, the President did not pursue the matter further.[344]

Three other witnesses confirm that the President knew why Ms. Lewinsky was transferred to the Pentagon. In 1997, the President told Chief of Staff Erskine Bowles "that there was a young woman—her name was Monica Lewinsky—who used to work at the White House; that Evelyn . . . thought she hung around the Oval Office too much and transferred her to the Pentagon."[345] According to Betty Currie, the President believed that Ms. Lewinsky had been unfairly transferred.[346] The President's close friend, Vernon Jordan, testified that the President said to him in December 1997 that "he knew about [Ms. Lewinsky's] situation, which was that she was pushed out of the White House."[347]

V. APRIL-DECEMBER 1996: NO PRIVATE MEETINGS

After Ms. Lewinsky began her Pentagon job on April 16, 1996, she had no further physical contact with the President for the remainder of the year. She and the President spoke by phone (and had phone sex) but saw each other only at public functions. Ms. Lewinsky grew frustrated after the election because the President did not bring her back to work at the White House.

A. PENTAGON JOB

On April 16, 1996, Ms. Lewinsky began working at the Pentagon as Confidential Assistant to the Assistant Secretary of Defense for Public Affairs.[348]

B. NO PHYSICAL CONTACT

According to Ms. Lewinsky, she had no physical contact with the President for the rest of 1996.[349] "I wasn't alone with him so when I saw him it was in some sort of event or group setting," she testi-fied.[350]

C. TELEPHONE CONVERSATIONS

Ms. Lewinsky and the President did talk by telephone, especially in her first weeks at the new job.[351] By Ms. Lewinsky's estimate, the President phoned her (sometimes leaving a message) four or five times in the month after she started working at the Pentagon, then two or three times a month thereafter for the rest of 1996.[352] During the fall 1996 campaign, the President sometimes called from trips when Mrs. Clinton was not accompanying him.[353] During at least seven of the 1996 calls, Ms. Lewinsky and the President had phone sex.[354]

According to Ms. Lewinsky, the President telephoned her at about 6:30 a.m. on July 19, the day he was leaving for the 1996 Olympics in Atlanta, and they had phone sex, after which the President exclaimed, "[G]ood morning!" and then said: "What a way to start a day."[355] A call log shows that the President called the White House operator at 12:11 a.m. on July 19 and asked for a wake-up call at 7 a.m., then at 6:40 a.m., the President called and said he was already up.[356] In Ms. Lewinsky's recollection, she and the President also had phone sex on May 21, July 5 or 6, October 22, and December 2, 1996.[357] On those dates, Mrs. Clinton was in Denver (May 21), Prague and Budapest (July 5-6), Las Vegas (October 22), and en route to Bolivia (December 2).[358]

Ms. Lewinsky repeatedly told the President that she disliked her Pentagon job and wanted to return to the White House.[359] In a recorded conversation, Ms. Lewinsky recounted one call:

> [A] month had passed and—so he had called one night, and I said, "Well," I said, "I'm really unhappy," you know. And [the President] said, "I don't want to talk about your job tonight. I'll call you this week, and then we'll talk about it. I want to talk about other things"—which meant phone sex.[360]

She expected to talk with him the following weekend, and she was "ready to broach the idea of . . . going to the campaign," but he did not call.[361]

Ms. Lewinsky and the President also talked about their relationship. During a phone conversation on September 5, according to Ms. Lewinsky, she told the President that she wanted to have intercourse with him. He responded that he could not do so because of the possible consequences. The two of them argued, and he asked if he should stop calling her. No, she responded.[362]

D. PUBLIC ENCOUNTERS

During this period, Ms. Lewinsky occasionally saw the President in public. She testified:

> I'm an insecure person . . . and I was insecure about the relationship at times and thought that he would come to forget me easily and if I hadn't heard from him . . . it was very difficult for me . . . . [U]sually when I'd see him, it would kind of prompt him to call me. So I made an effort. I would go early and stand in the front so I could see him . . . .[363]

On May 2, 1996, Ms. Lewinsky saw the President at a reception for the Saxophone Club, a political organization.[364] On June 14, Ms. Lewinsky and her family attended the taping of the President's weekly radio address and had photos taken with the President.[365] On August 18, Ms. Lewinsky attended the President's 50th birthday party at Radio City Music Hall, and she got into a cocktail party for major donors where she saw the President.[366] According to Ms. Lewinsky, when the President reached past her at the rope line to shake hands with another guest, she reached out and touched his crotch in a "playful" fashion.[367] On October 23, according to Ms. Lewinsky, she talked with the President at a fundraiser for Senate Democrats.[368] The two were photographed together at the event.[369] The President was wearing a necktie she had given him, according to Ms. Lewinsky, and she said to him, "Hey, Handsome—I like your tie."[370] The President telephoned her that night. She said she planned to be at the White House on Pentagon business the next day, and he told her to stop by the Oval Office. At the White House the next day, Ms. Lewinsky did not see the President because Ms. Lieberman was nearby.[371] On December 17, Ms. Lewinsky attended a holiday reception at the White House.[372] A photo shows her shaking hands with the President.[373]

E. Ms. Lewinsky's Frustrations

Continuing to believe that her relationship with the President was the key to regaining her White House pass, Ms. Lewinsky hoped that the President would get her a job immediately after the election. "I kept a calendar with a countdown until election day," she later wrote in an unsent letter to him. The letter states:

> I was so sure that the weekend after the election you would call me to come visit and you would kiss me passionately and tell me you couldn't wait to have me back. You'd ask me where I wanted to work and say something akin to "Consider it done" and it would be. Instead I didn't hear from you for weeks and subsequently your phone calls became less frequent.[374]

Ms. Lewinsky grew increasingly frustrated over her relationship with President Clinton.[375] One friend understood that Ms. Lewinsky complained to the President about not having seen each other privately for months, and he replied, "Every day can't be sunshine."[376] In email to another friend in early 1997, Ms. Lewinsky wrote: "I just don't understand what went wrong, what happened? How could he do this to me? Why did he keep up contact with me for so long and now nothing, now when we could be together?"[377]

VI. Early 1997: Resumption of Sexual Encounters

In 1997, President Clinton and Ms. Lewinsky had further private meetings, which now were arranged by Betty Currie, the President's secretary. After the taping of the President's weekly radio address on February 28, the President and Ms. Lewinsky had a sexual encounter. On March 24, they had what proved to be their final sexual encounter. Throughout this period, Ms. Lewinsky continued to press for a job at the White House, to no avail.

A. RESUMPTION OF MEETINGS WITH THE PRESIDENT

1. ROLE OF BETTY CURRIE

A. ARRANGING MEETINGS

In 1997, with the presidential election past, Ms. Lewinsky and the President resumed their one-on-one meetings and sexual encounters. The President's secretary, Betty Currie, acted as intermediary.

According to Ms. Currie, Ms. Lewinsky would often call her and say she wanted to see the President, sometimes to discuss a particular topic.[378] Ms. Currie would ask President Clinton, and, if he agreed, arrange the meeting.[379] Ms. Currie also said it was "not unusual" that Ms. Lewinsky would talk by phone with the President and then call Ms. Currie to set up a meeting.[380] At times, Ms. Currie placed calls to Ms. Lewinsky for President Clinton and put him on the line.[381]

The meetings between the President and Ms. Lewinsky often occurred on weekends.[382] When Ms. Lewinsky would arrive at the White House, Ms. Currie generally would be the one to authorize her entry and take her to the West Wing.[383] Ms. Currie acknowledged that she sometimes would come to the White House for the sole purpose of having Ms. Lewinsky admitted and bringing her to see the President.[384] According to Ms. Currie, Ms. Lewinsky and the President were alone together in the Oval Office or the study for 15 to 20 minutes on multiple occasions.[385]

Secret Service officers and agents took note of Ms. Currie's role. Officer Steven Pape once observed Ms. Currie come to the White House for the duration of Ms. Lewinsky's visit, then leave.[386] When calling to alert the officer at the West Wing lobby that Ms. Lewinsky was en route, Ms. Currie would sometimes say, "[Y]ou know who it is."[387] On one occasion, Ms. Currie instructed Officer Brent Chinery to hold Ms. Lewinsky at the lobby for a few minutes because she needed to move the President to the study.[388] On another occasion, Ms. Currie told Officer Chinery to have Ms. Lewinsky held at the gate for 30 to 40 minutes because the President already had a visitor.[389]

Ms. Lewinsky testified that she once asked the President why Ms. Currie had to clear her in, and why he could not do so himself. "[H]e said because if someone comes to see him, there's a list circulated among the staff members and then everyone would be questioning why I was there to see him."[390]

B. Intermediary for Gifts

Ms. Lewinsky also sent over a number of packages—six or eight, Ms. Currie estimated.[391] According to Ms. Currie, Ms. Lewinsky would call and say she was sending something for the President.[392] The package would arrive addressed to Ms. Currie.[393] Courier receipts show that Ms. Lewinsky sent seven packages to the White House between October 7 and December 8, 1997.[394] Evidence indicates that Ms. Lewinsky on occasion also dropped parcels off with Ms. Currie or had a family member do so,[395] and brought gifts to the President when visiting him.[396] Ms. Currie testified that most packages from Ms. Lewinsky were intended for the President.[397]

Although Ms. Currie generally opened letters and parcels to the President, she did not open these packages from Ms. Lewinsky.[398] She testified that "I made the determination not to open" such letters and packages because "I felt [they were] probably personal."[399] Instead, she would leave the package in the President's box, and "[h]e would pick it up."[400] To the best of her knowledge, such parcels always reached the President.[401]

C. Secrecy

Ms. Currie testified that she suspected impropriety in the President's relationship with Ms. Lewinsky.[402] She told the grand jury that she "had concern." In her words: "[H]e was spending a lot of time with a 24-year-old young lady. I know he has said that young people keep him involved in what's happening in the world, so I knew that was one reason, but there was a concern of mine that she was spending more time than most."[403] Ms. Currie understood that "the majority" of the President's meetings with Ms. Lewinsky were "more personal in nature as opposed to business."[404]

Ms. Currie also testified that she tried to avoid learning details of the relationship between the President and Ms. Lewinsky. On one occasion, Ms. Lewinsky said of herself and the President, "As long as no one saw us—and no one did—then nothing happened." Ms. Currie responded: "Don't want to hear it. Don't say any more. I don't want to hear any more."[405]

Ms. Currie helped keep the relationship secret. When the President wanted to talk with Ms. Lewinsky, Ms. Currie would dial the call herself rather than go through White House operators, who keep logs of presidential calls made through the switchboard.[406] When Ms. Lewinsky phoned and Ms. Currie put the President on the line, she did not log the call, though the standard procedure was to note all calls, personal and professional.[407] According to Secret Service uniformed officers, Ms. Currie sometimes tried to persuade them to admit Ms. Lewinsky to the White House compound without making a record of it.[408]

In addition, Ms. Currie avoided writing down or retaining most messages from Ms. Lewinsky to the President. In response to a grand jury subpoena, the White House turned over only one note to the President concerning Ms. Lewinsky—whereas evidence indicates that Ms. Lewinsky used Ms. Currie to convey requests and messages to the President on many occasions.[409]

When bringing Ms. Lewinsky in from the White House gate, Ms. Currie said she sometimes chose a path that would reduce the likelihood of being seen by two White House employees who disapproved of Ms. Lewinsky: Stephen Goodin and Nancy Hernreich.[410] Ms. Currie testified that she once brought Ms. Lewinsky directly to the study, "sneaking her back" via a roundabout path to avoid running into Mr. Goodin.[411] When Ms. Lewinsky visited the White House on weekends and at night, being spotted was not a prob-

lem—in Ms. Currie's words, "there would be no need to sneak"—
so Ms. Lewinsky would await the President in Ms. Currie's office.[412]

According to Ms. Lewinsky, she once expressed concern about
records showing the President's calls to her, and Ms. Currie told her
not to worry.[413] Ms. Lewinsky also suspected that Ms. Currie was
not logging in all of her gifts to the President.[414] In Ms. Lewinsky's
evaluation, many White House staff members tried to regulate the
President's behavior, but Ms. Currie generally did as he wished.[415]

2. OBSERVATIONS BY SECRET SERVICE OFFICERS

Officers of the Secret Service Uniformed Division noted Ms.
Lewinsky's 1997 visits to the White House. From radio traffic about
the President's movements, several officers observed that the President often would head for the Oval Office within minutes of Ms.
Lewinsky's entry to the complex, especially on weekends, and some
noted that he would return to the Residence a short time after her
departure.[416] "It was just like clockwork," according to one officer.[417] Concerned about the President's reputation, another officer
suggested putting Ms. Lewinsky on a list of people who were not to
be admitted to the White House. A commander responded that it
was none of their business whom the President chose to see, and, in
any event, nobody would ever find out about Ms. Lewinsky.[418]

B. VALENTINE'S DAY ADVERTISEMENT

On February 14, 1997, the Washington Post published a Valentine's Day "Love Note" that Ms. Lewinsky had placed. The ad said:

> *HANDSOME*
> *With love's light wings did*
> *I o'er perch these walls*
> *For stony limits cannot hold love out,*
> *And what love can do that dares love attempt.*
> *— Romeo and Juliet 2:2*
> *Happy Valentine's Day.*
> *M*[419]

C. FEBRUARY 24 MESSAGE

On February 24, Ms. Lewinsky visited the White House on Pentagon business.[420] She went by Ms. Currie's office.[421] Ms. Currie sent a note to the President—the only such note turned over by the White House in response to a grand jury subpoena: "Monica Lewinsky stopped by. Do you want me to call her?"[422]

D. FEBRUARY 28 SEXUAL ENCOUNTER

According to Ms. Lewinsky, she and the President had a sexual encounter on Thursday, February 28—their first in nearly 11 months. White House records show that Ms. Lewinsky attended the taping of the President's weekly radio address on February 28.[423] She was at the White House from 5:48 to 7:07 p.m.[424] The President was in the Roosevelt Room (where the radio address was taped) from 6:29 to 6:36 p.m., then moved to the Oval Office, where he remained until 7:24 p.m.[425] He had no telephone calls while Ms. Lewinsky was in the White House.[426]

Wearing a navy blue dress from the Gap, Ms. Lewinsky attended the radio address at the President's invitation (relayed by Ms. Currie), then had her photo taken with the President.[427] Ms. Lewinsky had not been alone with the President since she had worked at the White House, and, she testified, "I was really nervous."[428] President Clinton told her to see Ms. Currie after the photo was taken because he wanted to give her something.[429] "So I waited a little while for him and then Betty and the President and I went into the back office," Ms. Lewinsky testified.[430] (She later learned that the reason Ms. Currie accompanied them was that Stephen Goodin did not want the President to be alone with Ms. Lewinsky, a view that Mr. Goodin expressed to the President and Ms. Currie.[431]) Once they had passed from the Oval Office toward the private study, Ms. Currie said, "I'll be right back," and walked on to the back pantry or the dining room, where, according to Ms. Currie, she waited for 15 to 20 minutes while the President and Ms. Lewinsky were in the study.[432] Ms. Currie (who said she acted on her own initiative) testified that she accompanied the President and Ms. Lewinsky out of the Oval Office because "I didn't want any perceptions, him being alone with someone."[433]

In the study, according to Ms. Lewinsky, the President "started to say something to me and I was pestering him to kiss me, because . . . it had been a long time since we had been alone."[434] The President told her to wait a moment, as he had presents for her.[435] As belated Christmas gifts, he gave her a hat pin and a special edition of Walt Whitman's *Leaves of Grass*.[436] Ms. Lewinsky described the Whitman book as "the most sentimental gift he had given me . . . it's beautiful and it meant a lot to me."[437] During this visit, according to Ms. Lewinsky, the President said he had seen her Valentine's Day message in the Washington Post, and he talked about his fondness for "Romeo and Juliet."[438]

Ms. Lewinsky testified that after the President gave her the gifts, they had a sexual encounter:

> [W]e went back over by the bathroom in the hallway, and we kissed. We were kissing and he unbuttoned my dress and fondled my breasts with my bra on, and then took them out of my bra and was kissing them and touching them with his hands and with his mouth.
>
> And then I think I was touching him in his genital area through his pants, and I think I unbuttoned his shirt and was kissing his chest. And then . . . I wanted to perform oral sex on him . . . and so I did. And then . . . I think he heard something, or he heard someone in the office. So, we moved into the bathroom.
>
> And I continued to perform oral sex and then he pushed me away, kind of as he always did before he came, and then I stood up and I said . . . I care about you so much; . . . I don't understand why you won't let me . . . make you come; it's important to me; I mean, it just doesn't feel complete, it doesn't seem right.[439]

Ms. Lewinsky testified that she and the President hugged, and "he said he didn't want to get addicted to me, and he didn't want me to get addicted to him." They looked at each other for a moment.[440]

Then, saying that "I don't want to disappoint you," the President consented.[441] For the first time, she performed oral sex through completion.[442]

When Ms. Lewinsky next took the navy blue Gap dress from her closet to wear it, she noticed stains near one hip and on the chest.[443] FBI Laboratory tests revealed that the stains are the President's semen.[444]

In his grand jury testimony, the President—who, because the OIC had asked him for a blood sample (and had represented that it had ample evidentiary justification for making such a request), had reason to suspect that Ms. Lewinsky's dress might bear traces of his semen—indicated that he and Ms. Lewinsky had had sexual contact on the day of the radio address. He testified:

> I was sick after it was over and I, I was pleased at that time that it had been nearly a year since any inappropriate contact had occurred with Ms. Lewinsky. I promised myself it wasn't going to happen again. The facts are complicated about what did happen and how it happened. But, nonetheless, I'm responsible for it.[445]

Later the President added, referring to the evening of the radio address: "I do believe that I was alone with her from 15 to 20 minutes. I do believe that things happened then which were inappropriate."[446] He said of the intimate relationship with Ms. Lewinsky: "I never should have started it, and I certainly shouldn't have started it back after I resolved not to in 1996."[447]

E. MARCH 29 SEXUAL ENCOUNTER

According to Ms. Lewinsky, she had what proved to be her final sexual encounter with the President on Saturday, March 29, 1997. Records show that she was at the White House from 2:03 to 3:16 p.m., admitted by Ms. Currie.[448] The President was in the Oval Office during this period (he left shortly after Ms. Lewinsky did, at 3:24 p.m.), and he did not have any phone calls during her White House visit.[449]

According to Ms. Lewinsky, Ms. Currie arranged the meeting

after the President said by telephone that he had something important to tell her. At the White House, Ms. Currie took her to the
study to await the President. He came in on crutches, the result of a
knee injury in Florida two weeks earlier.[450]

According to Ms. Lewinsky, their sexual encounter began with a
sudden kiss: "[T]his was another one of those occasions when I was
babbling on about something, and he just kissed me, kind of to shut
me up, I think."[451] The President unbuttoned her blouse and
touched her breasts without removing her bra.[452] "[H]e went to go
put his hand down my pants, and then I unzipped them because it
was easier. And I didn't have any panties on. And so he manually
stimulated me."[453] According to Ms. Lewinsky, "I wanted him to
touch my genitals with his genitals," and he did so, lightly and without penetration.[454] Then Ms. Lewinsky performed oral sex on him,
again until he ejaculated.[455]

According to Ms. Lewinsky, she and the President had a lengthy
conversation that day. He told her that he suspected that a foreign
embassy (he did not specify which one) was tapping his telephones,
and he proposed cover stories. If ever questioned, she should say
that the two of them were just friends. If anyone ever asked about
their phone sex, she should say that they knew their calls were being
monitored all along, and the phone sex was just a put-on.[456]

In his grand jury testimony, the President implicitly denied this
encounter. He acknowledged "inappropriate intimate contact" with
Ms. Lewinsky "on certain occasions in early 1996 and once in early
1997."[457] The President indicated that "the one occasion in 1997"
was the radio address.[458]

F. CONTINUING JOB EFFORTS

With the 1996 election past, meanwhile, Ms. Lewinsky had continued striving to get a job at the White House. She testified that she
first broached the issue in a telephone call with the President in January 1997, and he said he would speak to Bob Nash, Director of
Presidential Personnel.[459] She understood that Mr. Nash was sup-

posed to "find a position for me to come back to the White House."[460]

Over the months that followed, Ms. Lewinsky repeatedly asked the President to get her a White House job. In her recollection, the President replied that various staff members were working on it, including Mr. Nash and Marsha Scott, Deputy Assistant to the President and Deputy Director for Presidential Personnel.[461] According to Ms. Lewinsky, the President told her:

> "Bob Nash is handling it," "Marsha's going to handle it" and "We just sort of need to be careful." You know, and . . . he would always sort of . . . validate what I was feeling by telling me something that I don't necessarily know is true. "Oh, I'll talk to her," "I'll—you know, I'll see blah, blah, blah," and it was just "I'll do," "I'll do," "I'll do." And didn't, didn't, didn't.[462]

Ms. Lewinsky came to wonder if she was being "strung along."[463]

Testifying before the grand jury, the President acknowledged that Ms. Lewinsky had complained to him about her job situation:

> You know, she tried for months and months to get a job back in the White House, not so much in the West Wing but somewhere in the White House complex, including the Old Executive Office Building. . . . She very much wanted to come back. And she interviewed for some jobs but never got one. She was, from time to time, upset about it.[464]

VII. MAY 1997: TERMINATION OF SEXUAL RELATIONSHIP

In May 1997, amid indications that Ms. Lewinsky had been indiscreet, President Clinton terminated the sexual relationship.

A. QUESTIONS ABOUT MS. LEWINSKY'S DISCRETION

In April or May 1997, according to Ms. Lewinsky, the President asked if she had told her mother about their intimate relationship. She responded: "No. Of course not."[465] (In truth, she had told her mother.[466]) The President indicated that Ms. Lewinsky's mother possibly had said something about the nature of the relationship to Walter Kaye, who had mentioned it to Marsha Scott, who in turn had alerted the President.[467]

Corroborating Ms. Lewinsky's account, Mr. Kaye testified that he told Ms. Lewinsky's aunt, Debra Finerman, that he understood that "her niece was very aggressive," a remark that angered Ms. Finerman. Ms. Finerman told Mr. Kaye that the President was the true aggressor: He was telephoning Ms. Lewinsky late at night. Ms. Finerman, in Mr. Kaye's recollection, attributed this information to Marcia Lewis, Ms. Lewinsky's mother (and Ms. Finerman's sister). Mr. Kaye—who had disbelieved stories he had heard from Democratic National Committee people about an affair between Ms. Lewinsky and the President—testified that he was "shocked" to hear of the late-night phone calls.[468]

B. MAY 24: BREAK-UP

On Saturday, May 24, 1997, according to Ms. Lewinsky, the President ended their intimate relationship. Ms. Lewinsky was at the White House that day from 12:21 to 1:54 p.m.[469] The President was in the Oval Office during most of this period, from 11:59 a.m. to 1:47 p.m.[470] He did not have any telephone calls.[471]

According to Ms. Lewinsky, she got a call from Ms. Currie at about 11 a.m. that day, inviting her to come to the White House at about 1 p.m. Ms. Lewinsky arrived wearing a straw hat with the hat pin the President had given her, and bringing gifts for him, including a puzzle and a Banana Republic shirt. She gave him the gifts in the dining room, and they moved to the area of the study.[472]

According to Ms. Lewinsky, the President explained that they had to end their intimate relationship.[473] Earlier in his marriage, he told her, he had had hundreds of affairs; but since turning 40, he had made a concerted effort to be faithful.[474] He said he was attracted to Ms. Lewinsky, considered her a great person, and hoped they would remain friends. He pointed out that he could do a great deal for her. The situation, he stressed, was not Ms. Lewin-

sky's fault.[475] Ms. Lewinsky, weeping, tried to persuade the President
not to end the sexual relationship, but he was unyielding, then and
subsequently.[476] Although she and the President kissed and hugged
thereafter, according to Ms. Lewinsky, the sexual relationship was
over.[477]

Three days after this meeting, on May 27, 1997, the Supreme
Court unanimously rejected President Clinton's claim that the Constitution immunized him from civil lawsuits. The Court ordered the
sexual harassment case Jones v. Clinton to proceed.[478]

VIII. JUNE-OCTOBER 1997: CONTINUING MEETINGS AND CALLS

Ms. Lewinsky tried to return to the White House staff and to
revive her sexual relationship with the President, but she failed at
both.

A. CONTINUING JOB EFFORTS

Although Ms. Lewinsky was not offered another White House
job, some testimony indicates that the President tried to get her
one.

According to Betty Currie, the President instructed her and Marsha Scott to help Ms. Lewinsky find a White House job.[479] Ms. Currie testified that she resisted the request, because her opinion of Ms.
Lewinsky had shifted over time. At first, she testified, she considered
Ms. Lewinsky "a friend" who "had been wronged" and had been
"maligned improperly."[480] But "[l]ater on, I considered her as a pain
in the neck, more or less."[481] The change of heart resulted in part
from Ms. Currie's many phone calls in 1997 from Ms. Lewinsky,
who was often distraught and sometimes in tears over her inability
to get in touch with the President.[482] Deeming her "a little bit
pushy," Ms. Currie argued against bringing Ms. Lewinsky back to
work at the White House, but the President told her and Ms. Scott,
in Ms. Currie's words, "to still pursue her coming back."[483] Indeed,
according to Ms. Currie, the President "was pushing us hard" on

the matter.[484] To the best of Ms. Currie's recollection, it was the only time the President instructed her to try to get someone a White House job.[485]

According to Ms. Lewinsky, the President told her to talk with Ms. Scott about a White House job in spring 1997.[486] On June 16, she met with Ms. Scott.[487] The meeting did not go as Ms. Lewinsky anticipated. She later recounted in an email message:

> There is most certainly a disconnect on what [the President] said he told her and how she acted. She didn't even know what my title or my job was . . . . She didn't have any job openings to offer. Instead, she made me go over what happened when I had to leave (who told me), and then proceeded to confirm the Evelyn [Lieberman] story about my "inappropriate behavior." Then she asked me: with such nasty women there and people gossiping about me, why did I want to come back? I was so upset. I really did not feel it was her place to question me about that. Later on, I said something about being told I could come back after November and she wanted to know who told me that! So I have placed a call to him but I don't know what is going to happen.

Ms. Lewinsky added that she was inclined "to walk away from it all," but acknowledged that "I'm always saying this and then I change my mind."[488]

Though she characterized her recollection as "all jumbled," Ms. Scott corroborated much of Ms. Lewinsky's account.[489] Ms. Scott said that at some point she did ask Ms. Lewinsky why she wanted to return to the White House.[490] Ms. Scott also said that she was unaware of Ms. Lewinsky's job title before their meeting.[491]

Over the next three weeks, Ms. Lewinsky tried repeatedly, without success, to talk with the President about her job quest. In a draft of a letter to Ms. Currie, she wrote that the President "said to me that he had told [Ms. Scott] I had gotten a bum deal, and I should get a good job in the West Wing," but Ms. Scott did not seem eager to arrange for Ms. Lewinsky's return. Ms. Lewinsky wrote:

I was surprised that she would question his judgment and not just do what he asked of her. Is it possible that, in fact, he did not tell her that? Does he really not want me back in the complex? He has not responded to my note, nor has he called me. Do you know what is going on? If so, are you able to share it with me?[492]

Ms. Currie testified to "a vague recollection" of having seen this letter.[493]

On June 29, 1997, Ms. Lewinsky wrote several notes. In a draft letter to Ms. Scott, Ms. Lewinsky wrote that "our last conversation was very upsetting to me," and added:

Marsha, I was told that I could come back after the election. I knew why I had to leave last year by mid-April, and I have been beyond patient since then. I do not think it is fair to . . . be told by the person whom I was told would get me a job that there is nothing for me and she doesn't really hear about positions [in] the complex anyway. I know that in your eyes I am just a hindrance—a woman who doesn't have a certain someone's best interests at heart, but please trust me when I say I do.[494]

Ms. Lewinsky also drafted a note to the President pleading for a brief meeting the following Tuesday. Referring to her inability to get in touch with him, she wrote: "Please do not do this to me. I feel disposable, used and insignificant. I understand your hands are tied, but I want to talk to you and look at some options."[495] Around this time, Ms. Lewinsky told a friend that she was considering moving to another city or country.[496]

B. JULY 3 LETTER

"[V]ery frustrated" over her inability to get in touch with the President to discuss her job situation, Ms. Lewinsky wrote him a peevish letter on July 3, 1997.[497] Opening "Dear Sir," the letter took the President to task for breaking his promise to get her another White House job.[498] Ms. Lewinsky also obliquely threatened to disclose their relationship. If she was not going to return to work at the

White House, she wrote, then she would "need to explain to my parents exactly why that wasn't happening." Some explanation was necessary because she had told her parents that she would be brought back after the election.[499] (Ms. Lewinsky testified that she would not actually have told her father about the relationship—she had already told her mother—but she wanted to remind the President that she had "left the White House like a good girl in April of '96," whereas other people might have threatened disclosure in order to retain the job.[500])

Ms. Lewinsky also raised the possibility of a job outside Washington. If returning to the White House was impossible, she asked in this letter, could he get her a job at the United Nations in New York?[501] It was the first time that she had told the President that she was considering moving.[502]

Although not questioned about this particular letter, the President testified that he believed Ms. Lewinsky might disclose their intimate relationship once he stopped it. He testified:

> After I terminated the improper contact with her, she wanted to come in more than she did. She got angry when she didn't get in sometimes. I knew that that might make her more likely to speak, and I still did it because I had to limit the contact.[503]

After receiving the July 3 letter, though, the President agreed to see Ms. Lewinsky. In her account, Ms. Currie called that afternoon and told her to come to the White House at 9 a.m. the next day.[504]

C. July 4 Meeting

On Friday, July 4, 1997, Ms. Lewinsky had what she characterized as a "very emotional" visit with the President.[505] Records show that Ms. Lewinsky entered the White House at 8:51 a.m.; no exit time is recorded.[506] Logs indicate that the President was in the Oval Office from 8:40 until after 11 a.m.[507]

In Ms. Lewinsky's recollection, their meeting began contentiously, with the President scolding her: "[I]t's illegal to threaten the President of the United States."[508] He then told her that he had not read her July 3 letter beyond the "Dear Sir" line; he surmised that it was threatening because Ms. Currie looked upset when she brought it to him. (Ms. Lewinsky suspected that he actually had read the whole thing.)[509] Ms. Lewinsky complained about his failure to get her a White House job after her long wait. Although the President claimed he wanted to be her friend, she said, he was not acting like it. Ms. Lewinsky began weeping, and the President hugged her. While they hugged, she spotted a gardener outside the study window, and they moved into the hallway by the bathroom.[510]

There, the President was "the most affectionate with me he'd ever been," Ms. Lewinsky testified. He stroked her arm, toyed with her hair, kissed her on the neck, praised her intellect and beauty.[511] In Ms. Lewinsky's recollection:

> [H]e remarked . . . that he wished he had more time for me. And so I said, well, maybe you will have more time in three years. And I was . . . thinking just when he wasn't President, he was going to have more time on his hands. And he said, well, I don't know, I might be alone in three years. And then I said something about . . . us sort of being together. I think I kind of said, oh, I think we'd be a good team, or something like that. And he . . . jokingly said, well, what are we going to do when I'm 75 and I have to pee 25 times a day? And . . . I told him that we'd deal with that. . . .[512]

Ms. Lewinsky testified that "I left that day sort of emotionally stunned," for "I just knew he was in love with me."[513]

Just before leaving, according to Ms. Lewinsky, she told the President "that I wanted to talk to him about something serious and that while I didn't want to be the one to talk about this with him, I thought it was important he know."[514] She informed him that Newsweek was working on an article about Kathleen Willey, a former White House volunteer who claimed that the President had sexually harassed her during a private meeting in the Oval Office on November 23, 1993. (Ms. Lewinsky knew of the article from Ms. Tripp, who had worked at the White House at the time of the alleged incident and had heard about the incident from Ms. Willey. Michael Isikoff of Newsweek had talked with Ms. Tripp about the episode in March 1997 and again shortly before July 4, and Ms. Tripp had subsequently related the Isikoff conversations to Ms. Lewinsky.[515]) Ms. Lewinsky told the President what she had learned from Ms. Tripp (whom she did not name), including the fact that Ms. Tripp had tried to get in touch with Deputy White House Counsel Bruce Lindsey, who had not returned her calls.[516]

Ms. Lewinsky testified about why she conveyed this information to the President: "I was concerned that the President had no idea this was going on and that this woman was going to be another Paula Jones and he didn't really need that."[517] She understood that Ms. Willey was looking for a job, and she thought that the President might be able to "make this go away" by finding her a job.[518]

The President responded that the harassment allegation was ludicrous, because he would never approach a small-breasted woman like Ms. Willey.[519] He further said that, during the previous week, Ms. Willey had called Nancy Hernreich to warn that a reporter was working on a story about Ms. Willey and the President; Ms. Willey wondered how she could get out of it.[520]

According to Ms. Lewinsky, the President had no telephone calls during her time with him. At 10:19 a.m., probably after her departure (her exit time is not shown on logs), he placed two calls, both potentially follow-ups to the conversation about the Newsweek article. First, he spoke with Bruce Lindsey for three minutes, then with Nancy Hernreich for 11 minutes.[521]

D. July 14-15 Discussions of Linda Tripp

On the evening of Monday, July 14, 1997, just after Ms. Lewinsky had returned from an overseas trip, the President had her come to the White House to discuss Linda Tripp and Newsweek.[522] Ms. Lewinsky entered the White House at 9:34 p.m. and exited at 11:22 p.m.[523] The President was in the Oval Office area from 9:28 to 11:25 p.m.[524]

Ms. Lewinsky testified that, at around 7:30 p.m. that evening,

Ms. Currie telephoned and said that the President wanted to talk to her or see her. At about 8:30 or 9:00 p.m., Ms. Currie called again and asked Ms. Lewinsky to come to the White House.[525]

Ms. Lewinsky testified that the President met her in Ms. Currie's office, then took her into Ms. Hernreich's office.[526] (Records show that seven minutes after Ms. Lewinsky's entry to the White House complex, the President left the Oval Office for the appointment secretary's office.)[527] According to Ms. Lewinsky:

> It was an unusual meeting . . . . It was very distant and very cold. . . . [A]t one point he asked me if the woman that I had mentioned on July 4th was Linda Tripp. And I hesitated and then answered yes, and he talked about that there was some issue . . . to do with Kathleen Willey and that, as he called it, that there was something on the Sludge Report, that there had been some information.[528]

The President told Ms. Lewinsky that Ms. Willey had called the White House again, this time to report that Mr. Isikoff somehow knew of her earlier White House call.[529] The President wondered if Ms. Lewinsky had mentioned the Willey call to Ms. Tripp, who in turn might have told Mr. Isikoff. Ms. Lewinsky acknowledged that she had done so. Ms. Lewinsky testified: "[H]e was concerned about Linda, and I reassured him. He asked me if I trusted her, and I said yes."[530] The President asked Ms. Lewinsky to try to persuade Ms. Tripp to call Mr. Lindsey.[531] The President, according to Ms. Lewinsky, also asked if she had confided anything about their relationship to Ms. Tripp. Ms. Lewinsky said (falsely) that she had not.[532]

The President left to participate in a conference call, which Ms. Lewinsky understood was with his attorneys, while Ms. Lewinsky sat with Ms. Currie.[533] According to White House records, at 10:03 p.m. the President participated in a 51-minute conference call with Robert Bennett, his private attorney in the Jones case, and Charles Ruff, White House Counsel. Immediately after completing that call, the President had a six-minute phone conversation with Bruce Lindsey.[534]

Afterward, the President returned and told Ms. Lewinsky, in her recollection, to notify Ms. Currie the following day, "without getting into details with her, even mentioning names with her," whether Ms. Lewinsky had "'mission-accomplished' . . . with Linda."[535]

The next day, according to Ms. Lewinsky, she did talk with Ms. Tripp, then called Ms. Currie and said she needed to talk with the President. He called her that evening. She told him "that I had tried to talk to Linda and that she didn't seem very receptive to trying to get in touch with Bruce Lindsey again, but that I would continue to try."[536] The President was in a sour mood, according to Ms. Lewinsky, and their conversation was brief.[537]

E. July 16 Meeting with Marsha Scott

On July 16, 1997, Ms. Lewinsky met again with Ms. Scott about returning to the White House.[538] Ms. Scott said she would try to detail Ms. Lewinsky from the Pentagon to Ms. Scott's office on a temporary basis, according to Ms. Lewinsky.[539] In that way, Ms. Scott said, Ms. Lewinsky could prove herself. Ms. Scott also said that "they had to be careful and protect [the President]."[540] Both Ms. Scott and Ms. Currie confirmed that Ms. Scott talked with Ms. Lewinsky about the possibility of being detailed to work at the White House.[541] Ms. Scott testified that she tried to arrange the detail on her own, without any direction from the President; Ms. Currie, however, testified that the President instructed her and Ms. Scott to try to get Ms. Lewinsky a job.[542]

F. July 24 Meeting

On Thursday, July 24, 1997, the day after her 24th birthday, Ms. Lewinsky visited the White House from 6:04 to 6:26 p.m., admitted by Ms. Currie.[543] The President was in the Oval Office when she arrived; he moved to the study at 6:14 p.m. and remained there until her departure.[544] He had no telephone calls during Ms. Lewinsky's visit.[545]

According to Ms. Lewinsky, she went to the White House to pick up a photograph from Ms. Currie, who said the President might be available for a quick meeting. Ms. Currie put Ms. Lewinsky in the

Cabinet Room while the President finished another meeting, then took her to see him. They chatted for five to ten minutes, and the President gave Ms. Lewinsky, as a birthday present, an antique pin.[546]

G. NEWSWEEK ARTICLE AND ITS AFTERMATH

Newsweek published the Kathleen Willey story in its August 11, 1997, edition (which appeared a week before the cover date). The article quoted Ms. Tripp as saying that Ms. Willey, after leaving the Oval Office on the day of the President's alleged advances, looked "disheveled," "flustered, happy, and joyful." The article also quoted Robert Bennett as saying that Ms. Tripp was "not to be believed."[547]

After the article appeared, Ms. Tripp wrote a letter to Newsweek charging that she had been misquoted, but the magazine did not publish it.[548] Ms. Lewinsky subsequently told the President about Ms. Tripp's letter. He replied, Ms. Lewinsky said in a recorded conversation, "Well, that's good because it sure seemed like she screwed me from that article."[549]

H. AUGUST 16 MEETING

On Saturday, August 16, 1997, Ms. Lewinsky tried, unsuccessfully, to resume her sexual relationship with the President. She visited the White House on that day from 9:02 to 10:20 a.m.[550] The President moved from the Residence to the Oval Office at 9:20 a.m. and remained in the Oval Office until 10:03 a.m.[551] After a one-minute call to Betty Currie at her desk at 9:18 a.m., evidently from the Residence, the President had no calls while Ms. Lewinsky was at the White House.[552] The next day he left for a vacation on Martha's Vineyard.[553]

Ms. Lewinsky testified that she brought birthday gifts for the President (his birthday is August 19):

> I had set up in his back office, I had brought an apple square and put a candle and had put his birthday presents out. And after he came back in and I sang happy birthday and he got his presents, I

asked him . . . if we could share a birthday kiss in honor of our
birthdays, because mine had been just a few weeks before. So, he
said that that was okay and we could kind of bend the rules that
day. And so . . . we kissed.[554]

Ms. Lewinsky touched the President's genitals through his pants
and moved to perform oral sex, but the President rebuffed her.[555] In
her recollection: "[H]e said, I'm trying not to do this and I'm trying
to be good. . . . [H]e got visibly upset. And so . . . I hugged him and
I told him I was sorry and not to be upset."[556] Later, in a draft note
to "Handsome," Ms. Lewinsky referred to this visit: "It was awful
when I saw you for your birthday in August. You were so distant
that I missed you as I was holding you in my arms."[557]

I. CONTINUING JOB EFFORTS

Ms. Lewinsky and Ms. Scott talked by phone on September 3,
1997, for 47 minutes.[558] According to notes that Ms. Lewinsky
wrote to two friends, Ms. Scott told her that the detail slot in her
office had been eliminated.[559] Ms. Lewinsky told one friend:

> So for now, there isn't any place for me to be detailed. So I should
> be PATIENT. I told her I was very upset and disappointed (even
> though I really didn't want to work for her) and then she and I got
> into it. She didn't understand why I wanted to come back when
> there were still people there who would give me a hard time and
> that it isn't the right political climate for me to come back. . . . She
> asked me why I kept pushing the envelope on coming back there—
> after all, I had the experience of being there already. So it's over. I
> don't know what I will do now but I can't wait any more and I
> can't go through all of this crap anymore. In some ways I hope I
> never hear from him again because he'll just lead me on because he
> doesn't have the balls to tell me the truth.[560]

Ms. Scott testified that "[t]he gist" of Ms. Lewinsky's email message
describing the conversation "fits with what I remember telling
her."[561]

Ms. Lewinsky expressed her escalating frustration in a note to the President that she drafted (but did not send).[562] She wrote:

I believe the time has finally come for me to throw in the towel. My conversation with Marsha left me disappointed, frustrated, sad and angry. I can't help but wonder if you knew she wouldn't be able to detail me over there when I last saw you. Maybe that would explain your coldness. The only explanation I can reason for your not bringing me back is that you just plain didn't want to enough or care about me enough.

Ms. Lewinsky went on to discuss other women rumored to be involved with the President who enjoy "golden positions," above criticism, "because they have your approval." She continued: "I just loved you—wanted to spend time with you, kiss you, listen to you laugh—and I wanted you to love me back." She closed: "As I said in my last letter to you I've waited long enough. You and Marsha win. I give up. You let me down, but I shouldn't have trusted you in the first place.[563]

Ms. Lewinsky continued trying to discuss her situation with the President. On Friday, September 12, 1997, she arrived at the White House without an appointment, called Ms. Currie, and had a long wait at the gate. When Ms. Currie came to meet her, Ms. Lewinsky was crying. Ms. Currie explained that sometimes the President's hands are tied—but, she said, she had gotten his authorization to ask John Podesta, the Deputy Chief of Staff, to help Ms. Lewinsky return to work at the White House.[564]

J. BLACK DOG GIFTS

Before the President had left for vacation, Ms. Lewinsky had sent a note asking if he could bring her a T-shirt from the Black Dog, a popular Vineyard restaurant.[565] In early September, Ms. Currie gave several Black Dog items to Ms. Lewinsky.[566] In an email message to Catherine Davis, Ms. Lewinsky wrote: "Well, I found out from Betty yesterday that he not only brought me a t-shirt, he got me 2 t-shirts, a hat and a dress!!!! Even though he's a big schmuck, that is surprisingly sweet—even that he remembered!"[567]

K. Lucy Mercer Letter and Involvement of Chief of Staff

A letter dated September 30, 1997, styled as an official memo, was found in Ms. Lewinsky's apartment. According to Ms. Lewinsky, she sent this letter or a similar one to the President.[568] Addressed to "Handsome" and bearing the subject line "The New Deal," the faux memo proposed a visit that evening after "everyone else goes home." Ms. Lewinsky wrote: "You will show me that you will let me visit you sans a crisis, and I will be on my best behavior and not stressed out when I come (to see you, that is)." She closed with an allusion to a woman rumored to have been involved with an earlier President: "Oh, and Handsome, remember FDR would never have turned down a visit with Lucy Mercer!"[569]

Ms. Lewinsky did not visit the White House the night of September 30, but the President called her late the night of September 30 or October 1.[570] According to Ms. Lewinsky, he may have mentioned during this call that he would get Erskine Bowles to help her find a White House job.[571]

At around this time, the President did ask the White House Chief of Staff to help in the job search. Mr. Bowles testified about a conversation with the President in the Oval Office: "He told me that there was a young woman—her name was Monica Lewinsky—who used to work at the White House; that Evelyn . . . thought she hung around the Oval Office too much and transferred her to the Pentagon."[572] The President asked Mr. Bowles to try to find Ms. Lewinsky a job in the Old Executive Office Building.[573] Mr. Bowles assigned his deputy, John Podesta, to handle it.[574]

L. News of Job Search Failure

On October 6, 1997, according to Ms. Lewinsky, she was told that she would never work at the White House again. Ms. Tripp conveyed the news, which she indicated had come from a friend on the White House staff. Ms. Lewinsky testified:

> Linda Tripp called me at work on October 6th and told me that her friend Kate in the NSC . . . had heard rumors about me and that I would never work in the White House again . . . . [Kate's] advice to me was "get out of town."[575]

For Ms. Lewinsky, who had previously considered moving to New York, this call was the "straw that broke the camel's back."[576] She was enraged.[577]

In a note she drafted (but did not send), Ms. Lewinsky expressed her frustration. She wrote:

> Any normal person would have walked away from this and said, "He doesn't call me, he doesn't want to see me—screw it. It doesn't matter." I can't let go of you. . . . I want to be a source of pleasure and laughter and energy to you. I want to make you smile.

She went on to relate that she had heard second-hand from a White House employee "that I was 'after the President' and would never be allowed to work [in] the complex." Ms. Lewinsky said she could only conclude "that all you have promised me is an empty promise. . . . I am once again totally humiliated. It is very clear that there is no way I am going to be brought back." She closed the note: "I will never do anything to hurt you. I am simply not that kind of person. Moreover, I love you."[578]

When terminating their sexual relationship on May 24, the President had told Ms. Lewinsky that he hoped they would remain friends, for he could do a great deal for her.[579] Now, having learned that he could not (or would not) get her a White House job, Ms. Lewinsky decided to ask him for a job in New York, perhaps at the United Nations—a possibility that she had mentioned to him in passing over the summer. On the afternoon of October 6, Ms. Lewinsky spoke of this plan to Ms. Currie, who quoted the President as having said earlier: "Oh, that's no problem. We can place her in the UN like that."[580]

In a recorded conversation later on October 6, Ms. Lewinsky said she wanted two things from the President. The first was contrition: He needed to "acknowledge . . . that he helped fuck up my life."[581] The second was a job, one that she could obtain without much effort: "I don't want to have to work for this position . . . . I just want it to be given to me."[582] Ms. Lewinsky decided to write the President a note proposing that the two of them "get together and work on some way that I can come out of this situation not feeling the way I do."[583] After composing the letter, she said: "I want him to feel a little guilty, and I hope that this letter did that."[584]

In this letter, which was sent via courier on October 7, Ms. Lewinsky said she understood that she would never be given a White House job, and she asked for a prompt meeting to discuss her job situation.[585] She went on to advance a specific request:

> I'd like to ask you to help me secure a position in NY beginning 1 December. I would be very grateful, and I am hoping this is a solution for both of us. I want you to know that it has always been and remains more important to me to have you in my life than to come back. . . . Please don't let me down.[586]

IX. OCTOBER-NOVEMBER 1997: UNITED NATIONS' JOB OFFER

Having learned that she would not be able to return to the White House, Ms. Lewinsky sought the President's help in finding a job in New York City. The President offered to place her at the United Nations. After initial enthusiasm, Ms. Lewinsky cooled on the idea of working at the U.N., and she prodded the President to get her a job in the private sector.

A. OCTOBER 10: TELEPHONE CONVERSATION

According to Ms. Lewinsky, the President telephoned her at approximately 2:00 to 2:30 a.m. on Friday, October 10.[587] They spent much of the hour-and-a-half call arguing. "[H]e got so mad at me, he must have been purple," she later recalled.[588]

According to Ms. Lewinsky, the President said: "If I had known what kind of person you really were, I wouldn't have gotten involved with you."[589] He reminded Ms. Lewinsky that she had earlier promised, "[i]f you just want to stop doing this, I'll . . . be no trouble."[590] Ms. Lewinsky said she challenged the President: "[T]ell me . . . when I've caused you trouble."[591] The President responded, "I've never worried about you. I've never been worried you would do something to hurt me."[592]

When the conversation shifted to her job search, Ms. Lewinsky complained that the President had not done enough to help her. He responded that, on the contrary, he was eager to help.[593] The President said that he regretted Ms. Lewinsky's transfer to the Pentagon and assured her that he would not have permitted it had he foreseen the difficulty in returning her to the White House.[594] Ms. Lewinsky told him that she wanted a job in New York by the end of October, and the President promised to do what he could.[595]

B. OCTOBER 11 MEETING

At approximately 8:30 a.m. on Saturday, October 11, according to Ms. Lewinsky, Ms. Currie called and told her that the President wished to see her.[596] Ms. Lewinsky entered the White House at 9:36 a.m. and departed at 10:54 a.m.[597] The President entered the Oval Office at 9:52 a.m.[598]

Ms. Lewinsky met with the President in the study, and they discussed her job search.[599] Ms. Lewinsky told the President that she wanted to pursue jobs in the private sector, and he told her to prepare a list of New York companies that interested her.[600] Ms. Lewinsky asked the President whether Vernon Jordan, a well-known Washington attorney who she knew was a close friend of the President and had many business contacts, might help her find a job.[601] According to Ms. Lewinsky, the President was receptive to the idea.[602]

In a recorded conversation, Ms. Lewinsky said that, at the end of the October 11 meeting, she and the President joined Ms. Currie in the Oval Office. The President grabbed Ms. Lewinsky's arm and kissed her on the forehead.[603] He told her: "I talked to Erskine [Bowles] about . . . trying to get John Hilley to give you . . . a good recommendation for your work here."[604]

Later, Ms. Lewinsky and Ms. Tripp discussed their concerns about the President's involvement in Ms. Lewinsky's job search. Specifically, Ms. Lewinsky was nervous about involving the President's Chief of Staff:

> Ms. Lewinsky: Well, see, I don't really think—I'm going to tell him that I don't think Erskine should have anything to do with this. I don't think anybody who works there should.
> Ms. Tripp: I don't see how that's—how that's a problem.
> Ms. Lewinsky: Because look at what happened with Webb Hubbell.[605]

Ms. Lewinsky preferred that Vernon Jordan assist her in her job search:

> Ms. Tripp: Well, I don't remember during the Webb Hubbell thing, was Vernon mentioned?
>
> Ms. Lewinsky: Yeah, but there's a big difference. I think somebody could construe, okay? Somebody could construe or say, "Well, they gave her a job to shut her up. They made her happy. . . . And he [Mr. Bowles] works for the government and shouldn't have done that." And with the other one [Mr. Jordan] you can't say that.[606]

C. OCTOBER 16-17: THE "WISH LIST"

On October 16, Ms. Lewinsky sent the President a packet, which included what she called a "wish list" describing the types of jobs that interested her in New York City.[607] The note began:

> My dream had been to work in Communications or Strategic Planning at the White House. I am open to any suggestions that you may have on work that is similar to that or may intrigue me.

The most important things to me are that I am engaged and interested in my work, I am not someone's administrative/ executive
assistant, and my salary can provide me a comfortable living in
NY.[608]

She identified five public relations firms where she would like to
work.[609] Ms. Lewinsky concluded by saying of the United Nations:

I do not have any interest in working there. As a result of what
happened in April '96, I have already spent a year and a half at an
agency in which I have no interest. I want a job where I feel challenged, engaged, and interested. I don't think the UN is the right
place for me.[610]

In a recorded conversation, Ms. Lewinsky said she wanted the President to take her list seriously and not ask her to settle for a U.N.
job.[611] She said she hoped "that if he starts to pick a bone with me
and the U.N., he sure as hell doesn't do it on the phone. . . . I don't
want to start getting into a screaming match with him on the
phone."[612]

In addition to the "wish list," Ms. Lewinsky said she enclosed in
the packet a pair of sunglasses and "a lot of things in a little enve-
lope," including some jokes, a card, and a postcard.[613] She said that
she had written on the card: "Wasn't I right that my hugs are better
in person than in cards?"[614] The postcard featured a "very erotic"
Egon Schiele painting.[615] Ms. Lewinsky also enclosed a note with her
thoughts on education reform.[616]

Ms. Lewinsky testified that she felt that the President owed her a
job for several reasons: Her relationship with him was the reason
she had been transferred out of the White House; he had promised
her a job and so far had done nothing to help her find one; and she
had left the White House "quietly," without making an issue of her
relationship with the President.[617]

D. THE PRESIDENT CREATES OPTIONS

At some point around this time in the fall of 1997, Ms. Currie asked John Podesta, the Deputy Chief of Staff, to help Ms. Lewinsky find a job in New York.[618] Mr. Podesta testified that, during a Presidential trip to Latin America, he approached then-U.N. Ambassador William Richardson while aboard Air Force One and asked the Ambassador to consider a former White House intern for a position at the U.N.[619] At the time, Mr. Podesta could not recall the intern's name.[620] Ambassador Richardson and the President both testified that they never discussed Ms. Lewinsky with each other.[621]

Ambassador Richardson returned from Latin America on Sunday, October 19.[622] Within a few days, his Executive Assistant, Isabelle Watkins, called Mr. Podesta's secretary and asked whether "she knew anything about a resume that John was going to send us."[623] Mr. Podesta's secretary knew nothing about it and asked Mr. Podesta what to do; he instructed her to call Ms. Currie.[624] At 3:09 p.m. on October 21, Ms. Currie faxed Ms. Lewinsky's resume to the United Nations.[625]

At 7:01 p.m., a six-minute call was placed to Ms. Lewinsky's apartment from a U.N. telephone number identified in State Department records as "Ambassador Richardson's line."[626] Ms. Lewinsky testified that she spoke to Ambassador Richardson. A woman called, Ms. Lewinsky testified, and said, "[H]old for Ambassador Richardson."[627] Then the Ambassador himself came on the line: "I remember, because I was shocked and I was . . . very nervous."[628] The purpose of the call was to schedule a job interview at a Watergate apartment the following week.[629] At odds with Ms. Lewinsky, the Ambassador and Ms. Watkins both testified that Ms. Watkins, not the Ambassador, spoke with Ms. Lewinsky.[630]

A few days later, according to Ms. Lewinsky, the President called her. She had been upset because no one at the White House had prepared her for the Ambassador's recent call and because she did not want the White House to railroad her into taking the U.N. job.[631] She reiterated that she was eager to pursue other opportunities, especially in the private sector.[632] The President reassured her, promising that a U.N. position was just one of many options.[633]

Ms. Lewinsky spoke to the President again one week later. Ms. Lewinsky testified that she told Ms. Currie to ask the President to call her to assuage her nervousness before the U.N. interview.[634]

According to Ms. Lewinsky, on October 30, the night before the interview, the President did call. She characterized the conversation as a "pep talk": "[H]e was trying to kind of build my confidence and reassure me."[635] The President told her to call Ms. Currie after the interview.[636] In his Jones deposition, the President indicated that he learned of her interview with Ambassador Richardson not from Ms. Lewinsky herself but from Ms. Currie.[637]

E. THE U.N. INTERVIEW AND JOB OFFER

On Friday morning, October 31, Ambassador Richardson and two of his assistants, Mona Sutphen and Rebecca Cooper, interviewed Ms. Lewinsky at the Watergate.[638] According to Ambassador Richardson, he "listen[ed] while Mona and Rebecca were interviewing her."[639] Neither Ambassador Richardson nor any of his staff made inquiries, before or after the interview, about Ms. Lewinsky's prior work performance.[640]

On Sunday, November 2, Ms. Lewinsky drafted a letter to Ms. Currie asking what to do in the event she received an offer from the U.N.[641] She wrote:

> I became a bit nervous this weekend when I realized that Amb. Richardson said his staff would be in touch with me this week. As you know, the UN is supposed to be my back-up, but because VJ [Vernon Jordan] has been out of town, this is my only option right now. What should I say to Richardson's people this week when they call?[642]

Ms. Lewinsky asked Ms. Currie to speak to the President about her problem: "If you feel it's appropriate, maybe you could ask 'the big guy' what he wants me to do. Ahhhhh . . . anxiety!!!!!"[643] Ms.

Lewinsky also mentioned the President's promise to involve Vernon Jordan in her job search:

> I don't think I told you that in my conversation last Thursday night with him that he said that he would ask you to set up a meeting between VJ and myself, once VJ got back. I assume he'll mention this to you at some point—hopefully sooner rather than later![644]

Before Ms. Lewinsky sent this letter, in her recollection, she received an offer from the U.N.[645] Phone records reflect that, at 11:02 a.m. on November 3, a three-minute call was placed to Ms. Lewinsky from the U.N. line identified in State Department records as Ambassador Richardson's.[646] Ms. Lewinsky stated that she believes she spoke to Ambassador Richardson, who extended her a job offer.[647]

According to his assistant, Ambassador Richardson made the decision to hire Ms. Lewinsky. Ms. Sutphen testified:

> I said, are you sure; and he said, yeah, yeah, I'm sure, why. And I said . . . are you sure, though you don't want to talk to anyone else . . . . And he said, no, no, I think it's fine; why don't you go ahead and give her an offer?[648]

Ambassador Richardson and Ms. Sutphen both testified that Ms. Sutphen, not the Ambassador, extended the job offer to Ms. Lewinsky. They recalled that the offer was made a week or 10 days after the interview, though Ms. Sutphen, when shown the phone records, testified that the November 3 call to Ms. Lewinsky probably was the job offer.[649]

Ms. Lewinsky testified that she told Ms. Currie about the offer and she probably also told the President directly.[650] Ms. Currie first testified that she had "probably" told the President about Ms. Lewinsky's U.N. offer, then testified that she had in fact told him, then testified that she could not remember, though she acknowledged that the President was interested in Ms. Lewinsky's getting a job.[651]

When the President was asked in the Jones deposition whether he

knew that Ms. Lewinsky had received the offer of a job at the U.N.,
he testified: "I know that she interviewed for one. I don't know if
she was offered one or not."[652]

F. THE U.N. JOB OFFER DECLINED

Three weeks after she received an offer, on November 24, Ms.
Lewinsky called Ms. Sutphen and asked for more time to consider
the offer because she wanted to pursue possibilities in the private
sector.[653] Ms. Sutphen told Ambassador Richardson, who, according to Ms. Sutphen, said the delay would be fine.[654] Over a month
later, on January 5, 1998, Ms. Lewinsky finally turned down the
job.[655]

X. NOVEMBER 1997: GROWING FRUSTRATION

Ms. Lewinsky met with Vernon Jordan, who promised to help
her find a job in New York. November proved, however, to be a
month of inactivity with respect to both Ms. Lewinsky's job search
and her relationship with the President. Mr. Jordan did not meet
with Ms. Lewinsky again, nor did he contact anyone in New York
City on her behalf. Ms. Lewinsky became increasingly anxious
about her inability to see the President. Except for a momentary
encounter in mid-November, Ms. Lewinsky did not meet with the
President between October 11 and December 5.

A. INTERROGATORIES ANSWERED

On November 3, 1997, the President answered Paula Jones's Second Set of Interrogatories. Two of those interrogatories asked the
President to list any woman other than his wife with whom he had
"had," "proposed having," or "sought to have" sexual relations
during the time that he was Attorney General of Arkansas, Governor of Arkansas, and President of the United States.[656] President
Clinton objected to the scope and relevance of both interrogatories
and refused to answer them.[657]

B. First Vernon Jordan Meeting

In mid-October, the President had agreed to involve Vernon Jordan in Ms. Lewinsky's job search.[658] In a draft letter to Ms. Currie dated November 2, Ms. Lewinsky wrote that the President had "said he would ask you to set up a meeting between VJ and myself."[659] According to Ms. Lewinsky, on November 3 or November 4, Ms. Currie told her to call Vernon Jordan's secretary to arrange a meeting.[660] Ms. Currie said she had spoken with Mr. Jordan and he was expecting Ms. Lewinsky's call.[661] In Ms. Lewinsky's account, Ms. Currie sought Mr. Jordan's aid at the President's direction.[662] Mr. Jordan likewise testified that, in his understanding, the President was behind Ms. Currie's request.[663]

Ms. Currie testified at various points that she contacted Mr. Jordan on her own initiative; that the President "probably" talked with her about Ms. Lewinsky's New York job hunt; and that she could not recall whether the President was involved.[664] In his Jones deposition, the President was asked whether he did anything to facilitate a meeting between Mr. Jordan and Ms. Lewinsky. He testified:

> I can tell you what my memory is. My memory is that Vernon said something to me about her coming in, Betty had called and asked if he [Mr. Jordan] would see her [Ms. Lewinsky]. . . . I'm sure if he said something to me about it I said something positive about it. I wouldn't have said anything negative about it.[665]

When pressed, the President testified that he did not think that he was the "precipitating force" in arranging the meeting between Mr. Jordan and Ms. Lewinsky.[666]

At 8:50 a.m. on November 5, Mr. Jordan spoke with the President by telephone for five minutes.[667] Later that morning, Mr. Jordan and Ms. Lewinsky met in his office for about twenty minutes.[668] She told him that she intended to move to New York, and she named several companies where she hoped to work.[669] She showed him the "wish list" that she had sent the President on October 16.[670] Mr. Jordan said that he had spoken with the President about her and that she came "highly recommended."[671] Concerning her job search, Mr. Jordan said: "We're in business."[672]

In the course of the day, Mr. Jordan placed four calls to Ms. Hernreich (whom he acknowledged calling when he wished to speak to the President[673]) and one to Ms. Currie.[674] Mr. Jordan testified that he could not remember the calls, but "[i]t is entirely possible" that they concerned Monica Lewinsky.[675]

Mr. Jordan also visited the White House and met with the President at 2:00 p.m. that day.[676] Again, Mr. Jordan testified that he had "no recollection" of the substance of his conversation with the President.[677]

On November 6, the day after meeting with Mr. Jordan, Ms. Lewinsky wrote him a thank-you letter: "It made me happy to know that our friend has such a wonderful confidant in you."[678] Also on November 6, Ms. Lewinsky wrote in an email to a friend that she expected to hear from Mr. Jordan "later next week."[679] The evidence indicates, though, that Mr. Jordan took no steps to help Ms. Lewinsky until early December, after she appeared on the witness list in the Jones case.

Mr. Jordan initially testified that he had "no recollection of having met with Ms. Lewinsky on November 5."[680] When shown documentary evidence demonstrating that his first meeting with Ms. Lewinsky occurred in early November, he acknowledged that an early November meeting was "entirely possible."[681] Mr. Jordan's failure to remember his November meeting with Ms. Lewinsky may indicate the low priority he attached to it at the time.

C. NOVEMBER 13: THE ZEDILLO VISIT

On Thursday, November 13, while Ernesto Zedillo, the President of Mexico, was in the White House, Ms. Lewinsky met very briefly with President Clinton in the private study.[682] Ms. Lewinsky's visit, which she described in an email as a "hysterical escapade," was the culmination of days of phone calls and notes to Ms. Currie and the President.[683]

Over the course of the week that preceded November 13, Ms.

Lewinsky made several attempts to arrange a visit with the President. On Monday, November 10, in addition to making frequent calls to Ms. Currie, she sent the President a note asking for a meeting.[684]

She hoped to see him on Tuesday, November 11 (Veterans Day), but he did not respond.[685] By courier,[686] she sent the President another note:

> I asked you three weeks ago to please be sensitive to what I am going through right now and to keep in contact with me, and yet I'm still left writing notes in vain. I am not a moron. I know that what is going on in the world takes precedence, but I don't think what I have asked you for is unreasonable.[687]

She added: "This is so hard for me. I am trying to deal with so much emotionally, and I have nobody to talk to about it. I need you right now not as president, but as a man. PLEASE be my friend."[688]

That evening, November 12, according to Ms. Lewinsky, the President called and invited her to the White House the following day.[689] In an email to a friend, Ms. Lewinsky wrote that she and the President "talked for almost an hour."[690] She added: "[H]e thought [N]ancy [Hernreich] (one of the meanies) would be out for a few hours on Thursday and I could come see him then."[691]

The following morning, November 13, Ms. Lewinsky tried to arrange a visit with the President. She called repeatedly but suspected that Ms. Currie was not telling the President of her calls.[692] Around noon, Ms. Currie told Ms. Lewinsky that the President had left to play golf. Ms. Lewinsky, in her own words, "went ballistic."[693]

After the President returned from the Army-Navy Golf Course in the late afternoon, Ms. Lewinsky told Ms. Currie that she was coming to the White House to give him some gifts.[694] Ms. Currie suggested that Ms. Lewinsky wait in Ms. Currie's car in the White House parking lot. Ms. Lewinsky went to the White House only to find that the doors to Ms. Currie's car were locked. Ms. Lewinsky waited in the rain.[695]

Ms. Currie eventually met her in the parking lot, and, in Ms. Lewinsky's words, they made a "bee-line" into the White House, sneaking up the back stairs to avoid other White House employees, particularly Presidential aide Stephen Goodin.[696] Ms. Lewinsky left two small gifts for the President with Ms. Currie, then waited alone for about half an hour in the Oval Office study.[697] In the study, Ms. Lewinsky saw several gifts she had given the President, including Oy Vey! The Things They Say: A Guide to Jewish Wit, Nicholson Baker's novel Vox, and a letter opener decorated with a frog.[698]

The President finally joined Ms. Lewinsky in the study, where they were alone for only a minute or two.[699] Ms. Lewinsky gave him an antique paperweight in the shape of the White House.[700] She also showed him an email describing the effect of chewing Altoid mints before performing oral sex. Ms. Lewinsky was chewing Altoids at the time, but the President replied that he did not have enough time for oral sex.[701] They kissed, and the President rushed off for a State Dinner with President Zedillo.[702]

D. NOVEMBER 14-DECEMBER 4: INABILITY TO SEE THE PRESIDENT

After this brief November 13 meeting, Ms. Lewinsky did not see the President again until the first week in December. Hoping to arrange a longer rendezvous, she sent the President several notes, as well as a cassette on which she recorded a message.[703]

Along with her chagrin over not seeing the President, Ms. Lewinsky was frustrated that her job search had apparently stalled. A few days before Thanksgiving, she complained to Ms. Currie that she had not heard from Mr. Jordan.[704] Ms. Currie arranged for her to speak with him "before Thanksgiving," while Ms. Lewinsky was in Los Angeles. Mr. Jordan told her to call him the following week to arrange another meeting.[705]

In draft letters to the President, which were recovered from her Pentagon computer, Ms. Lewinsky reflected on the change in their relationship: "[B]oth professionally and personally, . . . our personal relationship changing has caused me more pain. Do you realize that?"[706] She asked for the President's understanding: "I don't want you to think that I am not grateful for what you are doing for me now—I'd probably be in a mental institute without it—but I am consumed with this disappointment, frustration, and anger." Ms. Lewinsky rued the brevity of her November 13 visit with the President: "All you . . . . ever have to do to pacify me is see me and hold me," she wrote. "Maybe that's asking too much."[707]

XI. December 5-18, 1997: The Witness List and Job Search

On Friday, December 5, Paula Jones's attorneys faxed a list of their potential witnesses—including Ms. Lewinsky—to the President's personal attorneys. The following day, President Clinton saw Ms. Lewinsky in an unscheduled visit and then discussed the Jones case with his attorneys and Deputy White House Counsel Bruce Lindsey. A few days later, Ms. Lewinsky met with Mr. Jordan at his office, and he arranged interviews for Ms. Lewinsky at three companies. In the middle of the night on December 17, the President called and informed Ms. Lewinsky that she was on the witness list and that she might have to testify under oath in the Jones case.

A. December 5: The Witness List

On Friday December 5, 1997, attorneys for Paula Jones identified Ms. Lewinsky as a potential witness in Ms. Jones's sexual harassment case.[708] At 5:40 p.m., they faxed their witness list to the President's attorney, Robert Bennett.[709] Ms. Lewinsky, however, would not learn of her potential involvement in the Jones case for twelve more days, when the President informed her.[710]

President Clinton was asked in the grand jury when he learned that Ms. Lewinsky's name was on the witness list. The President responded: "I believe that I found out late in the afternoon on the sixth."[711]

B. DECEMBER 5: CHRISTMAS PARTY AT THE WHITE HOUSE

On Friday, December 5, Ms. Lewinsky returned from Department of Defense travel in Europe.[712] She asked Ms. Currie if the President could see her the next day, but Ms. Currie said he was busy meeting with his lawyers.[713] In the late afternoon, she attended a Christmas party at the White House with a Defense Department colleague.[714] Ms. Lewinsky exchanged a few words with the President in the reception line.[715]

The Christmas reception encounter heightened Ms. Lewinsky's frustration. On the evening of December 5, she drafted an anguished letter to the President.[716] "[Y]ou want me out of your life," she wrote. "I guess the signs have been made clear for awhile—not wanting to see me and rarely calling. I used to think it was you putting up walls."[717] She had purchased several gifts for him, and, she wrote, "I wanted to give them to you in person, but that is obviously not going to happen."[718] Ms. Lewinsky reminded the President of his words during their October 10 telephone argument:

> I will never forget what you said that night we fought on the phone—if you had known what I was really like you would never have gotten involved with me. I'm sure you're not the first person to have felt that way about me. I am sorry that this has been such a bad experience.[719]

She concluded the letter: "I knew it would hurt to say goodbye to you; I just never thought it would have to be on paper. Take care."[720]

C. DECEMBER 6: THE NORTHWEST GATE INCIDENT

1. INITIAL VISIT AND REJECTION

On the morning of Saturday, December 6, Ms. Lewinsky went to the White House to deliver the letter and gifts to the President. The gifts included a sterling silver antique cigar holder, a tie, a mug, a

"Hugs and Kisses" box, and an antique book about Theodore Roosevelt.[721] Ms. Lewinsky planned to leave the parcel with Ms. Currie, who had told Ms. Lewinsky that the President would be busy with his lawyers and unable to see her.[722]

Ms. Lewinsky arrived at the White House at approximately 10:00 a.m. She told the Secret Service uniformed officers at the Northwest Gate that she had gifts to drop off for the President, but that Ms. Currie did not know she was coming.[723] Ms. Lewinsky and the officers made several calls in an attempt to locate Ms. Currie.[724] The officers eventually invited Ms. Lewinsky inside the guard booth.[725] When Ms. Currie learned that Ms. Lewinsky was at the Northwest Gate, she sent word that the President "already had a guest in the [O]val," so the officers should have Ms. Lewinsky wait there for about 40 minutes.[726]

While Ms. Lewinsky was waiting, one officer mentioned that Eleanor Mondale was in the White House.[727] Ms. Lewinsky correctly surmised that the President was meeting with Ms. Mondale, rather than his lawyers, and she was "livid."[728] She stormed away, called and berated Ms. Currie from a pay phone, and then returned to her Watergate apartment.[729]

Hands shaking and almost crying, Ms. Currie informed several Secret Service officers that the President was "irate" that someone had disclosed to Ms. Lewinsky whom he was meeting with.[730] Ms. Currie told Sergeant Keith Williams, a supervisory uniformed Secret Service Officer, that if he "didn't find out what was going on, someone could be fired."[731] She also told Captain Jeffrey Purdie, the Secret Service watch commander for the uniformed division at the time, that the President was "so upset he wants somebody fired over this."[732]

2. MS. LEWINSKY RETURNS TO THE WHITE HOUSE

From her apartment, Ms. Lewinsky reached the President on the phone.[733] According to Ms. Lewinsky, the President was angry that she had "made a stink" and said that "it was none of my business . . . what he was doing."[734]

Then, to Ms. Lewinsky's surprise, the President invited her to visit him.[735] She testified that "none of the other times that we had really fought on the phone did it end up resulting in a visit that day."[736] WAVES records reflect that Ms. Lewinsky was cleared to enter the White House at 12:52 p.m. and exited at 1:36 p.m.[737]

During their meeting, Ms. Lewinsky told the President that Mr. Jordan had done nothing to help her find a job.[738] The President responded, "Oh, I'll talk to him. I'll get on it."[739]

Ms. Lewinsky testified that, overall, she had a "really nice" and "affectionate" visit with the President.[740] In an email to a friend a few days later, she wrote that, although "things have been crazy with the creep, . . . I did have a wonderful visit with him on Saturday. When he doesn't put his walls up, it is always heavenly."[741]

3. "WHATEVER JUST HAPPENED DIDN'T HAPPEN"

Later that day (December 6), the uniformed Secret Service officers at the Northwest Gate were told that no one would be fired—so long as they remained quiet. According to Sergeant Williams, Ms. Currie said that, if the officers did not "tell a lot of people what had happened, then nothing would happen."[742]

The President told Captain Jeffrey Purdie, the Secret Service watch commander for the uniformed division at the time, "I hope you use your discretion."[743] Captain Purdie interpreted the President's remark to mean that Captain Purdie "wasn't going to say anything," and he in turn told all of the officers involved not to discuss the incident.[744] One officer recalled that Captain Purdie told him and other officers, "Whatever just happened didn't happen."[745] Captain Purdie told another officer, "I was just in the Oval Office with the President and he wants somebody's ass out here. . . . As far as you're concerned, . . . [t]his never happened."[746] In response, that officer, who considered the Northwest Gate incident a "major event," "just shook [his] head" and "started making a set of [his] own notes" in order to document the incident.[747]

Captain Purdie recommended to his supervisor, Deputy Chief Charles O'Malley, that "no paperwork be generated" regarding the

Northwest Gate incident because "Ms. Currie was satisfied with the way things were handled."[748] According to Captain Purdie, Deputy Chief O'Malley agreed, and no record of the incident was made.[749] Deputy Chief O'Malley testified that the meeting between the President and Captain Purdie was the only occasion he could recall in fourteen years at the White House where a President directly addressed a job performance issue with a uniformed division supervisor.[750]

The President was questioned in the grand jury about the incident at the Northwest Gate. He testified that he knew that Ms. Lewinsky had become upset upon learning that Ms. Mondale was in the White House "to see us that day."[751] He testified: "As I remember, I had some other work to do that morning. . . . "[752] The President said that the disclosure of information that day was "inappropriate" and "a mistake," but he could not recall whether he wanted a Secret Service officer fired or gave any such orders.[753] He thought that the officers "were . . . told not to let it happen again, and I think that's the way it should have been handled."[754] When asked if he told Captain Purdie that he hoped that he could count on his discretion, the President stated, "I don't remember anything I said to him in that regard."[755]

According to Ms. Lewinsky, the President later indicated to her that he had concerns about the discretion of the Secret Service uniformed officers. On December 28 she asked how Paula Jones's attorneys could have known enough to place her on the witness list. The President replied that the source might be Linda Tripp or "the uniformed officers."[756]

D. THE PRESIDENT CONFERS WITH HIS LAWYERS

Deputy Counsel Bruce Lindsey testified that he met with the President and the President's personal attorney, Robert Bennett, at around 5:00 p.m. on December 6 to discuss the Jones case.[757] According to Mr. Lindsey, it was "likely" that he learned about Ms. Lewinsky's appearance on the witness list in that meeting.[758] Earlier in the day, at around 12:00 p.m. (after Ms. Lewinsky stormed away from the Northwest Gate but before she returned and saw the President), Mr. Lindsey had received a page: "Call Betty ASAP."[759] Mr. Lindsey testified that he did not recall the page, nor did he know, at the time, that Ms. Lewinsky had visited the White House.[760]

E. SECOND JORDAN MEETING

The next day (Sunday, December 7), Mr. Jordan visited the White House and met with the President.[761] Mr. Jordan testified that he was "fairly certain" that he did not discuss the Jones suit or Ms. Lewinsky.[762]

On Thursday, December 11, Ms. Lewinsky had her second meeting with Mr. Jordan.[763] Ms. Lewinsky testified that they discussed her job search, and Mr. Jordan told her to send letters to three business contacts that he provided her. Mr. Jordan noted that Ms. Lewinsky was anxious to get a job as quickly as possible, and he took action.[764] In the course of the day, Mr. Jordan placed calls on her behalf to Peter Georgescu, Chairman and Chief Executive Officer at Young & Rubicam; Richard Halperin, Executive Vice President and Special Counsel to the Chairman of MacAndrews & Forbes Holdings, Inc. (majority stockholder of Revlon); and Ursula Fairbairn, Executive Vice-President, Human Resources and Quality, of American Express.[765] Mr. Jordan told Ms. Lewinsky to keep him informed of the progress of her job search.[766]

At one point in the conversation, according to Ms. Lewinsky, Mr. Jordan said, "[Y]ou're a friend of the President."[767] This prompted Ms. Lewinsky to reveal that she "didn't really look at him as the President"; rather, she "reacted to him more as a man and got angry at him like a man and just a regular person."[768] When Mr. Jordan asked why Ms. Lewinsky got angry at the President, she replied that she became upset "when he doesn't call me enough or see me enough."[769] Ms. Lewinsky testified that Mr. Jordan advised her to take her frustrations out on him rather than the President.[770] According to Ms. Lewinsky, Mr. Jordan summed up the situation: "You're in love, that's what your problem is."[771]

Mr. Jordan recalled a similar conversation, in which Ms. Lewinsky complained that the President did not see her enough, although he thought it took place during a meeting eight days later. He testified that he felt the need to remind Ms. Lewinsky that the President is the "leader of the free world" and has competing obligations.[772]

Mr. Jordan is "certain" that he had a conversation with the President about Ms. Lewinsky at some point after this December 11 meeting.[773] He told the President that he would be trying to get Ms. Lewinsky a job in New York.[774] Mr. Jordan testified that the President "was aware that people were trying to get jobs for her, that Podesta was trying to help her, that Bill Richardson was trying to help her, but that she really wanted to work in the private sector."[775]

F. EARLY MORNING PHONE CALL

On December 15, 1997, Paula Jones's lawyers served President Clinton with her second set of document requests by overnight mail. These requests asked the President to "produce documents that related to communications between the President and Monica Lewisky" [sic].[776] This was the first Paula Jones discovery request to refer to Monica Lewinsky by name.

Ms. Lewinsky testified that in the early-morning hours of December 17, at roughly 2:00 or 2:30 a.m., she received a call from the President.[777] The call lasted about half an hour.[778]

The President gave Ms. Lewinsky two items of news: Ms. Currie's brother had died in a car accident, and Ms. Lewinsky's name had appeared on the witness list in the Jones case.[779] According to Ms. Lewinsky, the President said "it broke his heart" to see her name on the witness list.[780] The President told her that she would not necessarily be subpoenaed; if she were, he "suggested she could sign an affidavit to try to satisfy [Ms. Jones's] inquiry and not be deposed."[781]

The President told Ms. Lewinsky to contact Ms. Currie in the event she were subpoenaed.[782] He also reviewed one of their established cover stories. He told Ms. Lewinsky that she "should say she visited the [White House] to see Ms. Currie and, on occasion when working at the [White House], she brought him letters when no one else was around."[783] The President's advice "was . . . instantly familiar to [Ms. Lewinsky]."[784] She testified that the President's use of this "misleading" story amounted to a continuation of their pre-existing pattern.[785]

Later in the conversation, according to Ms. Lewinsky, the President said he would try to get Ms. Currie to come in over the weekend so that Ms. Lewinsky could visit and he could give her several Christmas presents.[786] Ms. Lewinsky replied that, since Ms. Currie's brother had just died, perhaps they should "let Betty be."[787]

In his grand jury appearance, the President was questioned about the December 17 phone call. He testified that, although he could not rule it out, he did not remember such a call.[788] The President was also asked whether in this conversation, or a conversation before Ms. Lewinsky's name came up in the Jones case, he instructed her to say that she was coming to bring letters. The President answered: "I might well have said that."[789]

But when asked whether he ever said anything along these lines after Ms. Lewinsky had been identified on the witness list, the President answered: "I don't recall whether I might have done something like that."[790] He speculated that he might have suggested this explanation in the context of a call from a reporter.[791] Nonetheless, he testified, in the context of the Jones case, "I never asked her to lie."[792]

G. JOB INTERVIEWS

On December 18, Ms. Lewinsky had two job interviews in New York City. At MacAndrews & Forbes, she met with Executive Vice President and Special Counsel to the Chairman Richard Halperin, who viewed the interview as "an accommodation for Vernon Jordan."[793] At Burson-Marstellar, she interviewed with Celia Berk, Managing Director of Human Resources.[794] A few days later, on December 23, Ms. Lewinsky interviewed in Washington, D.C., with Thomas Schick, Executive Vice President, Corporate Affairs and Communications, of American Express.[795]

XII. DECEMBER 19, 1997 - JANUARY 4, 1998: THE SUBPOENA

Ms. Lewinsky was served with a subpoena in the Jones case on Friday, December 19. She immediately called Mr. Jordan, and he invited her to his office. Mr. Jordan spoke with the President that afternoon and again that evening. He told the President that he had met with Ms. Lewinsky, that she had been subpoenaed, and that he planned to obtain an attorney for her. On Sunday, December 28, the President met with Ms. Lewinsky, who expressed concern about the subpoena's demand for the gifts he had given her. Later that day, Ms. Currie drove to Ms. Lewinsky's apartment and collected a box containing some of the subpoenaed gifts. Ms. Currie took the box home and hid it under her bed.

A. DECEMBER 19: MS. LEWINSKY IS SUBPOENAED

On Friday, December 19, 1997, sometime between 3:00 p.m. and 4:00 p.m., Ms. Lewinsky was served with a subpoena at her Pentagon office.[796] The subpoena commanded her to appear for a deposition in Washington, D.C., at 9:30 a.m. on January 23, 1998.[797] The subpoena also required the production of certain documents and gifts. Among the items that Ms. Lewinsky was required to produce were "each and every gift including, but not limited to, any and all dresses, accessories, and jewelry, and/or hat pins given to you by, or on behalf of, Defendant Clinton," as well as "[e]very document constituting or containing communications between you and Defendant Clinton, including letters, cards, notes, memoranda, and all telephone records."[798]

Ms. Lewinsky testified that, after being served with the subpoena, she "burst into tears," and then telephoned Mr. Jordan from a pay phone at the Pentagon.[799] Mr. Jordan confirmed Ms. Lewinsky's account; he said he tried to reassure Ms. Lewinsky: "[C]ome and talk to me and I will see what I can do about finding you counsel."[800]

According to records maintained by Mr. Jordan's law firm, Ms.

Lewinsky arrived at his office at 4:47 p.m.[801] White House phone records show that, at 4:57 p.m., the President telephoned Mr. Jordan; the two men spoke from 5:01 p.m. to 5:05 p.m.[802] At 5:06 p.m., Mr. Jordan placed a two-minute call to a Washington, D.C., attorney named Francis Carter.[803]

Ms. Lewinsky and Mr. Jordan gave somewhat different accounts of their meeting that day. According to Ms. Lewinsky, shortly after her arrival, Mr. Jordan received a phone call, and she stepped out of his office. A few minutes later, Ms. Lewinsky was invited back in, and Mr. Jordan called Mr. Carter.[804]

Mr. Jordan testified that he spoke to the President before Ms. Lewinsky ever entered his office.[805] He told the President: "Monica Lewinsky called me up. She's upset. She's gotten a subpoena. She is coming to see me about this subpoena. I'm confident that she needs a lawyer, and I will try to get her a lawyer."[806] Mr. Jordan told the President that the lawyer he had in mind was Francis Carter.[807] According to Mr. Jordan, the President asked him: "You think he's a good lawyer?" Mr. Jordan responded that he was.[808] Mr. Jordan testified that informing the President of Ms. Lewinsky's subpoena "was the purpose of [his] call."[809]

According to Mr. Jordan, when Ms. Lewinsky entered his office, "[H]er emotional state was obviously one of dishevelment and she was quite upset. She was crying. She was—she was highly emotional, to say the least."[810] She showed him the subpoena as soon as she entered.[811]

Ms. Lewinsky also testified that she discussed the subpoena with Mr. Jordan.[812] She told him that she found the specific reference to a hat pin alarming—how could the Jones's attorneys have known about it?[813] Mr. Jordan told her it was "a standard subpoena."[814] When he indicated to Ms. Lewinsky that he would be seeing the President that night, Ms. Lewinsky told him "to please make sure that he told the President" about her subpoena.[815]

At some point, according to Mr. Jordan, Ms. Lewinsky asked him about the future of the Clintons' marriage.[816] Because Ms. Lewinsky seemed "mesmerized" by President Clinton,[817] he "asked her directly had there been any sexual relationship between [her] and the President."[818] Mr. Jordan explained, "You didn't have to be Einstein to know that that was a question that had to be asked by me at that particular time, because heretofore this discussion was about a job. The subpoena changed the circumstances."[819] Ms. Lewinsky said she had not had a sexual relationship with the President.[820]

Ms. Lewinsky testified, however, that at this time she assumed that Mr. Jordan knew "with a wink and a nod that [she] was having a relationship with the President."[821] She therefore interpreted Mr. Jordan's questions as "What are you going to say?" rather than "What are the [actual] answers . . .?"[822] When the meeting ended, she "asked [Mr. Jordan] if he would give the President a hug."[823]

That evening, Mr. Jordan visited the President at the White House. According to Mr. Jordan, the two met alone in the Residence and talked for about ten minutes.[824] He testified:

> I told him that Monica Lewinsky had been subpoenaed, came to me with a subpoena. I told him that I was concerned by her fascination, her being taken with him. I told him how emotional she was about having gotten the subpoena. I told him what she said to me about whether or not he was going to leave the First Lady at the end of the term.[825]

Mr. Jordan asked the President "[t]he one question that I wanted answered."[826] That question was, "Mr. President, have you had sexual relations with Monica Lewinsky?" The President told Mr. Jordan, "No, never."[827]

Mr. Jordan told the President: "I'm trying to help her get a job and I'm going to continue to do that. I'm going to get her counsel and I'm going to try to be helpful to her as much as I possibly can, both with the lawyer, and I've already done what I could about the job, and I think you ought to know that."[828] Mr. Jordan testified: "He thanked me for telling him. Thanked me for my efforts to get her a job and thanked me for getting her a lawyer."[829]

In his grand jury testimony, the President recalled that he met with Mr. Jordan on December 19; however, he testified that his memory of that meeting was somewhat vague:

> I do not remember exactly what the nature of the conversation was. I do remember that I told him that there was no sexual relationship between me and Monica Lewinsky, which was true. And that—then all I remember for the rest is that he said he had referred her to a lawyer, and I believe it was Mr. Carter.[830]

Asked whether he recalled that Mr. Jordan told him that Ms. Lewinsky appeared fixated on him and hoped that he would leave Mrs. Clinton, the President testified: "I recall him saying he thought that she was upset with—somewhat fixated on me, that she acknowledged that she was not having a sexual relationship with me, and that she did not want to be [brought] into that Jones lawsuit."[831]

B. DECEMBER 22: MEETING WITH VERNON JORDAN

Mr. Jordan arranged for Ms. Lewinsky to meet with attorney Francis Carter at 11:00 a.m. on Monday, December 22.[832] On that morning, according to Ms. Lewinsky, she called Mr. Jordan and asked to meet before they went to Mr. Carter's office.[833] She testified: "I was a little concerned. I thought maybe [Mr. Jordan] didn't really understand . . . what it was that was happening here with me being subpoenaed and what this really meant."[834] She also wanted to find out whether he had in fact told the President of her subpoena. Mr. Jordan said that he had.[835] Ms. Lewinsky also told Mr. Jordan that she was worried that someone might have been eavesdropping on her telephone conversations with the President.[836] When Mr. Jordan asked why she thought that would be of concern, Ms. Lewinsky said, "Well, we've had phone sex."[837]

Ms. Lewinsky testified that she brought some of her gifts from the President, showed them to Mr. Jordan, and implied that these items were not all of the gifts that the President had given her.[838] Mr. Jordan, in contrast, testified that Ms. Lewinsky never showed him any gifts from the President.[839]

C. December 22: First Meeting with Francis Carter

Mr. Jordan drove Ms. Lewinsky to Mr. Carter's office.[840] There, he introduced Ms. Lewinsky to Mr. Carter, explaining that she needed not only a lawyer but a "counselor."[841] Mr. Carter testified that, after the initial referral, he expected to have no further contact with Mr. Jordan about Ms. Lewinsky or her case.[842]

Mr. Carter and Ms. Lewinsky then met for approximately an hour.[843] She explained that she did not want to be drawn into the Jones case and would strongly prefer not to be deposed.[844] He said that he would try to persuade Paula Jones's attorneys not to depose her.[845] Ms. Lewinsky testified that she suggested filing an affidavit to avert a deposition.[846]

According to Ms. Lewinsky, she asked Mr. Carter to get in touch with the President's personal attorney, Robert Bennett, just "to let him know that I had been subpoenaed in this case."[847] She wanted to make clear that she was "align[ing] [her]self with the President's side."[848] Mr. Carter testified that, while Ms. Lewinsky was in his office, he placed a call to Mr. Bennett to arrange a meeting.[849]

On the morning of Tuesday, December 23, Mr. Carter met for an hour with two of the President's personal attorneys, Mr. Bennett and Katherine Sexton.[850] The President's attorneys told Mr. Carter that other witnesses had filed motions to quash their subpoenas, and they offered legal research to support such a motion.[851]

D. December 23: Clinton Denials to Paula Jones

Throughout the sexual harassment case, Ms. Jones's attorneys attempted to obtain information about President Clinton's sexual relationships with any woman other than his wife. On December 11, 1997, the judge overseeing the Jones case, Susan Webber Wright, ruled that the President had to answer a written interrogatory naming every state and federal employee since 1986 with whom he had sexual relations or with whom he had proposed to have sexual relations. On December 23, 1997, the President answered the interrogatory: "None."[852]

E. DECEMBER 28: FINAL MEETING WITH THE PRESIDENT

A day or two after Christmas, Ms. Lewinsky called Ms. Currie and told her that the President had mentioned that he had presents for her.[853] Ms. Currie called back and told her to come to the White House at 8:30 a.m. on Sunday, December 28.[854]

That morning, Ms. Lewinsky met with the President in the Oval Office. WAVES records reflect that the visit was requested by Ms. Currie and that Ms. Lewinsky entered the White House at 8:16 a.m.[855]

After she arrived at the Oval Office, she, the President, and Ms. Currie played with Buddy, the President's dog, and chatted. Then, the President took her to the study and gave her several Christmas presents: a marble bear's head, a Rockettes blanket, a Black Dog stuffed animal, a small box of chocolates, a pair of joke sunglasses, and a pin with a New York skyline on it.[856]

Ms. Lewinsky testified that, during this visit, she and the President had a "passionate" and "physically intimate" kiss.[857]

Ms. Lewinsky and the President also talked about the Jones case.[858] In Ms. Lewinsky's account, she asked the President "how he thought [she] got put on the witness list."[859] He speculated that Linda Tripp or one of the uniformed Secret Service officers had told the Jones attorneys about her.[860] When Ms. Lewinsky mentioned her anxiety about the subpoena's reference to a hat pin, he said "that sort of bothered [him], too."[861] He asked whether she had told anyone about the hat pin, and she assured him that she had not.[862]

At some point in the conversation, Ms. Lewinsky told the President, "[M]aybe I should put the gifts away outside my house somewhere or give them to someone, maybe Betty."[863] Ms. Lewinsky recalled that the President responded either "I don't know" or "Let me think about that."[864]

When Ms. Lewinsky was asked whether she thought it odd for

the President to give her gifts under the circumstances (with a subpoena requiring the production of all his gifts), she testified that she
did not think of it at the time, but she did note some hesitancy on
the President's part:

> [H]e had hesitated very briefly right before I left that day in kind of
> packaging . . . all my stuff back up . . . I don't think he said any-
> thing that indicated this to me, but I thought to myself, "I wonder
> if he's thinking he shouldn't give these to me to take out." But he
> did.[865]

When asked in the Jones deposition about his last meeting with
Ms. Lewinsky, the President remembered only that she stopped by
"[p]robably sometime before Christmas" and he "stuck [his] head
out [of the office], said hello to her."[866] The deposition occurred
three weeks after this December 28 meeting with Ms. Lewinsky.

In the grand jury, the President acknowledged "talking with Ms.
Lewinsky about her testimony, or about the prospect that she might
have to give testimony. And she, she talked to me about that."[867] He
maintained, however, that they did not discuss Ms. Lewinsky's subpoena: "[S]he was upset. She—well, she—we—she didn't—we did-
n't talk about a subpoena. But she was upset."[868] In the President's
recollection, Ms. Lewinsky said she knew nothing about sexual
harassment; why did she have to testify? According to the President,
"I explained to her that it was a political lawsuit. They wanted to
get whatever they could under oath that was damaging to me."[869]

Ms. Lewinsky's friend, Catherine Allday Davis, testified about a
conversation with Ms. Lewinsky on January 3, 1998. Ms. Lewinsky
told Ms. Davis that she had met with the President and discussed
the Jones case a few days earlier. Ms. Davis testified that Ms. Lewinsky and the President had "noted [that] there was no evidence" of
their relationship.[870]

E (SIC). DECEMBER 28: CONCEALMENT OF GIFTS

In the afternoon of December 28, a few hours after Ms. Lewinsky's White House visit, Ms. Currie drove to Ms. Lewinsky's Water-

gate apartment and collected a box containing the President's gifts. Ms. Currie then took the box home and hid it under her bed. Ms. Lewinsky, Ms. Currie, and the President were all questioned as to why Ms. Currie retrieved the box of gifts from Ms. Lewinsky.

According to Ms. Lewinsky, the transfer originated in a phone call from Ms. Currie that afternoon. Ms. Lewinsky testified that Ms. Currie said, "I understand you have something to give me," or, "The President said you have something to give me."[871] Ms. Lewinsky understood that Ms. Currie was alluding to the gifts.[872] Ms. Currie said that she would stop by Ms. Lewinsky's apartment and pick up the items.[873] Ms. Lewinsky testified that she put many, but not all, of her gifts from the President into a box. Ms. Currie drove by her apartment and picked it up.[874]

Ms. Lewinsky was concerned because the gifts were under subpoena; she did not throw them away, however, because "they meant a lot to [her]."[875] The reason she gave the gifts to Ms. Currie, and not to one of her friends or her mother, was "a little bit of an assurance to the President . . . that everything was okay."[876] She felt that, because the gifts were with Ms. Currie, they were within the President's control: "Not that [the gifts] were going to be in his possession, but that he would understand whatever it was I gave to Betty and that that might make him feel a little bit better."[877]

Ms. Lewinsky's account of the events of December 28 in her sworn statement of February 1, 1998, corroborates her later grand jury testimony:

> "Ms. L . . . asked if she should put away (outside her home) the gifts he had given her or, maybe, give them to someone else. Ms. Currie called Ms. L later that afternoon as said that the Pres. had told her Ms. L. wanted her to hold onto something for her. Ms. L boxed up most of the gifts she had received and gave them to Ms. Currie. It is unknown if Ms. Currie knew the contents of the box."[878]

Ms. Currie's testimony was somewhat at odds with Ms. Lewinsky's. Though her overall recollection was hazy, Ms. Currie believed that Ms. Lewinsky had called her and raised the idea of the gifts transfer.[879] Ms. Currie was asked about the President's involvement in the transfer:

> Q: And did the President know you were holding these things for Monica?
> BC: I don't know. I don't know.
> Q: Didn't he say to you that Monica had something for you to hold?
> BC: I don't remember that. I don't.
> Q: Did you ever talk to the President and tell him you had this box from Monica?
> BC: I don't remember that either.
> Q: Do you think it happened, though?
> BC: I don't know. I don't know.[880]

When asked whether a statement by Ms. Lewinsky indicating that Ms. Currie had in fact spoken to the President about the gift transfer would be false, Ms. Currie replied: "Then she may remember better than I. I don't remember."[881]

According to Ms. Currie, Ms. Lewinsky said that she was uncomfortable retaining the gifts herself because "people were asking questions" about them.[882] Ms. Currie said she drove to Ms. Lewinsky's residence after work, collected the box, brought it home, and put it under her bed.[883] Written on the top of the box were the words "Please do not throw away!!!"[884] Ms. Currie testified that she knew that the box contained gifts from the President.[885]

For his part, the President testified that he never asked Ms. Currie to collect a box of gifts from Ms. Lewinsky.[886] He said that he had no knowledge that Ms. Currie had held those items "until that was made public."[887]

The President testified that he has no distinct recollection of discussing the gifts with Ms. Lewinsky on December 28: "[M]y memory is that on some day in December, and I'm sorry I don't remember when it was, she said, well, what if they ask me about the gifts you have given me. And I said, well, if you get a request to produce those, you have to give them whatever you have."[888]

D (sic). December 31: Breakfast with Vernon Jordan

Ms. Lewinsky testified that in late December 1997 she realized that she needed to "come up with some sort of strategy as to [what to do] if Linda Tripp" divulged what she knew.[889] On December 30, Ms. Lewinsky telephoned Mr. Jordan's office and conveyed either directly to him or through one of his secretaries that she was concerned about the Jones case.[890]

The following day, Ms. Lewinsky and Mr. Jordan had breakfast together at the Park Hyatt Hotel.[891] According to Ms. Lewinsky, she told Mr. Jordan that a friend of hers, Linda Tripp, was involved in the Jones case. She told Mr. Jordan: "I used to trust [Ms. Tripp], but I didn't trust her any more."[892] Ms. Lewinsky said that Ms. Tripp might have seen some notes in her apartment. Mr. Jordan asked: "Notes from the President to you?" Ms. Lewinsky responded: "No, notes from me to the President." According to Ms. Lewinsky, Mr. Jordan said: "Go home and make sure they're not there." Ms. Lewinsky testified that she understood that Mr. Jordan was advising her to "throw . . . away" any copies or drafts of notes that she had sent to the President.[893]

After breakfast, Mr. Jordan gave Ms. Lewinsky a ride back to his office.[894] When Ms. Lewinsky returned home to her apartment that day, she discarded approximately 50 draft notes to the President.[895]

E (sic). January 4: The Final Gift

On Sunday, January 4, 1998, Ms. Lewinsky called Ms. Currie at home and told her that she wanted to drop off a gift for the President.[896] Ms. Currie invited Ms. Lewinsky to her home, and Ms. Lewinsky gave her the package.[897] The package contained a book entitled The Presidents of the United States and a love note inspired by the movie Titanic.[898]

XIII. JANUARY 5–JANUARY 16, 1998: THE AFFIDAVIT

On January 5, 1998, Ms. Lewinsky's attorney, Francis Carter, drafted an affidavit for Ms. Lewinsky in an attempt to avert her deposition. She spoke with the President that evening. On January 6, Ms. Lewinsky talked to Mr. Jordan about the affidavit, which denied any sexual relations between her and the President. On January 7, Ms. Lewinsky signed the affidavit. On January 8, she interviewed for a job in New York City. After the interview went poorly, Mr. Jordan placed a phone call to the company's chairman on her behalf, and Ms. Lewinsky was given a second interview. The following week, after Ms. Lewinsky told Ms. Currie that she would need a reference from the White House, the President asked Chief of Staff Erskine Bowles to arrange one.

A. JANUARY 5: FRANCIS CARTER MEETING

At 3:00 p.m. on Monday, January 5, 1998, Ms. Lewinsky met with Mr. Carter at his office for approximately one hour.[899] Ms. Lewinsky testified that Mr. Carter described what a deposition was like and "threw out a bunch of different questions."[900] The questions that most concerned her related to the circumstances of her departure from the White House.[901]

Mr. Carter told Ms. Lewinsky that he would draft an affidavit for her to sign in hopes of averting her deposition. They arranged for Ms. Lewinsky to pick up a draft of the affidavit the next day.[902]

B. JANUARY 5: CALL FROM THE PRESIDENT

After her meeting with Mr. Carter, Ms. Lewinsky sent word via Ms. Currie that she needed to speak to the President about an important matter.[903] Specifically, Ms. Lewinsky told Ms. Currie she was anxious about something she needed to sign.[904]

A few hours later, according to Ms. Lewinsky, the President returned her call.[905] She mentioned an affidavit she would be signing and asked if he wanted to see it. According to Ms. Lewinsky, the President responded that he did not, as he had already seen about fifteen others.[906] Ms. Lewinsky testified that she told the President that she was troubled by potential questions about her transfer from the White House to the Pentagon. She was concerned that "people at the White House who didn't like [her]" might contradict her and "get [her] in trouble."[907] The President, according to Ms. Lewinsky, advised her: "[Y]ou could always say that the people in Legislative Affairs got it [the Pentagon job] for you or helped you get it."[908]

The President acknowledged in the grand jury that he was aware that Ms. Lewinsky had signed an affidavit in early January, but had no specific recollection of a conversation with her in that time period.[909] He testified that he did not recall telling Ms. Lewinsky that she could say, if asked, that persons in the Legislative Affairs Office of the White House had helped her obtain the job at the Pentagon.[910]

According to Ms. Lewinsky, she and the President also briefly discussed an antique book that she had dropped off with Ms. Currie the day before. With the book, she enclosed a letter telling the President that she wanted to have sexual intercourse with him at least once.[911] In their phone conversation, Ms. Lewinsky told the President, "I shouldn't have written some of those things in the note."[912] She testified that the President agreed.[913]

Although the President had testified in the Jones case that any personal messages from Ms. Lewinsky to him had been "unremarkable," he told the grand jury that he had received "quite affectionate" messages from Ms. Lewinsky, even after their intimate relationship ended.[914] The President testified that he cautioned Ms. Lewinsky about such messages: "I remember telling her she should be careful what she wrote, because a lot of it was clearly inappropriate and would be embarrassing if somebody else read it. I don't remember when I said that. I don't remember whether it was in '96 or when it was."[915] The President did remember the antique book Ms. Lewinsky had given him, but said he did not recall a romantic note enclosed with it.[916]

C. JANUARY 6: THE DRAFT AFFIDAVIT

According to Ms. Lewinsky, in the afternoon of January 6, 1998, she visited Mr. Carter's office and picked up a draft of the affidavit.[917] Later that day, according to Ms. Lewinsky, she and Mr. Jordan discussed the draft by telephone.[918] Ms. Lewinsky testified that having Mr. Jordan review the affidavit was like getting it "blessed" by the President.[919] Ms. Lewinsky testified that she told Mr. Jordan that she was worried about a sentence that implied that she had been alone with the President and thus might incline Paula Jones's attorneys to question her.[920] She eventually deleted it.[921]

In addition, Paragraph 8 of the draft affidavit provided in part:

> I have never had a sexual relationship with the President. . . . The occasions that I saw the President, with crowds of other people, after I left my employment at the White House in April, 1996 related to official receptions, formal functions or events related to the U.S. Department of Defense, where I was working at the time.[922]

Deeming the reference to "crowds" "too far out of the realm of possibility,"[923] Ms. Lewinsky deleted the underscored phrase and wrote the following sentence at the end of this paragraph: "There were other people present on all of these occasions."[924] She discussed this proposed sentence, as well as her general anxiety about Paragraph 8, with Mr. Jordan.[925]

When questioned in the grand jury, Mr. Jordan acknowledged that Ms. Lewinsky called him with concerns about the affidavit,[926] but maintained that he told her to speak with her attorney.[927]

Phone records for January 6 show that Mr. Jordan had a number of contacts with Ms. Lewinsky, the President, and Mr. Carter. Less than thirty minutes after Mr. Jordan spoke by phone to Ms. Lewinsky, he talked with the President for thirteen minutes. Immediately after this call, at 4:33 p.m., Mr. Jordan called Mr. Carter. Less than an hour later, Mr. Jordan placed a four-minute call to the main White House number. Over the course of the day, Mr. Jordan called a White House number twice, Ms. Lewinsky three times, and Mr. Carter four times.[928]

Mr. Carter testified that his phone conversations with Mr. Jordan this day and the next "likely" related to Ms. Lewinsky and his litigation strategy for her.[929] In fact, Mr. Carter billed Ms. Lewinsky for time for "[t]elephone conference with Atty Jordan."[930]

When questioned in the grand jury, Mr. Jordan testified that he could not specifically remember the January 6 calls. He said he "assumed" that he talked with Ms. Lewinsky about her job search, and he believed that he called Mr. Carter to see "how he was dealing with this highly emotional lady."[931] He said that he might have talked with the President about Ms. Lewinsky, but he maintained that "there [was] no connection" between his 13-minute conversation with the President and the call he placed immediately thereafter to Mr. Carter.[932]

D. JANUARY 7: MS. LEWINSKY SIGNS AFFIDAVIT

Ms. Lewinsky set an appointment with Mr. Carter to finalize the affidavit for 10 a.m. on January 7, 1998.[933] She signed the affidavit; however, she acknowledged in the grand jury that statements in it were false.[934] Mr. Carter indicated to her that he "intend[ed] to hold onto this until after I talk to plaintiff's lawyers." He told her to "keep in touch," and said: "Good luck on your job search."[935]

According to Mr. Jordan, Ms. Lewinsky came to his office on January 7 and showed him the signed affidavit.[936] Over the course of the day, Mr. Jordan placed three calls of significant duration to the White House.[937] He testified: "I knew the President was concerned about the affidavit and whether it was signed or not."[938] When asked whether the President understood that the affidavit denied a sexual relationship, Mr. Jordan testified: "I think that's a reasonable assumption."[939] According to Mr. Jordan, when he informed the President that Ms. Lewinsky had signed the affidavit, the President said, "Fine, good."[940] Mr. Jordan said he was continuing to work on her job, and the President responded, "Good."[941]

Ten days after this conversation, in the Jones deposition, President Clinton was asked whether he knew that Ms. Lewinsky had met with Vernon Jordan and talked about the Jones case. He answered:

I knew he met with her. I think Betty suggested that he meet with her. Anyway, he met with her. I, I thought that he talked to her about something else. I didn't know that—I thought he had given her some advice about her move to New York. Seems like that's what Betty said.[942]

In his grand jury appearance, however, President Clinton testified that Mr. Jordan informed "us" on January 7 that Ms. Lewinsky had signed an affidavit to be used in connection with the Jones case.[943] The President defended his deposition testimony by stating:

> [M]y impression was that, at the time, I was focused on the meetings. I believe the meetings he had were meetings about her moving to New York and getting a job.
>
> I knew at some point that she had told him that she needed some help, because she had gotten a subpoena. I'm not sure I know whether she did that in a meeting or a phone call. And I was not, I was not focused on that. I know that, I know Vernon helped her get a lawyer, Mr. Carter. And I, I believe that he did it after she had called him, but I'm not sure. But I knew that the main source of their meetings was about her move to New York and her getting a job.[944]

E. JANUARY 8: THE PERELMAN CALL

The day after she signed the affidavit, January 8, 1998, Ms. Lewinsky interviewed in New York with Jaymie Durnan, Senior Vice President and Special Assistant to the Chairman at MacAndrews & Forbes Holdings, Inc. (MFH).[945] Mr. Durnan testified that, although impressive, Ms. Lewinsky was not suited for any MFH opening.[946] He told her that he would pass on her resume to Revlon, an MFH company.[947] Ms. Lewinsky called Mr. Jordan and reported that she felt that the interview had gone "very poorly."[948] Mr. Jordan indicated in response that "he'd call the chairman."[949]

At 4:54 p.m., Mr. Jordan called Ronald Perelman, chairman and chief executive officer of MFH.[950] Mr. Jordan told the grand jury with respect to Mr. Perelman, one "[c]an't get any higher—or any richer."[951] Asked why he chose to call Mr. Perelman, Mr. Jordan responded: "I have spent a good part of my life learning institutions and people, and, in that process, I have learned how to make things happen. And the call to Ronald Perelman was a call to make things happen, if they could happen."[952]

According to Mr. Perelman, Mr. Jordan spoke of "this bright young girl, who I think is terrific," and said that he wanted "to make sure somebody takes a look at her."[953] Mr. Perelman testified that, in the roughly twelve years that Mr. Jordan had been on Revlon's Board of Directors, he did not recall Mr. Jordan ever calling to recommend someone.[954]

After he spoke with Mr. Perelman, Mr. Jordan telephoned Ms. Lewinsky and told her, "I'm doing the best I can to help you out."[955] Ms. Lewinsky soon received a call from Revlon, inviting her to another interview.[956]

Over the course of January 8, Mr. Jordan placed three calls to the White House—twice to a number at the White House Counsel's Office, once to the main White House number.[957] As to the Counsel's Office calls, Mr. Jordan speculated that he was trying to reach Cheryl Mills, Deputy White House Counsel, to express his "frustration" about Ms. Lewinsky.[958] According to Mr. Jordan, Ms. Mills knew who Ms. Lewinsky was: "[T]hat was no secret, I don't think, around the White House, that I was helping Monica Lewinsky."[959]

F. January 9: "Mission Accomplished"

On the morning of Friday, January 9, 1998, Ms. Lewinsky interviewed with Allyn Seidman, Senior Vice President of MFH, and two individuals at Revlon.[960] Ms. Lewinsky testified that the interviews went well and that Ms. Seidman called her back that day and "informally offered [her] a position, and [she] informally accepted."[961]

Ms. Lewinsky then called Mr. Jordan and relayed the good news.[962] When shown records of a seven-minute call at 4:14 p.m., Mr. Jordan testified: "I have to assume that if she got the job and we have a seven-minute conversation and the day before I had talked to the chairman [Ronald Perelman], I have to assume the Jordan magic worked." [963]

According to Mr. Jordan, he believed that he notified Ms. Currie and the President as soon as he learned that Ms. Lewinsky had obtained an offer: "I am certain that at some point in time I told Betty Currie, 'Mission accomplished.'" [964] Mr. Jordan testified that he also told the President directly that, "'Monica Lewinsky's going to work for Revlon,' and his response was, 'Thank you very much.'" [965]

G. January 12: Pre-Trial Hearing in Jones Case

On January 12, 1998, Judge Wright held a hearing in the Jones case to discuss pre-trial issues, including the President's upcoming deposition. [966] At that hearing, Judge Wright required Ms. Jones's counsel to list all the witnesses that they planned to call at trial. Ms. Jones's witness list named many women, among them Ms. Lewinsky, to support her theory that the President had a pattern of rewarding women based on their willingness to engage in sexual relations with him. At the hearing, Judge Wright indicated that she would permit Ms. Jones to call as witnesses some of the women she listed in support of her case.

H. January 13: References from the White House

On Tuesday, January 13, 1998, Jennifer Sheldon, Manager of Corporate Staffing of Revlon, called Ms. Lewinsky and formally extended her a position as a public relations administrator. Asked whether this was a relatively quick hiring process, Ms. Sheldon responded, "In totality of how long open positions normally stay open, yes. This was pretty fast." [967] Ms. Sheldon told Ms. Lewinsky that she needed to send her some references. [968]

According to Ms. Lewinsky, she then called Ms. Currie because she was "concerned that if I put [Mr. Hilley] down as a reference, he might not say flattering things about me." [969] At 11:11 a.m. on January 13, Ms. Currie paged Ms. Lewinsky and left the following message: "Will know something this afternoon. Kay."[970]

That day, January 13, the President talked with Chief of Staff Erskine Bowles about a reference for Ms. Lewinsky.[971] The President told Mr. Bowles that Ms. Lewinsky "had found a job in the . . . private sector, and she had listed John Hilley as a reference, and could we see if he could recommend her, if asked." Mr. Bowles assured the President that Mr. Hilley would give Ms. Lewinsky a recommendation commensurate with her job performance.[972]

Thereafter, Mr. Bowles took the President's request to Mr. Podesta, the Deputy Chief of Staff, who in turn spoke with Mr. Hilley.[973] Mr. Hilley responded that, because he did not know Ms. Lewinsky personally, he would have his office write a recommendation.[974] It would be a generic letter, simply confirming the dates of employment, because of the less than favorable circumstances surrounding Ms. Lewinsky's departure from the White House.[975]

Ms. Lewinsky testified that Ms. Currie called later that day and told her that "Mr. Podesta took care of it and everything would be fine with Mr. Hilley."[976] At 11:17 a.m. the next day, Wednesday, January 14, Ms. Lewinsky faxed her acceptance to Revlon and listed John Hilley and her Defense Department supervisor as references.[977]

The President was asked in the grand jury whether he ever spoke to Mr. Bowles about obtaining a reference from Mr. Hilley for Ms. Lewinsky. He testified that he did, at Ms. Lewinsky's request, although he thought he had done so earlier than January 13 or 14.[978]

I. JANUARY 13: FINAL JORDAN MEETING

According to Ms. Lewinsky, on Tuesday, January 13, she stopped by Mr. Jordan's office to drop off some thank-you gifts for helping her find a job. Ms. Lewinsky offered to show him a copy of her signed affidavit in the Jones case, but he indicated that he did not need to see it.[979]

J. January 13-14: Lewinsky-Tripp Conversation and Talking Points

In a face-to-face conversation on January 13, Ms. Lewinsky told Linda Tripp: "This is what my lawyer taught me. You really don't—you don't very often say 'no' unless you really need to. The best is, 'Well, not that I recall, not that I really remember. Might have, but I don't really remember.'"[980] Ms. Lewinsky said that, if asked in a deposition, "Were you ever alone with the President?" she could say, "Um, it's possible I may have taken a letter on the weekend, but, you know—I might have, but I don't really. . . ."[981]

Ms. Lewinsky and Ms. Tripp then discussed the situation:

> Ms. Lewinsky: I don't think the way that man thinks, I don't think he thinks of lying under oath. . . .
>
> Ms. Tripp: Yes, he is because he's the one who said, "Deny, deny, deny." Of course he knows.
>
> Ms. Lewinsky: Right. But it's—hard to explain this. It's like—(sigh)
>
> Ms. Tripp: You know what I mean. I mean, I don't know—do I think he is consciously —
>
> Ms. Lewinsky: If— if—if I said, if somebody said to him, "Is Monica lying under oath," he would say yes. But when he on his own thinks about it, he doesn't think about it in those terms. Okay?
>
> Ms. Tripp: Probably.
>
> Ms. Lewinsky: Okay? He thinks of it as, "We're safe. We're being smart." Okay? "We're being smart, we're being safe, it's good for everybody."[982]

On January 14, Ms. Lewinsky gave Ms. Tripp a three-page document regarding "points to make in [Ms. Tripp's] affidavit."[983] Ms. Lewinsky testified that she wrote the document herself, although some of the ideas may have been inspired by conversations with Ms. Tripp.[984]

K. JANUARY 15: THE ISIKOFF CALL

In the grand jury, Betty Currie testified that on Thursday, January 15, 1998, she received a telephone call from Michael Isikoff of Newsweek, who inquired about courier receipts reflecting items sent by Ms. Lewinsky to the White House.[985]

Ms. Currie called Mr. Jordan and asked for guidance in responding to Mr. Isikoff's inquiry because, in her words, she had a "comfort level with Vernon."[986] After Ms. Currie arranged to meet with Mr. Jordan at his office,[987] Ms. Lewinsky drove her there.[988]

Mr. Jordan confirmed in the grand jury that Ms. Currie expressed concern about a call from Mr. Isikoff.[989] He invited her to his office but advised her to "talk to Mike McCurry and Bruce Lindsey . . . because I cannot give you that advice."[990]

In a recorded conversation that day, January 15, Ms. Lewinsky encouraged Ms. Tripp not to disclose her (Lewinsky's) relationship with the President. Ms. Lewinsky tried to persuade Ms. Tripp to lie by telling her that others planned to lie: "I'm not concerned all that much anymore because I'm not going to get in trouble because you know what? The story I've signed . . . under oath is what someone else is saying under oath." When Ms. Tripp asked, "Who?" Ms. Lewinsky responded: "He will," referring to the President.[991] Ms. Lewinsky stated that she did not think the President would "slip up" at his deposition because she was not a "big issue" like Gennifer Flowers and Paula Jones. In contrast, she regarded herself as nothing more than "rumor and innuendo."[992]

One of Ms. Lewinsky's friends, Natalie Ungvari, testified that, when Ms. Lewinsky was implicated in the Jones case, "it seemed to me that Monica was just confident everybody would say the right thing, that everything would be orchestrated to come out a secret."[993]

L. JANUARY 15-16: DEVELOPMENTS IN THE JONES LAW SUIT

On January 15, 1998, President Clinton's counsel served Ms. Jones's attorneys with the President's responses to Ms. Jones's document requests.[994] One of the requests specifically sought all documents reflecting communications between the President and Monica Lewinsky.[995] President Clinton objected to the scope of this request, but, notwithstanding his objection, he stated that he did not have any responsive documents.

Also on January 15, Mr. Carter drafted a motion to quash the subpoena issued by Paula Jones's attorneys to Ms. Lewinsky. Attached to the motion was Ms. Lewinsky's signed affidavit.[996] At the request of Katherine Sexton, one of the President's personal attorneys, Mr. Carter faxed a copy of the affidavit to her law offices. Mr. Carter testified that he asked Ms. Sexton why she needed the affidavit that day:

> I said, "Well, Katie, you're going to get it tomorrow because I'm filing it, and it's going to be attached as an exhibit to the motion." She said, "Well, but you've already provided it to the other side, so can I get a copy"—words to that effect. I said, "I have no problem." And so I faxed it to her.[997]

On January 16, 1998, Mr. Carter arranged for the overnight delivery of the motion to quash and the accompanying affidavit to Judge Susan Webber Wright's law clerk and Paula Jones's attorneys.[998]

XIV. JANUARY 17, 1998-PRESENT: THE DEPOSITION AND AFTERWARD

The President was asked a number of questions about Ms. Lewinsky during his January 17, 1998, deposition in the Jones case. In sworn testimony, the President denied having a sexual affair or sexual relations with her. That evening, the President called Ms. Currie and asked her to meet him the following day to discuss Ms. Lewinsky. After allegations that the President had an affair with a White House intern became public, the President emphatically denied the reports to aides and to the American public.

A. JANUARY 17: THE DEPOSITION

On Saturday, January 17, 1998, the President testified under oath at a deposition in the Jones case.[999] Judge Susan Webber Wright traveled from Little Rock, Arkansas, to preside at the deposition in Washington, D.C.[1000]

Prior to any questions, Judge Wright reminded the parties about her standing Protective Order. She specifically stated: "[I]f anyone reveals anything whatsoever about this deposition, . . . it will be in violation of the Protective Order. This includes the questions that were asked, . . . You may acknowledge that [the deposition] took place, but that is it."[1001] Judge Wright accepted the following definition of the term "sexual relations:"

> For the purposes of this deposition, a person engages in "sexual relations" when the person knowingly engages in or causes . . . contact with the genitalia, anus, groin, breast, inner thigh, or buttocks of any person with an intent to arouse or gratify the sexual desire of any person . . . . "Contact" means intentional touching, either directly or through clothing.[1002]

After the President had answered a few questions about Ms. Lewinsky, his attorney, Robert Bennett, urged Judge Wright to limit further inquiries. Mr. Bennett stated that Ms. Lewinsky had executed an affidavit "saying that there is absolutely no sex of any kind of any manner, shape or form, with President Clinton."[1003] When Judge Wright cautioned Mr. Bennett not to make remarks that "could be arguably coaching the witness," Mr. Bennett represented to Judge Wright: "In preparation of the witness for this deposition, the witness is fully aware of Ms. Lewinsky's affidavit, so I have not told him a single thing he doesn't know . . . ."[1004] President Clinton, who was present when Mr. Bennett made his objection, did not contradict his attorney's comment. Rejecting Mr. Bennett's argument, Judge Wright permitted the questioning about Ms. Lewinsky to continue.[1005]

Over the course of extensive questioning, the President testified that he had seen Ms. Lewinsky "on two or three occasions" during the government shutdown in the fall of 1995, including one occasion when she brought pizza to him, and one or two other occasions when she delivered documents to him.[1006] He could not recall whether he had been alone with Ms. Lewinsky on such occasions, although he acknowledged that it was possible.[1007] The President further testified that he could not remember the subject of any conversations with Ms. Lewinsky.[1008]

President Clinton recalled that he received only a couple of unremarkable personal messages from Ms. Lewinsky, and he could not recall ever having received a cassette tape from her.[1009] He received presents from her "[o]nce or twice"—a book or two and a tie.[1010] The President originally testified that he could not recall any gifts he might have given her; later in the deposition, however, he remembered that some merchandise he had purchased from a Martha's Vineyard restaurant might have reached her through Ms. Currie.[1011] The President stated that he might have given Ms. Lewinsky a hat pin, though he could not recall for certain.[1012]

The President testified that his last conversation with Ms. Lewinsky had been before Christmas, when she had visited the White House to see Ms. Currie. The President stated: "I stuck my head out, said hello to her."[1013] He said it was also possible that, during that encounter, he had joked with Ms. Lewinsky that the plaintiff's attorneys were going to subpoena "every woman I ever talked to" and Ms. Lewinsky "would qualify."[1014]

The President testified that he was unaware that Mr. Jordan had talked with Ms. Lewinsky about the Jones case, in which she had also been subpoenaed to testify at a deposition.[1015]

The President emphatically denied having had sexual relations with Ms. Lewinsky.[1016]

At the conclusion of the deposition, Judge Wright said: "Before [the President] leaves, I want to remind him, as the witness in this matter, and everyone else in the room, that this case is subject to a Protective Order regarding all discovery, . . . and . . . all parties present, including . . . the witness are not to say anything whatsoever about the questions they were asked, the substance of the deposition, . . . any details, . . . and this is extremely important to this Court." [1017]

Sometime after the President's deposition, Mr. Podesta saw Bruce Lindsey, Deputy White House Counsel, at the White House and inquired how the deposition went. According to Mr. Podesta, Mr. Lindsey said that the President had been asked about Monica Lewinsky. [1018] Mr. Lindsey testified that, during a break in the President's deposition, the President had told him that Ms. Lewinsky's name had come up. [1019]

That same evening, Mr. Lindsey met with the President in the Oval Office, where they discussed the deposition. [1020] Mr. Lindsey, relying on the attorney-client, presidential communication, deliberative process, and work-product privileges, declined to say what specifically was discussed at this meeting.

B. THE PRESIDENT MEETS WITH MS. CURRIE

Soon after the deposition, the President called Ms. Currie and asked her to come to the White House the next day. [1021] Ms. Currie acknowledged that, "It's rare for [the President] to ask me to come in on Sunday." [1022] The President wanted to discuss Ms. Lewinsky's White House visits. [1023]

At approximately 5:00 p.m. on Sunday, January 18, 1998, Ms. Currie met with the President. [1024] The meeting took place at her desk outside the Oval Office. According to Ms. Currie, the President appeared "concerned." [1025] He told Ms. Currie that, during his deposition the previous day, he had been asked questions about Monica Lewinsky. [1026] Ms. Currie testified: "I think he said, 'There are several things you may want to know.'" [1027] He proceeded to make a series of statements, [1028] one right after the other: [1029]

* "You were always there when she was there, right?"
* "We were never really alone."
* "Monica [Lewinsky] came on to me, and I never touched her, right?"
* "You can see and hear everything, right?" [1030]

Ms. Currie testified that, based on his demeanor and the way he made the statements, the President wanted her to agree with them.[1031]

Ms. Currie testified that she did, in fact, agree with the President when he said, "You were always there when she was there, right?"[1032] Before the grand jury, however, Ms. Currie acknowledged the possibility that Ms. Lewinsky could have visited the President when she was not at the White House.[1033]

With respect to whether the President was "never really alone" with Ms. Lewinsky, Ms. Currie testified that there were several occasions when the President and Ms. Lewinsky were either in the Oval Office or in the study without anyone else present.[1034] Ms. Currie explained that she did not consider the President and Ms. Lewinsky to be "alone" on such occasions because she was at her desk outside the Oval Office; accordingly, they were all together in the same "general area."[1035] Ms. Currie testified that "the President, for all intents and purposes, is never alone. There's always somebody around him."[1036]

As to whether Ms. Lewinsky "came on" to him, Ms. Currie testified that she "would have no reason to know" whether Ms. Lewinsky ever "came on" to the President because Ms. Currie was not present all the time.[1037] Finally, as to whether she "could see and hear everything," Ms. Currie testified that she should not have agreed with the President.[1038] She testified that when the President and Ms. Lewinsky were alone together in the study, while Ms. Currie was at her desk, she could "hear nothing."[1039]

The President also made the following statement during their January 18, 1998 meeting, according to Ms. Currie: "[Monica Lewinsky] wanted to have sex with me, but I told her I couldn't do that."[1040]

When the President was questioned about this meeting with Ms. Currie in the grand jury, he testified that he recalled the conversation, but he denied that he was "trying to get Betty Currie to say something that was untruthful."[1041] Rather, the President testified that he asked a "series of questions" in an effort to quickly "refresh

[his] memory."[1042] The President explained: "I wanted to establish . . . that Betty was there at all other times in the complex, and I wanted to know what Betty's memory was about what she heard, what she could hear . . . . [a]nd I was trying to figure [it] out . . . in a hurry because I knew something was up."[1043]

In his grand jury testimony, the President acknowledged that, "in fairness," Ms. Currie "may have felt some ambivalence about how to react" to his statements.[1044] The President maintained that he was trying to establish that Ms. Currie was "always there," and could see and hear everything.[1045] At the same time, he acknowledged that he had always tried to prevent Ms. Currie from learning about his relationship with Ms. Lewinsky.[1046] "[I] did what people do when they do the wrong thing. I tried to do it where nobody else was looking at it."[1047]

The President was also asked about his statement that Ms. Currie was always in the Oval Office when Ms. Lewinsky visited. He explained that he may have intended the term "Oval Office" to include the entire Oval Office complex.[1048] The President further explained, "I was talking about 1997. I was never, ever trying to get Betty Currie to claim that on the occasions when Monica Lewinsky was there when she wasn't anywhere around, that she was."[1049] When asked whether he restricted his remarks to the year 1997, the President responded, "Well, I don't recall whether I did or not, but . . . I assumed [Ms. Currie] knew what I was talking about."[1050]

When questioned about his statement to Ms. Currie, "you could see and hear everything," the President responded:

> My memory of that was that, that she had the ability to hear what was going on if she came in the Oval Office from her office. And a lot of times, you know, when I was in the Oval Office, she just had the door open to her office. Then there was—the door was never completely closed to the hall. So, I think there was—I'm not entirely sure what I meant by that, but I could have meant that she generally would be able to hear conversations, even if she couldn't see them. And I think that's what I meant.[1051]

Finally, when asked about his statement to Ms. Currie that "Monica came on to me and I never touched her," the President refused to answer.[1052]

C. January 18-19: Attempts to Reach Ms. Lewinsky

In the wake of her Sunday afternoon session, Ms. Currie paged Ms. Lewinsky four times.[1053] She testified that the President "may have asked me to call [Ms. Lewinsky] to see what she knew or where she was or what was happening."[1054] Later that evening, at 11:02 p.m., the President called Ms. Currie to ask whether she had spoken to Ms. Lewinsky.[1055]

Over a two-hour span the next morning, Monday, January 19, 1998, Ms. Currie made eight unsuccessful attempts to contact Ms. Lewinsky, by either pager or telephone.[1056] After speaking with the President to let him know that she was unable to reach Ms. Lewinsky, Ms. Currie again paged her.[1057] The purpose of these calls, according to Ms. Currie, was to tell Ms. Lewinsky that her name had been mentioned in the President's deposition.[1058]

Mr. Jordan also tried unsuccessfully to reach Ms. Lewinsky that morning.[1059] That afternoon, Mr. Jordan met with the President in the Oval Office.[1060] Later, Ms. Lewinsky's attorney, Frank Carter, called Mr. Jordan and told him that Ms. Lewinsky had obtained new counsel, William Ginsburg and Nathaniel Speights.[1061] Mr. Jordan passed this information on to the President that evening in a seven-minute phone conversation.[1062]

D. January 20-22: Lewinsky Story Breaks

After the publication of an article alleging a sexual relationship with Ms. Lewinsky, President Clinton conferred with his attorneys and issued a number of denials to his aides and to the American public.

1. "CLINTON ACCUSED"

On Wednesday, January 21, 1998, the Washington Post pub-
lished a story entitled "Clinton Accused of Urging Aide to Lie; Starr
Probes Whether President Told Woman to Deny Alleged Affair to
Jones's Lawyers."[1063] The White House learned the essentials of the
Post story on the night of January 20, 1998.[1064]

President Clinton placed a number of phone calls that night and
the following morning.[1065] From 12:08 a.m. to 12:39 a.m., he spoke
with his personal attorney, Robert Bennett. Mr. Bennett would be
quoted in the Post article as saying, "The President adamantly
denies he ever had a relationship with Ms. Lewinsky and she has
confirmed the truth of that."[1066] He added: "This story seems ridicu-
lous and I frankly smell a rat."[1067]

Immediately after his call to Mr. Bennett, President Clinton
called Deputy White House Counsel Bruce Lindsey; they spoke for
about half an hour, until 1:10 a.m.[1068]

At 1:16 a.m., the President called Ms. Currie at home and spoke
to her for 20 minutes. Ms. Currie testified that the President was
concerned that her name was mentioned in the Post article.[1069] Soon
after this call, the President called Mr. Lindsey.[1070]

A few hours later, at approximately 6:30 a.m., the President
called Mr. Jordan in New York City to tell him, according to Mr.
Jordan, that the Post story was untrue.[1071] From 7:14 a.m. to 7:22
a.m., the President spoke again with Mr. Lindsey.[1072]

Responding to the Post story that day, the White House issued a
statement, personally approved by the President, declaring that he
was "outraged by these allegations" and that "he has never had an
improper relationship with this woman." White House spokesperson Mike McCurry said that the statement "was prepared by the
Counsel's office, and I reviewed it with the President to make sure
that it reflected what he wanted me to say . . . He looked at it, and
he said fine. . . . It was prepared in consultation between the
lawyers and the President. The Counsel's Office gave it to me. I

wanted to, of course, verify that that's exactly what the President wanted me to say."[1073]

2. DENIALS TO AIDES

According to Mr. Lindsey, the remainder of the morning was spent in a series of meetings about the Lewinsky matter, including preparing the President for anticipated Lewinsky-related questions in three previously scheduled media interviews.[1074] At these meetings, President Clinton denied the allegations to several of his top aides.

The President met with Chief of Staff Erskine Bowles, along with his two deputies, John Podesta and Sylvia Matthews. According to Mr. Bowles, the President told them, "I want you to know I did not have sexual relationships with this woman, Monica Lewinsky. I did not ask anybody to lie. And when the facts come out, you'll understand."[1075] The President made a similar denial that morning to Harold Ickes, his former Deputy Chief of Staff.[1076]

The President also discussed the matter with Ms. Currie for a second time.[1077] According to Ms. Currie, the President called her into the Oval Office and gave a "sort of a recapitulation of what we had talked about on Sunday—you know, 'I was never alone with her'— that sort of thing."[1078] The President spoke with the same tone and demeanor that he used during his previous session with her.[1079] Ms. Currie testified that the President may have mentioned that she might be asked about Ms. Lewinsky.[1080]

Later that day, the President summoned Sidney Blumenthal to the Oval Office. They spoke for about 30 minutes.[1081] The President said to Mr. Blumenthal, "I haven't done anything wrong."[1082] Mr. Blumenthal testified that the President told him, "Monica Lewinsky came on to me and made a sexual demand on me." The President said that he "rebuffed her."[1083] The President also told Mr. Blumenthal that Ms. Lewinsky had "threatened him. She said that she would tell people they'd had an affair, that she was known as the stalker among her peers, and that she hated it and if she had an affair or said she had an affair then she wouldn't be the stalker any more."[1084] Mr. Blumenthal then asked the President whether he and Ms. Lewinsky were alone when she threatened him. The President responded, "Well, I was within eyesight or earshot of someone."[1085]

According to Mr. Blumenthal, the President complained: "I feel like a character in a novel. I feel like somebody who is surrounded by an oppressive force that is creating a lie about me and I can't get the truth out. I feel like the character in the novel Darkness at Noon."[1086]

Soon thereafter, in the course of a meeting about the progress of the President's State of the Union address, the President made a second denial of the allegations to Mr. Podesta.[1087] Mr. Podesta testified:

> [H]e said to me that he had never had sex with her, and that—and that he never asked—you know, he repeated the denial, but he was extremely explicit in saying he never had sex with her . . . . Well, I think he said—he said that—there was some spate of, you know, what sex acts were counted, and he said that he had never had sex with her in any way whatsoever—that they had not had oral sex.[1088]

The President was asked during his grand jury appearance whether he recalled denying a sexual relationship with Ms. Lewinsky to his senior aides and advisors, including Mr. Bowles, Mr. Podesta, Mr. Blumenthal, Mr. Ickes, and Mr. Jordan.[1089] The President did not recall specific details but did remember the following:

> I met with certain people, and [to] a few of them I said I didn't have sex with Monica Lewinsky, or I didn't have an affair with her or something like that. I had a very careful thing I said, and I tried not to say anything else . . . . I remember that I issued a number of denials to people that I thought needed to hear them, but I tried to be careful and to be accurate.

And I believe, sir, that—you'll have to ask them what they thought. But I was using those terms in the normal way people use them.[1090]

The President testified that he had said "things that were true about this relationship. That I used—in the language I used, I said, there's nothing going on between us. That was true.[1091] I said I did not have sex with her as I defined it. That was true."[1092] The President qualified this answer, however: "I said things that were true. They may have been misleading, and if they were I have to take responsibility for it, and I'm sorry."[1093]

3. INITIAL DENIALS TO THE AMERICAN PUBLIC

On the afternoon of January 21, the President made his first of a series of previously scheduled media appearances. In an interview on National Public Radio's "All Things Considered," the following colloquy took place:

> Q: Mr. President, ... [m]any Americans woke up to the news today that the Whitewater independent counsel is investigating an allegation that you . . . encouraged a young woman to lie to lawyers in the Paula Jones civil suit. Is there any truth to that allegation?
> WJC: No, sir, there's not. It's just not true.
> Q: Is there any truth to the allegation of an affair between you and the young woman?
> WJC: No. That's not true either. . . . The charges are not true. And I haven't asked anybody to lie.[1094]

That evening, the President appeared on the PBS program "The News Hour with Jim Lehrer." He was asked again whether the allegation of an affair with a White House intern was true. The President replied, "That is not true. That is not true. I did not ask anyone to tell anything other than the truth. There is no improper relationship. And I intend to cooperate with this inquiry. But that is not true." When asked to define what he meant by the term "improper relationship," the President answered, "Well, I think you know what it means. It means that there is not a sexual relationship, an improper sexual relationship, or any other kind of improper relationship."[1095]

The following morning, on January 22, 1998, the President again denied he had done anything improper. Speaking at a televised White House photo opportunity with Palestinian Authority Chairman Yasser Arafat, the President stated: "[T]he allegations are false, and I would never ask anybody to do anything other than tell the truth. That is false."[1096]

The President also gave an interview to Roll Call that day. He stated: "[T]he relationship was not improper, and I think that's important enough to say. . . . But let me answer—it is not an improper relationship and I know what the word means. . . . The relationship was not sexual. And I know what you mean, and the answer is no."[1097]

At each of these interviews, the President pledged he would cooperate fully with the investigation. On NPR, the President stated: "I have told people that I would cooperate in the investigation, and I expect to cooperate with it. I don't know any more about it, really, than you do. But I will cooperate. . . . I'm doing my best to cooperate with the investigation."[1098] To Mr. Lehrer, he said: "[W]e are doing the best to cooperate here, but we don't know much yet. . . . I think it's important that we cooperate, I will cooperate, but I want to focus on the work at hand."[1099]

In his photo opportunity with Mr. Arafat, the President stated:

[T]he American people have a right to get answers. We are working very hard to comply, get all the requests for information up here. And we will give you as many answers as we can, as soon as we can, at the appropriate time, consistent with our obligation to also cooperate with the investigations. And that's not a dodge; that's really what I've—I've talked with our people. I want to do that. I'd like for you to have more rather than less, sooner rather than later. So we will work through it as quickly as we can and get all those questions out there to you.[1100]

Finally, in his Roll Call interview, the President vowed: "I'm going to cooperate with this investigation. . . . And I'll cooperate."[1101]

4. "WE JUST HAVE TO WIN"

Amidst the flurry of press activity on January 21, 1998, the President's former political consultant, Dick Morris, read the Post story and called the President.[1102] According to Mr. Morris, he told the President, "You poor son of a bitch. I've just read what's going on."[1103] The President responded, Mr. Morris recalled, "Oh, God. This is just awful. . . . I didn't do what they said I did, but I did do something. I mean, with this girl, I didn't do what they said, but I did . . . do something[1104]. . . . And I may have done enough so that I don't know if I can prove my innocence. . . . There may be gifts. I gave her gifts, ... [a]nd there may be messages on her phone answering machine."[1105]

Mr. Morris assured the President, "[t]here's a great capacity for forgiveness in this country and you should consider tapping into it."[1106] The President said, "But what about the legal thing? You know, the legal thing? You know, Starr and perjury and all. . . . You know, ever since the election, I've tried to shut myself down. I've tried to shut my body down, sexually, I mean. . . . But sometimes I slipped up and with this girl I just slipped up."[1107]

Mr. Morris suggested that he take a poll on the voters' willingness to forgive confessed adultery. The President agreed.[1108]

Mr. Morris telephoned the President later that evening with the poll results, which showed that the voters were "willing to forgive [the President] for adultery, but not for perjury or obstruction of justice[.]"[1109] When Mr. Morris explained that the poll results suggested that the President should not go public with a confession or explanation, he replied, "Well, we just have to win, then."[1110]

The President had a follow-up conversation with Mr. Morris during the evening of January 22, 1998, when Mr. Morris was considering holding a press conference to "blast Monica Lewinsky 'out of the water.'"[1111] The President told Mr. Morris to "be careful". According to Mr. Morris, the President warned him not to "be too hard on [Ms. Lewinsky] because there's some slight chance that she may not be cooperating with Starr and we don't want to alienate her by anything we're going to put out."[1112]

Meanwhile, in California, the President's good friend and Hollywood producer, Harry Thomason, had seen the President's interview with Jim Lehrer on televison.[1113] Mr. Thomason, who had occasionally advised the President on matters relating to the media, traveled to Washington, D.C., and met with him the next day.[1114] Mr. Thomason told the President that "the press seemed to be saying that [the President's comments were] weak" and that he, Mr. Thomason, "thought his response wasn't as strong as it could have been."[1115] Mr. Thomason recommended that the President "should explain it so there's no doubt in anybody's mind that nothing happened."[1116] The President agreed: "You know, you're right. I should be more forceful than that."[1117]

In the ensuing days, the President, through his Cabinet, issued a number of firm denials. On January 23, 1998, the President started a Cabinet meeting by saying the allegations were untrue.[1118] Afterward, several Cabinet members appeared outside the White House. Madeline Albright, Secretary of State, said: "I believe that the allegations are completely untrue." The others agreed. "I'll second that, definitely," Commerce Secretary William Daley said. Secretary of Education Richard Riley and Secretary of Health and Human Services Donna Shalala concurred.[1119]

The next day, Ann Lewis, White House Communications Director, publicly announced that "those of us who have wanted to go out and speak on behalf of the president" had been given the green light by the President's legal team.[1120] She reported that the President answered the allegations "directly" by denying any improper relationship. She believed that, in issuing his public denials, the President was not "splitting hairs, defining what is a sexual relationship, talking about 'is' rather than was.[1121] You know, I always thought, perhaps I was naive, since I've come to Washington, when you said a sexual relationship, everybody knew what that meant." Ms. Lewis expressly said that the term includes "oral sex."[1122]

On Monday, January 26, 1998, in remarks in the Roosevelt Room in the White House, President Clinton gave his last public statement for several months on the Lewinsky matter. At an event promoting after-school health care, the President denied the allegations in the strongest terms: "I want to say one thing to the American people. I want you to listen to me. I'm going to say this again: I did not have sexual relations with that woman, Miss Lewinsky. I never told anybody to lie, not a single time. Never. These allegations are false."[1123]

Grounds for Impeachment

There is Substantial and Credible Information that President Clinton Committed Acts that May Constitute Grounds for an Impeachment

INTRODUCTION

Pursuant to Section 595(c) of Title 28, the Office of Independent Counsel (OIC) hereby submits substantial and credible information that President Clinton obstructed justice during the Jones v. Clinton sexual harassment lawsuit by lying under oath and concealing evidence of his relationship with a young White House intern and federal employee, Monica Lewinsky. After a federal criminal investigation of the President's actions began in January 1998, the President lied under oath to the grand jury and obstructed justice during the grand jury investigation. There also is substantial and credible information that the President's actions with respect to Monica Lewinsky constitute an abuse of authority inconsistent with the President's constitutional duty to faithfully execute the laws.

There is substantial and credible information supporting the following eleven possible grounds for impeachment:

1. President Clinton lied under oath in his civil case when he denied a sexual affair, a sexual relationship, or sexual relations with Monica Lewinsky.

2. President Clinton lied under oath to the grand jury about his sexual relationship with Ms. Lewinsky.

3. In his civil deposition, to support his false statement about the sexual relationship, President Clinton also lied under oath about being alone with Ms. Lewinsky and about the many gifts exchanged between Ms. Lewinsky and him.

4. President Clinton lied under oath in his civil deposition about his discussions with Ms. Lewinsky concerning her involvement in the Jones case.

5. During the Jones case, the President obstructed justice and had an understanding with Ms. Lewinsky to jointly conceal the truth about their relationship by concealing gifts subpoenaed by Ms. Jones's attorneys.

6. During the Jones case, the President obstructed justice and had an understanding with Ms. Lewinsky to jointly conceal the truth of their relationship from the judicial process by a scheme that included the following means: (i) Both the President and Ms. Lewinsky understood that they would lie under oath in the Jones case about their sexual relationship; (ii) the President suggested to Ms. Lewinsky that she prepare an affidavit that, for the President's purposes, would memorialize her testimony under oath and could be used to prevent questioning of both of them about their relationship; (iii) Ms. Lewinsky signed and filed the false affidavit; (iv) the President used Ms. Lewinsky's false affidavit at his deposition in an attempt to head off questions about Ms. Lewinsky; and (v) when that failed, the President lied under oath at his civil deposition about the relationship with Ms. Lewinsky.

7. President Clinton endeavored to obstruct justice by helping Ms. Lewinsky obtain a job in New York at a time when she would have been a witness harmful to him were she to tell the truth in the Jones case.

8. President Clinton lied under oath in his civil deposition about

his discussions with Vernon Jordan concerning Ms. Lewinsky's involvement in the Jones case.

9. The President improperly tampered with a potential witness by attempting to corruptly influence the testimony of his personal secretary, Betty Currie, in the days after his civil deposition.

10. President Clinton endeavored to obstruct justice during the grand jury investigation by refusing to testify for seven months and lying to senior White House aides with knowledge that they would relay the President's false statements to the grand jury—and did thereby deceive, obstruct, and impede the grand jury.

11. President Clinton abused his constitutional authority by (i) lying to the public and the Congress in January 1998 about his relationship with Ms. Lewinsky; (ii) promising at that time to cooperate fully with the grand jury investigation; (iii) later refusing six invitations to testify voluntarily to the grand jury; (iv) invoking Executive Privilege; (v) lying to the grand jury in August 1998; and (vi) lying again to the public and Congress on August 17, 1998—all as part of an effort to hinder, impede, and deflect possible inquiry by the Congress of the United States.

The first two possible grounds for impeachment concern the President's lying under oath about the nature of his relationship with Ms. Lewinsky. The details associated with those grounds are, by their nature, explicit. The President's testimony unfortunately has rendered the details essential with respect to those two grounds, as will be explained in those grounds.

I. THERE IS SUBSTANTIAL AND CREDIBLE INFORMATION THAT PRESIDENT CLINTON LIED UNDER OATH AS A DEFENDANT IN JONES V. CLINTON REGARDING HIS SEXUAL RELATIONSHIP WITH MONICA LEWINSKY.

(1) He denied that he had a "sexual relationship" with Monica Lewinsky.

(2) He denied that he had a "sexual affair" with Monica Lewinsky.

(3) He denied that he had "sexual relations" with Monica Lewinsky.

(4) He denied that he engaged in or caused contact with the genitalia of "any person" with an intent to arouse or gratify (oral sex performed on him by Ms. Lewinsky).

(5) He denied that he made contact with Monica Lewinsky's breasts or genitalia with an intent to arouse or gratify.

On May 6, 1994, former Arkansas state employee Paula Corbin Jones filed a federal civil rights lawsuit against President Clinton claiming that he had sexually harassed her on May 8, 1991, by requesting her to perform oral sex on him in a suite at the Excelsior Hotel in Little Rock. Throughout the pretrial discovery process in Jones v. Clinton, United States District Judge Susan Webber Wright ruled, over the President's objections, that Ms. Jones's lawyers could seek various categories of information, including information about women who had worked as government employees under Governor or President Clinton and allegedly had sexual activity with him. Judge Wright's rulings followed the prevailing law in sexual harassment cases: The defendant's sexual relationships with others in the workplace, including consensual relationships, are a standard subject of inquiry during the discovery process. Judge Wright recognized the commonplace nature of her discovery rulings and stated that she was following a "meticulous standard of materiality" in allowing such questioning.

At a hearing on January 12, 1998, Judge Wright required Ms. Jones to list potential trial witnesses. Ms. Jones's list included several "Jane Does."[1] Ms. Jones's attorneys said they intended to call a Jane Doe named Monica Lewinsky as a witness to support Ms. Jones's claims. Under Ms. Jones's legal theory, women who had sexual relationships with the President received job benefits because of the sexual relationship, but women who resisted the President's sexual advances were denied such benefits.[2]

On January 17, 1998, Ms. Jones's lawyers deposed President

Clinton under oath with Judge Wright present and presiding over the deposition. Federal law requires a witness testifying under oath to provide truthful answers. The intentional failure to provide truthful answers is a crime punishable by imprisonment and fine.[3] At the outset of his deposition, the President took an oath administered by Judge Wright: "Do you swear or affirm . . . that the testimony you are about to give in the matter before the court is the truth, the whole truth, and nothing but the truth, so help you God?" The President replied: "I do."[4] At the beginning of their questioning, Ms. Jones's attorneys asked the President: "And your testimony is subject to the penalty of perjury; do you understand that, sir?" The President responded, "I do."[5]

Based on the witness list received in December 1997 (which included Ms. Lewinsky) and the January 12, 1998, hearing, the President and his attorneys were aware that Ms. Jones's attorneys likely would question the President at his deposition about Ms. Lewinsky and the other "Jane Does." In fact, the attorneys for Ms. Jones did ask numerous questions about "Jane Does," including Ms. Lewinsky.

There is substantial and credible information that President Clinton lied under oath in answering those questions.

A. Evidence that President Clinton Lied Under Oath During the Civil Case

1. President Clinton's Statements Under Oath About Monica Lewinsky

During pretrial discovery, Paula Jones's attorneys served the President with written interrogatories.[6] One stated in relevant part:

Please state the name, address, and telephone number of each and every [federal employee] with whom you had sexual relations when you [were] . . . President of the United States.[7]

The interrogatory did not define the term "sexual relations." Judge Wright ordered the President to answer the interrogatory, and on December 23, 1997, under penalty of perjury, President Clinton answered "None."[8]

At the January 17, 1998, deposition of the President, Ms. Jones's attorneys asked the President specific questions about possible sexual activity with Monica Lewinsky. The attorneys used various terms in their questions, including "sexual affair," "sexual relationship," and "sexual relations." The terms "sexual affair" and "sexual relationship" were not specially defined by Ms. Jones's attorneys. The term "sexual relations" was defined:

> For the purposes of this deposition, a person engages in "sexual relations" when the person knowingly engages in or causes . . . contact with the genitalia, anus, groin, breast, inner thigh, or buttocks of any person with an intent to arouse or gratify the sexual desire of any person. . . . "Contact" means intentional touching, either directly or through clothing.[9]

President Clinton answered a series of questions about Ms. Lewinsky, including:

Q: Did you have an extramarital sexual affair with Monica Lewinsky?

WJC: *No.*

Q: If she told someone that she had a sexual affair with you beginning in November of 1995, would that be a lie?

WJC: *It's certainly not the truth. It would not be the truth.*

Q: I think I used the term "sexual affair." And so the record is completely clear, have you ever had sexual relations with Monica Lewinsky, as that term is defined in Deposition Exhibit 1, as modified by the Court?

Mr. Bennett:[10]

I object because I don't know that he can remember—

Judge Wright:

Well, it's real short. He can—I will permit the question and you may show the witness definition number one.

WJC: *I have never had sexual relations with Monica Lewinsky. I've never had an affair with her.*[11]

President Clinton reiterated his denial under questioning by his own attorney:

Q: In paragraph eight of [Ms. Lewinsky's] affidavit, she says this, "I have never had a sexual relationship with the President, he did not propose that we have a sexual relationship, he did not offer me employment or other benefits in exchange for a sexual relationship, he did not deny me employment or other benefits for rejecting a sexual relationship." Is that a true and accurate statement as far as you know it?

WJC: *That is absolutely true.*[12]

2. MONICA LEWINSKY'S TESTIMONY

Monica Lewinsky testified under oath before the grand jury that, beginning in November 1995, when she was a 22-year-old White House intern, she had a lengthy relationship with the President that included substantial sexual activity. She testified in detail about the times, dates, and nature of ten sexual encounters that involved some form of genital contact. As explained in the Narrative section of this Referral, White House records corroborate Ms. Lewinsky's testimony in that the President was in the Oval Office area during the encounters. The records of White House entry and exit are incomplete for employees, but they do show her presence in the White House on eight of those occasions.[13]

The ten incidents are recounted here because they are necessary to assess whether the President lied under oath, both in his civil deposition, where he denied any sexual relationship at all, and in his grand jury testimony, where he acknowledged an "inappropriate intimate contact" but denied any sexual contact with Ms. Lewinsky's breasts or genitalia. When reading the following descriptions, the President's denials under oath should be kept in mind.

Unfortunately, the nature of the President's denials requires that the contrary evidence be set forth in detail. If the President, in his grand jury appearance, had admitted the sexual activity recounted by Ms. Lewinsky and conceded that he had lied under oath in his civil deposition, these particular descriptions would be superfluous. Indeed, we refrained from questioning Ms. Lewinsky under oath about particular details until after the President's August 17 testimony made that questioning necessary. But in view of (i) the President's denials, (ii) his continued contention that his civil deposition testimony was legally accurate under the terms and definitions employed, and (iii) his refusal to answer related questions, the detail is critical. The detail provides credibility and corroboration to Ms. Lewinsky's testimony. It also demonstrates with clarity that the President lied under oath both in his civil deposition and to the federal grand jury.[14] There is substantial and credible information that the President's lies about his relationship with Ms. Lewinsky were abundant and calculating.

(1) WEDNESDAY, NOVEMBER 15, 1995

Ms. Lewinsky testified that she had her first sexual contact with the President on the evening of Wednesday, November 15, 1995, while she was an intern at the White House. Two times that evening, the President invited Ms. Lewinsky to meet him near the Oval Office.[15] On the first occasion, the President took Ms. Lewinsky back into the Oval Office study, and they kissed.[16] On the second, she performed oral sex on the President in the hallway outside the Oval Office study.[17] During this encounter, the President directly touched and kissed Ms. Lewinsky's bare breasts.[18] In addition, the President put his hand down Ms. Lewinsky's pants and directly stimulated her genitalia (acts clearly within the definition of "sexual relations" used at the Jones deposition).[19]

(ii) Friday, November 17, 1995

Ms. Lewinsky testified that she met with the President again two days later, on Friday, November 17, 1995.[20] During that encounter, Ms. Lewinsky stated, she performed oral sex on the President in the private bathroom outside the Oval Office study.[21] The President initiated the oral sex by unzipping his pants and exposing his genitals. Ms. Lewinsky understood the President's actions to be a sign that he wanted her to perform oral sex on him.[22] During this encounter, the President also fondled Ms. Lewinsky's bare breasts with his hands and kissed her breasts.[23]

(iii) Sunday, December 31, 1995

Ms. Lewinsky testified that she met with the President on New Year's Eve, Sunday, December 31, 1995, after the President invited her to the Oval Office.[24] Once there, the President lifted Ms. Lewinsky's sweater, fondled her bare breasts with his hands, and kissed her breasts. She stated that she performed oral sex on the President in the hallway outside the Oval Office study.[25]

(iv) Sunday, January 7, 1996

Monica Lewinsky testified that she performed oral sex on the President in the bathroom outside the Oval Office study during the late afternoon on Sunday, January 7, 1996.[26] The President arranged this encounter by calling Ms. Lewinsky at home and inviting her to visit.[27] On that occasion, the President and Ms. Lewinsky went into the bathroom, where he fondled her bare breasts with his hands and mouth. During this encounter, the President stated that he wanted to perform oral sex on Ms. Lewinsky, but she stopped him for a physical reason.[28]

(v) Sunday, January 21, 1996

Ms. Lewinsky testified that she and the President had a sexual encounter on the afternoon of Sunday, January 21, 1996, after he invited her to the Oval Office.[29] The President lifted Ms. Lewinsky's top and fondled her bare breasts.[30] The President unzipped his pants and exposed his genitals, and she performed oral sex on him in the hallway outside the Oval Office study.[31]

(VI) SUNDAY, FEBRUARY 4, 1996

Ms. Lewinsky testified that she and the President had sexual contact in the Oval Office study and in the adjacent hallway on the afternoon of Sunday, February 4, 1996.[32] That day, the President had called Ms. Lewinsky.[33] During their encounter, the President partially removed Ms. Lewinsky's dress and bra and touched her bare breasts with his mouth and hands. He also directly touched her genitalia.[34] Ms. Lewinsky performed oral sex on the President.[35]

(VII) SUNDAY, MARCH 31, 1996

Ms. Lewinsky testified that she and the President had sexual contact in the hallway outside the Oval Office study during the late afternoon of Sunday, March 31, 1996.[36] The President arranged this encounter by calling Ms. Lewinsky and inviting her to the Oval Office. During this encounter, Ms. Lewinsky did not perform oral sex on the President. The President fondled Ms. Lewinsky's bare breasts with his hands and mouth and fondled her genitalia directly by pulling her underwear out of the way. In addition, the President inserted a cigar into Ms. Lewinsky's vagina.[37]

(VIII) SUNDAY, APRIL 7, 1996

Ms. Lewinsky testified that she and the President had sexual contact on Easter Sunday, April 7, 1996, in the hallway outside the Oval Office study and in the study itself.[38] On that occasion, the President touched Ms. Lewinsky's breasts, both through her clothing and directly. After the President unzipped his pants, Ms. Lewinsky also performed oral sex on him.[39]

This was their last in-person sexual encounter for over nine months.

(IX) FRIDAY, FEBRUARY 28, 1997

Ms. Lewinsky testified that her next sexual encounter with the President occurred on Friday, February 28, 1997, in the early evening.[40] The President initiated this encounter by having his secretary Betty Currie call Ms. Lewinsky to invite her to the White House for a radio address. After the address, Ms. Lewinsky and the President kissed by the bathroom. The President unbuttoned her dress and fondled her breasts, first with her bra on and then directly. He touched her genitalia through her clothes, but not directly, on this occasion. Ms. Lewinsky performed oral sex on him.[41] On this day, Ms. Lewinsky was wearing a blue dress that forensic tests have conclusively shown was stained with the President's semen.[42]

(X) SATURDAY, MARCH 29, 1997

Ms. Lewinsky testified that she and the President had sexual contact on the afternoon of March 29, 1997, in the Oval Office study.[43] On that occasion, the President unbuttoned Ms. Lewinsky's blouse and touched her breasts through her bra, but not directly. He also put his hands inside Ms. Lewinsky's pants and stimulated her genitalia.[44] Ms. Lewinsky performed oral sex on him, and they also had brief, direct genital-to-genital contact.[45]

(XI) TWO SUBSEQUENT MEETINGS

Ms. Lewinsky testified that she met with President Clinton in the Oval Office study on the morning of Saturday, August 16, 1997. They kissed, and Ms. Lewinsky touched the President's genitals through his clothing, but he rebuffed her efforts to perform oral sex. No other sexual acts occurred during this encounter.[46]

On Sunday, December 28, 1997, three weeks before the President's civil deposition in the Jones case, the President and Ms. Lewinsky met in the Oval Office. In addition to discussing a number of issues that are analyzed below, they engaged in "passionate" kissing—she said, "I don't call it a brief kiss." No other sexual contact occurred.[47]

3. PHONE SEX

Ms. Lewinsky testified that she and the President engaged in "phone sex" approximately fifteen times. The President initiated each phone sex encounter by telephoning Ms. Lewinsky.[48]

4. PHYSICAL EVIDENCE

Ms. Lewinsky produced to OIC investigators a dress she wore during the encounter on February 28, 1997, which she believed might be stained with the President's semen. At the request of the OIC, the FBI Laboratory examined the dress and found semen stains.[49] At that point, the OIC requested a DNA sample from the President. On August 3, 1998, two weeks before the President's grand jury testimony, a White House physician drew blood from the President in the presence of a senior OIC attorney and a FBI special agent.[50] Through the most sensitive DNA testing, RFLP testing, the FBI Laboratory determined conclusively that the semen on Ms. Lewinsky's dress was, in fact, the President's.[51] The chance that the semen is not the President's is one in 7.87 trillion.[52]

5. TESTIMONY OF MS. LEWINSKY'S FRIENDS, FAMILY MEMBERS, AND COUNSELORS

During her relationship with the President, Monica Lewinsky spoke contemporaneously to several friends, family members, and counselors about the relationship. Their testimony corroborates many of the details of the sexual activity provided by Ms. Lewinsky to the OIC.

(1) CATHERINE ALLDAY DAVIS

Catherine Allday Davis, a college friend of Monica Lewinsky's,[53] testified that Ms. Lewinsky told her in late 1995 or early 1996 about Ms. Lewinsky's sexual relationship with the President.[54] According to Ms. Davis, Ms. Lewinsky told her that the relationship included mutual kissing and hugging, as well as oral sex performed by Ms. Lewinsky on the President. She also stated that the President touched Monica "on her breasts and on her vagina."[55] Ms. Davis also described the cigar incident discussed above.[56] Ms. Davis added that Monica said that she had "phone sex" with the President five to ten times in 1996 or 1997.[57]

(ii) Neysa Erbland

Neysa Erbland, a high school friend of Ms. Lewinsky's,[58] testified that Ms. Lewinsky told her in 1995 that she was having an affair with President Clinton.[59] According to Ms. Erbland, Ms. Lewinsky said that the sexual relationship began when Ms. Lewinsky was an intern.[60] Ms. Lewinsky told Ms. Erbland that the sexual contact included oral sex, kissing, and fondling.[61] On occasion, as Ms. Erbland described it, the President put his face in Ms. Lewinsky's bare chest.[62] Ms. Erbland also said that Ms. Lewinsky described the cigar incident discussed above.[63] Ms. Erbland also understood from Ms. Lewinsky that she and the President engaged in phone sex, normally after midnight.[64]

(iii) Natalie Rose Ungvari

Ms. Lewinsky told another high school friend, Natalie Rose Ungvari,[65] of her sexual relationship with the President. Ms. Lewinsky first informed Ms. Ungvari of the sexual relationship on November 23, 1995. Ms. Ungvari specifically remembers the date because it was her birthday.[66] Ms. Ungvari recalled that Ms. Lewinsky said that she performed oral sex on the President and that he fondled her breasts.[67] Ms. Lewinsky told Ms. Ungvari that the President sometimes telephoned Ms. Lewinsky late at night and would ask her to engage in phone sex.[68]

(iv) Ashley Raines

Ashley Raines, a friend of Ms. Lewinsky who worked in the White House Office of Policy Development Operations,[69] testified that Ms. Lewinsky described the sexual relationship with the President. Ms. Raines testified that Ms. Lewinsky told her that the relationship began around the time of the government furlough in late 1995.[70] Ms. Raines understood that the President and Ms. Lewinsky engaged in kissing and oral sex, usually in the President's study.[71] Ms. Lewinsky also told Ms. Raines that she and the President had engaged in phone sex on several occasions.[72]

(V) ANDREW BLEILER

In late 1995, Monica Lewinsky told Andrew Bleiler, a former boyfriend, that she was having an affair with a high official at the White House.[73] According to Mr. Bleiler, Ms. Lewinsky said that the relationship did not include sexual intercourse, but did include oral sex. She also told Mr. Bleiler about the cigar incident discussed above, and sexual activity in which the man touched Ms. Lewinsky's genitals and caused her to have an orgasm.[74]

(VI) DR. IRENE KASSORLA

Dr. Irene Kassorla counseled Ms. Lewinsky from 1992 through 1997.[75] Ms. Lewinsky told her of the sexual relationship with the President. Ms. Lewinsky said she performed oral sex on the President in a room adjacent to the Oval Office, that the President touched Ms. Lewinsky causing her to have orgasms, and that they engaged in fondling and touching of one another.[76] The President was in charge of scheduling their sexual encounters and "became Lewinsky's life."[77]

(VII) LINDA TRIPP

When she worked at the Pentagon, Ms. Lewinsky told a co-worker, Linda Tripp, that she had a sexual relationship with President Clinton.[78] Ms. Tripp stated that Ms. Lewinsky first told her about the relationship in September or October 1996. Ms. Lewinsky told Ms. Tripp that the first sexual encounter with the President had occurred on November 15, 1995, when Ms. Lewinsky performed oral sex on him. Ms. Lewinsky told Ms. Tripp that, during the course of this sexual relationship, she performed oral sex on the President, the President fondled Ms. Lewinsky's breasts, the President touched Ms. Lewinsky's genitalia, and they engaged in phone sex.[79]

(VIII) DEBRA FINERMAN

Ms. Lewinsky's aunt, Debra Finerman, testified that Monica told her about her sexual relationship with President Clinton.[80] Ms. Finerman testified that Ms. Lewinsky described a particular sexual encounter with the President.[81] Ms. Finerman otherwise did not ask and was not told the specifics of the sexual activity between the President and Ms. Lewinsky.[82]

(IX) DALE YOUNG

Dale Young, a family friend, testified that Ms. Lewinsky told her that she had engaged in oral sex with President Clinton.[83]

(X) KATHLEEN ESTEP

Kathleen Estep, a counselor for Ms. Lewinsky,[84] met with Ms. Lewinsky on three occasions in November 1996.[85] Based on her limited interaction with Ms. Lewinsky, Ms. Estep stated that she considered Ms. Lewinsky to be credible.[86] During their second session, Ms. Lewinsky told Ms. Estep about her sexual relationship with President Clinton.[87] Ms. Lewinsky told Ms. Estep that the physical part of the relationship involved kissing, Ms. Lewinsky performing oral sex on the President, and the President fondling her breasts.[88]

6. SUMMARY

The detailed testimony of Ms. Lewinsky, her corroborating prior consistent statements to her friends, family members, and counselors, and the evidence of the President's semen on Ms. Lewinsky's dress establish that Ms. Lewinsky and the President engaged in substantial sexual activity between November 15, 1995, and December 28, 1997.[89]

The President, however, testified under oath in the civil case—both in his deposition and in a written answer to an interrogatory—that he did not have a "sexual relationship" or a "sexual affair" or "sexual relations" with Ms. Lewinsky. In addition, he denied engaging in activity covered by a more specific definition of "sexual relations" used at the deposition.[90]

In his civil case, the President made five different false statements related to the sexual relationship. For four of the five statements, the President asserts a semantic defense: The President argues that the terms used in the Jones deposition to cover sexual activity did not cover the sexual activity in which he engaged with Ms. Lewinsky. For his other false statements, the President's response is factual—namely, he disputes Ms. Lewinsky's account that he ever touched her breasts or genitalia during sexual activity.[91]

The President's denials—semantic and factual—do not withstand scrutiny.

First, in his civil deposition, the President denied a "sexual affair" with Ms. Lewinsky (the term was not defined). The President's response to lying under oath on this point rests on his definition of "sexual affair"—namely, that it requires sexual intercourse, no matter how extensive the sexual activities might otherwise be. According to the President, a man could regularly engage in oral sex and fondling of breasts and genitals with a woman and yet not have a "sexual affair" with her.

Second, in his civil deposition, the President also denied a "sexual relationship" with Ms. Lewinsky (the term was not defined). The President's response to lying under oath on this point similarly rests on his definition of "sexual relationship"—namely, that it requires sexual intercourse. Once again, under the President's theory, a man could regularly engage in oral sex and fondling of breasts and genitals with a woman, yet not have a "sexual relationship" with her.

The President's claim as to his interpretation of "sexual relationship" is belied by the fact that the President's own lawyer—earlier at that same deposition—equated the term "sexual relationship" with "sex of any kind in any manner, shape or form." The President's lawyer offered that interpretation when requesting Judge Wright to limit the questioning to prevent further inquiries with respect to Monica Lewinsky. As the videotape of the deposition reveals, the President was present and apparently looking in the direction of his attorney when his attorney offered that statement.[92] The President gave no indication that he disagreed with his attorney's straightforward interpretation that the term "sexual relationship" means "sex of any kind in any manner, shape, or form." Nor did the President thereafter take any steps to correct the attorney's statement.

Third, in an answer to an interrogatory submitted before his deposition, the President denied having "sexual relations" with Ms. Lewinsky (the term was not defined). Yet again, the President's apparent rejoinder to lying under oath on this point rests on his definition of "sexual relations"—that it, too, requires sexual intercourse. According to President Clinton, oral sex does not constitute sexual relations.

Fourth, in his civil deposition, the President denied committing any acts that fell within the specific definition of "sexual relations" that was in effect for purposes of that deposition. Under that specific definition, sexual relations occurs "when the person knowingly engages in or causes contact with the genitalia, anus, groin, breast, inner thigh, or buttocks of any person with an intent to arouse or gratify the sexual desire of any person."[93] Thus, the President denied engaging in or causing contact with the genitalia, breasts, or anus of "any person" with an intent to arouse or gratify the sexual desire of "any person."

Concerning oral sex, the President's sole answer to the charge that he lied under oath at the deposition focused on his interpretation of "any person" in the definition. Ms. Lewinsky testified that she performed oral sex on the President on nine occasions. The President said that by *receiving* oral sex, he would not "engage in" or "cause"[94] contact with the genitalia, anus, groin, breast, inner thigh, or buttocks of "any person" because "any person" really means "any *other* person." The President further testified before the grand jury: "[I]f the deponent is the person who has oral sex performed on him, then the contact is with—*not with anything on that list, but with the lips of another person.*"[95]

The President's linguistic parsing is unreasonable. Under the President's interpretation (which he says he followed at his deposition), in an oral sex encounter, one person is engaged in sexual relations, but the other person is not engaged in sexual relations.[96]

Even assuming that the definitional language can be manipulated to exclude the deponent's receipt of oral sex, the President is still left with the difficulty that reasonable persons would not have understood it that way. And in context, the President's semantics become even weaker: The *Jones* suit rested on the allegation that the President sought to have Ms. Jones perform oral sex on him. Yet the President now claims that the expansive definition devised for deposition questioning should be interpreted to exclude that very act.

Fifth, by denying at his civil deposition that he had engaged in any acts falling within the specific definition of "sexual relations," the President denied engaging in or causing contact with the breasts or genitalia of Ms. Lewinsky with an intent to arouse or gratify one's sexual desire. In contrast to his explanations of the four preceding false statements under oath, the President's defense to lying under oath in this instance is purely factual.

As discussed above, Ms. Lewinsky testified credibly that the President touched and kissed her bare breasts on nine occasions, and that he stimulated her genitals on four occasions.[97] She also testified about a cigar incident, which is discussed above. In addition, a deleted computer file from Ms. Lewinsky's home computer contained an apparent draft letter to the President that explicitly referred to an incident in which the President's "mouth [was] on [her] breast" and implicitly referred to direct contact with her genitalia.[98] This draft letter further corroborates Ms. Lewinsky's testimony.

Ms. Lewinsky's prior consistent statements to various friends, family members, and counselors—made when the relationship was ongoing—likewise corroborate her testimony on the nature of the President's touching of her body. Ms. Lewinsky had no apparent motive to lie to her friends, family members, and counselors. Ms. Lewinsky especially had no reason to lie to Dr. Kassorla and Ms. Estep, to whom she related the facts in the course of a professional relationship. And Ms. Lewinsky's statements to some that she did not have intercourse with the President, even though she wanted to do so, enhances the credibility of her statements. Moreover, the precise nature of the sexual activity only became relevant after the President interposed his semantic defense regarding oral sex on August 17, 1998.

By contrast, the President's testimony strains credulity. His apparent "hands-off" scenario—in which he would have received oral sex on nine occasions from Ms. Lewinsky but never made direct contact with Ms. Lewinsky's breasts or genitalia—is not credible. The President's claim seems to be that he maintained a hands-off policy in ongoing sexual encounters with Ms. Lewinsky, which coincidentally happened to permit him to truthfully deny "sexual relations" with her at a deposition occurring a few years in the future. As Ms. Lewinsky noted, it suggests some kind of "service contract—that all I did was perform oral sex on him and that that's all this relationship was."[99]

The President also had strong personal, political, and legal motives to lie in the Jones deposition: He did not want to admit that he had committed extramarital sex acts with a young intern in the Oval Office area of the White House. Such an admission could support Ms. Jones's theory of liability and would embarrass him. Indeed, the President admitted that during the relationship he did what he could to keep the relationship secret, including "misleading" members of his family and Cabinet.[100] The President testified, moreover, that he "hoped that this relationship would never become public."[101]

At the time of his civil deposition, the President also could have presumed that he could lie under oath without risk because—as he knew—Ms. Lewinsky had already filed a false affidavit denying a sexual relationship with the President. Indeed, they had an understanding that each would lie under oath (explained more fully in Ground VI below). So the President might have expected that he could lie without consequence on the belief that no one could ever successfully challenge his denial of a sexual relationship with her.

In sum, based on all of the evidence and considering the President's various responses, there is substantial and credible information that the President lied under oath in his civil deposition and his interrogatory answer in denying a sexual relationship, a sexual affair, or sexual relations with Ms. Lewinsky.[102]

II. THERE IS SUBSTANTIAL AND CREDIBLE INFORMATION THAT PRESIDENT CLINTON LIED UNDER OATH TO THE GRAND JURY ABOUT HIS SEXUAL RELATIONSHIP WITH MONICA LEWINSKY.

A. BACKGROUND

In January 1998, upon application of the Attorney General, the Special Division of the United States Court of Appeals for the District of Columbia Circuit expanded the OIC's jurisdiction to investigate, among other matters, whether Monica Lewinsky and the President obstructed justice in the Jones case. The criminal investigation was triggered by specific and credible evidence that Monica Lewinsky denied her relationship with President Clinton in a false affidavit in the Jones case, that she had spoken to the President and Vernon Jordan about her testimony, and that she may have been influenced to lie by the President through the assistance of Vernon Jordan and others in finding her a job. After the President, in his January 17 deposition, denied any sexual relationship with Monica Lewinsky and otherwise minimized his overall relationship with her, the President's testimony became an additional subject of the OIC investigation.

The threshold factual question was whether the President and Monica Lewinsky in fact had a sexual relationship. If they did, the President would have committed perjury in his civil deposition and interrogatory answer: The President, as noted in Ground I above, had denied a sexual affair, sexual relationship, or sexual relations with Monica Lewinsky, including any direct contact with her breasts or genitalia. The answer to the preliminary factual question also could alter the interpretation of several possibly obstructionist acts by the President—the employment assistance for Ms. Lewinsky, the concealment of gifts he had given to Ms. Lewinsky, the discussion between the President and Ms. Lewinsky of her testimony or affidavit, the President's post-deposition communications with Betty Currie, and the President's emphatic denials of a relationship to his aides who later testified before the grand jury.

During the investigation, the OIC gathered a substantial body of information that established that the President and Monica Lewinsky did, in fact, have a sexual relationship. That information is outlined in Ground I above. In particular, the information includes: (i) the detailed and credible testimony of Ms. Lewinsky regarding the 10 sexual encounters; (ii) the President's semen stain on Ms. Lewinsky's dress; and (iii) the testimony of friends, family members, and counselors to whom she made near-contemporaneous statements about the relationship.

All of this evidence pointed to a single conclusion—that she and the President did have a sexual relationship.

B. THE PRESIDENT'S GRAND JURY TESTIMONY

The President was largely aware of that extensive body of evidence before he testified to the grand jury on August 17, 1998. Not only did the President know that Ms. Lewinsky had reached an immunity agreement with this Office in exchange for her truthful testimony, but the President knew from public reports and his own knowledge that his semen might be on one of Ms. Lewinsky's dresses. The OIC had asked him for a blood sample on August 3, 1998 (two weeks before his grand jury testimony) and assured his counsel that there was a substantial predicate for the request, which reasonably implied that there was semen on the dress.

As a result, the President had three apparent choices in his testimony to the grand jury. First, the President could adhere to his previous testimony in his civil case, as well as in his public statements, and deny any sexual relationship. But he knew (or at least, had reason to know) that the contrary evidence was overwhelming, particularly if his semen were in fact on Ms. Lewinsky's dress. Second, the President could admit a sexual relationship, which would cause him also to simultaneously admit that he lied under oath in the Jones case. Third, the President could invoke his Fifth Amendment privilege against compelled self-incrimination.

Confronting those three options, the President attempted to avoid them altogether. The President admitted to an "inappropriate intimate" relationship, but he maintained that he had not committed perjury in the Jones case when he denied having a sexual relationship, sexual affair, or sexual relations with her.[103] The President contended that he had believed his various statements in the Jones case to be legally accurate.[104] He also testified that the inappropriate relationship began not in November 1995 when Ms. Lewinsky was an intern, as Ms. Lewinsky and other witnesses have testified, but in 1996.

During his grand jury testimony, the President was asked whether Monica Lewinsky performed oral sex on him and, if so, whether he had committed perjury in his civil deposition by denying a sexual relationship, sexual affair, or sexual relations with her. The President refused to say whether he had oral sex. Instead, the President said (i) that the undefined terms "sexual affair," "sexual relationship," and "sexual relations" necessarily require sexual intercourse, (ii) that he had not engaged in intercourse with Ms. Lewinsky, and (iii) that he therefore had not committed perjury in denying a sexual relationship, sexual affair, or sexual relations.[105]

A more specific definition of "sexual relations" had also been used at the civil deposition. As to that definition, the President said to the grand jury that he does not and did not believe oral sex was covered.

> Q: [I]s oral sex performed on you within that definition as you understood it, the definition in the Jones—
>
> A: As I understood it, it was not; no.[106]

The President thus contended that he had not committed perjury on that question in the Jones deposition—even assuming that Monica Lewinsky performed oral sex on him.

There still was the question of his contact with Ms. Lewinsky's breasts and genitalia, which the President conceded would fall within the Jones definition of sexual relations. The President denied that he had engaged in such activity and said, in effect, that Monica Lewinsky was lying:

> Q: The question is, if Monica Lewinsky says that while you were in the Oval Office area you touched her breasts would she by lying?

A: That is not my recollection. My recollection is that I did not have sexual relations with Ms. Lewinsky and I'm staying on my former statement about that. . . . My, my statement is that I did not have sexual relations as defined by that.

Q: If she says that you kissed her breasts, would she be lying?

A: I'm going to revert to my former statement [that is, the prepared statement denying "sexual relations"].

Q: Okay. If Monica Lewinsky says that while you were in the Oval Office area you touched her genitalia, would she be lying? And that calls for a yes, no, or reverting to your former statement.

A: I will revert to my former statement on that.[107]

The President elaborated that he considered kissing or touching breasts or genitalia during sexual activity to be covered by the Jones definition, but he denied that he had ever engaged in such conduct with Ms. Lewinsky:

Q: So touching, in your view then and now—the person being deposed touching or kissing the breast of another person would fall within the definition?

A: That's correct, sir.

Q: And you testified that you didn't have sexual relations with Monica Lewinsky in the Jones deposition, under that definition, correct?

A: That's correct, sir.

Q: If the person being deposed touched the genitalia of another person, would that be—and with the intent to arouse the sexual desire, arouse or gratify, as defined in definition[1], would that be, under your understanding then and now—

A: Yes, sir.

Q:—sexual relations.

A: Yes, sir.

Q: Yes it would?

A: Yes it would. If you had a direct contact with any of these places in the body, if you had direct contact with intent to arouse or gratify, that would fall within the definition.

Q: So you didn't do any of those three things—

A: You—

Q:—with Monica Lewinsky.

A: You are free to infer that my testimony is that I did not have sexual relations, as I understood this term to be defined.

Q: Including touching her breast, kissing her breast, touching her genitalia?

A: That's correct.[108]

C. SUMMARY

In the foregoing testimony to the grand jury, the President lied under oath three times.

1. The President testified that he believed oral sex was not covered by any of the terms and definitions for sexual activity used at the Jones deposition. That testimony is not credible: At the Jones deposition, the President could not have believed that he was telling "the truth, the whole truth, and nothing but the truth" in denying a sexual relationship, sexual relations, or a sexual affair with Monica Lewinsky.

2. In all events, even putting aside his definitional defense, the President made a second false statement to the grand jury. The President's grand jury testimony contradicts Ms. Lewinsky's grand jury testimony on the question whether the President touched Ms. Lewinsky's breasts or genitalia during their sexual activity. There

can be no contention that one of them has a lack of memory or is mistaken. On this issue, either Monica Lewinsky lied to the grand jury, or President Clinton lied to the grand jury. Under any rational view of the evidence, the President lied to the grand jury.

First, Ms. Lewinsky's testimony about these encounters is detailed and specific. She described with precision nine incidents of sexual activity in which the President touched and kissed her breasts and four incidents involving contacts with her genitalia.

Second, Ms. Lewinsky has stated repeatedly that she does not want to hurt the President by her testimony.[109] Thus, if she had exaggerated in her many prior statements, she presumably would have said as much, rather than adhering to those statements. She has confirmed those details, however, even though it clearly has been painful for her to testify to the details of her relationship with the President.

Third, the testimony of many of her friends, family members, and counselors corroborate her testimony in important detail. Many testified that Ms. Lewinsky had told them that the President had touched her breasts and genitalia during sexual activity. These statements were made well before the President's grand jury testimony rendered these precise details important. Ms. Lewinsky had no motive to lie to these individuals (and obviously not to counselors). Indeed, she pointed out to many of them that she was upset that sexual intercourse had not occurred, an unlikely admission if she were exaggerating the sexual aspects of their relationship.

Fourth, a computer file obtained from Ms. Lewinsky's home computer contained a draft letter that referred in one place to their sexual relationship. The draft explicitly refers to "watching your mouth on my breast" and implicitly refers to direct contact with Ms. Lewinsky's genitalia.[110] This draft letter further corroborates Ms. Lewinsky's testimony and indicates that the President's grand jury testimony is false.

Fifth, as noted above, the President's "hands-off" scenario—in which he would have received oral sex on nine occasions from Ms. Lewinsky but never made direct contact with Ms. Lewinsky's breasts or genitalia—is implausible. As Ms. Lewinsky herself testified, it suggests that she and the President had some kind of "service contract—that all I did was perform oral sex on him and that that's all this relationship was."[111] But as the above descriptions and the Narrative explain, the nature of the relationship, including the sexual relationship, was far more than that.

Sixth, in the grand jury, the President had a motive to lie by denying he had fondled Ms. Lewinsky in intimate ways. The President clearly sought to deny any acts that would show that he committed perjury in his civil case (implying that the President understood how seriously the public and the courts would view perjury in a civil case). To do that, the President had to deny touching Ms. Lewinsky's breasts or genitalia—no matter how implausible his testimony to that effect might be.

Seventh, the President refused to answer specific questions before the grand jury about what activity he did engage in (as opposed to what activity he did not engage in)—even though at the Jones deposition only seven months before, his attorney stated that he was willing to answer specific questions when there was a sufficient factual predicate.[112] The President's failure in the grand jury to answer specific follow-up questions suggests that he could not supply responses in a consistent or credible manner.

3. Finally, the President made a third false statement to the grand jury about his sexual relationship with Monica Lewinsky. He contended that the intimate contact did not begin until 1996. Ms. Lewinsky has testified that it began November 15, 1995, during the government shutdown—testimony corroborated by statements she made to friends at the time.[113] A White House photograph of the evening shows the President and Ms. Lewinsky eating pizza.[114] White House records show that Ms. Lewinsky did not depart the White House until 12:18 a.m. and show that the President was in the Oval Office area until 12:35 a.m.[115]

Ms. Lewinsky was still an intern when she says the President began receiving oral sex from her, whereas she was a full-time employee by the time that the President admits they began an "inappropriate intimate" relationship. The motive for the President to make a false statement about the date on which the sexual relationship started appears to have been that the President was unwilling to admit sexual activity with a young 22-year-old White House intern in the Oval Office area. Indeed, Ms. Lewinsky testified that, at that first encounter, the President tugged at her intern pass. He said that "this" may be a problem; Ms. Lewinsky interpreted that statement to reflect his awareness that there would be a problem with her obtaining access to the West Wing.[116]

For all these reasons, there is substantial and credible information that the President lied to the grand jury about his sexual relationship with Monica Lewinsky.[117]

III. THERE IS SUBSTANTIAL AND CREDIBLE INFORMATION THAT PRESIDENT CLINTON LIED UNDER OATH DURING HIS CIVIL DEPOSITION WHEN HE STATED THAT HE COULD NOT RECALL BEING ALONE WITH MONICA LEWINSKY AND WHEN HE MINIMIZED THE NUMBER OF GIFTS THEY HAD EXCHANGED.

The President testified to the grand jury and stated to the Nation on August 17 that his testimony in his civil deposition had been "legally accurate." Even apart from his answers about the sexual relationship, the President's deposition testimony was inaccurate on several other points.

During President Clinton's deposition in the Jones case, Ms. Jones's attorneys asked the President many detailed questions about the nature of his relationship with Ms. Lewinsky, apart from whether the relationship was sexual. The questions included: (i) whether the President had been alone with Ms. Lewinsky in the White House and, if so, how many times; and (ii) whether he and Ms. Lewinsky exchanged gifts.[118] Both issues were important in determining the nature of the relationship.[119]

There is substantial and credible information that the President lied under oath about those subjects.

A. THERE IS SUBSTANTIAL AND CREDIBLE INFORMATION THAT PRESIDENT CLINTON LIED UNDER OATH WHEN HE TESTIFIED THAT HE COULD NOT SPECIFICALLY RECALL INSTANCES IN WHICH HE WAS ALONE WITH MONICA LEWINSKY.

1. THE PRESIDENT'S CIVIL DEPOSITION TESTIMONY

President Clinton was asked at his deposition whether he had ever been alone with Ms. Lewinsky. He testified as follows:

> Q: . . . At any time were you and Monica Lewinsky together alone in the Oval Office?
>
> [videotape shows approximately five-second pause before answer]
>
> WJC: I don't recall, but as I said, when she worked at the legislative affairs office, they always had somebody there on the weekends. I typically worked some on the weekends. Sometimes they'd bring me things on the weekends. She—it seems to me she brought things to me once or twice on the weekends. In that case, whatever time she would be in there, drop it off, exchange a few words and go, she was there. I don't have any specific recollections of what the issues were, what was going on, but when the Congress is there, we're working all the time, and typically I would do some work on one of the days of the weekends in the afternoon.
>
> Q: So I understand, your testimony is that it was possible, then, that you were alone with her, but you have no specific recollection of that ever happening?
>
> WJC: Yes, that's correct. It's possible that she, in, while she was working there, brought something to me and that at the time she brought it to me, she was the only person there. That's possible.[120]

The President also was asked whether he had ever been alone with Ms. Lewinsky in the hallway that runs from the Oval Office, past the study, to the dining room and kitchen area.[121]

> Q: At any time were you and Monica Lewinsky alone in the hallway between the Oval Office and this kitchen area?

> WJC: I don't believe so, unless we were walking back to the back dining room with the pizza.[122] I just, I don't remember. I don't believe we were alone in the hallway, no.[123]

The President was then asked about any times he may have been alone in any room with Ms. Lewinsky:

> Q: At any time have you and Monica Lewinsky ever been alone together in any room of the White House?

> WJC: I think I testified to that earlier. I think that there is a, it is—I have no specific recollection, but it seems to me that she was on duty on a couple of occasions working for the legislative affairs office and brought me some things to sign, something on the weekend. That's—I have a general memory of that.[124]

2. EVIDENCE THAT CONTRADICTS THE PRESIDENT'S TESTIMONY

In the seven months preceding the President's grand jury testimony on August 17, the OIC gathered substantial and credible information that the President lied under oath in his deposition statements about being alone with Monica Lewinsky.

First, Monica Lewinsky testified before the grand jury that she was alone with the President on numerous occasions[125] and in numerous areas, including the Oval Office,[126] Nancy Hernreich's office,[127] the President's private study,[128] the private bathroom across from the study,[129] and the hallway that leads from the Oval Office to the private dining room.[130] Ms. Lewinsky confirmed that she and the President were alone during sexual activity.[131]

Second, Betty Currie testified that President Clinton and Ms. Lewinsky were alone together in the Oval Office area a number of times.[132] She specifically remembered three occasions when the President and Ms. Lewinsky were alone together: February 28, 1997,[133] early December 1997,[134] and December 28, 1997.[135]

Third, six current or former members of the Secret Service testified that the President and Ms. Lewinsky were alone in the Oval Office area—Robert Ferguson,[136] Lewis Fox,[137] William Bordley,[138] Nelson Garabito,[139] Gary Byrne,[140] and John Muskett.[141]

Fourth, White House steward Glen Maes testified that on some weekend day after Christmas 1997,[142] the President came out of the Oval Office, saw Ms. Lewinsky with a gift, and escorted her into the Oval Office. Mr. Maes testified that the President and Ms. Lewinsky were alone together for approximately eight minutes, and then Ms. Lewinsky left.[143]

3. THE PRESIDENT'S GRAND JURY TESTIMONY

On August 17, 1998, the President testified to the grand jury and began his testimony by reading a statement admitting that he had been alone with Ms. Lewinsky:

When I was alone with Ms. Lewinsky on certain occasions in early 1996 and once in early 1997, I engaged in conduct that was wrong.[144]

The President acknowledged being alone with Ms. Lewinsky on multiple occasions, although he could not pinpoint the precise number.[145] Perhaps most important, the President admitted that he was alone with Ms. Lewinsky on December 28, 1997,[146] less than three weeks before his deposition in the Jones case. Indeed, he acknowledged that he would have to have been an "exhibitionist" for him not to have been alone with Ms. Lewinsky when they were having sexual encounters.[147]

4. SUMMARY

Substantial and credible information demonstrates that the President made three false statements under oath in his civil deposition regarding whether he had been alone with Ms. Lewinsky.

First, the President lied when he said "I don't recall" in response to the question whether he had ever been alone with Ms. Lewinsky. The President admitted to the grand jury that he had been alone with Ms. Lewinsky. It is not credible that he actually had no memory of this fact six months earlier, particularly given that they were obviously alone when engaging in sexual activity.

Second, when asked whether he had been alone with Ms. Lewinsky in the hallway in the Oval Office, the President answered, "I don't believe so, unless we were walking back to the back dining room with the pizza."[148] That statement, too, was false: Most of the sexual encounters between the President and Ms. Lewinsky occurred in that hallway (and on other occasions, they walked through the hallway to the dining room or study), and it is not credible that the President would have forgotten this fact.

Third, the President suggested at his civil deposition that he had no specific recollection of being alone with Ms. Lewinsky in the Oval Office, but had a general recollection that Ms. Lewinsky may have brought him "papers to sign" on certain occasions when she worked at the Legislative Affairs Office.[149] This statement was false. Ms. Lewinsky did not bring him papers for official purposes. To the contrary, "bringing papers" was one of the sham "cover stories" that the President and Ms. Lewinsky had originally crafted to conceal their sexual relationship.[150] The fact that the President resorted to a previously designed cover story when testifying under oath at the Jones deposition confirms that he made these false denials in a calculated manner with the intent and knowledge that they were false.

The President had an obvious motive to lie in this respect. He knew that it would appear odd for a President to have been alone with a female intern or low-level staffer on so many occasions. Such

an admission might persuade Judge Wright to deny any motion by
Ms. Lewinsky to quash her deposition subpoena. It also might
prompt Ms. Jones's attorneys to oppose efforts by Ms. Lewinsky
not to be deposed and to ask specific questions of Ms. Lewinsky
about the times she was alone with the President. It also might raise
questions publicly if and when the President's deposition became
public; at least parts of the deposition were likely to become public
at trial, if not at the summary judgment stage.

Because lying about their sexual relationship was insufficient to
avoid raising further questions, the President also lied about being
alone with Ms. Lewinsky—or at least feigned lack of memory as to
specific occurrences.[151]

B. THERE IS SUBSTANTIAL AND CREDIBLE INFORMATION THAT THE PRESIDENT LIED UNDER OATH IN HIS CIVIL DEPOSITION ABOUT GIFTS HE EXCHANGED WITH MONICA LEWINSKY.

During his civil deposition, the President also was asked several
questions about gifts he and Monica Lewinsky had exchanged. The
evidence demonstrates that he answered the questions falsely. As
with the questions about being alone, truthful answers to these
questions would have raised questions about the nature of the relationship. Such answers also would have been inconsistent with the
understanding of the President and Ms. Lewinsky that, in response
to her subpoena, Ms. Lewinsky would not produce all of the gifts
she had received from the President (an issue discussed more fully in
Ground V).

1. THE PRESIDENT'S CIVIL DEPOSITION TESTIMONY ABOUT HIS GIFTS TO MONICA LEWINSKY

During the President's deposition in the Jones case, Ms. Jones's
attorneys asked several questions about whether he had given gifts
to Monica Lewinsky.

Q: Well, have you ever given any gifts to Monica Lewinsky?

WJC: I don't recall. Do you know what they were?

Q: A hat pin?

WJC: I don't, I don't remember. But I certainly, I could have.

Q: A book about Walt Whitman?

WJC: I give—let me just say, I give people a lot of gifts, and when people are around I give a lot of things I have at the White House away, so I could have given her a gift, but I don't remember a specific gift.

Q: Do you remember giving her a gold broach?

WJC: No.[152]

2. EVIDENCE THAT CONTRADICTS THE PRESIDENT'S CIVIL DEPOSITION TESTIMONY

(i) Just three weeks before the President's deposition, on December 28, 1997, President Clinton gave Ms. Lewinsky a number of gifts, the largest number he had ever given her.[153] They included a large Rockettes blanket, a pin of the New York skyline, a marble-like bear's head from Vancouver, a pair of sunglasses, a small box of cherry chocolates, a canvas bag from the Black Dog, and a stuffed animal wearing a T-shirt from the Black Dog.[154] Ms. Lewinsky produced the Rockettes blanket, the bear's head, the Black Dog canvas bag, the Black Dog stuffed animal, and the sunglasses to the OIC on July 29, 1998.[155]

(ii) The evidence also demonstrates that the President gave Ms. Lewinsky a hat pin as a belated Christmas gift on February 28, 1997.[156] The President and Ms. Lewinsky discussed the hatpin on December 28, 1997, after Ms. Lewinsky received a subpoena calling for her to produce all gifts from the President, including any hat pins.[157] In her meeting with the President on December 28, 1997, according to Ms. Lewinsky, "I mentioned that I had been concerned about the hat pin being on the subpoena and he said that that had sort of concerned him also and asked me if I had told anyone that he had given me this hat pin and I said no."[158] The President's secretary Betty Currie also testified that she had previously discussed the hat pin with the President.[159]

(iii) Ms. Lewinsky testified that the President gave her additional gifts over the course of their relationship, such as a brooch,[160] the book Leaves of Grass by Walt Whitman,[161] an Annie Lennox compact disk,[162] and a cigar.[163]

3. PRESIDENT'S CIVIL DEPOSITION TESTIMONY ABOUT GIFTS FROM MONICA LEWINSKY TO THE PRESIDENT

When asked at his civil deposition in the Jones case whether Monica Lewinsky had ever given him gifts, President Clinton testified as follows:

> Q: Has Monica Lewinsky ever given you any gifts?
>
> WJC: Once or twice. I think she's given me a book or two.
>
> Q: Did she give you a silver cigar box?
>
> WJC: No.
>
> Q: Did she give you a tie?
>
> WJC: Yes, she has given me a tie before. I believe that's right. Now, as I said, let me remind you, normally when I get these ties, I get ties, you know, together, and then they're given to me later, but I believe that she has given me a tie.[164]

4. EVIDENCE THAT CONTRADICTS THE PRESIDENT'S TESTIMONY

(I) MONICA LEWINSKY'S TESTIMONY

The evidence reveals that Ms. Lewinsky gave the President approximately 38 gifts; she says she almost always brought a gift or two when she visited.[165]

a. Ms. Lewinsky testified before the grand jury that she gave the President six neckties.[166]

b. Ms. Lewinsky testified that she gave the President a pair of sunglasses on approximately October 22, 1997.[167] The President's attorney, David E. Kendall, stated in a letter on March 16, 1998: "We believe that Ms. Lewinsky might have given the President a few additional items, such as ties and a pair of sunglasses, but we have not been able to locate these items."[168]

c. On November 13, 1997, Ms. Lewinsky gave the President an antique paperweight that depicted the White House.[169] Ms. Lewinsky testified that on December 6, 1997, and possibly again on December 28, 1997, she saw this paperweight in the dining room, where the President keeps many items of political memorabilia.[170] The President turned over the paperweight to the OIC in response to a second subpoena calling for it.[171]

d. Ms. Lewinsky gave the President at least seven books:

- The Presidents of the United States, on January 4, 1998;[172]

- Our Patriotic President: His Life in Pictures, Anecdotes, Sayings, Principles and Biography,[173] on December 6, 1997;[174]

- an antique book on Peter the Great, on August 16, 1997;[175]

- The Notebook, on August 16, 1997;[176]

- Oy Vey, in early 1997;[177]

- a small golf book, in early 1997;[178] and

- her personal copy of Vox, a novel about phone sex, on March 29, 1997.[179]

e. Ms. Lewinsky gave the President an antique cigar holder, on December 6, 1997.[180]

f. Ms. Lewinsky testified that she gave the President a number of additional gifts.[181]

5. GRAND JURY TESTIMONY OF THE PRESIDENT AND MS. CURRIE

When he testified to the grand jury, President Clinton acknowledged giving Monica Lewinsky several gifts, stating that "it was a right thing to do to give her gifts back."[182] He acknowledged giving her gifts on December 28, 1997,[183] just three weeks before the civil deposition.

During the criminal investigation, the President has produced seven gifts that Ms. Lewinsky gave him. He testified to the grand jury that Ms. Lewinsky had given him "a tie, a coffee cup, a number of other things I had."[184] In addition, the President acknowledged that "there were some things that had been in my possession that I no longer had, I believe."[185]

Betty Currie testified that Ms. Lewinsky sent a number of packages for the President—six or eight, she estimated.[186] Ms. Lewinsky also sometimes dropped parcels off or had family members do so.[187] When the packages came to the White House, Ms. Currie would leave the packages from Ms. Lewinsky in the President's box outside the Oval Office, and "[h]e would pick [them] up."[188] To the best of her knowledge, such parcels always reached the President: "The President got everything anyone sent him."[189] Ms. Currie testified that to her knowledge, no one delivered packages or something as many times as Ms. Lewinsky did.[190]

6. SUMMARY

The President stated in his civil deposition that he could not recall whether he had ever given any gifts to Ms. Lewinsky;[191] that he could not remember whether he had given her a hat pin although "certainly, I could have"; and that he had received a gift from Ms. Lewinsky only "once or twice."[192] In fact, the evidence demonstrates that they exchanged numerous gifts of various kinds at many points over a lengthy period of time. Indeed, on December 28, only three weeks before the deposition, they had discussed the hat pin. Also on December 28, the President had given Ms. Lewinsky a number of gifts, more than he had ever given her before.

A truthful answer to the questions about gifts at the Jones deposition would have raised further questions about the President's relationship with Monica Lewinsky. The number itself would raise questions about the relationship and prompt further questions about specific gifts; some of the specific gifts (such as Vox and Leaves of Grass) would raise questions whether the relationship was sexual and whether the President had lied in denying that their relationship was sexual. Ms. Lewinsky explained the point: Had they admitted the gifts, it would "at least prompt [the Jones attorneys] to want to question me about what kind of friendship I had with the President and they would want to speculate and they'd leak it and my name would be trashed and he [the President] would be in trouble."[193]

A truthful answer about the gifts to Ms. Lewinsky also would have raised the question of where they were. Ms. Lewinsky had been subpoenaed for gifts, as the President knew. The President knew also from his conversation with Ms. Lewinsky on December 28, 1997 (an issue discussed more fully in Ground V) that Ms. Lewinsky would not produce all of the gifts she had received from the President.

For those reasons, the President had a clear motive when testifying under oath to lie about the gifts.

IV. THERE IS SUBSTANTIAL AND CREDIBLE INFORMATION THAT THE PRESIDENT LIED UNDER OATH DURING HIS CIVIL DEPOSITION CONCERNING CONVERSATIONS HE HAD WITH MONICA LEWINSKY ABOUT HER INVOLVEMENT IN THE JONES CASE.

President Clinton was asked during his civil deposition whether he had discussed with Ms. Lewinsky the possibility of her testifying in the Jones case. He also was asked whether he knew that she had been subpoenaed at the time he last had spoken to her.

There is substantial and credible information that the President lied under oath in answering these questions. A false statement about these conversations was necessary in order to avoid raising questions whether the President had tampered with a prospective witness in the civil lawsuit against him.

A. CONVERSATIONS WITH MS. LEWINSKY REGARDING THE POSSIBILITY OF HER TESTIFYING IN THE JONES CASE

1. PRESIDENT CLINTON'S TESTIMONY IN HIS DEPOSITION

In the President's civil deposition, he was asked about any discussions he might have had with Monica Lewinsky about the Jones case:

Q: Have you ever talked to Monica Lewinsky about the possibility that she might be asked to testify in this lawsuit?

[videotape indicates an approximately 14-second pause before answer]

WJC: I'm not sure, and let me tell you why I'm not sure. It seems to me the, the, the—I want to be as accurate as I can here. Seems to me the last time she was there to see Betty before Christmas we were joking about how you-all [Ms. Jones's attorneys], with the help of the Rutherford Institute, were going to call every woman I'd ever talked to . . . and ask them that, and so I said you [Ms. Lewinsky] would qualify, or something like that. I don't, I don't think we ever had more of a conversation than that about it, but I might have mentioned something to her about it, because when I saw how long the witness list was, or I heard about it, before I saw, but actually by the time I saw it her name was on it, but I think that was after all this had happened. I might have said something like that, so I don't want to say for sure I didn't, because I might have said something like that.

•   •   •

Q: What, if anything, did Monica Lewinsky say in response?

WJC: Nothing that I remember. Whatever she said, I don't remember. Probably just some predictable thing.[194]

2. EVIDENCE THAT CONTRADICTS THE PRESIDENT'S CIVIL DEPOSITION TESTIMONY

(i) MS. LEWINSKY'S TESTIMONY

Ms. Lewinsky testified that she spoke three times to President Clinton about the prospect of testifying in the Jones lawsuit—once (December 17, 1997 after she was on the witness list and twice more (December 28, 1997, and January 5, 1998 after she had been subpoenaed.

a. December 17, 1997, Call. Ms. Lewinsky testified that President Clinton called her at about 2:00 a.m. on December 17, 1997. First, he told her that Ms. Currie's brother had died; then he told Ms. Lewinsky that she was on the witness list in the Jones case. According to Ms. Lewinsky, "[h]e told me that it didn't necessarily mean that I would be subpoenaed, but that that was a possibility, and if I were to be subpoenaed, that I should contact Betty and let Betty know that I had received the subpoena."[195] Ms. Lewinsky said that the President told her that she might be able to sign an affidavit to avoid being deposed.[196] According to Ms. Lewinsky, the President also told her, "You know, you can always say you were coming to see Betty or that you were bringing me letters."[197] Ms. Lewinsky took that statement to be a reminder of the false "cover stories" that they had used earlier in the relationship.[198]

b. December 28, 1997, Visit. Ms. Lewinsky was subpoenaed on December 19. At her request, Vernon Jordan told the President that Ms. Lewinsky had been subpoenaed.[199] She then met with President Clinton nine days later on December 28, less than three weeks before the President was deposed.

According to Ms. Lewinsky, she and the President discussed the Jones lawsuit and how the Jones lawyers might have learned about

her. Ms. Lewinsky said they also discussed the subpoena's requirement that she produce gifts she had received from the President,
including specifically a "hat pin."[200]

Because of their mutual concern about the subpoena, Ms. Lewinsky testified that she asked the President if she should put the gifts
away somewhere.[201] The President responded "I don't know" or
"Hmm" or "Let me think about it."[202] Later that day, according to
Ms. Lewinsky, Ms. Currie called to pick up the gifts, which she then
stored under her bed in her home in Virginia.[203] (This issue will be
discussed more fully in Ground V below.)

c. January 5, 1998, Call. Ms. Lewinsky also testified that she
spoke to the President by telephone on January 5, 1998, and they
continued to discuss her role in the Jones case. Ms. Lewinsky
expressed concern that, if she were deposed, she might have a difficult time explaining the circumstances of her transfer from the
White House to the Pentagon. According to Ms. Lewinsky, the President suggested that she answer by explaining that people in the
White House Legislative Affairs office had helped her get the Pentagon job—which Ms. Lewinsky understood to be a misleading
answer because she in fact had been transferred as a result of her
being around the Oval Office too much.[204]

(II) THE PRESIDENT'S GRAND JURY TESTIMONY

When the President testified to the grand jury, the President
admitted that Ms. Lewinsky visited him on December 28, 1997,[205]
and that during that visit, they discussed her involvement in the
Jones case:

> WJC: . . . I remember a conversation about the possibility of
> her testifying. I believe it must have occurred on the 28th.
>
> She mentioned to me that she did not want to testify. So, that's
> how it came up. Not in the context of, I heard you have a sub-
> poena, let's talk about it.

She raised the issue with me in the context of her desire to avoid testifying, which I certainly understood; not only because there were some embarrassing facts about our relationship that were inappropriate, but also because a whole lot of innocent people were being traumatized and dragged through the mud by these Jones lawyers with their dragnet strategy. . . .[206]

•   •   •

Q: . . . Do you agree that she was upset about being subpoenaed?

WJC: Oh, yes, sir, she was upset. She—well, she—we—she didn't—we didn't talk about a subpoena. But she was upset. She said, I don't want to testify; I know nothing about this; I certainly know nothing about sexual harassment; why do they want me to testify. And I explained to her why they were doing this, and why all these women were on these lists, people that they knew good and well had nothing to do with any sexual harassment.[207]

3. SUMMARY

There is substantial and credible information that President Clinton lied under oath in his civil deposition in answering "I'm not sure" when asked whether he had talked to Ms. Lewinsky about the prospect of her testifying. In fact, he had talked to Ms. Lewinsky about it on three occasions in the month preceding his civil deposition, as Ms. Lewinsky's testimony makes clear.

The President's motive to lie in his civil deposition on this point is evident. Had he admitted talking to Ms. Lewinsky about the possibility that she might be asked to testify, that would have raised the specter of witness tampering. Such an admission likely would have led Ms. Jones's attorneys to inquire further into that subject with both the President and Ms. Lewinsky. Furthermore, had the President admitted talking to Ms. Lewinsky about her testifying, that conversation would have attracted public inquiry into the conversa-

tion and the general relationship between the President and Ms.
Lewinsky.

B. THERE IS SUBSTANTIAL AND CREDIBLE INFORMATION THAT PRESIDENT CLINTON LIED UNDER OATH IN HIS CIVIL DEPOSITION WHEN HE DENIED KNOWING THAT MS. LEWINSKY HAD RECEIVED HER SUBPOENA AT THE TIME HE HAD LAST TALKED TO HER.

1. EVIDENCE

In his civil deposition, President Clinton testified that the last
time he had spoken to Ms. Lewinsky was in December 1997 (the
month before the deposition), "[p]robably sometime before Christmas."[208] The President was asked:

> Q: Did [Ms. Lewinsky] tell you she had been served with a
> subpoena in this case?

> WJC: No. I don't know if she had been.[209]

Vernon Jordan testified that he had told the President about the
subpoena on December 19, 1997, after he had talked to Ms. Lewinsky.

Ms. Lewinsky confirmed that Mr. Jordan had told her on December 22, 1997, that he (Mr. Jordan) had told the President of her subpoena.[210] When he testified to the grand jury, the President stated
that in his conversation with Ms. Lewinsky on December 28, 1997,
"my recollection is I knew by then, of course, that she had gotten a
subpoena. And I knew that she was, therefore, . . . slated to testify."[211] Ms. Lewinsky testified that she and the President had two
conversations after she was subpoenaed: the December 28, 1997,
meeting and a January 5, 1998, phone conversation.[212]

2. SUMMARY

There is substantial and credible information that the President lied under oath in his civil deposition by answering "I don't know if she had been" subpoenaed when describing his last conversation with Ms. Lewinsky. In fact, he knew that she had been subpoenaed. Given that the conversation with Ms. Lewinsky occurred in the few weeks immediately before the President's civil deposition, he could not have forgotten the conversation. As a result, there is no plausible conclusion except that the President intentionally lied in this answer.

During the civil deposition, the President also falsely dated his last conversation with Ms. Lewinsky as "probably sometime before Christmas," which implied that it might have been before the December 19 subpoena. Because Ms. Lewinsky had been subpoenaed on December 19, that false statement about the date of the conversation was a corollary to his other false statement (that he did not know she had been subpoenaed at the time of their last conversation).

The President's motive to lie in his civil deposition on the subpoena issue is evident. Had he admitted talking to Ms. Lewinsky after her subpoena, that would have raised the specter of witness tampering, which could have triggered legal and public scrutiny of the President.

V. THERE IS SUBSTANTIAL AND CREDIBLE INFORMATION THAT PRESIDENT CLINTON ENDEAVORED TO OBSTRUCT JUSTICE BY ENGAGING IN A PATTERN OF ACTIVITY TO CONCEAL EVIDENCE REGARDING HIS RELATIONSHIP WITH MONICA LEWINSKY FROM THE JUDICIAL PROCESS IN THE JONES CASE. THE PATTERN INCLUDED:

(i) concealment of gifts that the President had given Ms. Lewinsky and that were subpoenaed from Ms. Lewinsky in the Jones case; and

(ii) concealment of a note sent by Ms. Lewinsky to the President on January 5, 1998.

From the beginning, President Clinton and Monica Lewinsky hoped and expected that their relationship would remain secret. They took active steps, when necessary, to conceal the relationship. The President testified that "I hoped that this relationship would never become public."[213]

Once the discovery process in the Jones case became an issue (particularly after the Supreme Court's unanimous decision on May 27, 1997, that ordered the case to go forward), their continuing efforts to conceal the relationship took on added legal significance. The risks to the President of disclosure of the relationship dramatically increased.

An effort to obstruct justice by withholding the truth from the legal process—whether by lying under oath, concealing documents, or improperly influencing a witness's testimony—is a federal crime.[214] There is substantial and credible information that President Clinton engaged in such efforts to prevent the truth of his relationship with Monica Lewinsky from being revealed in the Jones case.

A. CONCEALMENT OF GIFTS

1. EVIDENCE REGARDING GIFTS

Ms. Lewinsky testified that in the early morning of December 17, at roughly 2:00 or 2:30 a.m., she received a call from the President.[215] Among other subjects, the President mentioned that he had Christmas presents for her.[216]

On December 19, 1997, Monica Lewinsky was served with a subpoena in connection with the Jones v. Clinton litigation. The subpoena required her to testify at a deposition on January 23, 1998.[217] The subpoena also required Ms. Lewinsky to produce "each and every gift including, but not limited to, any and all dresses, accessories, and jewelry, and/or hat pins given to you by, or on behalf of, Defendant Clinton."[218] After being served with the subpoena, Ms. Lewinsky became concerned because the list of gifts included the hat pin, which "screamed out at me because that was the first gift that the President had given me."[219]

Later that same day, December 19, 1997, Ms. Lewinsky met with Vernon Jordan and told him of her concern about the gifts, including the hat pin.[220] During that meeting, Ms. Lewinsky asked Mr. Jordan to inform the President that she had been subpoenaed.[221] Mr. Jordan acknowledged that Ms. Lewinsky "was concerned about the subpoena and I think for her the subpoena ipso facto meant trouble."[222]

Shortly after Christmas, Ms. Lewinsky called Ms. Currie and said that the President had mentioned that he had presents for her.[223] Ms. Currie called back and told her to come to the White House at 8:30 a.m. on Sunday, December 28, 1997.[224] On December 28, Ms. Lewinsky and the President met in the Oval Office. According to her testimony, Ms. Lewinsky "mentioned that [she] had been concerned about the hat pin being on the subpoena and he said that that had sort of concerned him also and asked [her] if [she] had told anyone that he had given [her] this hat pin and [she] said no."[225] According to Ms. Lewinsky, she and the President discussed the possibility of moving some of the gifts out of her possession:

[A]t some point I said to him, "Well, you know, should I—
maybe I should put the gifts away outside my house somewhere or give them to someone, maybe Betty." And he sort of
said—I think he responded, "I don't know" or "Let me think
about that." And [we] left that topic.²²⁶

Ms. Lewinsky testified that she was never under the impression
from anything the President said that she should turn over to Ms.
Jones's attorneys all the gifts that he had given her.²²⁷

On the 28th, the President also gave Ms. Lewinsky several
Christmas gifts. When asked why the President gave her more gifts
on December 28 when he understood she was under an obligation
to produce gifts in response to the subpoena, Ms. Lewinsky stated:

You know, I can't answer what [the President] was thinking,
but to me, it was—there was never a question in my mind and
I—from everything he said to me, I never questioned him, that
we were never going to do anything but keep this private, so
that meant deny it and that meant do—take whatever appropriate steps needed to be taken, you know, for that to happen. . . . So by turning over all these gifts, it would at least
prompt [the Jones attorneys] to want to question me about
what kind of friendship I had with the President and they
would want to speculate and they'd leak it and my name
would be trashed and he [the President] would be in trouble.²²⁸

Ms. Lewinsky testified that a few hours after their meeting on
December 28, 1997, Ms. Currie called her.²²⁹ According to Ms.
Lewinsky, Ms. Currie said: "'I understand you have something to
give me.' Or, 'The President said you have something to give me'—
[Something] [a]long those lines."²³⁰ In her February 1 handwritten
statement to the OIC, which Ms. Lewinsky has testified was truthful, she stated: "Ms. Currie called Ms. L later that afternoon a[nd]
said that the Pres. had told her [that] Ms. L wanted her to hold onto
something for her. Ms. L boxed up most of the gifts she had received
and gave them to Ms. Currie."²³¹

Ms. Lewinsky testified that she understood that Ms. Currie was referring to gifts from the President when she mentioned "something for me."[232] Ms. Lewinsky testified that she was not surprised to receive the call, given her earlier discussion with the President.[233]

Ms. Currie testified that Ms. Lewinsky, not Ms. Currie, placed the call and raised the subject of transferring the gifts. In Ms. Currie's account, Ms. Lewinsky said that she (Ms. Lewinsky) was uncomfortable retaining the gifts herself because "people were asking questions about the stuff she had gotten."[234] Ms. Currie also testified that she did not remember the President telling her that Ms. Lewinsky wanted her to hold some items, and she did not remember later telling the President that she was holding the gifts for Ms. Lewinsky.[235] When asked if a contrary statement by Ms. Lewinsky—indicating that Ms. Currie had in fact spoken to the President about the gift transfer—would be false, Ms. Currie replied: "Then she may remember better than I. I don't remember."[236]

According to both Ms. Currie and Ms. Lewinsky, Ms. Currie drove to Ms. Lewinsky's home later on December 28 for only the second time in her life.[237] Ms. Lewinsky gave her a sealed box that contained several gifts Ms. Lewinsky had received from the President, including the hat pin and one of the gifts he had given her that very morning.[238] Ms. Lewinsky wrote "Please do not throw away" on the box.[239] Ms. Currie then took the box and placed it in her home under her bed. Ms. Currie understood that the box contained gifts from the President, although she did not know the specific contents.[240] Ms. Lewinsky said that Ms. Currie did not seem at all confused when Ms. Lewinsky handed over the box of gifts[241] and never asked about the contents.[242]

When Ms. Currie later produced the box to the OIC in response to a subpoena, the box contained a hat pin, two brooches, an inscribed official copy of the 1996 State of the Union Address, a photograph of the President in the Oval Office, an inscribed photograph of the President and Ms. Lewinsky, a sun dress, two t-shirts, and a baseball cap with a Black Dog logo.[243]

2. THE PRESIDENT'S GRAND JURY TESTIMONY

President Clinton testified that he had spoken to Ms. Lewinsky about gifts he had given her, but said the conversation may have occurred before she received the subpoena on December 19. He testified:

> I did have a conversation with Ms. Lewinsky at some time about gifts, the gifts I'd given her. I do not know whether it occurred on the 28th, or whether it occurred earlier. I do not know whether it occurred in person or whether it occurred on the telephone. I have searched my memory for this, because I know it's an important issue. . . . The reason I'm not sure it happened on the 28th is that my recollection is that Ms. Lewinsky said something to me like, what if they ask me about the gifts you've given me. That's the memory I have. That's why I question whether it happened on the 28th, because she had a subpoena with her, request for production. And I told her that if they asked her for gifts, she'd have to give them whatever she had, that that's what the law was.[244]

The President denied that he had asked Betty Currie to pick up a box of gifts from Ms. Lewinsky:

> Q: After you gave her the gifts on December 28th [1997], did you speak with your secretary, Ms. Currie, and ask her to pick up a box of gifts that were some compilation of gifts that Ms. Lewinsky would have—
>
> WJC: No, sir, I didn't do that.
>
> Q:—to give to Ms. Currie?
>
> WJC: I did not do that.[245]

• • •

> Q: [D]id you ever have a conversation with Betty Currie about gifts, or picking something up from Monica Lewinsky?

WJC: I don't believe I did, sir. No.

Q: You never told her anything to this effect, that Monica has something to give you?

WJC: No, sir.[246]

3. SUMMARY OF GIFTS

The uncontroverted evidence demonstrates that the President had given gifts to Ms. Lewinsky before December 28, 1997; that the President told Ms. Lewinsky on the phone on December 17, 1997, that he had more gifts for her; that Ms. Lewinsky met with the President at the White House on December 28; that on the 28th, Ms. Lewinsky was concerned about retaining possession of the gifts the President had previously given her because they were under subpoena; that on the 28th, the President gave several Christmas gifts to Ms. Lewinsky; and that after that meeting, Ms. Lewinsky transferred some gifts (including one of the new gifts) to the President's personal secretary, Ms. Currie, who stored them under her bed in her home.

Ms. Lewinsky testified that she spoke to the President on December 28 about the gifts called for by the subpoena—in particular, the hat pin. The President agreed that they talked about gifts, but suggested that the conversation might have taken place before Ms. Lewinsky was subpoenaed on December 19. The President said, however, that his memory is unclear on the timing.[247]

The testimony conflicts as to what happened when Ms. Lewinsky raised the subject of gifts with the President and what happened later that day. The President testified that he told Ms. Lewinsky that "you have to give them whatever you have."[248] According to Ms. Lewinsky, she raised the possibility of hiding the gifts, and the President offered a somewhat neutral response.

Ms. Lewinsky testified that Betty Currie called her to retrieve the gifts soon after Ms. Lewinsky's conversation with the President. Ms. Currie says that she believes that Ms. Lewinsky called her about the gifts, but she says she has a dim memory of the events.[249]

The central factual question is whether the President orchestrated or approved the concealment of the gifts. The reasonable inference from the evidence is that he did.

1. The witnesses disagree about whether Ms. Currie called Ms. Lewinsky or Ms. Lewinsky called Ms. Currie. That issue is relevant because Ms. Currie would not have called Ms. Lewinsky about the gifts unless the President directed her to do so. Indeed, because she did not know of the gifts issue, there is no other way that Ms. Currie could have known to make such a call unless the President told her to do so.

Ms. Lewinsky's testimony on the issue is consistent and unequivocal. In her February 1, 1998, handwritten statement, she wrote: "Ms. Currie called Ms. L later that afternoon a[nd] said that the Pres. had told her Ms. L wanted her to hold onto something for her."[250] In her grand jury testimony, Ms. Lewinsky said that several hours after she left the White House, Ms. Currie called and said something along the lines of "The President said you have something to give me."[251]

Ms. Currie's testimony is contrary but less clear. Ms. Currie has stated that Ms. Lewinsky called her, but her memory of the conversation, in contrast to Ms. Lewinsky's, generally has been hazy and uncertain. As to whether she had talked to the President about the gifts, for example, Ms. Currie initially said she had not, but then said that Ms. Lewinsky (who said that Ms. Currie had talked to the President) "may remember better than I. I don't remember."[252]

Ms. Lewinsky's testimony makes more sense than Ms. Currie's testimony. First, Ms. Lewinsky stated that if Ms. Currie had not called, Ms. Lewinsky simply would have kept the gifts (and perhaps thrown them away).[253] She would not have produced the gifts to Ms. Jones's attorneys. And she would not have given them to a friend or mother because she did not want to get anyone else involved.[254] She was not looking for someone else to take them.[255]

Also, Ms. Currie drove to Ms. Lewinsky's house to pick up the gifts. That was only the second time that Ms. Currie had ever gone there.[256] More generally, the person making the extra effort (in this case, Ms. Currie) is ordinarily the person requesting the favor.

2. Even if Ms. Lewinsky is mistaken and she did call Ms. Currie first, the evidence still leads clearly to the conclusion that the President orchestrated this transfer.

First, it is unlikely that Ms. Lewinsky would have involved Ms. Currie in this matter unless the President had indicated his assent when Ms. Lewinsky raised the issue with him earlier in the day. Indeed, there is a logical flaw in the President's story: If the President had truly suggested that Ms. Lewinsky produce the gifts to Ms. Jones's attorneys, Ms. Lewinsky obviously would not have turned around and called the President's personal secretary to give the gifts to her, in direct contravention of the President's instruction.

Second, it also is unlikely that Ms. Currie would have driven to Ms. Lewinsky's home, retrieved the gifts from Ms. Lewinsky, and stored them under her bed at home without being asked to do so by the President—at least, without checking with him. It would have been out of character for Ms. Currie to have taken such an action without the President's approval. For example, when helping Ms. Lewinsky in her job search, Ms. Currie said that she told the President of her plans and agreed that she "would not have tried to get Ms. Lewinsky a job if . . . [I] thought the President didn't want [me] to."[257]

3. Even if the President did not orchestrate the transfer to Ms. Currie, there is still substantial evidence that he encouraged the concealment and non-production of the gifts by Ms. Lewinsky. The President "hoped that this relationship would never become public."[258] The President gave Ms. Lewinsky new gifts on December 28, 1997. Given his desire to conceal the relationship, it makes no sense that the President would have given Ms. Lewinsky more gifts on the 28th unless he and Ms. Lewinsky understood that she would not produce all of her gifts in response to her subpoena.

4. The President had a motive to orchestrate the concealment of gifts, whether accomplished through Ms. Currie indirectly or through Ms. Lewinsky directly. The President knew that Ms. Lewinsky was concerned about the subpoena. Both of them were concerned that the gifts might raise questions about the relation-

ship. By confirming that the gifts would not be produced, the President ensured that these questions would not arise.

The concealment of the gifts also ensured that the President could provide false and misleading statements about the gifts under oath at his deposition (as he did) without being concerned that Ms. Lewinsky might have produced gifts that the President was denying (or minimizing the number of). If Ms. Lewinsky had produced to Ms. Jones's attorneys all of the gifts that she had given to Ms. Currie, then the President could not plausibly have said "I don't recall" in response to the question, "[H]ave you ever given any gifts to Monica Lewinsky?" He could not have said, "I don't remember a specific gift."[259] Indeed, unless the President knew that Ms. Lewinsky had not complied with the subpoena, it is unlikely he would have risked lying about the number and nature of the gifts he had given her.

In analyzing the evidence on this issue, it also bears mention that President Clinton likely operated no differently with respect to the gifts than he did with respect to testimony. It is clear that he lied under oath and that Ms. Lewinsky filed a false affidavit after the President suggested she file an affidavit. So there is little reason that he would not have attempted to ensure (whether directly or subtly) that Ms. Lewinsky conceal the gifts as a corollary to their mutual lies under oath. (Also, it was the President's pattern to use Ms. Currie as an intermediary in dealing with Ms. Lewinsky.[260])

The President's apparent response to all of this is that Ms. Lewinsky on her own contacted Ms. Currie and involved her in this endeavor to hide subpoenaed evidence, and that Ms. Currie complied without checking with the President. Based on the testimony and behavior of both Ms. Currie and Ms. Lewinsky, those inferences fall outside the range of reasonable possibility.

There is substantial and credible information, therefore, that the President endeavored to obstruct justice by participating in the concealment of subpoenaed evidence.

B. January 5, 1998, Note to the President

1. Evidence Regarding the January 5, 1998 Note

On December 16, 1997, the President was served by Ms. Jones's attorneys with a request for production of documents, including documents relating to "Monica Lewisky" [sic]. The request placed upon the President a continuing obligation to preserve and produce responsive documents. Notes and letters from Ms. Lewinsky were responsive and relevant.

On January 4, 1998, Ms. Lewinsky left a book for the President with Ms. Currie.[261] Ms. Lewinsky had enclosed in the book a romantic note that she had written, inspired by a recent viewing of the movie Titanic.[262] In the note, Ms. Lewinsky told the President that she wanted to have sexual intercourse with him, at least once.[263]

On January 5, in the course of discussing her affidavit and possible testimony in a phone conversation with the President, Ms. Lewinsky says she told the President, "I shouldn't have written some of those things in the note."[264] According to Ms. Lewinsky, the President said that he agreed and that she should not write those kinds of things on paper.[265]

On January 15, President Clinton served responses to Ms. Jones's second set of document requests, which again asked for documents that related to "Monica Lewisky." The President stated that he had "no documents" responsive to this request.[266]

2. President Clinton's Testimony

The President remembered the book Ms. Lewinsky had given him about the Presidents and testified that he "did like it a lot."[267] President Clinton testified that he did not recall a romantic note enclosed in the book or when he had received it.[268]

3. Summary on January 5, 1998, Note

The request for production of documents that the President received from Ms. Jones's attorneys called for all documents reflecting communications between him and Ms. Lewinsky. The note given to him by Ms. Lewinsky on January 5, 1998, fell within that category and would have been revealing about the relationship. Indeed, had the note been produced, the President might have been foreclosed from denying a sexual relationship at his deposition. Based on Ms. Lewinsky's testimony, there is substantial and credible information that the President concealed or destroyed this note at a time when such documents were called for by the request for production of documents.[269]

VI. THERE IS SUBSTANTIAL AND CREDIBLE INFORMATION THAT

(i) President Clinton and Ms. Lewinsky had an understanding that they would lie under oath in the Jones case about their relationship; and

(ii) President Clinton endeavored to obstruct justice by suggesting that Ms. Lewinsky file an affidavit so that she would not be deposed, she would not contradict his testimony, and he could attempt to avoid questions about Ms. Lewinsky at his deposition.

Based on their conversations and their past practice, both the President and Ms. Lewinsky understood that they would lie under oath in the Jones case about their sexual relationship, as part of a scheme to obstruct justice in the Jones case. In pursuing this effort:

- the President suggested that Monica Lewinsky file an affidavit, which he knew would be false;

- the President had an interest in Ms. Lewinsky's false affidavit because it would "lock in" her testimony, allowing the President to deny the sexual relationship under oath without fear of contradiction;

- Ms. Lewinsky signed and, on January 16, sent to the Court the false affidavit denying a sexual relationship with the President as part of a motion to quash her deposition subpoena;

- the President's attorney used the affidavit to object to questions about Ms. Lewinsky at his January 17 deposition; and

- when that failed, the President also lied under oath about the relationship with Ms. Lewinsky at his civil deposition, including by the use of "cover stories" that he and Ms. Lewinsky had devised.

A. EVIDENCE REGARDING AFFIDAVIT AND USE OF AFFIDAVIT

Monica Lewinsky testified that President Clinton called her at around 2:00 or 2:30 a.m. on December 17, 1997,[270] and told her that her name was on the Jones case witness list.[271] As noted in her February 1 handwritten statement: "When asked what to do if she was subpoenaed, the Pres. suggested she could sign an affidavit . . . ."[272] Ms. Lewinsky said she is "100% sure" that the President suggested that she might want to sign an affidavit.[273]

Ms. Lewinsky understood the President's advice to mean that she might be able to execute an affidavit that would not disclose the true nature of their relationship. In order "to prevent me from being deposed," she said she would need an affidavit that "could range from anywhere between maybe just somehow mentioning, you know, innocuous things or going as far as maybe having to deny any kind of relationship."[274]

Ms. Lewinsky has stated that the President never explicitly told her to lie. Instead, as she explained, they both understood from their conversations that they would continue their pattern of covering up and lying about the relationship. In that regard, the President never said they must now tell the truth under oath; to the contrary, as Ms. Lewinsky stated:

[I]t wasn't as if the President called me and said, "You know, Monica, you're on the witness list, this is going to be really hard for us, we're going to have to tell the truth and be humiliated in front of the entire world about what we've done," which I would have fought him on probably. That was different. And by him not calling me and saying that, you know, I knew what that meant.[275]

Ms. Jones's lawyers served Ms. Lewinsky with a subpoena on December 19, 1997. Ms. Lewinsky contacted Vernon Jordan, who in turn put her in contact with attorney Frank Carter.[276] Based on the information that Ms. Lewinsky provided, Mr. Carter prepared an affidavit which stated: "I have never had a sexual relationship with the President."[277]

After Mr. Carter drafted the affidavit, Ms. Lewinsky spoke to the President by phone on January 5th.[278] She asked the President if he wanted to see the draft affidavit. According to Ms. Lewinsky, the President replied that he did not need to see it because he had already "seen 15 others."[279]

Mr. Jordan confirmed that President Clinton knew that Ms. Lewinsky planned to execute an affidavit denying a sexual relationship.[280] Mr. Jordan further testified that he informed President Clinton when Ms. Lewinsky signed the affidavit.[281] Ms. Lewinsky's affidavit was sent to the federal court in Arkansas on January 16, 1998—the day before the President's deposition—as part of her motion to quash the deposition subpoena.

Two days before the President's deposition, his lawyer, Robert Bennett, obtained a copy of Ms. Lewinsky's affidavit from Mr. Carter.[282] At the President's deposition, Ms. Jones's counsel asked questions about the President's relationship with Ms. Lewinsky. Mr. Bennett objected to the "innuendo" of the questions, noting that Ms. Lewinsky had signed an affidavit denying a sexual relationship, which according to Mr. Bennett, indicated that "there is absolutely no sex of any kind in any manner, shape or form."[283] Mr. Bennett said that the President was "fully aware of Ms. Lewinsky's affidavit."[284] Mr. Bennett affirmatively used the affidavit in an effort to cut off questioning. The President said nothing—even though, as he knew, the affidavit was false. Judge Wright overruled the objection and allowed the questioning to continue.

Later, Mr. Bennett read Ms. Lewinsky's affidavit denying a "sexual relationship" to the President and asked him: "Is that a true and accurate statement as far as you know it?" The President answered: "That is absolutely true."[285]

B. SUMMARY OF PRESIDENT'S GRAND JURY TESTIMONY

The President told the grand jury: "[D]id I hope [Ms. Lewinsky would] be able to get out of testifying on an affidavit? Absolutely. Did I want her to execute a false affidavit? No, I did not."[286] The President did not explain how a full and truthful affidavit—for example, an affidavit admitting that they engaged in oral sex and that Vernon Jordan had been involved, at the President's request, in late 1997 and early 1998 in obtaining Ms. Lewinsky a job—would have helped her avoid a deposition.

When questioned about his phone conversation with Ms. Lewinsky on December 17, 1997—during which the President suggested filing an affidavit—the President testified that he did not remember exactly what he had said.[287] The President also maintained that Ms. Lewinsky's affidavit, as it ultimately was filed denying a "sexual relationship," was not necessarily inaccurate. He testified that, depending on Ms. Lewinsky's state of mind, her statement denying a sexual relationship could have been true.

> I believe at the time that she filled out this affidavit, if she believed that the definition of sexual relationship was two people having intercourse, then this is accurate. And I believe that is the definition that most ordinary Americans would give it.[288]

At his grand jury appearance, the President also was asked about his counsel's statement to Judge Wright that Ms. Lewinsky's affidavit denying a "sexual relationship" was equivalent to saying "there is absolutely no sex of any kind in any manner, shape or form" with President Clinton. Given the President's interpretation of the term "sexual relationship" to require sexual intercourse, the President was asked how he lawfully could have sat silent while his attorney—in the President's presence and on his behalf—made a false statement to a United States District Judge in an effort to forestall further questioning. The President offered several responses.

First, the President maintained that he was not paying "much attention" when Mr. Bennett said that there is "absolutely no sex of any kind" between the President and Ms. Lewinsky.[289] The President further stated: "That moment, that whole argument just passed me by. I was a witness."[290] The President's explanation is difficult to reconcile with the videotape of the deposition, which shows that the President was looking in Mr. Bennett's direction when his counsel made this statement.

Alternatively, the President contended that when Mr. Bennett said that "there is absolutely no sex of any kind," Mr. Bennett was speaking only in the present tense and thus was making a completely true statement. The President further stated: "It depends on what the meaning of the word 'is' is,"[291] and that "actually, in the present tense that is an accurate statement."[292] Before the grand jury, counsel for the OIC then asked the President: "Do you mean today that because you were not engaging in sexual activity with Ms. Lewinsky during the deposition that the statement of Mr. Bennett might be literally true?"[293] The President responded: "No, sir. I mean that at the time of the deposition, it had been—that was well beyond any point of improper contact between me and Ms. Lewinsky."[294] The President's suggestion that he might have engaged in such a detailed parsing of the words at his deposition is at odds with his assertion that the "whole argument passed me by."

Finally, the President took issue with the notion that he had any duty to prevent his attorney from making a false statement to Judge Wright: "Mr. Bennett was representing me. I wasn't representing him."[295] That is a truism. Yet when a witness is knowingly responsible for a misstatement of fact to a federal judge that misleads the Court and attempts to prevent questioning on a relevant subject, that conduct rises to the level of an obstruction of justice.

C. Evidence Regarding Cover Stories

The affidavit was not the only part of the scheme in which both the President and Ms. Lewinsky would lie under oath. Ms. Lewinsky testified that, as part of their mutual concealment efforts, she and President Clinton formulated "cover stories" to explain Ms. Lewinsky's presence in the West Wing and Oval Office. When Ms. Lewinsky worked at the White House, she and the President agreed that Ms. Lewinsky would tell people that she was coming to the Oval Office to deliver papers or to have papers signed, when in truth she was going to the Oval Office to have a sexual encounter with the President.[296]

While employed at the White House, Ms. Lewinsky used this cover story on several occasions.[297] It worked: Several Secret Service officers testified that they understood that Ms. Lewinsky was at the Oval Office to deliver or to pick up papers.[298] In fact, however, Ms. Lewinsky stated that her White House job never required her to deliver papers or obtain the President's signature, although she carried papers as a prop.[299]

After she was transferred to the Pentagon, Ms. Lewinsky testified that she and the President formulated a second "cover story": that Ms. Lewinsky was going to the White House to visit Betty Currie rather than the President. Ms. Lewinsky testified that she and the President discussed how "Betty always needed to be the one to clear me in so that, you know, I could always say I was coming to see Betty."[300] Ms. Lewinsky testified that she met with the President privately on ten occasions after she left her job at the White House.[301] Ms. Currie signed her in for each of those private visits.[302]

Ms. Lewinsky has stated that her true purpose in visiting the White House on these occasions was to see President Clinton, not Ms. Currie.[303] President Clinton agreed that "just about every time" that Ms. Lewinsky came to see Ms. Currie when he was there, Ms. Lewinsky saw him as well.[304]

Ms. Lewinsky testified that President Clinton encouraged her to continue to use the cover stories to conceal their relationship after her name appeared on the witness list in the Jones case. In her early-morning phone conversation with President Clinton on December 17, 1997—the same conversation in which the President told her that her name was on the witness list and suggested that she file an affidavit if subpoenaed[305]—Ms. Lewinsky discussed cover stories with the President:

> ML: At some point in the conversation, and I don't know if it was before or after the subject of the affidavit came up, he sort of said, "You know, you can always say you were coming to see Betty or that you were bringing me letters." Which I understood was really a reminder of things that we had discussed before.
>
> Q: So when you say things you had discussed, sort of ruses that you had developed.
>
> ML: Right. I mean, this was—this was something that—that was instantly familiar to me.
>
> Q: Right.
>
> ML: And I knew exactly what he meant.
>
> Q: Had you talked with him earlier about these false explanations about what you were doing visiting him on several occasions?
>
> ML: Several occasions throughout the entire relationship. Yes. It was the pattern of the relationship, to sort of conceal it.[306]

President Clinton used those same deceptive cover stories during his deposition in the Jones case. In the civil deposition, when asked if he had met with Ms. Lewinsky "several times" while she worked at the White House, the President responded that he had seen her on two or three occasions during the government shutdown, "and then when she worked at the White House, I think there was one or two other times when she brought some documents to me."[307] When asked if he was ever alone with Ms. Lewinsky in the Oval Office, the President stated:

[W]hen she worked at the legislative affairs office, they always had somebody there on the weekends. . . . Sometimes they'd bring me things on the weekends. In that case, whatever time she would be in there, drop it off, exchange a few words and go, she was there. . . . It's possible that she, in, while she was working there, brought something to me and that at the time she brought it to me, she was the only person there, That's possible.[308]

The pattern of devising cover stories in an effort to forestall an inquiry into the relationship continued even after Ms. Lewinsky was subpoenaed to testify. On January 5, 1998, she met with her attorney, Frank Carter, and discussed questions that she might be asked at a deposition. One of the questions was how she had obtained her Pentagon job. Ms. Lewinsky worried that if the Jones lawyers checked with the White House about the transfer, some at the White House would say unflattering things about why she had been terminated.[309] Ms. Lewinsky spoke to President Clinton on the phone that evening and asked for advice on how to answer the question. Ms. Lewinsky testified that the President responded, "[Y]ou could always say that the people in Legislative Affairs got it for you or helped you get it"—a story that Ms. Lewinsky stated was misleading because Ms. Lewinsky in fact had been transferred because she was around the Oval Office too much.[310] President Clinton knew the truth.

D. THE PRESIDENT'S GRAND JURY TESTIMONY ON COVER STORIES

The President testified that before he knew that Ms. Lewinsky was a witness in the Jones case, he "might well" have told Ms.

Lewinsky that she could offer the cover stories if questioned about her presence in the West Wing and Oval Office:

> Q: Did you ever say anything like that, you can always say that you were coming to see Betty or bringing me letters? Was that part of any kind of a, anything you said to her or a cover story, before you had any idea she was going to be part of Paula Jones?
>
> WJC: I might well have said that.
>
> Q: Okay.
>
> WJC: Because I certainly didn't want this to come out, if I could help it. And I was concerned about that. I was embarrassed about it. I knew it was wrong.[311]

However, no doubt aware of the significance of the question, the President testified that he did not remember whether he had discussed the cover stories with Ms. Lewinsky during the December 17, 1997, conversation,[312] or at any time after Ms. Lewinsky's name appeared on the Jones witness list:

> Q: Did you tell [Ms. Lewinsky] anytime in December something to that effect: You know, you can always say that you were coming to see Betty or you were bringing me letters? Did you say that, or anything like that, in December '97 or January '98, to Monica Lewinsky?
>
> WJC: Well, that's a very broad question. I do not recall saying anything like that in connection with her testimony. I could tell you what I do remember saying, if you want to know. But I don't—we might have talked about what to do in a nonlegal context at some point in the past, but I have no specific memory of that conversation.
>
> I do remember what I said to her about the possible testimony.

•   •   •

Q: Did you say anything like [the cover stories] once you knew or thought she might be a witness in the Jones case? Did you repeat the statement, or something like it to her?

WJC: Well, again, I don't recall, and I don't recall whether I might have done something like that, for example, if somebody says, what if the reporters ask me this, that or the other thing. I can tell you this:

In the context of whether she could be a witness, I have a recollection that she asked me, well, what do I do if I get called as a witness, and I said, you have to get a lawyer. And that's all I said. And I never asked her to lie.

Q: Did you tell her to tell the truth?

WJC: Well, I think the implication was she would tell the truth.[313]

E. SUMMARY

There is substantial and credible information that the President and Ms. Lewinsky reached an understanding that both of them would lie under oath when asked whether they had a sexual relationship (a conspiracy to obstruct justice or to commit perjury, in criminal law terms). Indeed, a tacit or express agreement to make false statements would have been an essential part of their December and January discussions, lest one of the two testify truthfully in the Jones case and thereby incriminate the other as a perjurer.

There also is substantial and credible information that President Clinton endeavored to obstruct justice by suggesting that Ms. Lewinsky file an affidavit to avoid her deposition, which would "lock in" her testimony under oath, and to attempt to avoid questions at his own deposition—all to impede the gathering of discoverable evidence in the Jones v. Clinton litigation.[314]

During the course of their relationship, the President and Ms. Lewinsky also discussed and used cover stories to justify her pres-

ence in and around the Oval Office area. The evidence indicates—
given Ms. Lewinsky's unambiguous testimony and the President's
lack of memory, as well as the fact that they both planned to lie
under oath—that the President suggested the continued use of the
cover stories even after Ms. Lewinsky was named as a potential witness in the Jones litigation. At no time did the President tell Ms.
Lewinsky to abandon these stories and to tell the truth about her
visits, nor did he ever indicate to her that she should tell the truth
under oath about the relationship. While the President testified that
he could not remember such conversations about the cover stories,
he had repeated the substance of the cover stories in his Jones deposition. The President's use of false cover stories in testimony under
oath in his Jones deposition strongly corroborates Ms. Lewinsky's
testimony that he suggested them to her on December 17 as a means
of avoiding disclosure of the truth of their relationship.

VII. THERE IS SUBSTANTIAL AND CREDIBLE INFORMATION THAT PRESIDENT CLINTON ENDEAVORED TO OBSTRUCT JUSTICE BY HELPING MS. LEWINSKY OBTAIN A JOB IN NEW YORK AT A TIME WHEN SHE WOULD HAVE BEEN A WITNESS AGAINST HIM WERE SHE TO TELL THE TRUTH DURING THE JONES CASE.

The President had an incentive to keep Ms. Lewinsky from jeop-
ardizing the secrecy of the relationship. That incentive grew once
the Supreme Court unanimously decided in May 1997 that the case
and discovery process were to go forward.

At various times during the Jones discovery process, the President and those working on his behalf devoted substantial time and
attention to help Ms. Lewinsky obtain a job in the private sector.

A. EVIDENCE

The entire saga of Ms. Lewinsky's job search and the President's
assistance in that search is discussed in detail in the Narrative section of this Referral. We summarize and analyze the key events and
dates here.

Ms. Lewinsky first mentioned her desire to move to New York in a letter to the President on July 3, 1997. The letter recounted her frustration that she had not received an offer to return to work at the White House.[315]

On October 1, the President was served with interrogatories asking about his sexual relationships with women other than Mrs. Clinton.[316] On October 7, 1997, Ms. Lewinsky couriered a letter expressing dissatisfaction with her job search to the President.[317] In response, Ms. Lewinsky said she received a late-night call from President Clinton on October 9, 1997. She said that the President told her he would start helping her find a job in New York.[318]

The following Saturday, October 11, 1997, Ms. Lewinsky met with President Clinton alone in the Oval Office dining room from 9:36 a.m. until about 10:54 a.m. In that meeting, she furnished the President a list of New York jobs in which she was interested.[319] Ms. Lewinsky mentioned to the President that she would need a reference from someone in the White House; the President said he would take care of it.[320] Ms. Lewinsky also suggested to the President that Vernon Jordan might be able to help her, and President Clinton agreed.[321] Immediately after the meeting, President Clinton spoke with Mr. Jordan by telephone.[322]

According to White House Chief of Staff Erskine Bowles, at some time in the summer or fall of 1997, President Clinton raised the subject of Monica Lewinsky and stated that "she was unhappy where she was working and wanted to come back and work at the OEOB [Old Executive Office Building]; and could we take a look."[323] Mr. Bowles referred the matter to Deputy Chief of Staff John Podesta.[324]

Mr. Podesta said he asked Betty Currie to have Ms. Lewinsky call him, but heard nothing until about October 1997, when Ms. Currie told him that Ms. Lewinsky was looking for opportunities in New York.[325] The Ambassador to the United Nations, Bill Richardson, said that Mr. Podesta told him that Ms. Currie had a friend looking for a position in New York.[326]

According to Ms. Lewinsky, Ambassador Richardson called her on October 21, 1997,[327] and interviewed her soon thereafter. She was then offered a position at the UN.[328] Ms. Lewinsky was unenthusiastic.[329] During the latter part of October 1997, the President and Ms. Lewinsky discussed enlisting Vernon Jordan to aid in pursuing private-sector possibilities.[330]

On November 5, 1997, Ms. Lewinsky met Mr. Jordan in his law office. Mr. Jordan told Ms. Lewinsky that she came "highly recommended."[331] Ms. Lewinsky explained that she hoped to move to New York, and went over her list of possible employers.[332] Mr. Jordan telephoned President Clinton shortly after the meeting.[333]

Ms. Lewinsky had no contact with the President or Mr. Jordan for another month.[334] On December 5, 1997, however, the parties in the Jones case exchanged witness lists. Ms. Jones's attorneys listed Ms. Lewinsky as a potential witness. The President testified that he learned that Ms. Lewinsky was on the list late in the day on December 6.[335]

The effort to obtain a job for Ms. Lewinsky then intensified. On December 7, President Clinton met with Mr. Jordan at the White House.[336] Ms. Lewinsky met with Mr. Jordan on December 11 to discuss specific job contacts in New York. Mr. Jordan gave her the names of some of his business contacts.[337] He then made calls to contacts at MacAndrews & Forbes (the parent corporation of Revlon), American Express, and Young & Rubicam.[338]

Mr. Jordan also telephoned President Clinton to keep him informed of the efforts to help Ms. Lewinsky. Mr. Jordan testified that President Clinton was aware that people were trying to get jobs for her, that Mr. Podesta was trying to help her, that Bill Richardson was trying to help her, but that she wanted to work in the private sector.[339]

On the same day of Ms. Lewinsky's meeting with Mr. Jordan, December 11, Judge Wright ordered President Clinton, over his objection, to answer certain written interrogatories as part of the discovery process in Jones. Those interrogatories required, among other things, the President to identify any government employees since 1986 with whom he had engaged in sexual relations (a term undefined for purposes of the interrogatory).[340] On December 16, the President's attorneys received a request for production of documents that mentioned Monica Lewinsky by name.

On December 17, 1997, according to Ms. Lewinsky, President Clinton called her in the early morning and told her that she was on the witness list, and they discussed their cover stories.[341] On December 18 and December 23, she interviewed for jobs with New York-based companies that had been contacted by Mr. Jordan.[342] On December 19, Ms. Lewinsky was served with a deposition subpoena by Ms. Jones's lawyers.[343] On December 22, 1997, Mr. Jordan took her to her new attorney; she and Mr. Jordan discussed the subpoena, the Jones case, and her job search during the course of the ride.[344]

The President answered the "other women" interrogatory on December 23, 1997, by declaring under oath: "None."[345]

On Sunday, December 28, 1997, Monica Lewinsky and the President met in the Oval Office.[346] During that meeting, the President and Ms. Lewinsky discussed both her move to New York and her involvement in the Jones suit.[347]

On January 5, 1998, Ms. Lewinsky declined the United Nations offer.[348] On January 7, 1998, Ms. Lewinsky signed the affidavit denying the relationship with President Clinton (she had talked on the phone to the President on January 5 about it).[349] Mr. Jordan informed the President of her action.[350]

The next day, on January 8, 1998, Ms. Lewinsky interviewed in New York with MacAndrews & Forbes, a company recommended by Vernon Jordan. The interview went poorly. Mr. Jordan then called Ronald Perelman, the Chairman of the Board at MacAndrews & Forbes. Mr. Perelman said Ms. Lewinsky should not worry, and that someone would call her back for another interview. Mr. Jordan relayed this message to Ms. Lewinsky, and someone called back that day.[351]

Ms. Lewinsky interviewed again the next morning, and a few hours later received an informal offer for a position.[352] She told Mr. Jordan of the offer, and Mr. Jordan then notified President Clinton with the news: "Mission accomplished."[353]

On January 12, 1998, Ms. Jones's attorneys informed Judge Wright that they might call Monica Lewinsky as a trial witness.[354] Judge Wright stated that she would allow witnesses with whom the President had worked, such as Ms. Lewinsky, to be trial witnesses.[355]

In a call on January 13, 1998, a Revlon employee formalized the job offer, and asked Ms. Lewinsky to provide references.[356] Either that day or the next, President Clinton told Erskine Bowles that Ms. Lewinsky "had found a job in the . . . private sector, and she had listed John Hilley as a reference, and could we see if he could recommend her, if asked."[357] Thereafter, Mr. Bowles took the President's request to Deputy Chief of Staff John Podesta, who in turn spoke to Mr. Hilley about writing a letter of recommendation. After speaking with Mr. Podesta, Mr. Hilley agreed to write such a letter, but cautioned it would be a "generic" one.[358] On January 14, at approximately 11:17 a.m., Ms. Lewinsky faxed her letter of acceptance to Revlon and listed Mr. Hilley as a reference.[359]

On January 15, the President responded to the December 15 request for production of documents relating to Monica Lewinsky by answering "none." On January 16, Ms. Lewinsky's attorney sent to the District Court in the Jones case her affidavit denying a "sexual relationship" with the President.[360] The next day, on January 17, the President was deposed and his attorney used her affidavit as the President similarly denied a "sexual relationship."

B. SUMMARY

When a party in a lawsuit (or investigation) provides job or financial assistance to a witness, a question arises as to possible witness tampering. The critical question centers on the intent of the party providing the assistance. Direct evidence of that intent often is unavailable. Indeed, in some cases, the witness receiving the job assistance may not even know that the party providing the assistance was motivated by a desire to stay on good terms with the witness during the pending legal proceeding.[361] Similarly, others who are enlisted in the party's effort to influence the witness's testimony by providing job assistance may not be aware of the party's motivation and intent.

One can draw inferences about the party's intent from circumstantial evidence. In this case, the President assisted Ms. Lewinsky in her job search in late 1997, at a time when she would have become a witness harmful to him in the Jones case were she to testify truthfully. The President did not act half-heartedly. His assistance led to the involvement of the Ambassador to the United Nations, one of the country's leading business figures (Mr. Perelman), and one of the country's leading attorneys (Vernon Jordan).

The question, therefore, is whether the President's efforts in obtaining a job for Ms. Lewinsky were to influence her testimony[362] or simply to help an ex-intimate without concern for her testimony. Three key facts are essential in analyzing his actions: (i) the chronology of events, (ii) the fact that the President and Ms. Lewinsky both intended to lie under oath about the relationship, and (iii) the fact that it was critical for the President that Ms. Lewinsky lie under oath.

There is substantial and credible information that the President assisted Ms. Lewinsky in her job search motivated at least in part by his desire to keep her "on the team" in the Jones litigation.

VIII. THERE IS SUBSTANTIAL AND CREDIBLE INFORMATION THAT THE PRESIDENT LIED UNDER OATH IN DESCRIBING HIS CONVERSATIONS WITH VERNON JORDAN ABOUT MS. LEWINSKY.

President Clinton was asked during his civil deposition whether he had talked to Mr. Jordan about Ms. Lewinsky's involvement in the Jones case. The President stated that he knew Mr. Jordan had talked to Ms. Lewinsky about her move to New York, but stated that he did not recall whether Mr. Jordan had talked to Ms. Lewinsky about her involvement in the Jones case. The testimony was false. A lie under oath about these conversations was necessary to avoid inquiry into whether Ms. Lewinsky's job and her testimony were improperly related.

A. PRESIDENT'S TESTIMONY IN THE JONES CASE

The President was questioned in his civil deposition about his conversations with Vernon Jordan regarding Ms. Lewinsky and her role in the Jones case. Beforehand, the President was asked a general question:

> Q: Did anyone other than your attorneys ever tell you that Monica Lewinsky had been served with a subpoena in this case?
>
> WJC: I don't think so.[363]

The President later testified in more detail about conversations he may have had with Mr. Jordan concerning Ms. Lewinsky's role in the case:

> Q: Excluding conversations that you may have had with Mr. Bennett or any of your attorneys in this case, within the past two weeks has anyone reported to you that they had had a conversation with Monica Lewinsky concerning this lawsuit?
>
> WJC: I don't believe so. I'm sorry, I just don't believe so.

●   ●   ●

> Q. Has it ever been reported to you that [Vernon Jordan] met with Monica Lewinsky and talked about this case?
>
> WJC: I knew that he met with her. I think Betty suggested that he meet with her. Anyway, he met with her. I, I thought that he talked to her about something else. I didn't know that—I thought he had given her some advice about her move to New York. Seems like that's what Betty said.[364]

B. Evidence That Contradicts the President's Civil Deposition Testimony

Vernon Jordan testified that his conversations with the President about Ms. Lewinsky's subpoena were, in fact, "a continuing dialogue."[365] When asked if he had kept the President informed about Ms. Lewinsky's status in the Jones case in addition to her job search, Mr. Jordan responded: "The two—absolutely."[366]

On December 19, Ms. Lewinsky phoned Mr. Jordan and told him that she had been subpoenaed in the Jones case.[367] Following that call, Mr. Jordan telephoned the President to inform him "that Monica Lewinsky was coming to see me, and that she had a subpoena"[368]—but the President was unavailable.[369] Later that day, at 5:01 p.m., Mr. Jordan had a seven-minute telephone conversation with the President:[370]

> I said to the President, "Monica Lewinsky called me up. She's upset. She's gotten a subpoena. She is coming to see me about this subpoena. I'm confident that she needs a lawyer, and I will try to get her a lawyer."[371]

Later on December 19, after meeting with Ms. Lewinsky, Mr. Jordan went to the White House and met with the President alone in the Residence.[372] Mr. Jordan testified: "I told him that Monica Lewinsky had been subpoenaed, came to me with a subpoena."[373] According to Mr. Jordan, the President "thanked me for my efforts to get her a job and thanked me for getting her a lawyer."[374]

According to Mr. Jordan, on January 7, 1998, Ms. Lewinsky showed him a copy of her signed affidavit denying any sexual relationship with the President.[375] He testified that he told the President about the affidavit, probably in one of his two logged calls to the White House that day:[376]

> Q: [W]alk us through what exactly you would have said on the portion of the conversation that related to Ms. Lewinsky and the affidavit.
>
> VJ: Monica Lewinsky signed the affidavit.

●   ●   ●

Q: [L]et's say if it was January 7th, or whenever it was that you informed him that she signed the affidavit,[377] is it accurate that based on the conversations you had with him already, you didn't have to explain to him what the affidavit was?

VJ: I think that's a reasonable assumption.

Q: So that it would have made sense that you would have just said, "She signed the affidavit," because both you and he knew what the affidavit was?

VJ: I think that's a reasonable assumption.

Q: All right. When you indicated to the President that she had signed the affidavit, what, if anything, did he tell you?

VJ: I think he—his judgment was consistent with mine that that was—the signing of the affidavit was consistent with the truth.[378]

Mr. Jordan testified that "I knew that the President was concerned about the affidavit and whether or not it was signed. He was, obviously."[379] When asked why he believed the President was concerned, Mr. Jordan testified:

Here is a friend of his who is being called as a witness in another case and with whom I had gotten a lawyer, I told him about that, and told him I was looking for a job for her. He knew about all of that. And it was just a matter of course that he would be concerned as to whether or not she had signed an affidavit foreswearing what I told you the other day, that there was no sexual relationship.[380]

Mr. Jordan summarized his contacts with the President about Monica Lewinsky and her involvement in the Jones litigation as follows:

I made arrangements for a lawyer and I told the President that. When she signed the affidavit, I told the President that the affidavit had been signed and when Frank Carter told me that he had filed a motion to quash, as I did in the course of everything else, I said to the President that I saw Frank Carter and he had informed me that he was filing a motion to quash. It was as a simple information flow, absent a substantive discussion about her defense, about which I was not involved.[381]

The President himself testified in the grand jury that he talked to Mr. Jordan about Ms. Lewinsky's involvement in the case. Despite his earlier statements at the deposition, the President testified to the grand jury that he had no reason to doubt that he had talked to Mr. Jordan about Ms. Lewinsky's subpoena, her lawyer, and her affidavit.[382]

C. SUMMARY

In his civil deposition, the President stated that he had talked to Vernon Jordan about Ms. Lewinsky's job. But as the testimony of Mr. Jordan reveals, and as the President as much as conceded in his subsequent grand jury appearance,[383] the President did talk to Mr. Jordan about Ms. Lewinsky's involvement in the Jones case— including that she had been subpoenaed, that Mr. Jordan had helped her obtain a lawyer, and that she had signed an affidavit denying a sexual relationship with the President. Given their several communications in the weeks before the deposition, it is not credible that the President forgot the subject of their conversations during his civil deposition. His statements "seems like that's what Betty said" and "I didn't know that" were more than mere omissions; they were affirmative misstatements.

The President's motive for making false and misleading statements about this subject in his civil deposition was straightforward. If the President admitted that he had talked with Vernon Jordan both about Monica Lewinsky's involvement in the Jones case and about her job, questions would inevitably arise about whether Ms.

Lewinsky's testimony and her future job were connected. Such an admission by the President in his civil deposition likely would have prompted Ms. Jones's attorneys to inquire further into the subject. And such an admission in his deposition would have triggered public scrutiny when the deposition became public.

At the time of his deposition, moreover, the President was aware of the potential problems in admitting any possible link between those two subjects. A criminal investigation and substantial public attention had focused in 1997 on job assistance and payments made to Webster Hubbell in 1994. The jobs and money paid to Mr. Hubbell by friends and contributors to the President had raised serious questions about whether such assistance was designed to influence Mr. Hubbell's testimony about Madison-related matters.[384] Some of Mr. Hubbell's jobs, moreover, had been arranged by Vernon Jordan, which was likely a further deterrent to the President raising both Ms. Lewinsky's job and her affidavit in connection with Vernon Jordan.

IX. THERE IS SUBSTANTIAL AND CREDIBLE INFORMATION THAT PRESIDENT CLINTON ENDEAVORED TO OBSTRUCT JUSTICE BY ATTEMPTING TO INFLUENCE THE TESTIMONY OF BETTY CURRIE.

In a meeting with Betty Currie on the day after his deposition and in a separate conversation a few days later, President Clinton made statements to her that he knew were false. The contents of the statements and the context in which they were made indicate that President Clinton was attempting to influence the testimony that Ms. Currie might have been required to give in the Jones case or in a grand jury investigation.[385]

A. EVIDENCE

1. SATURDAY, JANUARY 17, 1998, DEPOSITION

President Clinton's deposition in Jones v. Clinton occurred on Saturday, January 17, 1998. In that deposition, the President testified that he could not recall being alone with Monica Lewinsky and that he had not had sexual relations, a sexual affair, or a sexual relationship with her. During his testimony, the President referred several times to Betty Currie and to her relationship with Ms. Lewinsky. He stated, for example, that the last time he had seen Ms. Lewinsky was when she had come to the White House to see Ms. Currie;[386] that Ms. Currie was present when the President had made a joking reference about the Jones case to Ms. Lewinsky;[387] that Ms. Currie was his source of information about Vernon Jordan's assistance to Ms. Lewinsky;[388] and that Ms. Currie had helped set up the meetings between Ms. Lewinsky and Mr. Jordan regarding her move to New York.[389]

At the deposition, Judge Wright imposed a protective order that prevented the parties from discussing their testimony with anyone else. "Before he leaves, I want to remind him, as the witness in this matter, . . . that this case is subject to a Protective Order regarding all discovery, . . . [A]ll parties present, including . . . the witness are not to say anything whatsoever about the questions they were asked, the substance of the deposition, . . ., any details . . . ."[390]

2. SUNDAY, JANUARY 18, 1998, MEETING WITH MS. CURRIE

Because the President referred so often to Ms. Currie, it was foreseeable that she might become a witness in the Jones matter, particularly if specific allegations of the President's relationship with Ms. Lewinsky came to light.[391] Indeed, according to Ms. Currie, President Clinton at some point may have told her that she might be asked about Monica Lewinsky.[392]

Shortly after 7:00 p.m. on Saturday, January 17, 1998, two and a half hours after he returned from the deposition, President Clinton called Ms. Currie at home[393] and asked her to come to the White House the next day.[394] Ms. Currie testified that "[i]t's rare for [President Clinton] to ask me to come in on Sunday."[395]

At about 5:00 p.m. on Sunday, January 18, Ms. Currie went to meet with President Clinton at the White House. She told the grand jury:

> He said that he had had his deposition yesterday, and they had asked several questions about Monica Lewinsky. And I was a little shocked by that or—(shrugging). And he said—I don't know if he said—I think he may have said, "There are several things you may want to know," or "There are things—" He asked me some questions.[396]

According to Ms. Currie, the President then said to her in succession:[397]

- "You were always there when she was there, right? We were never really alone."[398]

- "You could see and hear everything."[399]

- "Monica came on to me, and I never touched her, right?"[400]

- "She wanted to have sex with me, and I can't do that."[401]

Ms. Currie indicated that these remarks were "more like statements than questions."[402] Ms. Currie concluded that the President wanted her to agree with him.[403] She based that conclusion on the way he made most of the statements and on his demeanor.[404] Ms. Currie also said that she felt the President made these remarks to see her reaction.[405]

Ms. Currie said that she indicated her agreement with each of the President's statements,[406] although she knew that the President and Ms. Lewinsky had in fact been alone in the Oval Office and in the President's study.[407] Ms. Currie also knew that she could not or did not in fact hear or see the President and Ms. Lewinsky while they were alone.[408]

In the context of this conversation, President Clinton appeared to be "concerned," according to Ms. Currie.[409]

The President's concern over the questions asked at the civil deposition about Ms. Lewinsky also manifested itself in substantial efforts to contact Monica Lewinsky over the next two days. Shortly after her meeting with the President, Ms. Currie made several attempts to contact Ms. Lewinsky. Ms. Currie testified it was "possible" she did so at the President's suggestion, and said "he may have asked me to call [Ms. Lewinsky] to see what she knew or where she was or what was happening."[410] Later that same night, at 11:01 p.m., the President again called Ms. Currie at home.[411] Ms. Currie could not recall the substance but suggested that the President had called to ask whether she had spoken to Ms. Lewinsky.[412] The next day, January 19, 1998, which was a holiday, Ms. Currie made seven unsuccessful attempts to contact Monica Lewinsky, by pager, between 7:00 a.m. and 9:00 a.m.[413] The President called Ms. Currie at home twice, and Ms. Currie called the President at the White House once that day.[414]

3. CONVERSATION BETWEEN THE PRESIDENT AND MS. CURRIE ON TUESDAY, JANUARY 20, 1998, OR WEDNESDAY, JANUARY 21, 1998.

On either Tuesday, January 20 or Wednesday, January 21 of that week, the President again met with Ms. Currie and discussed the Monica Lewinsky matter. Ms. Currie testified as follows:

> BC: It was Tuesday or Wednesday. I don't remember which one this was, either. But the best I remember, when he called me in the Oval Office, it was sort of a recap[it]ulation of what we had talked about on Sunday—you know, "I was never alone with her"—that sort of thing.

> Q: Did he pretty much list the same—

> BC: To my recollection, sir, yes.

Q: And did he say it in sort of the same tone and demeanor that he used the first time he told you on Sunday?

BC: The best I remember, sir, yes.

•   •   •

Q: And the President called you into the Oval Office specifically to list these things?

BC: I don't know if that's specifically what he called me in for, but once I got inside, that's what he—

Q: That's what he told you?

BC: Uh-huh.[415]

B. THE PRESIDENT'S GRAND JURY TESTIMONY

The President was asked why he might have said to Ms. Currie in their meeting on Sunday, January 18, 1998, "we were never alone together, right?" and "you could see and hear everything." The President testified:

[W]hat I was trying to determine was whether my recollection was right and that she was always in the office complex when Monica was there, and whether she thought she could hear any conversations we had, or did she hear any.

•   •   •

I was trying to—I knew . . . to a reasonable certainty that I was going to be asked more questions about this. I didn't really expect you to be in the Jones case at the time. I thought what would happen is that it would break in the press, and I was trying to get the facts down. I was trying to understand what the facts were.[416]

Later, the President stated that he was referring to a larger area than simply the room where he and Ms. Lewinsky were located. He also testified that his statements to Ms. Currie were intended to cover a limited range of dates:

WJC:. . . . [W]hen I said, we were never alone, right, I think I also asked her a number of other questions, because there were several times, as I'm sure she would acknowledge, when I either asked her to be around. I remember once in particular when I was talking with Ms. Lewinsky when I asked Betty to be in the, actually, in the next room in the dining room, and, as I testified earlier, once in her own office.

But I meant that she was always in the Oval Office complex, in that complex, while Monica was there. And I believe that this was part of a series of questions I asked her to try to quickly refresh my memory. So, I wasn't trying to get her to say something that wasn't so. And, in fact, I think she would recall that I told her to just relax, go in the grand jury and tell the truth when she had been called as a witness.

Q: So, when you said to Mrs. Currie that, I was never alone with her, right, you just meant that you and Ms. Lewinsky would be somewhere perhaps in the Oval Office or many times in your back study, is that correct?

WJC: That's right. We were in the back study.

Q: And then—

WJC: Keep in mind, sir, I just want to make it—I was talking about 1997. I was never, ever trying to get Betty Currie to claim that on the occasions when Monica Lewinsky was there when she wasn't anywhere around, that she was. I would never have done that to her, and I don't think she thought about that. I don't think she thought I was referring to that.

Q: Did you put a date restriction? Did you make it clear to Mrs. Currie that you were only asking her whether you were never alone with her after 1997?

WJC: Well, I don't recall whether I did or not, but I assumed—if I didn't, I assumed she knew what I was talking about, because it was the point at which Ms. Lewinsky was out of the White House and had to have someone WAVE her in, in order to get in the White House. And I do not believe to this day that I was—in 1997, that she was ever there and that I ever saw her unless Betty Currie was there. I don't believe she was.[417]

With respect to the word "alone," the President also stated that "it depends on how you define alone" and "there were a lot of times when we were alone, but I never really thought we were."[418]

The President was also asked about his specific statement to Betty Currie that "you could see and hear everything." He testified that he was uncertain what he intended by that comment:

Q: When you said to Mrs. Currie, you could see and hear everything, that wasn't true either, was it, as far as you knew. You've already—. . .

WJC: . . . My memory of that was that, that she had the ability to hear what was going on if she came in the Oval Office from her office. And a lot of times, you know, when I was in the Oval Office, she just had the door open to her office. Then there was—the door was never completely closed to the hall. So I think there was—I'm not entirely sure what I meant by that, but I could have meant that she generally would be able to hear conversations, even if she couldn't see them. And I think that's what I meant.[419]

The President then testified that when he made the comment to Ms. Currie about her being able to hear everything, he again was referring to only a limited period of time:

Q: . . . .you would not have engaged in those physically intimate acts if you knew that Mrs. Currie could see or hear that, is that correct?

WJC: That's correct. But keep in mind, sir, I was talking about 1997.

That occurred, to the—and I believe that occurred only once in February of 1997. I stopped it. I never should have started it, and I certainly shouldn't have started it back after I resolved not to in 1996. And I was referring to 1997.

And I—what—as I say, I do not know—her memory and mine may be somewhat different. I do not know whether I was asking her about a particular time when Monica was upset and I asked her to stand, stay back in the dining area. Or whether I was, had reference to the fact that if she kept the door open to the Oval Office, because it was always—the door to the hallway was always somewhat open, that she would always be able to hear something if anything went on that was, you know, too loud, or whatever.

I do not know what I meant. I'm just trying to reconcile the two statements as best I can, without being sure.[420]

The President was also asked about his comment to Ms. Currie that Ms. Lewinsky had "come on" to him, but that he had "never touched her":

Q:. . . . [I]f [Ms. Currie] testified that you told her, Monica came on to me and I never touched her, you did, in fact, of course, touch Ms. Lewinsky, isn't that right, in a physically intimate way?

WJC: Now, I've testified about that. And that's one of those questions that I believe is answered by the statement that I made.[421]

Q: What was your purpose in making these statements to Mrs. Currie, if it weren't for the purpose to try to suggest to her what she should say if ever asked?

WJC: Now, Mr. Bittman, I told you, the only thing I remember is when all this stuff blew up, I was trying to figure out what the facts were. I was trying to remember. I was trying to remember every time I had seen Ms. Lewinsky.

. . . I knew this was all going to come out. . . . I did not know [at the time] that the Office of Independent Counsel was involved. And I was trying to get the facts and try to think of the best defense we could construct in the face of what I thought was going to be a media onslaught.[422]

Finally, the President was asked why he would have called Ms. Currie into his office a few days after the Sunday meeting and repeated the statements about Ms. Lewinsky to her. The President testified that although he would not dispute Ms. Currie's testimony to the contrary, he did not remember having a second conversation with her along these lines.[423]

C. SUMMARY

The President referred to Ms. Currie on multiple occasions in his civil deposition when describing his relationship with Ms. Lewinsky. As he himself recognized, a large number of questions about Ms. Lewinsky were likely to be asked in the very near future. The President thus could foresee that Ms. Currie either might be deposed or questioned or might need to prepare an affidavit.

The President called her shortly after the deposition and met with Ms. Currie the next day. The President appeared "concerned," according to Ms. Currie. He then informed Ms. Currie that questions about Ms. Lewinsky had been asked at the deposition.

The statements the President made to her on January 18 and again on January 20 or 21—that he was never alone with Ms. Lewinsky, that Ms. Currie could always hear or see them, and that he never touched Ms. Lewinsky—were false, but consistent with the testimony that the President provided under oath at his deposition. The President knew that the statements were false at the time he made them to Ms. Currie. The President's suggestion that he was simply trying to refresh his memory when talking to Ms. Currie conflicts with common sense: Ms. Currie's confirmation of false statements could not in any way remind the President of the facts. Thus, it is not plausible that he was trying to refresh his recollection.

The President's grand jury testimony reinforces that conclusion. He testified that in asking questions of Ms. Currie such as "We were never alone, right" and "Monica came on to me, and I never touched her, right," he intended a date restriction on the questions. But he did not articulate a date restriction in his conversations with Ms. Currie. Moreover, with respect to some aspects of this incident, the President was unable to devise any innocent explanation, testifying that he did not know why he had asked Ms. Currie some questions and admitting that he was "just trying to reconcile the two statements as best [he could]." On the other hand, if the most reasonable inference from the President's conduct is drawn—that he was attempting to enlist a witness to back up his false testimony from the day before—his behavior with Ms. Currie makes complete sense.

The content of the President's statements and the context in which those statements were made provide substantial and credible information that President Clinton sought improperly to influence Ms. Currie's testimony. Such actions constitute an obstruction of justice and improper influence on a witness.

X. THERE IS SUBSTANTIAL AND CREDIBLE INFORMATION THAT PRESIDENT CLINTON ENDEAVORED TO OBSTRUCT JUSTICE DURING THE FEDERAL GRAND JURY INVESTIGATION. WHILE REFUSING TO TESTIFY FOR SEVEN MONTHS, HE SIMULTANEOUSLY LIED TO POTENTIAL GRAND JURY WITNESSES KNOWING THAT THEY WOULD RELAY THE FALSEHOODS TO THE GRAND JURY.

The President's grand jury testimony followed seven months of investigation in which he had refused six invitations to testify before the grand jury. During this period, there was no indication that the President would admit any sexual relationship with Ms. Lewinsky. To the contrary, the President vehemently denied the allegations.

Rather than lie to the grand jury himself, the President lied about his relationship with Ms. Lewinsky to senior aides, and those aides then conveyed the President's false story to the grand jury.[424]

In this case, the President lied to, among others, three current

senior aides—John Podesta, Erskine Bowles, and Sidney Blumenthal—and one former senior aide, Harold Ickes. The President
denied any kind of sexual relationship with Monica Lewinsky; said
that Ms. Lewinsky had made a sexual demand on him; and denied
multiple telephone conversations with Monica Lewinsky. The President, by his own later admission, was aware that his aides were
likely to convey the President's version of events to the grand jury.

The President's aides took the President at his word when he
made these statements. Each aide then testified to the nature of the
relationship between Monica Lewinsky and the President based on
those statements—without knowing that they were calculated falsehoods by the President designed to perpetuate the false statements
that the President made during his deposition in the Jones case.

The aides' testimony provided the grand jury a false account of
the relationship between the President and Ms. Lewinsky. Their testimony thus had the potential to affect the investigation—including
decisions by the OIC and grand jury about how to conduct the
investigation (for example, whether to subpoena Secret Service
agents) and whether to indict particular individuals.

A. THE TESTIMONY OF CURRENT AND FORMER AIDES

1. JOHN PODESTA

John Podesta, Deputy Chief of Staff,[425] testified that on several
occasions shortly after the media first began reporting the Lewinsky
allegations, the President either denied having a relationship with
Ms. Lewinsky or otherwise minimized his involvement with her.

Mr. Podesta described a meeting with the President, Chief of
Staff Erskine Bowles, and Deputy Chief of Staff Sylvia Matthews, in
the morning of January 21, 1998.[426] During that meeting, the President stated: "Erskine, I want you to know that this story is not
true."[427] Mr. Podesta further recalled that the President said "that he
had not had a sexual relationship with her, and that he never asked
anybody to lie."[428]

Several days later, on January 23, 1998, the President more

adamantly told Mr. Podesta that he had not engaged in sex of any "kind, shape or manner" with Ms. Lewinsky. Mr. Podesta recalled:

> JP: [H]e said to me that he had never had sex with her, and that—and that he never asked—you know, he repeated the denial, but he was extremely explicit in saying he never had sex with her.
>
> Q: How do you mean?
>
> JP: Just what I said.
>
> Q: Okay. Not explicit, in the sense that he got more specific than sex, than the word "sex."
>
> JP: Yes, he was more specific than that.
>
> Q: Okay. Share that with us.
>
> JP: Well, I think he said—he said that—there was some spate of, you know, what sex acts were counted, and he said that he had never had sex with her in any way whatsoever—
>
> Q: Okay.
>
> JP:—that they had not had oral sex.[429]

Later, possibly that same day,[430] the President made a further statement to Mr. Podesta regarding his relationship with Ms. Lewinsky.

Mr. Podesta testified that the President "said to me that after [Monica] left [her job at the White House], that when she had come by, she came by to see Betty, and that he—when she was there, either Betty was with them—either that she was with Betty when he saw her or that he saw her in the Oval Office with the door open and Betty was around—and Betty was out at her desk."[431] The President relayed to Mr. Podesta one of the false "cover stories" that the President and Ms. Lewinsky had agreed to use.

Both the President and Mr. Podesta knew that Mr. Podesta was likely to be a witness in the ongoing grand jury criminal investigation.[432] Nonetheless, Mr. Podesta recalled that the President "volunteered" to provide information about Ms. Lewinsky to him[433] even though Mr. Podesta had not asked for these details.[434]

Mr. Podesta "believe[d]" the President, and testified that it was important to him that the President denied the affair.[435] Mr. Podesta repeated to the grand jury the false and misleading statements that the President told him.

2. ERSKINE BOWLES

Mr. Bowles, the White House Chief of Staff,[436] confirmed Mr. Podesta's account of the President's January 21, 1998, statement in which the President denied having a sexual relationship with Ms. Lewinsky.

Mr. Bowles testified:

> EB: And this was the day this huge story breaks. And the three of us walked in together—Sylvia Matthews, John Podesta, and me—into the Oval Office, and the President was standing behind his desk.

> Q: About what time of day is this?

> EB: This is approximately 9:00 in the morning, or something—you know, in that area. And he looked up at us and he said the same thing he said to the American people. He said, "I want you to know I did not have sexual relationships [sic] with this woman Monica Lewinsky. I did not ask anybody to lie. And when the facts come out, you'll understand."[437]

Mr. Bowles testified that he took the President's statements seriously:

> "All I can tell you is: This guy who I've worked for looked me in the eye and said he did not have sexual relationships with her. And if I didn't believe him, I couldn't stay. So I believe him."[438]
> Mr. Bowles repeated the President's false and misleading statement to the grand jury.

3. SIDNEY BLUMENTHAL

Sidney Blumenthal, an Assistant to the President,[439] similarly testified that the President made statements to him denying the Lewinsky allegations shortly after the first media report.

Mr. Blumenthal stated that he spoke to Mrs. Clinton on the afternoon of January 21, 1998, and to the President early that evening. During those conversations, both the President and Mrs. Clinton offered an explanation for the President's meetings with Ms. Lewinsky, and President Clinton offered an explanation for Ms. Lewinsky's allegations of a sexual relationship.[440]

Testifying before the grand jury, Mr. Blumenthal related his discussion with President Clinton:

> I said to the President, "What have you done wrong?" And he said, "Nothing. I haven't done anything wrong." . . . And it was at that point that he gave his account of what had happened to me and he said that Monica—and it came very fast. He said, "Monica Lewinsky came at me and made a sexual demand on me." He rebuffed her. He said, "I've gone down that road before, I've caused pain for a lot of people and I'm not going to do that again."
>
> She threatened him. She said that she would tell people they'd had an affair, that she was known as the stalker among her peers, and that she hated it and if she had an affair or said she had an affair then she wouldn't be the stalker any more.[441]

Mr. Blumenthal testified that the President appeared "upset" during this conversation.[442]

Finally, Mr. Blumenthal asked the President to explain alleged answering machine messages (a detail mentioned in press reports).

> He said that he remembered calling her when Betty Currie's brother died and that he left a message on her voice machine that Betty's brother had died and he said she was close to Betty and had been very kind to Betty. And that's what he recalled.[443]

According to Mr. Blumenthal, the President said that the call he made to Ms. Lewinsky relating to Betty's brother was the "only one he could remember."[444] That was false: The President and Ms. Lewinsky talked often on the phone, and the subject matter of the calls was memorable.

A grand juror asked Mr. Blumenthal whether the President had said that his relationship with Ms. Lewinsky included any kind of sexual activity. Mr. Blumenthal testified that the President's response was "the opposite. He told me that she came on to him and that he had told her he couldn't have sexual relations with her and that she threatened him. That is what he told me."[445]

Mr. Blumenthal testified that after the President relayed this information to him, he "certainly believed his story. It was a very heartfelt story, he was pouring out his heart, and I believed him."[446] Mr. Blumenthal repeated to the grand jury the false statements that the President made to him.

4. HAROLD ICKES

Mr. Ickes, a former Deputy Chief of Staff,[447] also related to the grand jury a conversation that he had with the President on the morning of January 26, 1998,[448] during which the President denied the Lewinsky allegations.

Regarding that conversation, Mr. Ickes testified: "The two things that I recall, the two things that he again repeated in public—had already said publicly and repeated in public that same Monday morning was that he had not had—he did not have a—or he had not had a sexual relationship with Ms. Lewinsky and that he had done nothing—now I'm paraphrasing—had done nothing to ask anybody to change their story or suborn perjury or obstruct justice."[449]

Mr. Ickes recalled that the President probably volunteered this information.[450] Mr. Ickes repeated the President's false statements to the grand jury.

B. The President's Grand Jury Testimony

The President admitted to the grand jury that, after the allegations were publicly reported, he made "misleading" statements to particular aides whom he knew would likely be called to testify before the grand jury. The President testified as follows:

Q: Do you recall denying any sexual relationship with Monica Lewinsky to the following people: Harry Thomasson, Erskine Bowles, Harold Ickes, Mr. Podesta, Mr. Blumenthal, Mr. Jordan, Ms. Betty Currie? Do you recall denying any sexual relationship with Monica Lewinsky to those individuals?

WJC: I recall telling a number of those people that I didn't have, either I didn't have an affair with Monica Lewinsky or didn't have sex with her. And I believe, sir, that—you'll have to ask them what they thought. But I was using those terms in the normal way people use them. You'll have to ask them what they thought I was saying.

Q: If they testified that you denied sexual relationship with Monica Lewinsky, or if they told us that you denied that, do you have any reason to doubt them, in the days after the story broke; do you have any reason to doubt them?

WJC: No.

The President then was specifically asked whether he knew that his aides were likely to be called before the grand jury.

Q: It may have been misleading, sir, and you knew though, after January 21st when the Post article broke and said that Judge Starr was looking into this, you knew that they might be witnesses. You knew that they might be called into a grand jury, didn't you?

WJC: That's right. I think I was quite careful what I said after that. I may have said something to all these people to that effect, but I'll also—whenever anybody asked me any details, I said, look, I don't want you to be a witness or I turn you into a witness or give you information that would get you in trouble. I just wouldn't talk. I, by and large, didn't talk to people about this.

Q: If all of these people—let's leave out Mrs. Currie for a minute. Vernon Jordan, Sid Blumenthal, John Podesta, Harold Ickes, Erskine Bowles, Harry Thomasson, after the story broke, after Judge Starr's involvement was known on January 21st, have said that you denied a sexual relationship with them. Are you denying that?

WJC: No.

Q: And you've told us that you—

WJC: I'm just telling you what I meant by it. I told you what I meant by it when they started this deposition.

Q: You've told us now that you were being careful, but that it might have been misleading. Is that correct?

WJC: It might have been. . . . So, what I was trying to do was to give them something they could—that would be true, even if misleading in the context of this deposition, and keep them out of trouble, and let's deal—and deal with what I thought was the almost ludicrous suggestion that I had urged someone to lie or tried to suborn perjury, in other words.[451]

C. SUMMARY

The President made the following misleading statements to his aides:

- The President told Mr. Podesta that he had not engaged in sex "in any way whatsoever" with Ms. Lewinsky, "including oral sex".

- The President told Mr. Podesta, Mr. Bowles, and Mr. Ickes that he did not have a "sexual relationship" with Ms. Lewinsky.

- The President told Mr. Podesta that "when [Ms. Lewinsky] came by, she came by to see Betty [Currie]."

- The President told Mr. Blumenthal that Ms. Lewinsky "came on to him and that he had told her he couldn't have sexual relations with her and that she threatened him."

- The President told Mr. Blumenthal that he couldn't remember making any calls to Ms. Lewinsky other than once when he left a message on her answering machine.

During the President's grand jury testimony, the President admitted that his statements to aides denying a sexual relationship with Ms. Lewinsky "may have been misleading."[452] The President also knew his aides likely would be called to testify regarding any communications with him about Ms. Lewinsky. And he presumably expected his aides to repeat his statements regarding Ms. Lewinsky to all questioners, including to the grand jury. Finally, he himself refused to testify for many months. The combination of the President's silence and his deception of his aides had the effect of presenting a false view of events to the grand jury.

The President says that at the time he spoke to his aides, he chose his words with great care so that, in his view, his statements would be literally true because he was referring only to intercourse. That explanation is undermined by the President's testimony before the grand jury that his denials "may have been misleading" and by the contradictory testimony by the aides themselves—particularly John Podesta, who says that the President specifically denied oral sex with Ms. Lewinsky. Moreover, on January 24, 1998, the White House issued talking points for its staff, and those talking points refute the President's literal truth argument: The talking points state as the President's view the belief that a relationship that includes oral sex is "of course" a "sexual relationship."[453]

For all of these reasons, there is substantial and credible information that the President improperly tampered with witnesses during the grand jury investigation.

XI. THERE IS SUBSTANTIAL AND CREDIBLE INFORMATION THAT PRESIDENT CLINTON'S ACTIONS SINCE JANUARY 17, 1998, REGARDING HIS RELATIONSHIP WITH MONICA LEWINSKY HAVE BEEN INCONSISTENT WITH THE PRESIDENT'S CONSTITUTIONAL DUTY TO FAITHFULLY EXECUTE THE LAWS.

Before, during, and after his January 17, 1998, civil deposition, the President attempted to conceal the truth about his relationship with Ms. Lewinsky from the judicial process in the Jones case. Furthermore, the President has since lied under oath to the grand jury and facilitated the provision of false information to the grand jury by others.

The President also misled the American people and the Congress in his public statement of January 26, 1998, in which he denied "sexual relations" with Ms. Lewinsky. The President misled his Cabinet and his senior aides by denying the relationship to them. The Cabinet and senior aides in turn misled the American people and the Congress by conveying the President's denials and professing their belief in the credibility of those denials.

The President promised in January 1998 to cooperate fully with the grand jury investigation and to provide "more rather than less, sooner rather than later." At that time, the OIC was conducting a criminal investigation and was obligated to report to Congress any substantial and credible information that may constitute grounds for an impeachment.

The President's conduct delayed the grand jury investigation (and thereby delayed any potential congressional proceedings). He asserted, appealed, withdrew, and reasserted Executive Privilege (and asserted other governmental privileges never before applied in federal criminal proceedings against the government). The President asserted these privileges concerning the investigation of factual questions about which the President already knew the answers. The President refused six invitations to testify voluntarily before the grand jury. At the same time, the President's aides and surrogates argued publicly that the entire matter was frivolous and that any investigation of it should cease.

After being subpoenaed in July, the President made false statements to the grand jury on August 17, 1998. That night, the President again made false statements to the American people and Congress, contending that his answers in his civil deposition had been "legally accurate." The President then made an implicit plea for Congress to take no action: "Our country has been distracted by this matter for too long."[454]

The President has pursued a strategy of (i) deceiving the American people and Congress in January 1998, (ii) delaying and impeding the criminal investigation for seven months, and (iii) deceiving the American people and Congress again in August 1998.

A. BEGINNING ON JANUARY 21, 1998, THE PRESIDENT MISLED THE AMERICAN PEOPLE AND CONGRESS REGARDING THE TRUTH OF HIS RELATIONSHIP WITH MS. LEWINSKY.

On January 21, 1998, the day the Washington Post first reported the Lewinsky matter, the President talked to his long-time advisor Dick Morris. With the President's approval, Mr. Morris commissioned a poll that evening. The results indicated that voters were willing to forgive the President for adultery but not for perjury or obstruction of justice.[467] When the President telephoned him that evening, Mr. Morris explained that the President thus should not go public with a confession or explanation.[468] According to Mr. Morris, the President replied, "Well, we just have to win, then."[457]

The next evening, the President dissuaded Mr. Morris from any plan to "blast[] Monica Lewinsky 'out of the water.'" The President indicated that "there's some slight chance that she may not be cooperating with Starr and we don't want to alienate her."[458]

The President himself spoke publicly about the matter several times in the initial days after the story broke. On January 26, the President was definitive: "I want to say one thing to the American people. I want you to listen to me. I'm going to say this again: I did not have sexual relations with that woman, Miss Lewinsky. I never told anybody to lie, not a single time. Never. These allegations are false."[459]

The President's emphatic denial to the American people was false. And his statement was not an impromptu comment in the heat of a press conference. To the contrary, it was an intentional and calculated falsehood to deceive the Congress and the American people.[460]

B. The First Lady, the Cabinet, the President's staff, and the President's associates relied on and publicly emphasized the President's denial.

After the President lied to the American people, the President's associates argued that the allegations against the President were false and even scurrilous.

Mrs. Clinton forcefully denied the allegations on January 27, 1998, one day after the President's public denial. She admitted that the American people "should certainly be concerned" if a President had an affair and lied to cover it up. She acknowledged that it would be a "very serious offense." But she emphasized that the allegations were false—a "pretty bad" smear. She noted that the President "has denied these allegations on all counts, unequivocally." And Mrs. Clinton shifted the focus away from the President, indicated that "this is a battle" and stated that "some folks are going to have a lot to answer for" when the facts come out.[461]

The most senior officials in the Executive Branch served as additional (albeit unwitting) agents of the President's deception. The Cabinet and White House aides stated emphatically that the allegations were false. For example, White House spokesperson Michael McCurry was asked whether the President's denial covered all forms of sexual contact, and Mr. McCurry stated that "I think every American that heard him knows exactly what he meant."[462] So, too, White House Communications Director Ann Lewis said on January 26, 1998: "I can say with absolute assurance the President of the

United States did not have a sexual relationship because I have heard the President of the United States say so. He has said it, he could not be more clear. He could not have been more direct."[463] She added: "Sex is sex, even in Washington. I've been assured."[464]

After a Cabinet meeting on January 23, 1998, in which the President offered denials, several members of the Cabinet appeared outside the White House. Secretary of State Albright stated: "I believe that the allegations are completely untrue."[465] Coupled with the President's firm denial, the united front of the President's closest advisors helped shape perception of the issue.

C. THE PRESIDENT REPEATEDLY AND UNLAWFULLY INVOKED THE EXECUTIVE PRIVILEGE TO CONCEAL EVIDENCE OF HIS PERSONAL MISCONDUCT FROM THE GRAND JURY.

When the allegations about Ms. Lewinsky first arose, the President informed the American people that he would cooperate fully. He told Jim Lehrer that "we are doing our best to cooperate here."[466] He told National Public Radio that "I have told people that I would cooperate in the investigation, and I expect to cooperate with it. . . . I'm going to do my best to cooperate with the investigation."[467] He told Roll Call "I'm going to cooperate with this investigation. . . . And I'll cooperate."[468]

Such cooperation did not occur. The White House's approach to the constitutionally based principle of Executive Privilege most clearly exposed the non-cooperation. In 1994, White House Counsel Lloyd Cutler issued an opinion that the Clinton Administration would not invoke Executive Privilege for cases involving personal wrongdoing by any government official.[469] By 1998, however, the President had blended the official and personal dimensions to the degree that the President's private counsel stated in a legal brief filed in the U.S. Court of Appeals for the District of Columbia Circuit: "In a very real and significant way, the objectives of William J. Clinton, the person, and his Administration (the Clinton White House) are one and the same."[470]

After the Monica Lewinsky investigation began, the President invoked Executive Privilege for the testimony of five witnesses: Bruce Lindsey, Cheryl Mills, Nancy Hernreich, Sidney Blumenthal, and Lanny Breuer. These claims were patently groundless. Even for official communications within the scope of the privilege, the Supreme Court ruled unanimously in 1974 in United States v. Nixon[471] that the Executive Privilege gives way in the face of the compelling need for evidence in criminal proceedings.

The President's assertion of Executive Privilege for Ms. Hernreich, an assistant who manages the secretarial work for the Oval Office,[472] was frivolous. At the time that the President was asserting Executive Privilege for one assistant, the President's other assistant (Betty Currie) had already testified extensively.

Based on Nixon, the OIC filed a motion to compel the testimony of Hernreich, Lindsey, and Blumenthal. The United States District Court held a hearing on March 20. Just before the hearing, the White House—without explanation—dropped its Executive Privilege claim as to Ms. Hernreich.[473]

On May 4, 1998, Chief Judge Norma Holloway Johnson ruled against the President on the Executive Privilege issue.[474] After the White House filed a notice of appeal, the OIC filed an expedited petition for certiorari before judgment in the Supreme Court. The President thereupon dropped his claim of Executive Privilege.

The tactics employed by the White House have not been confined to the judicial process. On March 24, while the President was traveling in Africa, he was asked about the assertion of Executive Privilege. He responded, "You should ask someone who knows." He also stated "I haven't discussed that with the lawyers. I don't know."[475]

This was untrue. Unbeknownst to the public, in a declaration filed in District Court on March 17 (seven days before the President's public expression of ignorance), White House Counsel Charles F.C. Ruff informed Chief Judge Johnson that he "ha[d] discussed" the matter with the President, who had directed the assertion of Executive Privilege.[476]

The deception has continued. Because the President withdrew his Executive Privilege claim while the case was pending in the Supreme Court of the United States, it was assumed that the President would no longer assert Executive Privilege. But that assumption proved incorrect. White House attorney Lanny Breuer appeared before the grand jury on August 4, 1998, and invoked Executive Privilege. He would not answer, for example, whether the President had told him about his relationship with Monica Lewinsky and whether they had discussed the gifts he had given to Monica Lewinsky.[477] On August 11, 1998, Chief Judge Johnson denied the Executive Privilege claim as a basis for refusing to testify, and ordered Mr. Breuer to testify.[478]

On August 11, 1998, Deputy White House Counsel Cheryl Mills testified and repeatedly asserted Executive Privilege at the President's direction.[479] The breadth of the claim was striking: The privilege was asserted not only for Ms. Mills's communications with the President, senior staff, and staff members of the White House Counsel's Office—but also for Ms. Mills's communications with private lawyers for the President, private lawyers for grand jury witnesses, and Betty Currie.[480]

On August 17, the President testified before the grand jury. At the request of a grand juror, the OIC asked the President about his assertions of Executive Privilege and why he had withdrawn the claim before the Supreme Court. The President replied that "I didn't really want to advance an executive privilege claim in this case beyond having it litigated, so that we, we had not given up on principal [sic] this matter, without having some judge rule on it. . . . I strongly felt we should not appeal your victory on the executive privilege issue."[481]

Four days after this sworn statement, on August 21, 1998, the President filed a notice of appeal with respect to the Executive Privilege claim for Lanny Breuer that Chief Judge Johnson had denied ten days earlier (and six days before the President's testimony). In addition, Bruce Lindsey appeared again before the grand jury on August 28, 1998, and the President again asserted Executive Privilege with respect to his testimony—even though the President had dropped the claim of Executive Privilege for Mr. Lindsey while the case was pending before the Supreme Court of the United States in June.[482]

The Executive Privilege was not the only claim of privilege interposed to prevent the grand jury from gathering relevant information. The President also acquiesced in the Secret Service's attempt to have the Judiciary craft a new protective function privilege (rejecting requests by this Office that the President order the Secret Service officers to testify). The District Court and the U.S. Court of Appeals for the District of Columbia Circuit rejected the privilege claim. The litigation was disruptive to the Secret Service and to the grand jury. The frivolity of the claim is evidenced by the Chief Justice's decision to reject the Secret Service's request for a stay without even referring the matter to the full Court. All of that litigation would have been unnecessary had the President testified in February instead of August, or had he taken the position that relevant facts should be fully available to the grand jury.

D. THE PRESIDENT REFUSED SIX INVITATIONS TO TESTIFY TO THE GRAND JURY, THEREBY DELAYING EXPEDITIOUS RESOLUTION OF THIS MATTER, AND THEN REFUSED TO ANSWER RELEVANT QUESTIONS BEFORE THE GRAND JURY WHEN HE TESTIFIED IN AUGUST 1998.

This Office extended six separate invitations to the President to testify before the grand jury. The first invitation was issued on January 28, 1998. The OIC repeated the invitations on behalf of the grand jury on February 4, February 9, February 21, March 2, and March 13. The President declined each invitation. His refusals substantially delayed this Office's investigation.

Finally, in the face of the President's actions, this Office asked the grand jury to consider issuing a subpoena to the President. The grand jury deliberated and approved the issuance of a subpoena. On July 17, 1998, the OIC served the subpoena, in accordance with the grand jury's action, on the President's private counsel. The subpoena required the President to appear on July 28.

The President sought to delay his testimony.[493] Shortly after a hearing before the District Court on the President's motion for a continuance, the President and the OIC reached an agreement by which the President would testify on August 17 via live video feed to the grand jury. In a Rose Garden ceremony on July 31, 1998, the President stated to the country: "I'm looking forward to the opportunity . . . of testifying. I will do so completely and truthfully."[484]

At the outset of his grand jury appearance, the President similarly stated: "I will answer each question as accurately and fully as I can."[485] The President then read a prepared statement in which he admitted "inappropriate intimate contact" with Ms. Lewinsky.[486] Despite his statement that he would answer each question, the President refused to answer specific questions about that contact (other than to indicate that it was not intercourse and did not involve the direct touching of Ms. Lewinsky's breasts or genitals).[487]

E. THE PRESIDENT MISLED THE AMERICAN PEOPLE AND THE CONGRESS IN HIS PUBLIC STATEMENT ON AUGUST 17, 1998, WHEN HE STATED THAT HIS ANSWERS AT HIS CIVIL DEPOSITION IN JANUARY HAD BEEN "LEGALLY ACCURATE."

The President addressed the Nation on the evening of August 17, 1998, after his grand jury appearance. The President did not tell the truth. He stated: "As you know, in a deposition in January, I was asked questions about my relationship with Monica Lewinsky. While my answers were legally accurate, I did not volunteer information."[488] As this Referral has demonstrated, the President's statements in his civil deposition were not "legally accurate," and he could not reasonably have thought they were. They were deliberate falsehoods designed to conceal the truth of the President's sexual relationship with Monica Lewinsky.

The President's claim that his testimony during the civil deposition was legally accurate—which he made to the grand jury and to the American people on August 17—perpetuates the deception and concealment that has accompanied his relationship with Monica

Lewinsky since his first sexual encounter with her on November 15, 1995.

F. SUMMARY

In this case, the President made and caused to be made false statements to the American people about his relationship with Ms. Lewinsky. He also made false statements about whether he had lied under oath or otherwise obstructed justice in his civil case. By publicly and emphatically stating in January 1998 that "I did not have sexual relations with that woman" and these "allegations are false," the President also effectively delayed a possible congressional inquiry, and then he further delayed it by asserting Executive Privilege and refusing to testify for six months during the Independent Counsel investigation. This represents substantial and credible information that may constitute grounds for an impeachment

CONCLUSION

This Referral is respectfully submitted on the Ninth day of September, 1998.

Kenneth W. Starr
Independent Counsel

NOTES

INTRODUCTION

1. Section 595(c) of Title 28 of the United States Code is part of the Ethics in Government Act. The section provides:

(c) Information relating to impeachment.—An independent counsel shall advise the House of Representatives of any substantial and credible information which such independent counsel receives, in carrying out the independent counsel's responsibilities under this chapter, that may constitute grounds for an impeachment. Nothing in this chapter or section 49 of this title [concerning the assignment of judges to the Special Division that appoints an independent counsel] shall prevent the Congress or either House thereof from obtaining information in the course of an impeachment proceeding.

2. Ms. Jones also named Arkansas State Trooper Danny Ferguson as a defendant. For a detailed background of the *Jones v. Clinton* lawsuit, see the accompanying Appendix, Tab C.

3. In 1991, Ms. Jones was an employee of the Arkansas Industrial Development Corporation. Ms. Jones alleged that while at work at a meeting at the Excelsior Hotel that day, she was invited into a hotel room with Governor Clinton, and that once she was there, the Governor exposed his genitals and asked her to perform oral sex on him. Ms. Jones alleged that she suffered various job detriments after refusing Governor Clinton's advances. This Referral expresses no view on the factual or legal merit, or lack thereof, of Ms. Jones's claims.

4. *Jones v. Clinton*, 117 S. Ct. 1636, 1652 (1997).

5. The purpose of discovery in a civil lawsuit is "to allow a broad search for facts, the names of witnesses, or any other matters which may aid a party in the preparation or presentation of his case." Fed. R. Civ. P. 26 advisory committee notes (1946). The discovery process allows the parties to obtain from their respective opponents written answers to interrogatories, oral testimony in depositions under oath, documents, and other tangible items so long as the information sought "appears reasonably calculated to lead to the discovery of admissible evidence." Fed. R. Civ. P. 26(b)(1).

6. 921-DC-00000461 (Dec. 11, 1997 Order at 3). Similarly, in a December 18, 1997 Order, Judge Wright noted that "the issue [was] one of discovery, not admissibility of evidence at trial. Discovery, as all counsel know, by its very nature takes unforeseen twists and turns and goes down numerous paths, and whether those

paths lead to the discovery of admissible evidence often simply cannot be predetermined." 1414-DC-00001012-13 (Dec. 18, 1997 Order at 7-8).

7. V002-DC-00000020 (President Clinton's Responses to Plaintiff's Second Set of Interrogatories at 5).

8. V002-DC-00000053 (President Clinton's Supplemental Responses to Plaintiff's Second Set of Interrogatories at 2). During discovery in a civil lawsuit, the parties must answer written questions ("interrogatories") that are served on them by their opponent. Fed. R. Civ. P. 33. The answering party must sign a statement under penalty of perjury attesting to the truthfulness of the answers. *Id.*

9. For a brief discussion of the scope of the OIC's jurisdiction, see "The Scope of the Referral," below.

10. The full text of the Special Division's Order is set forth in the Appendix, Tab A.

11. *Jones v. Clinton*, Motion of the United States for Limited Intervention and a Stay of Discovery, at 6. The overlap in the proceedings was significant. Witnesses called before the grand jury in the criminal investigation had been subpoenaed by both parties to the civil case; defendant's counsel had subpoenaed information from the OIC; and the plaintiff's attorneys had subpoenaed documents directly related to the criminal matter.

12. *Jones v. Clinton*, Order, Jan. 29, 1998, at 2.

13. *Id.*

14. *Id.* at 2-3.

15. *Id.* at 3.

16. *Jones v. Clinton*, 993 F. Supp. 1217, 1222 (E.D. Ark. 1998) (footnote and emphasis omitted).

17. *Jones v. Clinton*, 990 F. Supp. 657, 679 (E.D. Ark. 1998).

18. In the course of its investigation, the OIC gathered information from a variety of sources, including the testimony of witnesses before the grand jury. Normally a federal prosecutor is prohibited by Rule 6(e) of the Federal Rules of Criminal Procedure from disclosing grand jury material, unless it obtains permission from a court or is otherwise authorized by law to do so. This Office concluded that the statutory obligation of disclosure imposed on an Independent Counsel by 28 U.S.C. § 595(c) grants such authority. Nevertheless, out of an abundance of caution, the OIC obtained permission from the Special Division to disclose grand jury material as appropriate in carrying out its statutory duty. A copy of the disclosure order entered

by the Special Division is set forth in the Appendix, Tab B. We also advised Chief Judge Norma Holloway Johnson, who supervises the principal grand jury in this matter, of our determination on that issue.

19. U.S. Const., art. I, § 2, cl. 5; art. I, § 3, cl. 6.

20. 28 U.S.C. § 594(a).

21. Before the grand jury, the President refused to answer certain questions about his conduct with Ms. Lewinsky on the ground that he believed the inquiries were unnecessary "and . . . I think, frankly, go too far in trying to criminalize my private life." Clinton 8/17/98 GJ at 94.

Others have argued that alleged "lies about sex" have nothing to do with the President's performance in office, and thus, are inconsequential. Former White House Counsel Jack Quinn articulated this view:

This is a matter of sex between consenting adults, and the question of whether or not one or the other was truthful about it. . . . This doesn't go to the question of his conduct in office. And, in that sense, it's trivial.

John F. Harris, "In Political Washington, A Confession Consensus," *Washington Post*, Aug. 4, 1998, at A1 (quoting Quinn's statement on CBS's "Face the Nation").

The President echoed this theme in his address to the Nation on August 17, 1998, following his grand jury testimony:

. . . I intend to reclaim my family life for my family. It's nobody's business but ours. Even Presidents have private lives. It is time to stop the pursuit of personal destruction and the prying into private lives and get on with our national life.

Testing of a President: In His Own Words, Last Night's Address, *The New York Times*, Aug. 18, 1998, at A12.

22. Clinton 1/17/98 Depo. at 9. As two commentators have noted: "[T]o the extent that discovery is permitted with respect to the sexual activities of either the complainant or the alleged harasser, courts likely will freely entertain motions to limit the availability of such information to the parties and their counsel and to prohibit general dissemination of such sensitive data to third parties." *See* Barbara Lindeman & David D. Kadue, *Sexual Harassment in Employment Law* 563 (1992).

23. A sexual harassment case can sometimes boil down to a credibility battle between the parties, in which "the existence of corroborative evidence or the lack thereof is likely to be crucial." *Henson v. City of Dundee*, 682 F.2d 897, 912 n.25 (11th Cir. 1982). If there are no eyewitnesses, it can be critical for a plaintiff to learn in discovery whether the defendant has committed the same kind of acts before or

since. Thus, the Equal Employment Opportunity Commission explained in a 1990 policy statement that the plaintiff's allegations of an incident of sexual harassment "would be further buttressed if other employees testified that the supervisor propositioned them as well." EEOC Policy Guidance (1990). The rules of evidence establish that such corroboration may be used to show the defendant's "motive, opportunity, intent, preparation, plan, knowledge, identity, or absence of mistake or accident." Fed. R. Evid. 404(b). In short, a defendant's sexual history, at least with respect to other employees, is ordinarily discoverable in a sexual harassment suit.

24. *United States v. Mandujano*, 425 U.S. 564, 576 (1975) (plurality opinion).

25. *ABF Freight Sys., Inc. v. NLRB*, 510 U.S. 317, 323 (1994).

26. *United States v. Norris*, 300 U.S. 564, 574 (1937). There is occasional misunderstanding to the effect that perjury is somehow distinct from "obstruction of justice." While the crimes are distinct, they are in fact variations on a single theme: preventing a court, the parties, and the public from discovering the truth. Perjury, subornation of perjury, concealment of subpoenaed documents, and witness tampering are all forms of obstruction of justice.

27. *See* Eugene Lyons, *Herbert Hoover: A Biography* 337 (1964) (quoting Hoover).

28. U.S. Const., art. II, § 1, cl. 8.

29. U.S. Const., art. II, § 3; *see also* George Washington, Second Inaugural Address, March 4, 1793:

Previous to the execution of any official act of the President the Constitution requires an oath of office. This oath I am now about to take, and in your presence: That if it shall be found during my administration of the Government I have in any instance violated willingly or knowingly the injunctions thereof, I may (besides incurring constitutional punishment) be subject to the upbraidings of all who are now witnesses of the present solemn ceremony.

Inaugural Addresses of the Presidents of the United States, H.R. Doc. No. 82-540, at 4 (1954).

30. Jordan, House Testimony, 7/24/97, at 46.

31. From April through November 1994, 17 different persons or entities retained Mr. Hubbell as a consultant. In 1994, he collected $450,010 for this work. In 1995, he collected $91,750, despite beginning a 28-month prison term in August of that year.

NARRATIVE

1. Lewinsky 8/6/98 GJ at 31-32, 39-40; DB Photos 0004 (photo of dress).

2. FBI Lab Report, 8/3/98.

3. OIC letter to David Kendall, 7/31/98 (1st letter of day).

4. Kendall letter to OIC, 7/31/98; OIC letter to Kendall, 7/31/98 (2d letter of day); Kendall letter to OIC, 8/3/98; OIC letter to Kendall, 8/3/98.

5. FBI Observation Report (White House), 8/3/98.

6. FBI Lab Reports, 8/6/98 & 8/17/98. The FBI Laboratory performed polymerase chain reaction analysis (PCR) and restriction fragment length polymorphisim analysis (RFLP). RFLP, which requires a larger sample, is the more precise method. United States v. Hicks, 103 F.3d 837, 844–847 (9th Cir. 1996).

7. FBI Lab Report, 8/17/98, at 2.

8. Lewinsky 7/27/98 Int. During earlier negotiations with this Office, Ms. Lewinsky provided a 10–page handwritten proffer statement summarizing her dealings with the President and other matters under investigation. Lewinsky 2/1/98 Statement. Ms. Lewinsky later confirmed the accuracy of the statement in grand jury testimony. Lewinsky 8/20/98 GJ at 62–63. The negotiations in January and February 1998 (which produced the written proffer) did not result in a cooperation agreement because Ms. Lewinsky declined to submit to a face-to-face proffer interview, which the OIC deemed essential because of her perjurious Jones affidavit, her efforts to persuade Linda Tripp to commit perjury, her assertion in a recorded conversation that she had been brought up to regard lying as necessary, and her forgery of a letter while in college. In July 1998, Ms. Lewinsky agreed to submit to a face-to-face interview, and the parties were able to reach an agreement.

9. Ex. ML–7 to Lewinsky 8/6/98 GJ.

10. Lewinsky 8/26/98 Depo. at 5–6; Lewinsky 8/6/98 GJ at 27–28.

11. Lewinsky 8/26/98 Depo. at 69.

12. Lewinsky 8/6/98 GJ at 59–60, 87; Lewinsky 8/20/98 GJ at 82; Lewinsky 8/24/98 Int. at 8.

13. Ms. Tripp testified that she took notes on two occasions. Tripp 6/30/98 GJ at 141–42; Tripp 7/7/98 GJ at 153–54; Tripp 7/16/98 GJ at 112–13.

14. Kassorla 8/28/98 Int. at 2–3. Ms. Lewinsky (who voluntarily waived therapist-patient privilege) consulted Dr. Kassorla in person from 1992 to 1993 and by telephone thereafter. Id. at 1. Anticipating that the White House might fire Ms.

Lewinsky in order to protect the President, Dr. Kassorla cautioned her patient that workplace romances are generally ill-advised. Id. at 2.

15. Kassorla 8/28/98 Int. at 2, 4. Ms. Lewinsky also consulted another counselor, Kathleen Estep, three times in November 1996. While diagnosing Ms. Lewinsky as suffering from depression and low self-esteem, Ms. Estep considered her self-aware, credible, insightful, introspective, relatively stable, and not delusional. Estep 8/23/98 Int. at 1–4.

16. Catherine Davis 3/17/98 GJ at 21–22.

17. Young 6/23/98 GJ at 40. See also Catherine Davis 3/17/98 GJ at 73; Erbland 2/12/98 GJ at 25 ("I never had any reason to think she would lie to me. I never knew of her to lie to me before and we talked about our boyfriends and, you know, sexual relationships throughout our friendship and I never knew her as a liar."); Finerman 3/18/98 Depo. at 113–16 (characterizing Ms. Lewinsky as trustworthy and honest); Raines 1/29/98 GJ at 87 ("I have no reason to believe that [Ms. Lewinsky's statements] were lies or made up."); Tripp 7/29/98 GJ at 187 ("There were so many reasons why I believed her. She just had way too much detail. She had detail that none of us could really conceivably have if you had not been exposed in a situation that she claimed to be."); Ungvari 3/19/98 GJ at 19 ("[s]he's never lied to me before"); id. at 21, 61–62; Young 6/23/98 GJ at 38–40.

18. Ms. Lewinsky testified that she has "always been a date-oriented person." Lewinsky 8/6/98 GJ at 28. See also Tripp 6/30/98 GJ at 141–42 (Ms. Lewinsky "had a photographic memory for the entire relationship").

19. Clinton 1/17/98 Depo. at 78, 204. The transcript of this deposition testimony appears in Document Supp. A. For reasons of privacy, the OIC has redacted the names of three women from the transcript. The OIC will provide an unredacted transcript if the House of Representatives so requests.

20. Clinton 1/17/98 Depo. at 57.

21. Clinton 1/17/98 Depo. at 54.

22. Clinton 1/17/98 Depo. at 204. Beyond his denial of a sexual relationship with Ms. Lewinsky, the President testified that he could not recall many details of their encounters. He said he could not specifically remember whether he had ever been alone with Ms. Lewinsky, or any of their in-person conversations, or any notes or messages she had sent him, or an audiocassette she had sent him, or any specific gifts he had given her. Alone together: Clinton 1/17/98 Depo. at 52–53, 56–59. Conversations: Id. at 59. Cards and letters: Id. at 62. Audiocassette: Id. at 63–64. Gifts

from the President to Ms. Lewinsky: Id. at 75. When asked about their last conversation, the President referred to a December encounter when, he said, Ms. Lewinsky had been visiting his secretary and he had "stuck [his] head out" to say hello. Id. at 68. He did not mention a private meeting with Ms. Lewinsky on December 28, 1997, or a telephone conversation with her on January 5, 1998. Lewinsky 8/6/98 GJ at 27–28 & Ex. ML–7; Clinton 8/17/98 GJ at 34–36, 126–28.

23. Clinton 8/17/98 GJ at 10, 79, 81.

24. Clinton 8/17/98 GJ at 10.

25. Clinton 8/17/98 GJ at 31, 10. *See also id.* at 38–39.

26. Clinton 8/17/98 GJ at 10, 92–93.

27. Clinton 8/17/98 GJ at 22.

28. Clinton 8/17/98 GJ at 10, 12, 93–96.

29. 849–DC–00000586. The definition mirrors a federal criminal statute, 18 U.S.C. ß 2246(3). The ellipsis in the quotation omits two paragraphs of the definition that Judge Wright ruled inapplicable. Clinton 1/17/98 Depo. at 21–22. The President testified that he considered the definition "rather strange," and at one point he spoke of "people being drawn into a lawsuit and being given definitions, and then a great effort to trick them in some way." Clinton 8/17/98 GJ at 19, 22. He acknowledged, however, that the definition "was the one the Judge decided on and I was bound by it." Clinton 8/17/98 GJ at 19.

30. Clinton 8/17/98 GJ at 15, 93, 100, 102.

31. Clinton 8/17/98 GJ at 151.

32. Clinton 8/17/98 GJ at 168.

33. Clinton 8/17/98 GJ at 102–105, 167–68.

34. Clinton 8/17/98 GJ at 95–96, 100, 110, 139. The President did not always specify that the contact had to be direct. Id. at 15 ("[m]y understanding of the definition is it covers contact by the person being deposed with the enumerated areas, if the contact is done with an intent to arouse or gratify"); *id.* at 16 (definition covers "[a]ny contact with the areas there mentioned").

35. Lewinsky 8/6/98 GJ at 27–28 & Ex. ML–7. These numbers include occasions when one or both of them had direct contact with the other's genitals, but not occasions when they merely kissed. On the timing of some of their sexual encounters, Ms. Lewinsky's testimony is at odds with the President's. According to Ms. Lewinsky, she and the President had three sexual encounters in 1995 (the President said he recalled none) and two sexual encounters in 1997 (not one, as the President testi-

fied). Lewinsky 8/6/98 GJ at 27–28 & Ex. ML–7; Lewinsky 8/26/98 Depo. at 6; Clinton 8/17/98 GJ at 9–10. The President's account omits the two 1995 encounters when Ms. Lewinsky was an intern (as well as one 1995 encounter when she worked on the White House staff), and it treats the 1997 encounter that produced the semen-stained dress as a single aberration.

36. Lewinsky 8/6/98 GJ at 34–36; Lewinsky 8/20/98 GJ at 17; Lewinsky 7/27/98 Int. at 2; Lewinsky 7/31/98 Int. at 4; Catherine Davis 3/17/98 GJ at 16; Erbland 2/12/98 GJ at 27–28, 43–44; Finerman 3/18/98 Depo. at 32; Kassorla 8/28/98 Int. at 2; Raines 1/29/98 GJ at 32–33; Tripp 7/2/98 GJ at 54, 101; Tripp 7/7/98 GJ at 171; Ungvari 3/19/98 GJ at 19, 25.

37. Lewinsky 8/6/98 GJ at 35; Lewinsky 7/27/98 Int. at 2.

38. Lewinsky 8/6/98 GJ at 12, 21; Lewinsky 2/1/98 Statement at 1. See also Andrew Bleiler 1/28/98 Int. at 3; Catherine Davis 3/17/98 GJ at 21; Kassorla 8/28/98 Int. at 2; Tripp 7/2/98 GJ at 100, 104–107; Ungvari 3/19/98 GJ at 23.

39. Lewinsky 8/6/98 GJ at 19; Catherine Davis 3/17/98 GJ at 20; Erbland 2/12/98 GJ at 29, 44; Ungvari 3/19/98 GJ at 20; Young 6/23/98 GJ at 37–38; but see Raines 1/29/98 GJ at 43 (testifying that she was "pretty sure" that Ms. Lewinsky spoke of reciprocal oral sex); Tripp GJ 7/2/98 at 101 (testifying that she understood that, on rare occasions, the President reciprocated).

40. Lewinsky 8/6/98 GJ at 38–39. See also Lewinsky 8/20/98 GJ at 24.

41. Lewinsky 8/6/98 GJ at 19–20, 38–39; Ungvari 3/19/98 GJ at 23–24.

42. Lewinsky 7/30/98 Int. at 5–13, 15–16; Lewinsky 8/6/98 GJ at 19–21; Lewinsky 8/20/98 GJ at 31–32, 40, 67–69; Lewinsky 8/26/98 Depo. at 20, 30–31, 50; Andrew Bleiler 1/28/98 Int. at 3; Catherine Davis 3/17/98 GJ at 20–21, 169; Erbland 2/12/98 GJ at 29, 43–45; Estep 8/23/98 Int. at 2; Kassorla 8/28/98 Int. at 2; Ungvari 3/19/98 GJ at 23–24.

43. Clinton 8/17/98 GJ at 10; Lewinsky 8/26/98 Depo. at 5. In Ms. Lewinsky's recollection, the friendship started to develop following their sixth sexual encounter, when the President sat down and talked with her for about 45 minutes after she had complained that he was making no effort to get to know her. Lewinsky 8/26/98 Depo. at 23, 33–34.

44. Lewinsky 8/20/98 GJ at 59. See also id. at 52; Lewinsky 8/6/98 GJ at 168. After the President's August 1998 speech acknowledging improper conduct with Ms. Lewinsky, she testified that she was no longer certain of her feelings because, in her view, he had depicted their relationship as "a service contract, that all I did was per-

form oral sex on him and that that's all that this relationship was. And it was a lot more than that to me . . . ." Lewinsky 8/20/98 GJ at 54. *See also id.* at 53–56, 102–104.

45. MSL–55–DC–0178 (document retrieved from Ms. Lewinsky's home computer); Catherine Davis 3/17/98 GJ at 147; Erbland 2/12/98 GJ at 92.

46. Lewinsky 8/20/98 GJ at 52; T1 at 101. *See also* Marcia Lewis 2/11/98 GJ at 7; Catherine Davis 3/17/98 GJ at 182.

47. Lewinsky 8/6/98 GJ at 18.

48. Lewinsky 7/27/98 Int. at 6; Currie 5/7/98 GJ at 60; Catherine Davis 3/17/98 GJ at 27; Raines 1/29/98 GJ at 53; Ungvari 3/19/98 GJ at 45; Young 6/23/98 GJ at 47; 1037-DC-00000042 (email from Ms. Lewinsky: "Jeez, I hate being called 'dear.' The creep calls me that sometimes. It's an old person saying!») (spelling and punctuation corrected). When angry, Ms. Lewinsky referred to the President as «creep» or «big creep.» Lewinsky 8/4/98 Int. at 8; Marcia Lewis 2/11/98 GJ at 17; Raines 1/29/98 GJ at 52; Ungvari 3/19/98 GJ at 45.

49. Lewinsky 7/27/98 Int. at 6.

50. Lewinsky 8/26/98 Depo. at 55–57; Lewinsky 7/27/98 Int. at 6.

51. Marcia Lewis 2/11/98 GJ at 7–8.

52. Erbland 2/12/98 GJ at 84. *See also* Lewinsky 8/26/98 Depo. at 56–57; Catherine Davis 3/17/98 GJ at 166–67. In late 1997, Ms. Lewinsky asked Vernon Jordan whether he believed that the Clintons would remain married. Lewinsky 2/1/98 Statement at 8; Jordan 3/3/98 GJ at 150.

53. Lewinsky 8/6/98 GJ at 17. *See also* Lewinsky 8/26/98 Depo. at 24; Lewinsky 8/24/98 Int. at 6; Tripp 7/7/98 GJ at 172.

54. Raines 1/29/98 GJ at 39. *See also* Catherine Davis 3/17/98 GJ at 18; Finerman 3/18/98 Depo. 47–49; Raines 1/29/98 GJ at 47–48; Tripp 7/14/98 GJ at 77, 79–81.

55. Lewinsky 8/6/98 GJ at 52–53.

56. Lewinsky 8/6/98 GJ at 52.

57. Lewinsky 8/6/98 GJ at 21–23; Lewinsky 7/27/98 Int. at 2. *See also* Catherine Davis 3/17/98 GJ at 36; Erbland 2/12/98 GJ at 38–39, 43; Finerman 3/18/98 Depo. at 26–29, 110, 116–17; Raines GJ at 51; Tripp 7/7/98 GJ at 62–63, 65–66; Ungvari 3/19/98 GJ at 81.

58. Lewinsky 8/6/98 GJ at 44; Lewinsky 8/24/98 Int. at 5; Currie 5/14/98 GJ at 131–32, 136, 141; Currie 7/22/98 GJ at 35, 77.

59. Lewinsky 8/20/98 GJ at 55.

60. Lewinsky 8/6/98 GJ at 23.

61. Lewinsky 8/6/98 GJ at 23–24; Lewinsky 7/27/98 Int. at 2. *See also* Catherine Davis 3/17/98 GJ at 36–37; Erbland 2/12/98 GJ at 38–39; Raines 1/29/98 GJ at 51; Ungvari 3/19/98 GJ at 81. Ms. Lewinsky gave the President a novel about phone sex, Vox by Nicholson Baker. Lewinsky 7/27/98 Int. at 13; 1361–DC–00000030 (White House list of books in private study, including Vox).

62. Lewinsky 7/30/98 Int. at 15.

63. Lewinsky 8/6/98 GJ at 23; Lewinsky 8/20/98 GJ at 6. The messages, on tapes that Ms. Lewinsky turned over to the OIC, are as follows: "Aw, shucks." "Hey." "Come on. It's me." "Sorry I missed you." Lewinsky 8/6/98 GJ at 22–23; Lewinsky 7/29/98 Int. at 3, 5; Lewinsky 8/3/98 Int. at 6.

64. Lewinsky 8/6/98 GJ at 22–23; Catherine Davis 3/17/98 GJ at 28–29; Erbland 2/12/98 GJ at 49; Kassorla 8/28/98 Int. at 4; Raines 1/29/98 GJ at 89; Tripp 7/2/98 GJ at 89; Tripp 7/9/98 GJ at 95–97, 104–105; Ungvari 3/19/98 GJ at 31–33.

65. Lewinsky 8/6/98 GJ at 67–69.

66. Lewinsky 8/6/98 GJ at 74–75.

67. Lewinsky 8/6/98 GJ at 114.

68. Clinton 8/17/98 GJ at 10.

69. Clinton 8/17/98 GJ at 47, 51.

70. Clinton 8/17/98 GJ at 47, 124.

71. Lewinsky 8/6/98 GJ at 25–26.

72. Lewinsky 7/27/98 Int. at 12. *See also* MSL–55–DC–0184 – 186 (eight-line poem recovered from Ms. Lewinsky's home computer that refers to President as "the Boss with whom we're all smitten" and wishes him "Happy National Boss Day!").

73. V006–DC–00000167; V006–DC–00000181 (gift record and donor information); V006–DC–00003646 (correspondence history).

74. V006–DC–00000157 – 158 (gift record and donor information).

75. Lewinsky 8/11/98 Int. at 2; V006–DC–00000178 (autographed photo).

76. Few of Ms. Lewinsky's subsequent gifts were logged. Of the roughly 30 gifts (including several antiques) that, in her account, she gave the President, White House records show only the matted poem from interns, two or three neckties (records conflict), and a T-shirt. V006-DC-00000157; V006-DC-00000162; V006-DC-00000167; V006-DC-00000180; V006-DC-00000181; V006-DC-00003714; V006-DC-00003715.

77. MSL-55-DC-0177.

78. Lewinsky 8/26/98 Depo. at 5–6 & Ex. ML–7. In response to a January 20, 1998, subpoena seeking "any and all gifts . . . to or from Monica Lewinsky . . . including. . . any tie, mug, paperweight, book, or other article," the President turned over a necktie, two antique books, a mug, and a silver standing holder for cigars or cigarettes. Subpoena V002; V002-DC-00000001; V002-DC-00000469. A subpoena dated July 17, 1998, identified specific gifts, including Vox, a novel about phone sex by Nicholson Baker that, according to Ms. Lewinsky, she gave the President in March 1997. Lewinsky 8/6/98 GJ at 183–84; Lewinsky 7/27/98 Int. at 13; Subpoena D1415. The President did not produce Vox in response to either subpoena, though his attorney represented that "the President has complied with [the] grand jury subpoenas."David Kendall Letter to OIC, 8/31/98. Vox, however, does appear on an October 1997 list of books in the President's private study, and Ms. Lewinsky saw it in the study on November 13, 1997. 1361-DC-00000030; Lewinsky 8/6/98 GJ at 183–84.

79. Lewinsky 8/26/98 Depo. at 5–6 & Ex. ML-7.

80. Lewinsky 8/20/98 GJ at 36. *See also* Lewinsky 8/6/98 GJ at 236; Catherine Davis 3/17/98 GJ at 153.

81. Lewinsky 8/6/98 GJ at 236; Lewinsky 8/20/98 GJ at 36; Lewinsky 8/3/98 Int. at 8; Lewinsky 8/11/98 Int. at 2–3. For example, one day after the President and Ms. Lewinsky talked by telephone on February 7, 1996, and one day after they talked on August 4, 1996, he wore a necktie she had given him. Lewinsky 8/5/98 Int. at 1; Lewinsky 8/11/98 Int. at 2–3.

82. Lewinsky 8/6/98 GJ at 236.

83. Clinton 8/17/98 GJ at 47. *See also id.* at 33–36, 43–46.

84. Lewinsky 8/6/98 GJ at 26.

85. Lewinsky 8/6/98 GJ at 189.

86. Lewinsky 8/6/98 GJ at 26–27.

87. Clinton 8/17/98 GJ at 48–49. In the Jones deposition, in contrast, the President was asked if he remembered anything written in Ms. Lewinsky's notes or cards to him. He testified:"No. Sometimes, you know, just either small talk or happy birthday or sometimes, you know, a suggestion about how to get more young people involved in some project I was working on. Nothing remarkable. I don't remember anything particular about it."Clinton 1/17/98 Depo. at 62.

88. Lewinsky 2/1/98 Statement at 10. *See also* Lewinsky 8/20/98 GJ at 62–63;

Lewinsky 8/6/98 GJ at 141–42, 178–79. Ms. Lewinsky once told Betty Currie:"As long as no one saw us — and no one did — then nothing happened."Currie 1/27/98 GJ at 63–64.

89. Lewinsky 8/6/98 GJ at 78, 97–101; Lewinsky 7/27/98 Int. at 3.

90. Lewinsky 8/20/98 GJ at 22. *See also* Lewinsky 7/27/98 Int. at 9 (President assumed Ms. Lewinsky's Jones affidavit would be a denial, since their pattern had been to conceal and deny).

91. Lewinsky 8/20/98 GJ at 4; Lewinsky 8/6/98 GJ at 166–67. *See also* Lewinsky 7/27/98 Int. at 9–10, 12.

92. Lewinsky 8/6/98 GJ at 234.

93. Clinton 8/17/98 GJ at 38.

94. Clinton 8/17/98 GJ at 38, 119. See also id. at 80, 119, 136, 153.

95. Clinton 8/17/98 GJ at 37.

96. Lewinsky 8/6/98 GJ at 53-54. See also Lewinsky 7/27/98 Int. at 2, 11; Lewinsky 8/19/98 Int. at 4; Lewinsky 2/1/98 Statement at 1.

97. Lewinsky 8/6/98 GJ at 53-54.

98. Lewinsky 8/6/98 GJ at 54.

99. Lewinsky 8/6/98 GJ at 54-55; Lewinsky 7/30/98 Int. at 10.

100. Lewinsky 8/6/98 GJ at 54-55.

101. Lewinsky 8/6/98 GJ at 18, 53-54.

102. Lewinsky 8/6/98 GJ at 18-19; Lewinsky 2/1/98 Statement at 1.

103. Lewinsky 8/20/98 GJ at 105; Lewinsky 2/1/98 Statement at 1.

104. Lewinsky 8/20/98 GJ at 22.

105. Lewinsky 2/1/98 Statement at 4; Lewinsky 8/6/98 GJ at 123, 233.

106. Clinton 1/17/98 Depo. at 50-51, 68.

107. Clinton 8/17/98 GJ at 118-19.

108. Clinton 8/17/98 GJ at 119. The President did not elaborate on his understanding of the words "ask[]" or "lie" in that statement. In other exchanges, he indicated that he construes some words narrowly. Id. at 59 (accuracy of particular statement "depends on what the meaning of the word 'is' is"); Id. at 107 ("I have not had sex with her as I defined it"); Id. at 134 ("it depends on how you define alone"); Id. ("there were a lot of times when we were alone, but I never really thought we were").

109. Lewinsky 8/6/98 GJ at 47. Along with weekend visits, Ms. Lewinsky sometimes saw the President on holidays: New Year's Eve, President's Day, Easter Sunday,

July 4. In November 1997, she grew irritated that the President did not arrange to see her on Veterans Day. Lewinsky 9/3/98 Int. at 2.

110. Lewinsky 8/6/98 GJ at 18. See also Lewinsky 8/20/98 GJ at 7, 22.

111. Lewinsky 8/6/98 GJ at 84-85; Lewinsky 8/20/98 GJ at 7. Ms. Lewinsky told friends about White House people she tried to avoid. Tripp 6/30/98 GJ at 159-60, 164; Tripp 7/14/98 GJ at 75; T1 at 32; 1037-DC-00000318 (email from Ms. Lewinsky).

112. Lewinsky 8/6/98 GJ at 34-35; Lewinsky 8/20/98 GJ at 16-17; Lewinsky 7/31/98 Int. at 4. The study is one of the most private rooms in the White House. Fox 2/17/98 GJ at 76. See also Chinery 7/23/98 GJ at 52; Currie 5/6/98 GJ at 67; Ferguson 7/17/87 GJ at 32, 38; Maes 4/8/98 GJ at 89-90; Podesta 6/23/98 GJ at 72.

113. Lewinsky 7/31/98 Int. at 4.

114. Lewinsky 8/4/98 Int. at 4.

115. Lewinsky 8/6/98 GJ at 36. See also Lewinsky 7/31/98 Int. at 4.

116. Lewinsky 8/6/98 GJ at 36-37; Lewinsky 7/27/98 Int. at 2. According to a Secret Service officer who entered the Oval Office when the President and Ms. Lewinsky were in or near the study, the door leading from the Oval Office to the hallway was slightly ajar. Muskett 7/21/98 GJ at 36-37, 39. In his Jones deposition, the President was asked if there are doors at both ends of the hallway. He responded: "[There] are, and they're always open." Clinton 1/17/98 Depo. at 59. In early 1998, in the course of denying any sexual relationship with Ms. Lewinsky, the President repeatedly told Deputy Chief of Staff John Podesta that "the door was open." Podesta 6/16/98 GJ at 88-89.

117. Lewinsky 8/6/98 GJ at 56. See also Lewinsky 7/31/98 Int. at 3.

118. Lewinsky 7/31/98 Int. at 3.

119. Lewinsky 8/26/98 Depo. at 44-45; Lewinsky 7/30/98 Int. at 9; Lewinsky 7/31/98 Int. at 4. Ms. Lewinsky also testified about various steps she took on her own to ensure that the relationship remained secret, such as using different doors to enter and depart the Oval Office area, avoiding the President at a White House party, and referring to the President as "her" in pages to Betty Currie. Lewinsky 8/6/98 GJ at 44-45, 57, 218; Lewinsky 8/20/98 GJ at 5-6, 18; Lewinsky 7/29/98 Int. at 2-3.

120. Clinton 8/17/98 GJ at 38. See also Id. at 53 (to President's knowledge, Ms. Currie did not see intimate activity between President and Ms. Lewinsky); Id. at 54 ("I'd have to be an exhibitionist not to have tried to exclude everyone else.").

121. Lewinsky 8/6/98 GJ at 56.

122. Lewinsky 8/6/98 GJ at 189, 198. See also Lewinsky 8/2/98 Int. at 3. The President was under a legal obligation to turn this note over to the Jones attorneys but failed to do so.

123. Lewinsky 8/24/98 Int. at 8.

124. Clinton 8/17/98 GJ at 50. See also Id. at 130-131.

125. One of these tapes, T30, is a face-to-face conversation between Ms. Tripp and Ms. Lewinsky, recorded under FBI auspices. The other, T22, is a telephone conversation between Ms. Tripp and Ms. Lewinsky, recorded by Ms. Tripp.

From these and other transcripts of recorded conversations, the OIC has redacted various brief, irrelevant, and gratuitous passages, mostly references to Ms. Lewinsky's family members. Most of these redactions are only a word or two long; others are somewhat longer. The tapes themselves have not been edited by the OIC, and the OIC will provide unredacted transcripts if the House of Representatives so requests.

Ms. Tripp produced to the OIC 27 tapes (four of which proved inaudible or blank) of her telephone conversations with Ms. Lewinsky. Ms. Tripp testified that she turned over the original recordings. She testified that she knew nothing about any duplications of the recordings, though others had access to or control over the tapes at times before they were turned over. According to a preliminary FBI examination, several of the 23 tapes containing audible conversations exhibit signs of duplication, and one tape exhibiting signs of duplication was produced by a recorder that was stopped and restarted during the recording process. These preliminary results raise questions about the reliability and authenticity of at least one recording, which in turn raise questions about the accuracy of Ms. Tripp's testimony regarding her handling of the tapes. The OIC is continuing to investigate this matter. This Referral does not quote or rely on any tapes that exhibit signs of duplication. For a fuller discussion, see Appendix, Tab I.

126. T30 at 41.

127. T30 at 41.

128. T30 at 41-42.

129. T22 at 12.

130. T22 at 12.

131. 828-DC-00000012 (resume); Lewinsky 7/27/98 Int. at 1; Walter Kaye 5/21/98 GJ at 34, 51-52; Marcia Lewis 4/3/98 Depo. at 90; Abramson 2/20/98 Int.

at 1; Footlik 3/19/98 Int. at 1; 827-DC-00000003 (White House entry records for Ms. Lewinsky). President Clinton testified that Mr. Kaye is "a good friend of mine and a good friend of our administration." Clinton 1/17/98 Depo. at 61. Ms. Lewinsky turned 22 on July 23. 812-DC-00000002 (passport showing birthdate).

132. Lewinsky 8/6/98 GJ at 8; Lewinsky 8/20/98 GJ at 8; Bobowick 2/12/98 Int. at 1; Currie 1/27/98 GJ at 23-24; Panetta 1/28/98 GJ at 121-23; Palmieri 2/24/98 GJ at 12; V006-DC-00000020 (White House employee data form).

133. Lewinsky 8/3/98 Int. at 2.

134. Lewinsky 8/3/98 Int. at 2; 828-DC-00000012 (resume); V006-DC-00000225 (employment approval for the Legislative Affairs Office); V006-DC-00000198 (1995 White House intern directory); V006-DC-00002287 (record of Ms. Lewinsky's transfer).

135. Lewinsky 8/26/98 Depo. at 60.

136. Lewinsky 8/6/98 GJ at 10.

137. Lewinsky 8/6/98 GJ at 9; Lewinsky 7/27/98 Int. at 2; Lewinsky 8/3/98 Int. at 1; V006-DC-00001826 (photo showing President and Ms. Lewinsky).

138. Lewinsky 8/26/98 Depo. at 16-17 & Ex. ML-7.

139. Finerman 3/18/98 Depo. at 10-11; Ungvari 3/19/98 GJ at 15-17.

149. Facts on File 852, 868 (1995).

141. Washington Post, 11/20/95 at A19; Los Angeles Times, 11/14/95 at A15; USA Today, 11/17/95 at 4A.

142. Lewinsky 8/6/98 GJ at 10-11; Byrne 6/25/98 Depo. at 18; Byrne 7/30/98 GJ at 36; Palmieri 2/24/98 GJ at 16-19; Panetta 1/28/98 GJ at 122.

143. Goodin 2/17/98 GJ at 48-50; Griffin 5/11/98 Int. at 1; Lewinsky 8/6/98 GJ at 10-11; Palmieri 2/24/98 GJ at 20-22; Raines 1/29/98 GJ at 35-36; V006-DC-00003737 - 3744 (White House photos showing President and Ms. Lewinsky during furlough).

144. Lewinsky 8/6/98 GJ at 11.

145. Lewinsky 8/3/98 Int. at 2; Barry Toiv 3/11/98 Int. at 1 (job title).

146. Lewinsky 8/6/98 GJ at 10; Lewinsky 7/27/98 Int. at 1-2. She told others that her physical relationship with the President began during the November 1995 shutdown. Raines 1/29/98 GJ at 38; Tripp 7/2/98 GJ at 38-39. To one friend, Ms. Lewinsky specified that the relationship began on November 15, 1995. Tripp 6/30/98 GJ at 138; Tripp 7/2/98 GJ at 38-39, 80-82.

147. 827-DC-00000008. According to records, it was one of only two times dur-

ing Ms. Lewinsky's tenure at the White House that she exited after midnight. 827-DC-00000003 - 16. (The other post-midnight exit was not during the furlough; it was the night of December 6-7, 1995.) As the omission of Ms. Lewinsky's November 15 afternoon exit time illustrates, White House Epass and WAVES records do not reflect all entries and exits of staff and visitors. Secret Service Representatives Barry Smith et al. 3/16/98 Int. at 3-5. See also Appendix, Tab I.

148. 1222-DC-00000156, 1222-DC-00000083 - 85 (movement logs). Times are approximate, as different logs of the President's movements sometimes vary by a few minutes. With occasional exceptions, these logs do not distinguish the President's private study from the Oval Office.

149. Lewinsky 7/27/98 Int. at 2; Lewinsky 8/24/98 Int. at 5.

150. Lewinsky 7/30/98 Int. at 5; Lewinsky 8/11/98 Int. at 7; Erbland 2/12/98 GJ at 24-25.

151. Lewinsky 8/6/98 GJ at 11; Lewinsky 7/27/98 Int. at 2; Lewinsky 7/30/98 Int. at 5.

152. Lewinsky 8/6/98 GJ at 11; Lewinsky 7/27/98 Int. at 2; Lewinsky 7/30/98 Int. at 5.

153. Lewinsky 8/6/98 GJ at 11; Lewinsky 8/26/98 Depo. at 7. Ms. Lewinsky later told confidants that the relationship began with kissing. Catherine Davis 3/17/98 GJ at 19; Finerman 3/18/98 Depo. at 31-35; Tripp 7/7/98 GJ at 151-52.

154. Lewinsky 7/30/98 Int. at 5.

155. Lewinsky 8/26/98 Depo. at 7.

156. Lewinsky 8/6/98 GJ at 12; Lewinsky 7/30/98 Int. at 5.

157. Lewinsky 8/26/98 Depo. at 7.

158. Lewinsky 8/26/98 Depo. at 7; Lewinsky 8/6/98 GJ at 12, 13.

159. Lewinsky 8/26/98 Depo. at 8; Lewinsky 7/30/98 Int. at 5.

160. Lewinsky 8/26/98 Depo. at 7-8.

161. Lewinsky 8/26/98 Depo. at 8. See also Id. at 21. Earlier in the evening, Ms. Lewinsky had removed her underwear. Lewinsky Int. 9/3/98 at 1.

162. Lewinsky 8/6/98 GJ at 12-14; Lewinsky 8/26/98 Depo. at 9-10; Lewinsky 7/30/98 Int. at 6.

163. Lewinsky 8/26/98 Depo. at 10.

164. Lewinsky 8/26/98 Depo. at 11.

165. Lewinsky 9/3/98 Int. at 3; Lewinsky 8/24/98 Int. at 5; Lewinsky 7/30/98 Int. at 6.

166. Lewinsky 8/6/98 GJ at 11-12; Lewinsky 8/26/98 Depo. at 7.

167. 1362-DC-00000549 (movement logs).

168. Lewinsky 7/30/98 Int. at 6.

169. 1472-DC-00000006 - 08. Starting 11 minutes later, the President talked with other Members of Congress. Id.

170. 827-DC-00000008 (Epass records).

171. 1222-DC-00000085 (movement logs).

172. Lewinsky 8/6/98 GJ at 14. See also Lewinsky 7/30/98 Int. at 6-7.

173. Lewinsky 8/6/98 GJ at 14-15; Lewinsky 7/30/98 Int. at 7.

174. Lewinsky 8/6/98 GJ at 15-16.

175. In Ms. Currie's recollection, Ms. Lewinsky and the President were alone together for about 30 seconds. Currie 1/27/98 GJ at 33-34; Currie 5/14/98 GJ at 36-38. Ms. Hernreich testified that when delivering food during the government shutdown, Ms. Lewinsky was alone with the President for two to four minutes. Hernreich 2/26/98 GJ at 36-37. See also Hernreich 2/25/98 GJ at 12-17. Other witnesses also remembered Ms. Lewinsky's pizza delivery during the furlough. Keating 2/25/98 GJ at 31-32; Palmieri 2/24/98 GJ at 20, 53, 62. The President and Ms. Lewinsky (as well as others) appear in eight White House photographs taken on November 17; in three of them, the President is eating pizza. V006-DC-00003737 - 3744.

176. Lewinsky 8/6/98 GJ at 16; Lewinsky 8/26/98 GJ at 11-15; Lewinsky 7/30/98 Int. at 7.

177. Lewinsky 8/26/98 Depo. at 12-13; Lewinsky 7/30/98 Int. at 7.

178. Lewinsky 8/26/98 Depo. at 12; Lewinsky 7/30/98 Int. at 7.

179. Lewinsky 7/30/98 Int. at 7.

180. Lewinsky 8/26/98 Depo. at 13-14.

181. Lewinsky 8/26/98 Depo. at 13-14; Lewinsky 7/30/98 Int. at 7. One friend understood that Ms. Lewinsky and the President kissed when she brought pizza, and that Ms. Lewinsky performed oral sex on him in a later encounter. Ungvari 3/19/98 GJ at 18-19, 20, 23. One of Ms. Lewinsky's counselors understood that the relationship with the President began at a pizza party. Estep 8/23/98 Int. at 2.

182. Lewinsky 7/30/98 Int. at 7. See also Lewinsky 8/26/98 Depo. at 15.

183. 1472-DC-00000015 (phone logs). Ms. Lewinsky said that this probably was the name she heard on that date. Lewinsky 8/11/98 Int. at 5. She testified that

she could not recall whether the President was on the telephone the whole time that she performed oral sex. Lewinsky 8/26/98 Depo. at 14.

184. Clinton 1/17/98 Depo. at 58.

185. Clinton 8/17/98 GJ at 31-32.

186. 827-DC-00000011 (Epass records).

187. 1222-DC-00000179 (movement logs). The President had one telephone call during this period, from 12:53 to 12:58 p.m. 1506-DC-00000029 (phone logs).

188. Lewinsky 8/26/98 Depo. at 15-16; Lewinsky 7/27/98 Int. at 3-4; Lewinsky 7/30/98 Int. at 8.

189. Lewinsky 8/26/98 Depo. at 16.

190. Lewinsky 8/26/98 Depo. at 16; Lewinsky 7/27/98 Int. at 3-4; Lewinsky 7/30/98 Int. at 8.

191. Lewinsky 8/26/98 Depo. at 16.

192. Lewinsky 8/26/98 Depo. at 16-17. See also Lewinsky 7/30/98 Int. at 8.

193. Lewinsky 7/27/98 Int. at 3-4; Lewinsky 7/30/98 Int. at 8.

194. Lewinsky 8/26/98 Depo. at 17. See also Finerman 3/18/98 Depo. at 30-32, 35.

195. Lewinsky 7/30/98 Int. at 3.

196. 1222-DC-00000325 (Secret Service duty logs).

197. Clinton 8/17/98 GJ at 31-32.

198. Clinton 8/17/98 GJ at 9-10.

199. Ms. Lewinsky understood that the President may have thought there was something improper in having a sexual relationship with an intern. Lewinsky 8/24/98 Int. at 5.

200. Clinton 8/17/98 GJ at 10.

201. As noted above, White House entry and exit records are incomplete.

202. 1222-DC-00000183 (movement logs).

203. Lewinsky 8/26/98 Depo. at 18. See also Lewinsky 7/30/98 Int. at 2, 8.

204. Lewinsky 8/26/98 Depo. at 18.

205. Lewinsky 8/26/98 Depo. at 19.

206. Lewinsky 8/26/98 Depo. at 19.

207. Lewinsky 8/26/98 Depo. at 19.

208. Lewinsky 8/26/98 Depo. at 19.

209. Lewinsky 8/26/98 Depo. at 20. They engaged in oral-anal contact as well. Id.

210. Lewinsky 8/26/98 Depo. at 38.

211. 1222-DC-00000325, 1362-DC-00001171 (Secret Service duty logs).

212. Fox 2/17/98 GJ at 33. Although Mr. Fox believed that the incident occurred in late 1995, the totality of the evidence suggests that it was on this date, January 7, 1996.

213. Fox 2/17/98 GJ at 31.

214. Fox 2/17/98 GJ at 60-61, 66-67.

215. Fox 2/17/98 GJ at 33.

216. Fox 2/17/98 GJ at 19-20, 42, 49-50.

217. Fox 2/17/98 GJ at 34-35. Officer Fox testified that the President and Ms. Lewinsky were alone. Fox 2/17/98 GJ 36-37. His sworn testimony on this point differs from the public statements of his attorney, who told reporters that Officer Fox did not know whether the two were alone. Chicago Tribune, 2/17/98 at 1C.

218. 827-DC-00000013 (Epass records).

219. 1222-DC-00000189 (movement logs). While Ms. Lewinsky was in the White House, the President had a single phone call, at 3:47 p.m. for one minute. 1506-DC-00000050 (phone logs).

220. Lewinsky 7/30/98 Int. at 9; Lewinsky 8/24/98 Int. at 6.

221. Lewinsky 8/26/98 Depo. at 22-23.

222. Lewinsky 8/26/98 Depo. at 23.

223. Lewinsky 8/26/98 Depo. at 23.

224. Lewinsky 8/26/98 Depo. at 23-24. See also Lewinsky 7/30/98 Int. at 10.

225. Lewinsky 8/26/98 Depo. at 24-25.

226. Lewinsky 8/26/98 Depo. at 25.

227. Lewinsky 8/26/98 Depo. at 26.

228. Lewinsky 8/26/98 Depo. at 26. This interruption may have been occasioned by the President's one-minute phone call at 3:47 p.m. 1506-DC-00000050 (phone logs).

229. Lewinsky 8/26/98 Depo. at 26-27. Ms. Lewinsky stated that the Blairs from Arkansas were visiting the President. Lewinsky 7/30/98 Int. at 10. This is confirmed by a Secret Service itinerary for January 21, 1996, where Diane Blair is listed as a houseguest. 1222-DC-00000024 (presidential itinerary).

230. Lewinsky 8/26/98 Depo. at 27-28; Lewinsky 7/30/98 Int. at 10; Tripp 7/7/98 GJ at 124-26, 139-143; Tripp 7/9/98 GJ at 4-5; 845-DC-00000004 (Tripp notes).

231. 1222-DC-00000196 (movement logs).

232. 1506-DC-00000068 (phone logs).

233. Lewinsky 8/26/98 Depo. at 28-29; Lewinsky·8/24/98 Int. at 6.

234. Lewinsky 8/26/98 Depo. at 29-30.

235. Lewinsky 8/26/98 Depo. at 30-31.

236. Lewinsky 8/26/98 Depo. at 31-32. They engaged in oral-anal contact as well. Id. at 30-31.

237. Lewinsky 8/26/98 Depo. at 33.

238. Lewinsky 8/26/98 Depo. at 33-34.

239. Lewinsky 8/26/98 Depo. at 33.

240. Lewinsky 8/26/98 Depo. at 33-34; Lewinsky 8/24/98 Int. at 6; Tripp 7/7/98 GJ at 169-71; 845-DC-00000006 (Tripp notes).

241. 1222-DC-00000197, 1222-DC-00000102 (movement logs).

242. 1506-DC-00000102 (phone logs).

243. Lewinsky 7/30/98 Int. at 11; Lewinsky 8/24/98 Int. at 6.

244. Lewinsky 7/30/98 Int. at 3, 11-12.

245. Lewinsky 7/30/98 Int. at 3, 11.

246. Lewinsky 8/6/98 GJ at 24; Lewinsky 7/29/98 Int. at 3.

247. Lewinsky 7/30/98 Int. at 11. Ms. Lewinsky later recounted the episode to several others. Erbland 2/12/98 GJ at 46-47; Finerman 3/18/98 Depo. at 47; Tripp 7/7/98 GJ at 175-76; Ungvari 3/19/98 GJ at 80.

248. Lewinsky 8/24/98 Int. at 6. See also Lewinsky 7/30/98 Int. at 11.

249. Garabito 7/30/98 GJ at 16-17, 23-24. According to a colleague, Agent Garabito is over six feet tall, slender, and Hispanic. OIC Memo of Interview with Special Agent Thomas M. Powers, 9/7/98.

250. Garabito 7/30/98 GJ at 25, 30-31.

251. Garabito 7/30/98 GJ at 32. Agent Garabito later recounted the incident to Larry L. Cockell, the head of the Presidential Protective Division of the Secret Service. The OIC learned of the episode from Agent Cockell's testimony. Cockell 7/23/98 GJ at 25-26.

252. 1472-DC-00000017 (call logs).

253. 1506-DC-00000017 (call logs).

254. Forbes, 9/22/97 at 2.

255. Lewinsky 8/6/98 GJ at 90.

256. Lewinsky 8/6/98 GJ at 91. See also Lewinsky 8/26/98 Depo. at 34; Tripp 7/7/98 GJ at 179-80. Ms. Lewinsky offered to return to the White House to see him,

but the President said he needed to stay in the Residence because his daughter was ill. Lewinsky 7/30/98 Int. at 12; Lewinsky 8/24/98 Int. at 6.

257. Ungvari 3/19/98 GJ at 29-31; Lewinsky 8/3/98 Int. at 3; Ungvari 3/18/98 Int. at 4; Verna 6/11/98 Depo. at 10; 845-DC-00000009 (Tripp notes).

258. Ungvari 3/19/98 GJ at 30.

259. Lewinsky 8/11/98 Int. at 2.

260. Lewinsky 8/20/98 GJ at 19; Lewinsky 7/30/98 Int. at 12; 845-DC-00000010 - 11 (Tripp notes).

261. Lewinsky 8/26/98 Depo. at 34-35.

262. 1222-DC-00000112 (movement logs). The President and 32 guests saw Executive Decision that evening. 1506-DC-00000558 (White House daily diary).

263. 968-DC-00003459 (Hillary Clinton calendar).

264. Lewinsky 7/29/98 Int. at 3; Lewinsky 7/30/98 Int. at 12-13.

265. 827-DC-00000016 (Epass records).

266. 1222-DC-00000216 - 217; 1222-DC-00000112 - 113 (movement logs).

267. 1506-DC-00000139 (phone logs).

268. 968-DC-00003459 (Hillary Clinton calendar). Mrs. Clinton returned that evening. 1506-DC-00000559 (White House diary); 1222-DC-00000041 (Secret Service itinerary).

269. Lewinsky 8/26/98 Depo. at 35-36.

270. Lewinsky 8/26/98 Depo. at 36; Lewinsky 7/30/98 Int. at 12.

271. Lewinsky 8/26/98 Depo. at 38-39.

272. Lewinsky 8/26/98 Depo. at 37.

273. Lewinsky 7/30/98 Int. at 12-13; Lewinsky 8/26/98 Depo. at 37-38. In the grand jury, the President declined to answer whether Ms. Lewinsky would be lying if she said he had used a cigar as a sexual aid with her. Clinton 8/17/98 GJ at 110-11.

274. Lewinsky 7/30/98 Int. at 13.

275. Fox 2/17/98 GJ at 42-43.

276. Ludtke 6/5/98 Int. at 1-2.

277. Muskett 7/21/98 GJ at 124. Others also noted that Ms. Lewinsky spent time around the West Wing. Byrne 3/13/98 Depo. at 22-25; Byrne 6/25/98 Depo. at 23, 39-44, 55-62, 104-113; Byrne 7/30/98 GJ at 8, 39-40; Hannie 4/6/98 Int. at 2-3; Keating 2/25/98 GJ at 52.

278. Lewinsky 8/20/98 GJ at 12.

279. Bordley 8/13/98 GJ at 9-16.

280. Bordley 8/13/98 GJ at 20-23, 29.

281. Bordley 8/13/98 GJ at 25-29.

282. Ferguson 7/17/98 GJ at 14-17, 27-28; Ferguson 7/23/98 GJ at 14-17, 20.

283. Ferguson 7/17/98 GJ at 27.

284. Ferguson 7/17/98 GJ at 27-28; Ferguson 7/23/98 GJ at 20-21.

285. Ferguson 7/17/98 GJ at 29, 31.

286. Ferguson 7/17/98 GJ at 29. In addition, Officer Lewis Fox and Agent Nelson Garabito testified about admitting Ms. Lewinsky to the Oval Office on one occasion each, as recounted above. Fox 2/17/98 GJ at 32-37; Garabito 7/30/98 GJ at 16-32. Officer Fox also saw Ms. Lewinsky exit the Oval Office on another occasion, but he did not know how long she had been inside. Fox 2/17/98 GJ at 43-46. Officer Gary Byrne also testified about having seen Ms. Lewinsky in the Oval Office with the President, though some details of his account varied in different tellings. Byrne 7/30/98 GJ at 7-32; Byrne 7/17/98 GJ at 4-10.

287. Byrne 3/13/98 Depo. at 27-28, 46-47, 51-55; Byrne 6/25/98 Depo. at 31.

288. Lewinsky 8/20/98 GJ at 10-11; Lewinsky 7/31/98 Int. at 6.

289. Lieberman 1/30/98 GJ at 36-37. Ms. Lieberman testified that she continued to disapprove of Ms. Lewinsky. When she saw Ms. Lewinsky back in the White House after she no longer worked there, Ms. Lieberman asked Ms. Currie, "What is she doing here?" She also may have said to Ms. Currie, who told Ms. Lewinsky that she could watch a presidential helicopter departure, "What are you — nuts?" or otherwise "expressed my displeasure." Lieberman GJ 1/30/98 at 50-52.

290. Lewinsky 8/20/98 GJ at 8.

291. Lieberman 1/30/98 GJ at 41.

292. Panetta 1/28/98 GJ at 139-42.

293. Lieberman 1/30/98 GJ at 45. See also Panetta 1/28/98 GJ at 143 (describing precautions taken "to protect the President's office and protect his integrity," including preventing President from meeting alone with female acquaintances in circumstances that "could be misinterpreted").

294. Lewis 2/11/98 GJ at 37-40. See also T3 at 15; Lewinsky 7/31/98 Int. at 7. Ms. Lieberman testified that the conversation occurred in September 1997. Lieberman 1/30/98 GJ at 66. In her recollection, the exchange began with Ms. Lewis coming up to her and saying, "You ruined [Ms. Lewinsky's] life on the basis of something that she never dId." According to Ms. Lieberman, she made no response,

and Ms. Lewis walked away. Later Ms. Lewis returned and said that she understood what Ms. Lieberman had done and why. Lieberman 1/30/98 GJ at 64-66.

295. Abramson 2/20/98 Int. at 3; Band 2/25/98 Int. at 2-3; Currie 5/6/98 GJ at 40-41; Ganong 2/12/98 Int. at 2; Keating 2/25/98 GJ at 73; Panetta 1/28/98 GJ at 139-42.

296. 1089-DC-00000970 (memo from Mr. Hilley to Ms. Lieberman); Hilley 5/19/98 GJ at 34-35, 47-50. Mr. Hilley testified that "extracurricular activities" — which applied to Ms. Lewinsky and one of her colleagues who was also transferred — did not refer to anything sexual in nature. Hilley 5/19/98 GJ at 49-50. See also Byrne 6/25/98 Depo. at 22-25, 27-28, 38, 43, 54-55; Currie 5/14/98 GJ at 19-35; Fox 2/17/98 GJ at 46-48; Maes 5/7/98 GJ at 34-42.

297. Duncan 2/18/98 GJ at 24.

298. V006-DC-00001347.

299. Duncan 2/18/98 GJ at 13-14.

300. Duncan 2/18/98 GJ at 23, 41.

301. Duncan 2/18/98 GJ at 8, 23-24.

302. Lewinsky 8/6/98 GJ at 61. The President was traveling to Oklahoma City on that day. V006-DC-00000694 (President's schedule); 968-DC-00000841 (same).

303. Keating 2/25/98 GJ at 76. The Pentagon position had a higher salary than Ms. Lewinsky's White House job. Lewinsky 8/3/98 Int. at 5. Ms. Lewinsky's supervisor, Jocelyn Jolley, was also transferred that day. Keating 2/25/98 GJ at 76-79; Lewinsky 8/6/98 GJ at 171. Unlike Ms. Lewinsky, Ms. Jolley was given a demotion: a temporary job at the General Services Administration. Jolley 2/24/98 GJ at 36-39; Keating 2/25/98 GJ at 79.

304. Keating 2/25/98 GJ at 78-79; Lewinsky 8/3/98 Int. at 3; Capps 3/23/98 Int. at 2; Fox 2/17/98 GJ at 47; Lynn 8/5/98 GJ at 14-16; Verna 7/21/98 GJ at 21-23.

305. Lewinsky 8/6/98 GJ at 171. See also Lewinsky 8/3/98 Int. at 3. Ms. Lewinsky testified that Mr. Keating led her to believe that she could probably return to work at the White House after the election. Lewinsky 8/3/98 Int. at 4. Mr. Keating testified that he told her that if she performed well at the Pentagon, "she may be able to get a job back in the White House. But not now." Keating 2/25/98 GJ at 79.

306. Lewinsky 8/26/98 Depo. at 60.

307. Lewinsky 8/6/98 GJ at 62.

308. 827-DC-00000016 (Epass records).

309. 1222-DC-00000219 (movement log).

310. Lewinsky 8/6/98 GJ at 62. See also Lewinsky 8/26/98 Depo. at 39; Lewinsky 7/27/98 Int. at 4; Tripp 7/9/98 GJ at 29-30.

311. In Ms. Lewinsky's recollection, Officer Muskett first said he needed to get Evelyn Lieberman's authorization before admitting Ms. Lewinsky to the Oval Office, but Ms. Lewinsky talked him out of it. Lewinsky 8/6/98 GJ at 91; Lewinsky 8/20/98 GJ at 42; Lewinsky 8/26/98 Depo. at 39-40; Lewinsky 7/27/98 Int. at 4; Lewinsky 7/30/98 Int. at 13; Lewinsky 7/31/98 Int. at 6.

312. Lewinsky 7/27/98 Int. at 4.

313. Lewinsky 8/6/98 GJ at 63. See also Lewinsky 8/26/98 Depo. at 40; Lewinsky 7/30/98 Int. at 13; Erbland 2/12/98 GJ at 37; Tripp 7/9/98 GJ at 31; 833-DC-00001070 (document recovered from Ms. Lewinsky's computer referring to President's promise to arrange for her return); MSL-DC-00001052 (another recovered computer file, saying in part: "You promised you would bring me back after the election with a snap of [your] fingers."); Lewinsky Statement 2/1/98 at 1 ("he promised to bring her back to the WH after the election"); Tripp 7/9/98 GJ at 31, 37-38, 42.

314. In a recorded conversation, Ms. Lewinsky recounted part of this discussion:

[H]e said, "I promise you," you know, something like, "if I win in November, I'll have you back like that. You can do anything you want. You can be anything you want." And then I made a joke and I said, "Well, can I be Assistant to the President for Blow Jobs?" He said, "I'd like that."

T7 at 34-35.

315. Lewinsky 8/6/98 GJ at 64.

316. Clinton 8/17/98 GJ at 130.

317. Lewinsky 8/26/98 Depo. at 40.

318. Lewinsky 8/6/98 GJ at 94-97.

319. Lewinsky 8/26/98 Depo. at 40-41.

320. Lewinsky 8/26/98 Depo. at 41.

321. Lewinsky 8/26/98 Depo. at 41.

322. Lewinsky 8/6/98 GJ at 20, 95-97; Lewinsky 7/30/98 Int. at 13.

323. Lewinsky 8/6/98 GJ at 95; Lewinsky 8/26/98 Depo. at 41-44; Lewinsky 7/27/98 Int. at 4-5; Lewinsky 7/30/98 Int. at 13.

324. Lewinsky 8/6/98 GJ at 92; Lewinsky 7/27/98 Int. at 4-5; Lewinsky 7/30/98 Int. at 13.

325. 1248-DC-00000008 (phone logs).

326. Lewinsky 8/6/98 GJ at 93, 97.

327. Lewinsky 8/6/98 GJ at 93. See also Lewinsky 8/26/98 Depo. at 43; Lewinsky 7/27/98 Int. at 5; Lewinsky 7/30/98 Int. at 13. Ms. Lewinsky testified that she did not see Mr. Ickes but recognized his voice. Lewinsky 8/6/98 GJ at 97.

328. Lewinsky 8/6/98 GJ at 93; Lewinsky 8/26/98 Depo. at 45; Lewinsky 7/27/98 Int. at 5; Lewinsky 7/30/98 Int. at 13.

329. Lewinsky 8/6/98 GJ at 94. See also Lewinsky 7/30/98 Int. at 11; Tripp 7/9/98 GJ at 30-36; 845-DC-00000012 - 13 (Tripp notes).

330. Muskett 7/21/98 GJ at 9-13.

331. Muskett 7/21/98 GJ at 22-24.

332. Muskett 7/21/98 GJ at 25-26, 83.

333. Muskett 7/21/98 GJ at 27-28, 91-93.

334. Muskett 7/21/98 GJ at 28, 31-33.

335. Muskett 7/21/98 GJ at 34-37.

336. Lewinsky 8/6/98 GJ at 36-37; Lewinsky 7/27/98 Int. at 2.

337. Muskett 7/21/98 GJ at 36-37, 39-40. Officer Muskett recalled that the plainclothes agent on duty at the time was Reginald Hightower. Muskett 7/21/98 GJ at 22. While not "100 percent sure" that this incident occurred, Agent Hightower testified that "it probably did happen." Hightower 7/28/98 GJ at 46-49.

338. Muskett 7/21/98 GJ at 42-46. Mr. Ickes testified that he cannot recall this incident but cannot rule it out. Ickes 8/5/98 GJ at 58-59.

339. Muskett 7/21/98 GJ at 47-52, 89.

340. 1506-DC-00000144 (phone logs).

341. Lewinsky 8/6/98 GJ at 64-65. See also Lewinsky 2/1/98 Statement at 1; Lewinsky 7/31/98 Int. at 6-7; Lewinsky 8/3/98 Int. at 5; Tripp 7/9/98 GJ at 72-73; 845-DC-00000014 (Tripp notes); T2 at 17.

342. Lewinsky 8/6/98 GJ at 65; Lewinsky 7/29/98 Int. at 3-4; Lewinsky 8/3/98 Int. at 5.

343. Lieberman 1/30/98 GJ at 62.

344. Lieberman 1/30/98 GJ at 62.

345. Bowles 4/2/98 GJ at 66-67.

346. Currie 5/7/98 GJ at 49-50.

347. Jordan 3/3/98 GJ at 64-65.

348. V006-DC-00002289 (email noting departures of White House employees);
Lewinsky 8/6/98 GJ at 65. According to the job description for the position:

The incumbent of this Schedule C position will have access to highly confidential,
sensitive and frequently politically controversial information and must be a person
in whom the [Assistant Secretary of Defense for Public Affairs] has complete trust
and confidence.

833-DC-00002880. Ms. Lewinsky held clearance for Sensitive Compartmented
Information. Lewinsky 8/24/98 Int. at 3. According to a regulation:

Sensitive Compartmented Information is information that not only is classified
for national security reasons as Top Secret, Secret, or Confidential, but also is subject
to special access and handling requirements because it involves or derives from particularly sensitive intelligence sources and methods.

28 C.F.R. ß 17.18(a) (1998).

349. Lewinsky 7/29/98 Int. at 1.

350. Lewinsky 8/6/98 GJ at 66.

351. Tripp 7/9/98 GJ at 94-98.

352. Lewinsky 8/6/98 GJ at 28 & Ex. ML-7.

353. Tripp 7/14/98 GJ at 3-4, 11-12; 845-DC-00000019 (Tripp notes).

354. Lewinsky 7/29/98 Int. at 4-5.

355. Lewinsky 7/30/98 Int. at 14. See also Lewinsky 7/29/98 Int. at 4; Lewinsky
8/6/98 GJ at 27-28; Tripp 7/9/98 GJ at 118-19 (mistakenly indicating that this
occurred July 15, 1996); 845-DC-00000018 (Tripp notes).

356. 1506-DC-00000275 (call log); 1506-DC-000000638.

357. Lewinsky 7/29/98 Int. at 4-5; Lewinsky 7/30/98 Int. at 14-15; 845-DC-
00000016 - 17 (Tripp notes); 845-DC-00000020 - 22 (same); Tripp 7/9/98 GJ at
102-04, 115-16; Tripp 7/14/98 GJ at 11-12, 35-37.

358. 1506-DC-00000222 (5/21/96); 1506-DC-00000264 (7/5/96); 1506-DC-
00000268 (7/6/96); 1506-DC-00000328 (10/22/96); 1506-DC-00000353 (12/2/96)
(President's schedules).

359. Lewinsky 7/29/98 Int. at 3; Finerman 3/18/98 Depo. at 49-50; Tripp 7/9/98
GJ at 53, 61-62, 94. Along with talking with the President, Ms. Lewinsky also contacted former White House colleagues for help returning to work there. Lewinsky
8/3/98 Int. at 5.

360. T7 at 36.

361. T7 at 36-37.

362. Lewinsky 7/30/98 Int. at 14; Lewinsky 8/6/98 GJ at 21; Erbland 2/12/98 GJ at 30; Tripp 7/14/98 GJ at 4-6; 845-DC-00000020 (Tripp notes).

363. Lewinsky 8/20/98 GJ at 25.

364. Lewinsky 7/29/98 Int. at 3, 16; Tripp 7/9/98 GJ at 99-100; 845-DC-00000015 (Tripp notes). The President was at the Renaissance Hotel in Washington from 8:40 to 9:25 p.m. that day. 1506-DC-00000188 - 189 (President's schedules).

365. V006-DC-00000534 (radio address guest list); 1222-DC-00000045 (itinerary); V006-DC-00001841 - 1847 (photographs); V006-DC-00003735 (photo requests); V006-DC-00001865 (videotape).

366. Lewinsky 8/20/98 GJ at 28-31; Lewinsky 7/29/98 Int. at 16; Lewinsky 8/24/98 Int. at 6-7; V006-DC-00000682 (President's schedule for August 18); V006-DC-00003735 (photo request from Ms. Lewinsky); MSL-DC-0000489 - 490 (event invitation); Tripp 7/9/98 GJ at 125-26; 845-DC-00000019 (Tripp notes).

367. Lewinsky 8/20/98 GJ at 28-31. See also Lewinsky 7/30/98 Int. at 17.

368. Lewinsky 7/31/98 Int. at 7. Ms. Lewinsky thought that this might have been October 23 or 24. Id. The President was at the Sheraton Washington Hotel from 6:55 to 8:05 p.m. on October 23. 1506-DC-00000334 - 335 (President's schedule).

369. Newsweek, 8/10/98, cover photo.

370. Lewinsky 8/11/98 Int. at 2.

371. Lewinsky 8/20/98 GJ at 26-27.

372. Lewinsky 7/29/98 Int. at 5.

373. V006-DC-00000007 (WAVES records); V006-DC-00001855 - 1856 (photos from the reception); V006-DC-00000391 (White House event attendance records).

374. MSL-DC-00001052 (spelling and punctuation corrected). See also Lewinsky 2/1/98 Statement at 1-2; Tripp 7/14/98 GJ at 32-34. Ms. Lewinsky did not send this letter. Lewinsky 8/4/98 Int. at 5.

375. Catherine Davis 3/17/98 GJ at 23-24, 27; Finerman 3/18/98 Depo. at 12; Kassorla 8/28/98 Int. at 4; Raines 1/29/98 GJ at 31-32; Tripp 7/2/98 GJ at 41-43.

376. Tripp 7/14/98 GJ at 39-40; 845-DC-00000022 (Tripp notes).

377. 833-DC-00001974 (email to Ms. Tripp).

378. Currie 5/7/98 GJ at 63.

379. Currie 5/6/98 GJ at 97-98.

380. Currie 5/6/98 GJ 14-15.

381. Currie 5/6/98 GJ at 52-53, 94-96.

382. 827-DC-00000002, 827-DC-00000018 (Ms. Lewinsky's WAVES records).

383. Currie 5/6/98 GJ at 57-58.

384. Currie 5/6/98 GJ at 84-85. In a later appearance before the grand jury, Ms. Currie testified that she could no longer recall any occasions when she came just to admit Ms. Lewinsky, but she could not rule it out. Currie 7/22/98 GJ at 24.

385. Currie 1/27/98 GJ at 32-33. See also Currie 5/6/98 GJ at 98; Currie 7/22/98 GJ at 25-26, 41. Ms. Currie subsequently wavered on this point. Currie 7/22/98 GJ at 14 ("[t]he President, for all intents and purposes, is never alone"); Id. at 15-16 (testifying that President and Ms. Lewinsky, in study together, were "not alone" so long as Ms. Currie was at her desk); Id. at 25 (agreeing that Ms. Lewinsky and President were alone together); Id. at 131 ("I was always there. And I considered them not to be alone. . . . I always thought that my presence there meant that they were not alone."). Cf. Clinton 8/17/98 GJ at 134 ("there were a lot of times when we were alone, but I never really thought we were").

386. Pape 5/18/98 Int. at 3-4.

387. Chinery 6/11/98 Depo. at 33.

388. Chinery 6/11/98 Depo. at 44-45; Chinery 7/23/98 GJ at 49.

389. Chinery 7/23/98 GJ at 8; Chinery 6/11/98 Depo. at 13-17. For other Secret Service corroboration of Ms. Currie's role, see Chinery 7/23/98 GJ at 49-50; Chinery 6/11/98 Depo. at 33, 37, 44; Garabito 7/30/98 GJ at 44-47; Shegogue 8/4/98 GJ at 11, 14-19, 24-27.

390. Lewinsky 8/20/98 GJ at 5. See also Id. at 14; Lewinsky 8/19/98 Int. at 5.

391. Currie 5/6/98 GJ at 88-89. See also Id. at 184; Currie 5/14/98 GJ at 78.

392. Currie 5/6/98 GJ at 88-89.

393. Currie 5/14/98 GJ at 72-74, 91; Currie 1/24/98 Int. at 3.

394. 837-DC-00000001; 837-DC-00000004; 837-DC-00000006; 837-DC-0000008; 837-DC-00000011; 837-DC-00000014; 837-DC-00000018.

395. Lewinsky 7/31/98 Int. at 13; Marcia Lewis 2/11/98 GJ at 28-30; T1 at 63-64.

396. Dragotta 8/13/98 GJ at 10-11; Janney 8/13/98 GJ at 7, 9-11, 14; Niedzwiecki 7/30/98 GJ at 12-13, 20-21; Pape 8/5/98 GJ at 24; Keith Williams 7/23/98 GJ at 14.

397. Currie 5/14/98 GJ at 72-73.

398. Currie 5/14/98 GJ at 73-74, 86-89; Currie 7/22/98 GJ at 51-52.

399. Currie 5/14/98 GJ at 88-89. See also Id. at 91; Currie 7/22/98 GJ at 49-50 (testifying that she did not open sealed cards from Ms. Lewinsky to President but "may have read" unsealed ones).

400. Currie 5/6/98 GJ at 88-89. See also Currie 5/14/98 GJ at 78.

401. "The President got everything anyone sent him." Currie 5/6/98 GJ at 129.

402. Currie 5/14/98 GJ at 143-45; Currie 1/24/98 Int. at 8.

403. Currie 5/6/98 GJ at 157-58.

404. Currie 5/6/98 GJ at 156; Currie 7/22/98 GJ at 42-43.

405. Currie 1/27/98 GJ at 63-64. See also Currie 5/6/98 GJ at 164; Currie 7/22/98 GJ at 31-33. According to Ms. Lewinsky, the President at one point told her similarly that "if the two people who are involved [in a relationship] say it didn't happen — it didn't happen." Lewinsky 2/1/98 Statement at 10, ∂ 11.

406. Currie 5/14/98 GJ at 131-43. Ms. Currie testified: "I think . . . what I was trying to do was allow the President to have personal and private phone calls if he wanted to. And the appearance of any impropriety, I didn't want to have it." Id. at 141.

407. Currie 7/22/98 GJ at 33-35.

408. Dragotta 8/13/98 GJ at 8-10; Pape 8/5/98 GJ at 17-18. Asked if she had tried to persuade officers not to log in Ms. Lewinsky's visits, Ms. Currie testified: "I hope I didn't. I can't imagine — and I can't imagine that it could be." Currie 7/22/98 GJ at 115. None of the Uniformed Division officers interviewed by the OIC acknowledged having permitted Ms. Lewinsky to enter the White House without proper clearance. However, as noted elsewhere, there is clear evidence that Ms. Lewinsky was in the White House on days for which no records show her entry or exit.

409. V006-DC-00003712 (2/24/97 message). Records show seven calls from Ms. Lewinsky's line to Ms. Currie's line on December 5, 1997, for example, and six calls the following day. 1216-DC-00000022.

410. Currie 5/6/98 GJ at 16-17, 20-21, 68-70, 73-74, 85-86; Currie 5/7/98 GJ at 8. See also 1037-DC-00000341 (email).

411. Currie 5/6/98 GJ at 73-74, 85-86. Ms. Currie later said that "I don't want the impression of sneaking, but it's just that I brought her in without anyone seeing her." Id. at 156. Ms. Lewinsky confirmed that Ms. Currie helped her avoid Mr.

Goodin and others. Lewinsky 8/20/98 GJ at 15; Lewinsky 7/27/98 Int. at 4; Lewinsky 8/3/98 Int. at 5; Lewinsky 8/24/98 Int. at 7.

412. Currie 5/6/98 GJ at 84-85.

413. Lewinsky 7/31/98 Int. at 4.

414. Lewinsky 8/5/98 Int. at 3.

415. Lewinsky 7/31/98 Int. at 5. Ms. Lewinsky told confidants about Ms. Currie's role. Catherine Davis 3/17/98 GJ at 17, 33, 37-38; Erbland 2/12/98 GJ at 43; Finerman 3/18/98 Depo. at 39-40; Raines 1/29/98 GJ at 49; Ungvari 3/19/98 GJ at 38-40; 1037-DC-00000337 - 338 (email from Ms. Lewinsky); 1037-DC-00000001 - 02 (card from Ms. Lewinsky).

416. Carbonetti 6/16/98 Int. at 2; Chinery 6/11/98 Depo. at 39-40; Janney 5/27/98 Int. at 2; LaDow 5/27/98 Int. at 3; Ludtke 6/5/98 Int. at 2; Pape 8/5/98 GJ at 23-24; Pape 5/18/98 Int. at 3-6.

417. Chinery 7/23/98 GJ at 50.

418. Pape 5/18/98 Int. at 5.

419. Washington Post, 2/14/97, "Love Notes" at 44 (824-DC-00000013 - 14). See also 1078-DC-00000002. A copy of the ad was found in the box of gifts and other items that Ms. Lewinsky, after being subpoenaed in the Jones case, gave Ms. Currie for safekeeping. 824-DC-00000013 - 14; Lewinsky 8/20/98 GJ at 71-72. Ms. Lewinsky told several people about the ad. Catherine Davis 3/17/98 GJ at 28; Finerman 3/18/98 Depo. at 22-23; Marcia Lewis 2/10/98 GJ at 59-61; Raines 1/29/98 GJ at 109. In email on February 13, she said she planned to check her telephone messages from London (where she would be on Valentine's Day) "in the hopes that the creep will call and say 'Thank you for my love note. I love you. Will you run away with me?' What do ya think the likelihood of that happening is?" 833-DC-00001934. On February 19, she wrote in an email that the President had not left any message for her on Valentine's Day. 833-DC-00009446.

420. 827-DC-00000018 (Epass records); Kessinger 2/24/98 Int. at 2.

421. 833-DC-00001906 (email from Ms. Lewinsky to Ms. Tripp).

422. V006-DC-00003712.

423. V006-DC-00003720 (radio address attendance list).

424. 827-DC-00000018; V006-DC-00000008; V006-DC-00001796.

425. 1222-DC-00000234; 968-DC-00000073.

426. 968-DC-00003506.

427. Lewinsky 8/26/98 Depo. at 45-46, 48-49; Lewinsky 8/6/98 GJ at 30.

428. Lewinsky 8/6/98 GJ at 45-46.

429. Lewinsky 8/26/98 Depo. at 46.

430. Lewinsky 8/6/98 GJ at 30.

431. Lewinsky 8/6/98 GJ at 30-31, 46-47; Lewinsky 7/30/98 Int. at 15; Lewinsky 7/31/98 Int. at 5. Mr. Goodin and Ms. Currie confirmed that Ms. Lewinsky stayed behind and talked with the President after the radio address. Currie 1/27/98 GJ at 34; Goodin 2/17/98 GJ at 52, 55. Mr. Goodin testified that he approached the President and "basically offer[ed] to chase her away because I didn't know if that was a good use of his time," but the President replied that "she's a friend of a political supporter." Goodin 2/17/98 GJ at 56. Nancy Hernreich, who was not present at the radio address, testified that Mr. Goodin told her about Ms. Lewinsky's presence there on the following work day. Hernreich 2/26/98 GJ at 5-9.

432. Currie 7/22/98 GJ at 130-31; Currie 1/27/98 GJ at 34-35; Lewinsky 8/6/98 GJ at 31; Lewinsky 7/30/98 Int. at 15.

433. Currie 7/22/98 GJ at 131. Ms. Currie also maintained that the President and Ms. Lewinsky were "[n]ever out of eyesight." Id. at 135. The President, however, acknowledged "inappropriate intimate contact" with Ms. Lewinsky on February 28 and testified that, to the best of his knowledge, Ms. Currie never witnessed any such encounters between himself and Ms. Lewinsky. Clinton 8/17/98 GJ at 10, 53-54.

434. Lewinsky 8/26/98 Depo. at 46-47.

435. Lewinsky 8/26/98 Depo. at 46-47.

436. Lewinsky 8/26/98 Depo. at 47; Lewinsky 8/6/98 GJ at 31. Ms. Currie testified that the President later asked her, "Did Monica show you the hat pin I gave her?" Currie 5/6/98 GJ at 142.

437. Lewinsky 8/6/98 GJ at 156. See also Lewinsky 8/20/98 GJ at 72; Lewinsky 8/26/98 Depo. at 47; Currie 5/6/98 GJ at 101-102; Catherine Davis 3/17/98 GJ 30-31; Erbland 2/12/98 GJ at 40-41; Finerman 3/18/98 Depo. at 15-16; Marcia Lewis 2/10/98 GJ at 51-52; Raines 1/29/98 GJ at 53-55.

A draft of Ms. Lewinsky's thank-you note (to "Dear Mr. P") was found in her apartment. It says in part:

All of my life, everyone has always said that I am a difficult person for whom to shop, and yet, you managed to choose two absolutely perfect presents! A little phrase (with only eight letters) like "thank you" simply cannot begin to express what I feel for what you have given me. Art & poetry are gifts to my soul!

I just love the hat pin. It is vibrant, unique and a beautiful piece of art. My only hope is that I have a hat fit to adorn it (ahhh, I see another excuse to go shopping)! I know that I am bound to receive compliments on it.

I have only read excerpts from "Leaves of Grass" before — never in its entirety or in such a beautifully bound edition. Like Shakespeare, Whitman's writings are so timeless. I find solace in works from the past that remain profound and somehow always poignant. Whitman is so rich that one must read him like one tastes a fine wine or good cigar — take it in, roll it in your mouth, and savor it!

I hope you know how very grateful I am for these gifts, especially your gift of friendship. I will treasure them all . . . always.

MSL-DC-00000621 - 622 (emphasis in original) (ellipsis in original). Ms. Lewinsky said she sent a version of this letter to the President and enclosed a necktie. Lewinsky 8/4/98 Int. at 5.

438. Lewinsky 8/24/98 Int. at 7; Finerman 3/18/98 Depo. at 22; Raines 1/29/98 GJ at 109.

439. Lewinsky 8/26/98 Depo. at 47-48. See also Lewinsky 8/6/98 GJ at 31, 38-39.

440. Lewinsky 8/26/98 Depo. at 47-48. See also Lewinsky 8/6/98 GJ at 31, 38-39.

441. Lewinsky 7/30/98 Int. at 15.

442. Lewinsky 8/26/98 Depo. at 48.

443. Lewinsky 8/6/98 GJ at 32, 39-40. Ms. Lewinsky testified that she did not keep the soiled dress as a souvenir. She said she does not ordinarily clean her clothes until she is ready to wear them again. "I was going to clean it. I was going to wear it again." Lewinsky 8/6/98 GJ at 41. She also testified that she was not certain that the stains were semen. She had dined out after the radio address, "[s]o it could be spinach dip or something." Lewinsky 8/6/98 GJ at 40. See also Lewinsky 7/29/98 Int. at 17.

444. FBI Lab Reports, 8/6/98, 8/17/98.

445. Clinton 8/17/98 GJ at 55.

446. Clinton 8/17/98 GJ at 138.

447. Clinton 8/17/98 GJ at 136-37.

448. V006-DC-00000008 (WAVES records); V006-DC-00001792 (WAVES request). Phone records indicate that Ms. Lewinsky called Ms. Currie for one minute at 8:37 a.m. that day. 1014-DC-00000022.

449. 968-DC-00000236 (presidential diary); V006-DC-00002130 (movement log); 968-DC-00003510 (phone log). Mrs. Clinton was in Africa. 968-DC-00003843 (schedule).

450. Lewinsky 7/30/98 Int. at 16; Lewinsky 8/20/98 GJ at 67-69; Lewinsky 8/24/98 Int. at 7.

451. Lewinsky 8/26/98 Depo. at 49.

452. Lewinsky 8/26/98 Depo. at 50.

453. Lewinsky 8/26/98 Depo. at 50.

454. Lewinsky 8/26/98 Depo. at 51. See also Lewinsky 8/20/98 GJ at 68-69; Lewinsky 7/30/98 Int. at 16. Ms. Lewinsky testified that their genitals only briefly touched: "[W]e sort of had tried to do that, but because he's so tall and he couldn't bend because of his knee, it didn't really work." Lewinsky 8/26/98 Depo. at 51.

455. Lewinsky 8/20/98 GJ at 68-69; Lewinsky 8/26/98 Depo. at 50; Lewinsky 7/30/98 Int. at 16.

456. Lewinsky 7/30/98 Int. at 16.

457. Clinton 8/17/98 GJ at 10.

458. Clinton 8/17/98 GJ at 54-55, 137-38.

459. Lewinsky 8/6/98 GJ at 66; Lewinsky 7/27/98 Int. at 5; Lewinsky 7/31/98 Int. at 8; Lewinsky 2/1/98 Statement at 1-2; MSL-DC-00001052; T1 at 38. Mr. Nash said he had never heard of Ms. Lewinsky before January 1998. Nash 3/19/98 Int. at 1; Nash 9/2/98 Int. at 1.

460. Lewinsky 8/6/98 GJ at 67.

461. Lewinsky 8/6/98 GJ at 66-67; Lewinsky 7/27/98 Int. at 5; Lewinsky 8/5/98 Int. at 2.

462. Lewinsky 8/6/98 GJ at 86-87.

463. Lewinsky 8/26/98 Depo. at 62.

464. Clinton 8/17/98 GJ at 113-14. Later the President said: "I didn't order her to be hired at the White House. I could have done so. I wouldn't do it." Id. At 124. But see Scott 3/19/98 GJ at 76 (ìWhen Mr. Bowles came in, one of the agreements that I think he got from the President was that he would control the hiring within the White House and that no Assistant to the President would be forced to take people within their shop that they did not want and were not qualified.î).

465. Lewinsky 8/6/98 GJ at 97-99; Lewinsky 7/27/98 Int. at 3.

466. Lewinsky 8/6/98 GJ at 87; Lewinsky 7/27/98 Int. at 3.

467. Lewinsky 8/6/98 GJ at 98-99; Lewinsky 7/27/98 Int. at 3. See also Lewinsky 9/3/98 Int. at 1.

468. Kaye 5/21/98 GJ at 103-108. Ms. Finerman testified that she did have a conversation along these lines with Mr. Kaye. Finerman 3/18/98 Depo. at 52-57. Mr. Kaye testified that he could not recall having discussed Ms. Lewinsky with Ms. Scott. Kaye 5/21/98 GJ at 44. Ms. Scott testified that she could not recall talking to Mr. Kaye about Ms. Lewinsky in this period, or talking to him about phone calls between Ms. Lewinsky and the President at any time. Scott 3/31/98 GJ at 53.

469. 827-DC-00000018 (Epass records).

470. 1222-DC-00000242.

471. 968-DC-00003533.

472. Lewinsky 8/4/98 Int. at 2-3.

473. Lewinsky 8/6/98 GJ at 24-25, 101.

474. Lewinsky 8/4/98 Int. at 2; Lewinsky 7/31/98 Int. at 16.

475. Lewinsky 8/4/98 Int. at 2-3.

476. Lewinsky 8/4/98 Int. at 3. Ms. Lewinsky later told confidants about the May 24 break-up. Catherine Davis 3/17/98 GJ at 133-35; Erbland 2/12/98 GJ at 46-47; Kassorla 8/28/98 Int. at 4; Raines 1/29/98 GJ at 58-59; Tripp 7/14/98 GJ at 78-84; Ungvari 3/19/98 GJ at 80. Dr. Kassorla, Ms. Lewinsky's therapist, told Ms. Lewinsky that the President's statement sounded rehearsed and insincere. Kassorla 8/28/98 Int. at 4.

A fragment of a deleted file recovered from Ms. Lewinsky's home computer apparently refers to the President's May 24 announcement:

. . . cannot do anything but accept that. However, I also cannot ignore what we have shared together. I don't care what you say, but if you were 100% fulfilled in your marriage I never would have seen that raw, intense sexuality that I saw a few times — watching your mouth on my breast or looking in your eyes while you explored the depth of my sex. Instead, it would have been a routine encounter void of anything but a sexual release. I do not want you to breach your moral standard . . . .

MSL-55-DC-0094; MSL-55-DC-0124 (spelling and punctuation corrected).

477. Lewinsky 8/6/98 GJ at 25. See also Lewinsky 7/27/98 Int. at 3 (birthday kiss 8/16/97; Christmas kiss 12/28/97); Id. at 7 (President told her that Christmas kiss

was permissible). Ms. Lewinsky tried to initiate genital contact with the President on August 16, 1997, but he rebuffed her. Lewinsky 8/20/98 GJ at 70.

478. Clinton v. Jones, 117 S. Ct. 1636 (1997).

479. Currie 5/6/98 GJ at 31-33; Currie 5/7/98 GJ at 44, 68; Currie 5/14/98 GJ at 6-8, 148. Ms. Currie was uncertain when this occurred. Currie 5/6/98 GJ at 31.

480. Currie 5/6/98 GJ at 45; Currie 5/14/98 GJ at 146.

481. Currie 5/14/98 GJ at 146.

482. Currie GJ 5/14/98 at 121; Currie GJ 5/6/98 at 13, 81.

483. Currie 5/7/98 GJ at 43-44.

484. Currie 5/7/98 GJ at 68.

485. Currie 5/7/98 GJ at 69. Contrary to Ms. Currie's testimony, Ms. Scott testified that the President never asked her to help Ms. Lewinsky, though they may have discussed it. In

Ms. Scott's account, she met with Ms. Lewinsky as a favor to Ms. Currie. Scott 3/19/98 GJ at 20, 32, 37, 78-79, 84-85; Scott 3/26/98 GJ at 13, 15; Scott 3/31/98 GJ at 43-44. For his part, the President testified that he talked with Ms. Scott about bringing Ms. Lewinsky back to work at the White House, though he did not order her to hire Ms. Lewinsky. Clinton 8/17/98 GJ at 130.

486. Lewinsky 8/6/98 GJ at 67; Lewinsky 8/24/98 Int. at 7. Ms. Lewinsky also tried to get a White House job through other avenues. She applied for a position at the National Security Council and had interviews there on May 1 and June 11. Lewinsky 7/27/98 Int. at 5; Bailey 5/26/98 GJ at 23; Dimel 2/18/98 Int. at 1; Friedrich 7/17/98 Int. at 1; Stott 2/27/98 Int. at 2; V006-DC-00000008 (WAVES records); 827-DC-00000018 (Epass records); 833-DC-00001876 (Tripp email regarding a job announcement); V006-DC-00000221 - 224 (Dimel documents). She was not chosen for the job. V006-DC-00000223 - 224 (Dimel letter). She also pursued a job in the White House press office. Lewinsky 7/27/98 Int. at 5. At one point Ms. Lewinsky told the President that she had applied for these jobs, and he responded that he needed to know in advance if he was to help her. Lewinsky 7/27/98 Int. at 5.

487. 827-DC-00000018 (Epass records); V006-DC-00000008 (WAVES records); Scott GJ 3/19/98 at 17.

488. 1037-DC-00000265- 266 (spelling and punctuation corrected). See also Finerman 3/18/98 Depo. at 50-51 (recounting this meeting); Tripp 7/14/98 GJ at 89-91 (recounting this meeting).

489. Scott 3/19/98 GJ at 52. See also Scott 3/26/98 GJ at 16-17.

490. Scott 3/19/98 GJ at 74.

491. Scott 3/19/98 GJ at 87.

492. 833-DC-00001070.

493. Currie 5/7/98 GJ at 35; see Id. at 39.

494. MSL-DC-00001176 - 1177. A revised version of the letter was also found in Ms. Lewinsky's apartment. MSL-DC-00001192. Consistent with a statement in the draft, Ms. Scott testified that "I don't hear about White House jobs." Scott 3/19/98 GJ at 90. Ms. Scott also testified that she recalled only a short thank-you note after her June 16 meeting with Ms. Lewinsky, though she did receive a "real pissy letter" from Ms. Lewinsky at some point, which she threw away. Scott 3/19/98 GJ at 77; Scott 3/26/98 GJ at 18.

495. MSL-DC-00001227 (emphasis in original). Ms. Lewinsky sent a version of the note. Lewinsky 8/4/98 Int. at 6. Records indicate that Ms. Lewinsky was in Madrid the following week and in Los Angeles later in the month. MSL-DC-00001221; 852-DC-00000035; 929-DC-00000056; 852-DC-00000037.

496. 1037-DC-00000103, 1037-DC-00000280, 1037-DC-00000296 (email from Catherine Davis to Ms. Lewinsky referring to "[y]our idea about working in another city or country") (multiple copies of same message).

497. Lewinsky 7/29/98 Int. at 8.

498. Lewinsky 8/6/98 GJ at 68, 87; Lewinsky 7/29/98 Int. at 7-8; Lewinsky 8/11/98 Int. at 6.

499. Lewinsky 8/6/98 GJ at 68, 87. See also Lewinsky 7/29/98 Int. at 7-8; Lewinsky 8/11/98 Int. at 6.

500. Lewinsky 8/6/98 GJ at 68-69, 87-89. See also Lewinsky 8/26/98 Depo. at 62-63.

501. Lewinsky 8/6/98 GJ at 68, 87; Lewinsky 7/29/98 Int. at 7-8; Lewinsky 8/11/98 Int. at 6.

502. Lewinsky 7/29/98 Int. at 8; Lewinsky 8/13/98 Int. at 1. Ms. Lewinsky said she thought of the United Nations because a former Pentagon colleague worked there and liked it. Lewinsky 8/13/98 Int. at 1.

503. Clinton 8/17/98 GJ at 124.

504. Lewinsky 8/6/98 GJ at 69. See also Lewinsky 7/29/98 Int. at 8.

505. Lewinsky 8/6/98 GJ at 69. See also Lewinsky 7/29/98 Int. at 7.

506. 827-DC-00000018.

507. V006-DC-00002140; V006-DC-00002214.

508. Lewinsky 8/6/98 GJ at 75. See also Lewinsky 7/29/98 Int. at 8; Lewinsky 8/4/98 Int. at 4.

509. Lewinsky 7/29/98 Int. at 8-9.

510. Lewinsky 8/26/98 Depo. at 54-55; Lewinsky 7/27/98 Int. at 3.

511. Lewinsky 8/26/98 Depo. at 55-56.

512. Lewinsky 8/26/98 Depo. at 56-57. See also Lewinsky 7/28/98 Int. at 6.

513. Lewinsky 8/26/98 Depo. at 56-57. See also Catherine Davis 3/17/98 GJ at 180; Tripp 7/7/98 GJ at 55-56; 845-DC-00000193 (Tripp notes).

514. Lewinsky 8/6/98 GJ at 72. See also Lewinsky 8/4/98 Int. at 4.

515. Lewinsky 8/6/98 GJ at 70-71; Tripp 7/14/98 GJ at 107-116.

516. Lewinsky GJ 8/6/98 at 72, 77; Lewinsky 302 7/29/98 at 7. According to Ms. Tripp, she had tried to alert Mr. Lindsey about the contact from Mr. Isikoff, but Mr. Lindsey, with whom she had worked at the White House, did not return her calls and pages. Ms. Tripp testified that she tried to reach him because "he was one of the protectors" of the President. Tripp 7/14/98 GJ at 111. Mr. Lindsey testified that he returned a page from Ms. Tripp, but not until July or August. Lindsey 2/18/98 GJ at 132-33.

517. Lewinsky 8/6/98 GJ at 71.

518. Lewinsky 8/6/98 GJ at 73-74; Lewinsky 7/29/98 Int. at 7.

519. Lewinsky 7/29/98 Int. at 7; Lewinsky 8/11/98 Int. at 5.

520. Lewinsky 8/6/98 GJ at 73; Lewinsky 7/29/98 Int. at 7.

521. 968-DC-00003546.

522. Lewinsky 8/6/98 GJ at 75.

523. 827-DC-00000018; See also Steven Pape 5/18/98 Depo. at 3.

524. V006-DC-00002142 (movement logs).

525. Lewinsky 8/6/98 GJ at 75-76; Lewinsky 7/29/98 Int. at 9. Ms. Currie did not recall Ms. Lewinsky's visit of July 14. Currie 7/22/98 GJ at 81.

526. Lewinsky 8/6/98 GJ at 76.

527. 1222-DC-00000251 (movement logs).

528. Lewinsky 8/6/98 GJ at 76. The President was referring to the Drudge Report, carried on the Internet, which had reported on July 4 (the day of Ms. Lewinsky's previous White House visit) that Michael Isikoff of Newsweek was "hot on the trail" of a story involving "a federal employee sexually propositioned by the Presi-

dent on federal property." Drudge Report 7/4/97. See also Washington Post, 8/11/97 at D1 (on Drudge Report's scoop of Newsweek).

529. Lewinsky 8/6/98 GJ at 76-77.

530. Lewinsky 8/6/98 GJ at 77.

531. Lewinsky 8/6/98 GJ at 77-78; Tripp 7/16/98 GJ at 12.

532. Lewinsky 8/6/98 GJ at 78; Lewinsky 7/27/98 Int. at 3; Lewinsky 7/29/98 Int. at 10; Tripp 7/14/98 GJ at 117-19; Tripp 7/16/98 GJ at 9.

533. Lewinsky 8/6/98 GJ at 78-79.

534. 968-DC-00003550.

535. Lewinsky 8/6/98 GJ at 79; Tripp 7/16/98 at 12.

536. Lewinsky 8/6/98 GJ at 79-80.

537. Lewinsky 7/29/98 Int. at 10-11. Subsequently, Ms. Tripp did call Mr. Lindsey. He urged her to contact Robert Bennett, but she never did so. Lindsey 3/12/98 GJ at 3, 13; Lindsey 2/18/98 GJ at 132-40; Tripp 7/16/98 GJ at 12-14, 54-67, 75-80; Lewinsky 7/29/98 Int. at 11; T29 at 16; 880-DC-0000002 - 8.

538. Scott 3/19/98 GJ at 64-72.

539. Lewinsky 7/31/98 Int. at 9.

540. Lewinsky 2/1/98 Statement at 2.

541. Scott 3/26/98 GJ at 18-21; Currie 5/7/98 GJ at 68. Ms. Lewinsky also conferred with her supervisor, Kenneth Bacon, about being detailed back to the White House. He gave his approval and sent a letter recommending her. Bailey 2/6/98 Int. at 3; Bacon 2/26/98 Int. at 2-3; 1012-DC-00000001; MSL-DC-00001230.

542. Scott 3/19/98 GJ at 78-79; Scott 3/26/98 GJ at 13-15; Scott 3/31/98 GJ at 43-44; Currie 5/7/98 GJ at 68.

543. 827-DC-00000018 (Epass records); V006-DC-00000008 (WAVES records); V006-DC-00001770 (WAVES request).

544. 1222-DC-00000254 (movement logs).

545. 968-DC-00003556 (phone logs).

546. Lewinsky 8/6/98 GJ at 27-28 & Ex. ML-7; Lewinsky 8/24/98 Int. at 6.

547. Newsweek, 8/11/97 at 30.

548. 845-DC-00000190 (letter); Tripp 7/16/98 GJ at 85-88.

549. T30 at 166. Ms. Tripp responded: "Oh, God. He thinks I screwed him in the article. I'm dead." Id.

550. V006-DC-00000008 (WAVES records).

551. V006-DC-00002146 (movement logs). Secret Service Officer Steven Pape

testified about Ms. Lewinsky's August 16 visit. When Ms. Lewinsky entered the complex through the Southwest Gate, Officer Pape, who was familiar with Ms. Lewinsky's visits, predicted to another officer that the President would move to the Oval Office shortly. Officer Pape's prediction proved accurate: The President moved to the Oval Office, according to records, 18 minutes after Ms. Lewinsky entered the White House. Pape 8/5/98 GJ at 20-24; Myrick 8/13/98 GJ at 5-9; V006-DC-00002146 (movement logs); V006-DC-00002095 (movement logs); V006-DC-00002147 (movement logs). See also Shegogue 8/4/98 GJ at 10-11, 14-15, 17-20 (Secret Service officer recalling that Ms. Currie escorted Ms. Lewinsky into West Wing the day before President left for Martha's Vineyard).

552. 968-DC-00003558.

553. 968-DC-00002947.

554. Lewinsky 8/26/98 Depo. at 52. See also Lewinsky 8/20/98 GJ at 70.

555. Lewinsky 8/20/98 GJ at 70; Lewinsky 8/26/98 Depo. at 51-53.

556. Lewinsky 8/26/98 Depo. at 52.

557. DB-DC-00000022 (note dated 11/12/97). Ms. Lewinsky said that she sent this or a similar note to the President. Lewinsky 7/31/98 Int. at 2. See also 1037-DC-00000583 (email to Catherine Davis).

558. 1051-DC-00000003 (Pentagon phone records).

559. 1037-DC-00000086 - 87, 1037-DC-00000167, 1037-DC-00000255 - 256, 1037-DC-00000258 - 259 (email to Catherine Davis); 1318-DC-00000001 (card to Dale Young).

560. 1037-DC-00000086 - 87, 1037-DC-00000167, 1037-DC-00000255 - 256, 1037-DC-00000258 - 259 (email to Catherine Davis) (spelling and punctuation corrected).

561. Scott 3/26/98 GJ at 142.

562. Lewinsky 8/4/98 Int. at 5.

563. MSL-DC-00001052 (spelling and punctuation corrected).

564. Lewinsky 8/3/98 Int. at 6-7; Lewinsky 8/11/98 Int. at 5. See also 1037-DC-00000168 (email recounting episode). In mid or late September, according to Ms. Lewinsky, Ms. Currie told Ms. Lewinsky that she had spoken with Mr. Podesta. Lewinsky 7/31/98 Int. at 9; Lewinsky 8/13/98 Int. at 2; Lewinsky 2/1/98 Statement at 2. (Ms. Lewinsky thought that the President was having Ms. Currie do the "legwork" of getting her a job out of concern about appearances. Lewinsky 8/13/98 Int. at 3.) Mr. Podesta testified that he told Ms. Currie to have Ms. Lewinsky call him.

Podesta 2/5/98 GJ at 35; Podesta 6/16/98 GJ at 12-19. Ms. Currie testified that she does not remember getting that response from Mr. Podesta, and, if she had gotten it, she would have passed it on to Ms. Lewinsky. Currie 5/14/98 GJ at 149-51. According to Ms. Lewinsky, Ms. Currie mentioned Mr. Podesta to her in September 1997, but never told her to call him. Lewinsky 8/24/98 Int. at 7. Subsequently, Ms. Currie asked Mr. Podesta to help Ms. Lewinsky get a New York job. Lewinsky 2/1/98 Statement at 2-3; Podesta 2/5/98 GJ at 40-43; Podesta 6/16/98 GJ at 13.

565. 1037-DC-00000038 - 040; 1037-DC-00000167 - 169 (email to Catherine Davis).

566. Lewinsky 8/6/98 GJ at 27-28 & Ex. ML-7.

567. 1037-DC-00000038, 1037-DC-00000040, 1037-DC-00000167 - 169. Ms. Lewinsky told several people about the gifts. Catherine Davis 3/17/98 GJ at 31-32, 109-111; Erbland 2/12/98 at GJ 39-42; Finerman 3/18/98 Depo. at 14-15; Raines 1/29/98 GJ at 53-55; Tripp 7/16/98 GJ at 119-120; 845-DC-00000193 (Tripp notes). According to the President and Ms. Currie, he gave the Black Dog items to Ms. Currie to distribute as she wished; he did not bring them specifically for Ms. Lewinsky. Clinton 1/17/98 Depo. At 75-76; currie 5/7/98 GJ at 73-78. Ms. Currie acknowledged, though, that in presenting the items to Ms. Lewinsky, she might have implied that President Clinton had gotten them especially for her. Currie 5/7/98 GJ at 78.

568. Lewinsky 7/29/98 Int. at 16; Lewinsky 8/4/98 Int. at 5.

569. MSL-DC-00001050. Beneath the text of the document, at the bottom of the page, Ms. Lewinsky added: "JUST A REMINDER TO THROW THIS AWAY AND NOT SEND IT BACK TO THE STAFF SECRETARY!" Id. The statement that Ms. Lewinsky and the President had not spent time together in six weeks evidently refers to her August 16 visit, before his vacation.

570. Lewinsky 8/6/98 GJ at 27-28 & Ex. ML-7. On September 30, the President signed, under penalty of perjury, interrogatory responses in the sexual harassment case, answering Ms. Jones's allegations against him. V002-DC-00000008 - 15.

571. Lewinsky 8/13/98 Int. at 1. In email, Ms. Lewinsky indicated that it was Ms. Currie who told her that the President was going to talk to the Chief of Staff. 1037-DC-00000168.

572. Bowles 4/2/98 GJ at 12, 65-73.

573. Bowles 4/2/98 GJ at 67-68.

574. Bowles 4/2/98 GJ at 70, 74-75. Mr. Bowles placed this incident in late sum-

mer or early fall of 1997. Bowles 4/2/98 GJ at 65-66. Mr. Podesta's account largely matches Mr. Bowles's, except that Mr. Podesta placed the incident in late spring or summer of 1997; he understood that Ms. Lewinsky wanted a job in the White House or an agency; and he recalled being told by Mr. Bowles that Ms. Lewinsky, according to the President, "thought that she hadn't been treated fairly" in being transferred to the Pentagon. Podesta 2/5/98 GJ at 21-22.

575. Lewinsky 8/6/98 GJ at 102. See also Lewinsky GJ 8/6/98 at 102; Lewinsky 7/29/98 Int. at 13; Lewinsky 7/31/98 Int. at 9; Tripp 7/28/98 GJ at 110-111, 125-26. Ms. Tripp's friend Kate Friedrich, however, has denied having made the remarks that Ms. Tripp attributed to her. Friedrich 7/17/98 Int. at 1.

576. Lewinsky 7/31/98 Int. at 10.

577. Lewinsky 8/13/98 Int. at 1.

578. MSL-55-DC-0178 (spelling and punctuation corrected).

579. Lewinsky 8/4/98 Int. at 2-3.

580. T1 at 28.

581. T1 at 24.

582. T1 at 61.

583. T1 at 25.

584. T13 at 19.

585. MSL-55-DC-00000001 (letter); 837-DC-00000001 (courier receipts); T1 at 97.

586. MSL-55-DC-00000001.

587. Lewinsky 8/6/98 GJ at 103; Lewinsky 7/31/98 Int. at 10. See also Lewinsky 7/29/98 Int. at 6; Lewinsky 8/6/98 GJ at 27-28 & Ex. ML-7.

588. T13 at 20.

589. T8 at 30. See also Lewinsky 7/31/98 Int. at 10. See also MSL-55-DC-0177 (draft letter from Ms. Lewinsky to the President referring to this remark); DB-DC-00000017 (another draft of same letter).

590. T8 at 30.

591. T8 at 30.

592. T8 at 33.

593. Lewinsky 7/31/98 Int. at 10; Lewinsky 7/27/98 Int. at 5.

594. Lewinsky 7/31/98 Int. at 10.

595. Lewinsky 7/31/98 Int. at 10.

596. Lewinsky 7/31/98 Int. at 11.

597. 827-DC-00000018 (Epass records). Ms. Lewinsky's aunt, Debra Finerman, wrote in a note that "Monica was called by Betty to come at 9:30 this a.m." MSL-DC-00000456 (document found in Ms. Lewinsky's apartment in the course of a consensual search on January 22, 1998).

598. 952-DC-00000060 (movement logs).

599. Lewinsky 8/6/98 GJ at 27-28 & Exh. ML-7.

600. Lewinsky 8/6/98 GJ at 104; Lewinsky 8/13/98 Int. at 2-3; T2 at 5.

601. Lewinsky 8/6/98 GJ at 104; Lewinsky 7/31/98 Int. at 11-12. Ms. Lewinsky was not certain whether it was during the October 11 visit or their October 10 phone conversation that she first asked the President to speak to Mr. Jordan on her behalf. Lewinsky 8/6/98 GJ at 104.

602. Lewinsky 8/6/98 GJ at 104; Lewinsky 7/31/98 Int. at 11-12. Ms. Lewinsky later said that the President assured her that he would call her and give "a report." T13 at 17-18.

603. T2 at 14. In the grand jury, Ms. Currie was shown a transcript of this recorded conversation and acknowledged that the meeting described by Ms. Lewinsky "probably happened." Currie 5/6/98 GJ at 187.

604. T2 at 14. Although it is unclear whether the President spoke with Mr. Bowles about a recommendation for Ms. Lewinsky in October, there is evidence he did so on January 13, 1998. See infra at Section XIII.H.

605. T2 at 10-11.

606. T2 at 11-12.

607. Lewinsky 7/31/98 Int. at 12. Ms. Lewinsky produced a draft of this document to the OIC on July 31, 1998. Lewinsky 7/31/98 Int. at 3. See also Lewinsky 8/13/98 Int. at 3.

608. DB-DC-00000027 (punctuation corrected) (emphasis in original). Ms. Lewinsky produced a draft of this document to the OIC on July 31, 1998. Lewinsky 7/31/98 GJ at 3.

609. DB-DC-00000027. Ms. Lewinsky also indicated that she would consider a job at one of the networks; she mentioned "Kaplan," and added that "CNN has a NY office." DB-DC-00000027. In a recorded conversation, Ms. Lewinsky said that she had told the President about her interest in television during their October 11 meeting. The President had responded, "The only one I know in a network is Kaplan, . . . but his job is in Atlanta." T2 at 6. See also Lewinsky 7/31/98 Int. at 11. CNN President Rick Kaplan is a friend of the President.

610. DB-DC-00000027.

611. T7 at 26.

612. T7 at 30.

613. T2 at 21-27. See also Lewinsky 8/6/98 GJ at 27-28 & Ex. ML-7; Lewinsky 8/11/98 Int. at 4.

614. T2 at 23. In her description, the card was "kind of cartoony" and said: "This is a test of the emergency insanity system." T2 at 21. See also Lewinsky 8/13/98 Int at 3.

615. T2 at 26-27.

616. T2 at 27-30. Ms. Lewinsky asked Ms. Currie to leave the packet under the President's desk. T2 at 3. In a recorded conversation on October 17, Ms. Lewinsky indicated that Ms. Currie had received the package. T13 at 33.

617. Lewinsky 8/13/98 Int. at 4; Lewinsky 8/26/98 Depo. at 61-63.

618. Podesta 2/5/98 GJ at 40-41. See also Lewinsky 7/31/98 Int. at 10. As previously discussed, Ms. Currie had earlier asked Mr. Podesta to help Ms. Lewinsky obtain a White House job.(625)

619. Podesta 2/5/98 GJ at 40-45; Richardson 4/30/98 Depo. at 28. On Sunday, October 12, 1997, the President traveled to Latin America for one week. United States President, Weekly Compilations of Presidential Documents at 1608, 1609, 1653. On that trip, the President was accompanied by, among others, then-U.N. Ambassador William Richardson and the Deputy Chief of Staff, John Podesta. Richardson 4/30/98 Depo. at 28-29; Podesta 2/5/98 GJ at 44. Ambassador Richardson recalled that Mr. Podesta had first made the request prior to the trip to Latin America. Richardson 4/30/98 Depo. at 28.

620. Podesta 2/5/98 GJ at 45; Richardson 4/30/98 Depo. at 32.

621. Richardson 4/30/98 Depo. at 160-61; Clinton 1/17/98 Depo. at 73.

622. Richardson 4/30/98 Depo. at 26.

623. Watkins 5/27/98 Depo. at 11-12, 18.

624. Podesta 2/5/98 GJ at 46.

625. 828-DC-00000012 (faxed copy of Ms. Lewinsky's resume, produced by the U.N.); Currie 5/6/98 GJ at 174.

626. 828-DC-00000004 (U.N. phone records).

627. Lewinsky 8/13/98 Int. at 3.

628. Lewinsky 8/26/98 Depo. at 63-64. See also Lewinsky 8/26/98 Depo. at 63-64; Lewinsky 7/31/98 Int. at 12; Lewinsky 7/27/98 Int. at 5.

629. Lewinsky 7/27/98 Int. at 5.

630. Richardson 4/30/98 Depo. at 47-48; Watkins 5/27/98 Depo. at 27-29. Ms. Watkins further testified that she often placed calls from the Ambassador's line. Watkins 5/27/98 Depo. at 37-38.

630. Lewinsky 8/13/98 Int. at 3-4.

631. Lewinsky 8/13/98 Int. at 4.

632. Lewinsky 8/13/98 Int. at 4. See also Lewinsky 7/31/98 Int. at 12.

633. Lewinsky 8/26/98 Depo. at 64-65; Lewinsky 7/31/98 Int. at 13.

634. Lewinsky 8/26/98 Depo. at 65. Ms. Lewinsky wrote an email to her friend Catherine Allday Davis: "It was nice; the big creep called Thursday night to give me a pep talk because I was so afraid I'd sound like an idiot." 1037-DC-00000022 (spelling corrected).(643)

635. 1037-DC-000000022 (spelling corrected).

636. Lewinsky 7/31/98 Int. at 13. See also Lewinsky 8/26/98 Depo. at 65.

637. Clinton 1/17/98 Depo. at 74.

638. 828-DC-00000023 (Ambassador Richardson's diary reflecting 7:30 a.m. meeting with Monica Lewinsky). See also Ambassador Richardson 4/30/98 Depo. at 66-68; Sutphen 5/27/98 Depo. at 7; Cooper 1/27/98 Int. at 1-2; Lewinsky 7/31/98 Int. at 13-14. After meeting with Ms. Lewinsky, Ambassador Richardson spent the remainder of the day meeting individually with Senators and Members of Congress. 828-DC-00000023 (Ambassador Richardson's itinerary for October 31).

639. Richardson 4/30/98 Depo. at 68; Cooper 1/27/98 Int. at 1-2.

640. Richardson 4/30/98 Depo. at 39; Sutphen 5/27/98 Depo. at 15-16; Cooper 1/27/98 Int. at 2.

641. The draft was retrieved from Ms. Lewinsky's computer in the course of a consensual search on January 22, 1998.

642. MSL-55-DC-0179 (punctuation added)(italics in original).

643. MSL-55-DC-0179.

644. MSL-55-DC-0179. Ms. Lewinsky concluded the letter, "I was pleased the UN interview went well, but I'm afraid it will be like being at the Pentagon in NY. . . YUCK!" MSL-55-DC-0179 (ellipsis in original).

645. Lewinsky 8/13/98 Int. at 4-5; Lewinsky 7/31/98 Int. at 14; Lewinsky 7/27/98 Int. at 5.

646. 828-DC-00000003.

647. Lewinsky 8/26/98 Depo. at 67; Lewinsky 7/27/98 Int. at 5; Lewinsky 7/31/98 Int. at 14; Lewinsky 8/13/98 Int. at 5.

According to Ambassador Richardson, the position offered to Ms. Lewinsky was not newly created. He testified that he intended to expand an open position in the U.N.'s Washington office and move it to New York. Richardson 4/30/98 Depo. at 39-40. Although Ambassador Richardson did not recall whether this opening was publicized, he testified that it would be common for the office not to post Schedule C (political appointment) positions. Richardson 4/30/98 Depo. at 71-72. Peter Aronsohn, who filled the position Ms. Lewinsky was offered, characterized the job as a "new position." Aronsohn 8/27/98 Int. at 2.

648. Sutphen 5/27/98 Depo. at 26.

649. Richardson 4/30/98 Depo. at 90-91; Sutphen 5/27/98 Depo. at 21 23.

650. Lewinsky 8/26/98 Depo. at 65-66; Lewinsky 8/13/98 Int. at 4.

651. Currie 5/6/98 GJ at 174-75, 181; Currie 5/14/98 GJ at 65-66.

652. Clinton 1/17/98 Depo. at 73.

653. Sutphen 5/27/98 Depo. at 32-33; Lewinsky 8/13/98 Int. at 5.

654. Sutphen 5/27/98 Depo. at 33. See also Richardson 4/30/98 Depo. at 110-11 (recalling Ms. Lewinsky's request for additional time to consider the offer).

655. Lewinsky 7/27/98 Int. at 5; Sutphen 5/27/98 Depo. at 38; 1013-DC-00000095 (toll records for Debra Finerman).

656. 921-DC-00000101 - 118 (Second Set of Interrogatories from Plaintiff to Defendant Clinton).

657. V002-DC-00000016; V002-DC-00000020-21.

658. See supra at IX.B. See also Lewinsky 8/6/98 GJ at 104; Lewinsky 7/31/98 Int. at 11-12.

659. MSL-55-DC-0179.

660. Lewinsky 7/31/98 Int. at 14.

661. Lewinsky 7/31/98 Int. at 14. Phone records reflect that on November 4 at 3:54 p.m., Ms. Lewinsky placed a three-and-a-half-minute call to Mr. Jordan's office; at 4:09 p.m., Mr. Jordan placed a one-minute call to Ms. Currie; and at 4:38 p.m., Mr. Jordan placed a one-minute call to Ms. Currie. 833-DC-00017875 (Ms Lewinsky's phone records); V004-DC-00000134 (Akin, Gump phone records).

662. T2 at 11-12. See also Lewinsky 7/31/98 Int. at 11.

663. Jordan 5/5/98 GJ at 47 (Mr. Jordan testified that he believed the President had told Ms. Currie to "[c]all Vernon and ask Vernon to help her").

664. Currie 5/6/98 GJ at 169-70, 176-78, 182-83, 198.

665. Clinton 1/17/98 Depo. at 81.

666. Clinton 1/17/98 Depo. at 82.

667. 1178-DC-00000011 (call logs).

668. Lewinsky 7/31/98 Int. at 14.

669. Lewinsky 7/31/98 Int. at 14-15.

670. Lewinsky 8/13/98 Int. at 3.

671. Lewinsky 8/6/98 GJ at 106; Lewinsky 7/31/98 Int. at 14-15; Lewinsky 7/27/98 Int. at 8, 10. Ms. Lewinsky later quoted the remark in email to a friend.(680)

672. 1037-DC-00000017 (email retrieved from Ms. Davis's computer). —

673. 1037-DC-00000017 (email retrieved from Catherine Davis's computer).

673. Jordan 3/3/98 GJ at 13.

674. V004-DC-00000135 (Akin, Gump phone records).

675. Jordan 5/5/98 GJ at 54.

676. 1178-DC-00000026 (WAVES record). Ms. Lewinsky would learn of the meeting between the President and Mr. Jordan. In email to a friend dated November 6, Ms. Lewinsky wrote that Mr. Jordan had "[seen] the big creep yesterday afternoon." 1037-DC-00000017 (spelling corrected) (email to Catherine Davis).

677. Jordan 5/5/98 GJ at 34.

678. 833-DC-00000980 (letter retrieved from Ms. Lewinsky's Pentagon computer)(spelling corrected).

679. 1037-DC-00000017 (email retrieved from Catherine Davis's computer). Ms. Lewinsky wrote that she was "a little nervous to do the whole name of the BF. His first name is Vernon." Id. According to her aunt, Debra Finerman, Ms. Lewinsky used the code name "Gwen" when discussing Mr. Jordan because "he's an important person" and Ms. Lewinsky "always had the feeling somebody was listening in" on their phone conversations, they did not want an eavesdropper to know that Mr. Jordan was helping her find a job. Finerman 3/18/98 Depo. at 60. See also Lewinsky 8/5/98 Int. at 3; Lewinksy 8/3/98 Int. at 9.

680. Jordan 3/3/98 GJ at 50.

681. Jordan 5/5/98 GJ at 26-30, 34.

682. Epass records reflect that Ms. Lewinsky entered the White House at 6:20 p.m., admitted by Ms. Currie. 827-DC-00000018. Secret Service Movement logs

show that the President entered the State Floor at 5:23 and moved to the Oval Office at 6:34. V006-DC-00002156.

683. 1037-DC-00000318 (email retrieved from Catherine Davis's computer).

684. Lewinsky 8/13/98 Int. at 5.

685. Lewinsky 8/13/98 Int. at 5. Many of Ms. Lewinsky's previous visits with the President had occurred on holidays. See, e.g., Lewinsky 7/30/98 Int. at 3, 13, 17 (describing visits on New Year's Eve, Presidents' Day, Easter Sunday, and July 4).

686. 837-DC-00000008(courier receipt).

687. DB-DC-00000022. Ms. Lewinsky produced a draft of this letter to the OIC on July 31, 1998. See also Lewinsky 7/31/98 Int. at 1 (confirming that she delivered a substantially similar note).

688. DB-DC-00000022.

689. Lewinsky 8/13/98 Int. at 5-6. On November 12, 1997, the President responded to Paula Jones's Third Set of Interrogatories. In response to an interrogatory that asked the President to provide information about all individuals who have discoverable and relevant information regarding the disputed facts at issue in the case, the President provided a list of names that did not include Ms. Lewinsky. 849-DC-0000090 - 97.

690. 1037-DC-00000318 (email retrieved from Catherine Davis's computer).

691. 1037-DC-00000318 (spelling corrected). Lewinsky 8/13/98 Int. at 6. On November 13, Ms. Hernreich was testifying before Congress. Walsh, "Democratic Donor Chung Invokes 5th Amendment; House Members Informally Interview Businessman Edward Walsh," Washington Post, November 15, 1997, at A6.

692. MSL-1249-DC-0140; Lewinsky 8/13/98 Int. at 6.

693. 1037-DC-00000318 (email retrieved from Catherine Davis's computer).

694. Lewinsky 8/13/98 Int. at 6; 1234-DC-00000050 (movement log); 986-DC-00003799 (Kearney Diary).

695. Lewinsky 8/13/98 Int. at 6.

696. Lewinsky 8/13/98 Int. at 6; 1037-DC-00000318 (email to Catherine Davis).

697. In a note to the President the next week, Ms. Lewinsky would write of the gifts: "I forgot to tell you: . . . The Gingko Blowjoba or whatever it is called and the Zinc lozenges were from me." MSL-55-DC-0140 (spelling and grammar corrected).

698. Lewinsky 8/6/98 GJ at 183-85; Lewinsky 8/2/98 Int. at 4. Ms. Lewinsky also saw a clipping of the Valentine's Day ad she had placed in the Washington Post on the President's desk. Lewinsky 8/6/98 GJ at 183-84. In a document composed

soon after this visit, Ms. Lewinsky wrote: "When I was hiding out in your office for a half-hour, I noticed you had the new Sarah McLachlan CD. I have it, too, and it's wonderful. Whenever I listen to song #5 I think of you. That song and Billie Holiday's version of 'I'll be Seeing You' are guaranteed to put me to tears when it comes to you!" MSL-1249-DC-0140-41 (deleted file from Ms. Lewinsky's home computer) (spelling and grammar corrected).

699. 1037-DC-00000318 (email to Catherine Davis).

700. Lewinsky 8/13/98 Int. at 6.

701. OIC 8/27/98 Memo.

702. 968-DC-00000187 (presidential schedule); 968-DC-00000303 (Kearney Diary). Ms. Currie initially testified that she could not recall Ms. Lewinsky's November 13 visit. Currie 5/6/98 GJ at 12, 15. After viewing documentary evidence, she recalled that this was the only time she surreptitiously escorted Ms. Lewinsky into the White House. Id. at 85.

703. Lewinsky 8/11/98 Int. at 1; Lewinsky 7/31/98 Int. at 1-2; 837-DC-00000011 (courier receipt); MSL-1249-DC-0140-41 (document recovered from Ms. Lewinsky's home computer).

On November 17, 1997, the President responded to Paula Jones's First Set of Requests for Production of Documents and Things. One request sought documents sent to President Clinton by any woman (other than Mrs. Clinton) with whom President Clinton had sexual relations. V002-DC-00000056 - 92. President Clinton objected to this request as one designed "solely to harass, embarrass, and humiliate the President and the Office he occupies." V002-DC-00000075. Nonetheless, the President answered that he did not have any documents responsive to that request.

704. Lewinsky 8/6/98 GJ at 105.

705. Lewinsky 8/6/98 GJ at 105. Phone and pager records corroborate these contacts. 1205-DC-00000016; V004-DC-00000143; 831-DC-00000011. (Note that Ms. Lewinsky's pager records reflect Pacific Time; throughout this referral, time has been adjusted to Eastern Standard Time.)

706. MSL-1249-DC-0140 (spelling and punctuation corrected).

707. MSL-1249-DC-0139 (spelling and punctuation corrected).

708. 849-DC-00000128.

709. 849-DC-00000121-37

710. See infra at Section XI.F. See also Lewinsky 8/6/98 GJ at 121-26.

711. Clinton 8/17/98 GJ at 84-85. In his Jones deposition, the President

acknowledged that he may have heard of the witness list before he actually saw it. Clinton 1/17/98 Depo. at 70.

712. 833-DC-00003207 (Travel Voucher DOD).

713. Lewinsky 8/6/98 GJ at 107; Lewinsky 7/31/98 Int. at 1.

714. V006-DC-00000521 (guest list); VOO6-DC-00001859 (photograph of Ms. Lewinsky and the President at the reception).

715. Lewinsky 7/31/98 Int. at 1.

716. Lewinsky 7/31/98 Int. at 2; MSL-55-DC-0177. The wording of the letter resembles, in part, a message on a cassette found during the consensual search of Ms. Lewinsky's apartment: "Hi. [Sniffling, crying.] I was so sad seeing you last night. I was so angry with you that once again you had rejected me. . . . I wanted to feel the warmth of you and the smell of you and the touch of you. And it made me sad. And I — you confuse me so much. I mean I [sigh]. I thought I — I thought I fell in love with this person that — that I really felt was such a good — such a good person, such a good heart, someone who's had a life with a lot of experiences.î See Document Supplement B, Tab 36.

717. MSL-55-DC-0177 (punctuation corrected).

718. MSL-55-DC-0177 (punctuation corrected).

719. MSL-DC-55-0177 (punctuation corrected).

720. MSL-55-DC-0177 (punctuation corrected).

721. Lewinsky 8/6/98 GJ at 108-09; Lewinsky 8/6/98 GJ at 27-29 & Exh. ML-7. The cigar holder, the tie, the mug, and the book have been produced to the OIC. V002-PHOTOS-0011 (holder, tie, and book); V002-PHOTOS-0005 (mug).

722. Lewinsky 8/6/98 GJ at 111-12.

723. Bryan Hall 5/21 98 Int. at 2; Bryan Hall 7/23/98 GJ at 10-11, 15-16; Niedzwiecki 7/30/98 GJ at 12-13; Lewinsky 8/6/98 GJ at 109-11.

724. Lewinsky 8/6/98 GJ at 110-11; Niedzwiecki 7/30/98 GJ at 13-14.

725. Byran Hall 7/23/98 GJ at 12-13; Niedzwiecki 7/30/98 GJ at 13, 15. Officer Hall recognized Ms. Lewinsky from a previous occasion, when she was greeted by, and delivered something to, Ms. Currie. Byran Hall 7/23/98 GJ at 6-10.

726. Tyler 7/28/98 GJ at 40; Chinery 7/23/98 GJ at 8.

727. Lewinsky 8/6/98 GJ at 111-12. Ms. Mondale recalled visiting the President that morning. Mondale 7/16/98 Int. at 1. See also 843-DC-00000004 (Epass records reflect that Ms. Mondale entered the White House at 9:33 a.m.).

728. Lewinsky 8/6/98 GJ at 111-12. See also Currie 7/22/98 GJ at 88-89. Ms.

Lewinsky suspected that Ms. Mondale was romantically involved with the President. Lewinsky 8/6/98 GJ at 111-12.

729. Lewinsky 8/6/98 GJ at 112-13. Ms. Currie testified that Ms. Lewinsky angrily told her: "'You had lied to me, that the President is in the office, and he's meeting with someone.' And I said, 'Yeah, you're right.' She was not too happy about it, and words were exchanged." Currie 1/27/98 GJ at 37.

730. Keith Williams 7/23/98 GJ at 24. See also Chinery 7/23/98 GJ at 10; Purdie 7/23/98 GJ at 13.

731. Keith Williams 7/23/98 GJ at 12. Some testimony indicates that the President directly told Sergeant Williams about the Northwest Gate incident. Three officers testified that Sergeant Williams told them that the President had spoken to him and had indicated that he wanted the officer responsible for the disclosure of information fired. Niedzwiecki 7/30/98 GJ at 29, 37; Byran Hall 7/23/98 GJ at 25-26; Porter 8/13/98 GJ at 16-18. For example, Officer Niedzwiecki testified that soon after the incident, Sergeant Williams came to the Northwest Gate and said, "[t]he President wants somebody's job." Niedzwiecki 7/30/98 GJ at 29. Sergeant Williams testified, however, that the President did not speak to him directly about the incident. Keith Williams 7/23/98 GJ at 31-32. According to Sergeant Williams, when he met alone with Ms. Currie, he noticed that the door leading to the Oval Office was at first shut but then was cracked open. Keith Williams 7/23/98 GJ at 22, 30. Sergeant Williams testified that he heard what he assumed to be a male voice coming from within the Oval Office saying "[t]his person needs to be fired." Keith Williams 7/30/98 GJ at 10-11. Sergeant Williams told the officers at the gate that he spoke to the President only to get their attention. Keith Williams 7/30/98 GJ at 16-17. However, Sergeant Williams also told the supervisor who replaced him that afternoon that the President had spoken to him directly about the incident at the Northwest Gate. Deardoff 9/3/98 Depo. at 8-9.

732. Purdie 7/23/98 GJ at 13, 18-19. Captain Purdie testified that he thought that the remedy of firing was "out of proportion to the incident . . . [e]specially without doing an investigation or a fact-finding mission." Purdie 7/23/98 GJ at 19.

733. Lewinsky 8/6/98 GJ at 113.

734. Lewinsky 8/6/98 GJ at 113-14.

735. Lewinsky 8/6/98 GJ at 114.

736. Lewinsky 8/6/98 GJ at 114.

737. 827-DC-00000018. Secret Service logs reflect that the President was in the area of the Oval Office throughout this period. V006-DC-00002158.

738. Lewinsky 8/6/98 GJ at 115-16. Specifically, Ms. Lewinsky told the President "that I was supposed to get in touch with Mr. Jordan the previous week and that things didn't work out and that nothing had really happened yet." Id.

739. Lewinsky 8/6/98 GJ at 116. The President also told Ms. Lewinsky that he had already gotten a Christmas present for her and that he would give that to her during another visit. Lewinsky 8/1/98 Int. at 2.

740. Lewinsky 8/6/98 GJ at 115.

741. 1037-DC-00000011 (spelling corrected).

742. Keith Williams 7/23/98 GJ at 25. Ms. Currie confirmed that she told an officer, "Okay. Fine. This never happened." However, she testified that she said this so that no officer would get in trouble. Currie 7/22/98 GJ at 91-92.

When Ms. Currie left work that day, she stopped by a Secret Service post and told an officer that "she spoke to the President . . . and . . . they decided that the incident never happened, they weren't going to pursue . . . discipline actions against them, that they just wanted it to go away." Chinery 7/23/98 GJ at 22-23. Later that week, Ms. Currie told that officer to inform one of his supervisors "that everything was okay and just to keep quiet about it." Keith Williams 7/23/98 GJ at 27-28.

743. Purdie 7/23/98 GJ at 32; Purdie 7/17/98 GJ at 3.

744. Purdie 7/17/98 GJ at 6; Bryan Hall 7/23/98 GJ at 31-32; Chinery 7/23/98 GJ at 21.

745. Porter 8/13/98 GJ at 12.

746. Niedzwiecki 7/30/98 GJ at 30-31.

747. Niedzwiecki 7/30/98 GJ at 31, 44. See also Niedzwiecki 8/5/98 GJ at 4-6 (text of Niedzwiecki notes).

748. Purdie 7/23/98 GJ at 35.

749. Purdie 7/23/98 GJ at 34-36. While Deputy Chief O'Malley testified that Captain Purdie notified him of the incident, Deputy Chief O'Malley did not recall Captain Purdie discussing with him, at any time, a decision not to generate an incident report or a memorandum. Charles O'Malley 9/8/98 Depo. at 44, 47-48.

750. O'Malley 9/8/98 Depo. at 22, 40-41.

751. Clinton 8/17/98 GJ at 84-85, 87. Ms. Mondale stated that she met with the President alone in the Oval Office study that day. Mondale 7/16/98 Int. at 1.

752. Clinton 8/17/98 GJ at 86.

753. Clinton 8/17/98 GJ at 88-89.

754. Clinton 8/17/98 GJ at 89-90.

755. Clinton 8/17/98 GJ at 91-92.

756. Lewinsky 8/6/98 GJ at 151-52; Lewinsky 2/1/98 Statement at 6. On December 23, Paula Jones's attorneys issued a subpoena to the Secret Service.

757. Lindsey 3/12/98 GJ at 64-66; Lindsey 2/19/98 GJ at 9-10. WAVES records reflect that Robert Bennett entered the White House at 4:39 p.m. on Saturday, December 6. 1407-DC-00000005.

758. Lindsey 3/12/98 GJ at 65.

759. 964-DC-00000862 (Presidential mail notes).

760. Lindsey 3/12/98 GJ at 63-64. Mr. Lindsey refused to answer questions about his December 6 meeting with the President, claiming attorney-client privilege and Executive (presidential communications) Privilege. Id. at 66. The U.S. District Court for the District of Columbia Circuit rejected Mr. Lindsey's claim of privilege, In re Grand Jury Proceedings, 5 F. Supp.2d 21 (D.D.C. 1998), and the Court of Appeals denied Mr. Lindsey's appeal, In re Lindsey, 148 F.3d 1100(D.C. Cir. 1998). A petition for Supreme Court review is currently pending.

761. WAVES records reflect that Mr. Jordan entered the White House at 5:21 p.m. on Sunday, December 7. 1178-DC-00000026.

762. Jordan 5/5/98 GJ at 83. He later testified that the conversation was "[a]bsolutely not" about Ms. Lewinsky. Jordan 5/5/98 GJ at 116.

763. V004-DC-00000171 (Akin, Gump visitor records) (recording visit of "Malensky"). Ms. Lewinsky recalled arranging the meeting on December 8 or 9. Lewinsky 8/1/98 Int. at 3. See also 833-DC-00017886 (reflecting Ms. Lewinsky's call to Mr. Jordan on December 8).

On December 8, Ms. Lewinsky sent Mr. Jordan a hat, a box of chocolates, and a note gently reminding him of his promise to help her find a job. Lewinsky 7/31/98 Int. at 15. She also sent the President a note and some peach candies. Lewinsky 8/1/98 Int. at 2; Lewinsky 8/1/98 Int. at 2; 837-DC-00000017; 837-DC-00000020 (courier receipts).

764. Jordan 3/3/98 GJ at 41-42.

765. V004-DC-00000148 (Akin, Gump phone records). See also Jordan 3/3/98 GJ at 54, 62-63, 70.

Mr. Halperin testified that Mr. Jordan had told him that Ms. Lewinsky "was a bright young woman who was energetic and enthusiastic and . . . encouraged me to meet with her." Halperin 4/23/98 GJ at 13. Similarly, Ms. Fairbairn stated that Mr. Jordan had told her that he "would like to send [her] a resume of a talented young lady and see if she matches up with any company openings." Fairbairn 1/29/98 Int. at 1. Mr. Georgescu, however, stated that Mr. Jordan "did not engage in a 'sales pitch' about [Ms.] Lewinsky." Georgescu 3/25/98 Int. at 2.

766. Lewinsky 8/6/98 GJ at 121. Ms. Lewinsky left the meeting with Mr. Jordan on December 8 with the impression that Mr. Jordan was going to get her a job. Lewinsky 8/1/98 Int. at 4.

767. Lewinsky 8/6/98 GJ at 119.

768. Lewinsky 8/6/98 GJ at 120.

769. Lewinsky 8/6/98 GJ at 120.

770. Lewinsky 8/6/98 GJ at 120. In her handwritten proffer, Ms. Lewinsky gave a very similar account of her second meeting with Mr. Jordan: "Ms. L. met again with Mr. Jordan in the beginning of December '97, at which time he provided Ms. L. with a list of three people to contact and suggested language to use in her letters to them. At some point, Mr. Jordan remarked something about Ms. L. being a friend of the Pres. of the United States. Ms. L. responded that she never really saw him as "the President"; she spoke to him like a normal man and even got angry with him like a normal man. Mr. Jordan asked what Ms. L. got angry about. Ms. L. replied that the Pres. doesn't see or call her enough. Mr. Jordan said Ms. L. should take her frustrations out on him — not the President.î Lewinsky 2/1/98 Statement at 3-4.

771. Lewinsky 8/6/98 GJ at 120.

772. Jordan 3/3/98 GJ at 154.

773. Jordan 3/3/98 GJ at 64-65.

774. Jordan 3/3/98 GJ at 65.

775. Jordan 3/3/98 GJ at 65.

776. 1414-DC-00001534 - 46 (Plaintiff's Second Request for Production of Documents and Things).

777. Lewinsky 8/6/98 GJ at 121-26.

778. Lewinsky 8/6/98 GJ at 126. Ms. Lewinsky testified that the call came as a surprise because Mrs. Clinton was in town. Id. at 122. See also 968-DC-00003479 (Mrs. Clinton's schedule reflects that she was in Washington, D.C. on December 17).

779. Lewinsky 8/6/98 GJ at 122-23.

780. Lewinsky 8/6/98 GJ at 123.

781. Lewinsky 2/1/98 Statement at 4.

782. Lewinsky 8/6/98 GJ at 123.

783. Lewinsky 2/1/98 Statement at 4.

784. Lewinsky 8/6/98 GJ at 123-24. Ms. Lewinsky testified that, "on [s]everal occasions," they had resolved to use this cover story to conceal their relationship. Id.

785. Lewinsky 8/6/98 GJ at 232.

786. Lewinsky 8/6/98 GJ at 126.

787. Lewinsky 8/6/98 GJ at 126.

788. Clinton 8/17/98 GJ at 116.

789. Clinton 8/17/98 GJ at 119. The President himself gave this explanation of Ms. Lewinsky's visits to the Oval Office at his Jones deposition. Clinton 1/17/98 Depo. at 50-51.

790. Clinton 8/17/98 GJ at 119-20.

791. Clinton 8/17/98 GJ at 119-20.

792. Clinton 8/17/98 GJ at 120.

793. Halperin 1/26/98 Int. at 2.

794. Berk 3/31/98 Int. at 1-2. In her proffer, Ms. Lewinsky stated that, during the week following her December 11 meeting with Mr. Jordan, she "had two interviews in NY in response to her letters." Lewinsky 2/1/98 Statement at 4.

795. Schick 1/29/98 Int. at 2.

796. Lewinsky 8/6/98 GJ at 128; Harte 4/17/98 Int. at 1.

797. 902-DC-000000135 - 138 (Lewinsky subpoena).

798. 902-DC-000000137.

799. Lewinsky 8/6/98 GJ at 128-29; Lewinsky 7/27/98 Int. at 6; 8/1/98 Int. at 6-7. In the late-night December 17 call, the President told Ms. Lewinsky that, if she were subpoenaed, she should call Ms. Currie. Ms. Lewinsky did not do so on December 19 because Ms. Currie's brother had recently died and Ms. Lewinsky did not want to bother her. Lewinsky 8/6/98 GJ at 126.

800. Jordan 3/3/98 GJ at 92-93. Mr. Jordan said that he did not contemplate representing Ms. Lewinsky himself because "I represent companies. I don't represent individuals." Jordan 3/3/98 GJ at 101.

801. V004-DC-00000172 (Akin, Gump visitor logs).

802. V004-DC-00000151 (Akin, Gump telephone records, indicating the call ended at 5:05 p.m.); 1178-DC-00000014 (Presidential call logs, reflecting the call ended at 5:08 p.m.). Presidential call logs are recorded by hand, and thus are likely

to be less accurate. The President may have been returning a call that Mr. Jordan had placed at 3:51 p.m.

803. Lewinsky 8/6/98 GJ at 131; V004-DC-00000151 (Akin, Gump telephone records). Mr. Jordan asked whether he could bring a potential client to Mr. Carter's office on Monday morning. Jordan 5/5/98 GJ at 135-136; Carter 6/18/98 GJ at 7-8

804. Lewinsky 8/6/98 GJ at 131.

805. Jordan 5/5/98 GJ at 140, 152-53.

806. Jordan 5/5/98 GJ at 145.

807. Jordan 5/5/98 GJ at 145.

808. Jordan 5/5/98 GJ at 147.

809. Jordan 5/5/98 GJ at 147.

810. Jordan 3/3/98 GJ at 102.

811. Jordan 3/3/98 GJ at 103.

812. Lewinsky 8/6/98 GJ at 131-32.

813. Lewinsky 8/6/98 GJ at 132.

814. Lewinsky 8/6/98 GJ at 132. In her handwritten proffer, Ms. Lewinsky described her meeting with Mr. Jordan that afternoon: "Ms. L expressed anxiety with respect to her subpoena requesting production of any gifts from the Pres., specifically citing hat pins which the Pres. had in fact given her. Mr. Jordan allayed her concerns by telling her it was standard language." Lewinsky 2/1/98 Statement at 5.

815. Lewinsky 8/6/98 GJ at 133.

816. Jordan 3/3/98 GJ at 150. Ms. Lewinsky confirmed that she had such a conversation with Mr. Jordan, although she believed it took place after a breakfast meeting on December 31. Lewinsky 8/6/98 GJ at 188; Lewinsky 2/1/98 Statement at 8.

817. Jordan 3/3/98 GJ at 123.

818. Jordan 3/3/98 GJ at 122. He also said: "I did not get graphic, I did not get specific, I didn't ask her if they kissed, I didn't ask if they caressed, all of which, as I understand it, is a part of the act of sex." Id. at 130.

819. Jordan 3/3/98 GJ at 126.

820. Jordan 3/3/98 GJ at 122-24. See also Lewinsky 8/6/98 GJ at 133-35.

821. Lewinsky 8/6/98 GJ at 134.

822. Lewinsky 8/6/98 GJ at 134.

823. Lewinsky 8/6/98 GJ at 135. According to Ms. Lewinsky, Mr. Jordan responded, "I don't hug men." Id.

824. Jordan 3/3/98 GJ at 167-8.

825. Jordan 3/3/98 GJ at 169. According to Mr. Jordan, the President listened with "some amazement" when Mr. Jordan recounted the conversation. Id. at 170.

826. Jordan 3/3/98 GJ at 173-74.

827. Jordan 3/3/98 GJ at 170.

828. Jordan 3/3/98 GJ at 171.

829. Jordan 3/3/98 GJ at 172. In the days that followed, Mr. Jordan informed the President that he had succeeded in engaging Francis Carter to represent Ms. Lewinsky. Jordan 3/5/98 GJ at 27.

830. Clinton 8/17/98 GJ at 64.

831. Clinton 8/17/98 GJ at 65-66.

832. Jordan 3/3/98 GJ at 164-66, 183-84.

833. Lewinsky 8/6/98 GJ at 138.

834. Lewinsky 8/6/98 GJ at 138.

835. Lewinsky 8/6/98 GJ at 138-39.

836. Lewinsky 8/6/98 GJ at 139.

837. Lewinsky 8/6/98 GJ at 139. Mr. Jordan asked what "phone sex" was. Lewinsky 8/6/98 GJ at 139. Ms. Lewinsky stated that she may have explained it this way: "He's taking care of business on one end and I'm taking care of business on another." Lewinsky 8/6/98 GJ at 143.

838. Lewinsky 8/6/98 GJ at 139-140. In her proffer, Ms. Lewinsky wrote that she "showed Mr. Jordan the items she was producing in response to the subpoena. Ms. L believes she made it clear that this was not everything she had that could respond to the subpoena, but she thought it was enough to satisfy." Lewinsky 2/1/98 Statement at 6.

839. Jordan 3/3/98 GJ at 153.

840. The diaries of both Mr. Carter and Mr. Jordan reflect an 11:00 a.m. appointment on December 22, 1997. 902-DC-00000231 (Mr. Carter's diary) and 1034-DC-00000103 (Mr. Jordan's diary).

841. Carter 6/18/98 GJ at 12, 14. According to Mr. Carter, although Mr. Jordan had previously referred clients to him, Mr. Jordan had never personally driven them to his office. Id. at 160-61.(857)

842. Carter 6/18/98 GJ at 158-60, 15, 75.

843. According to Mr. Carter's bill, he met with Ms. Lewinsky for 1.1 hours. 902-DC-00000037.

844. Lewinsky 8/6/98 GJ at 146; Carter 6/18/98 GJ at 25.

845. Lewinsky 8/6/98 GJ at 146-47; Carter 6/18/98 GJ at 25.

846. Lewinsky 8/6/98 GJ at 146. Somewhat at odds with Ms. Lewinsky, Mr. Carter testified, "I thought I needed to develop an affidavit recounting what she said to me." Carter 6/18/98 GJ at 65.

847. Lewinsky 8/6/98 GJ at 147.

848. Lewinsky 8/6/98 GJ at 147.

849. Carter 6/18/98 GJ at 29-30; 902-DC-00000038.

850. Carter 6/18/98 GJ at 39.

851. Carter 6/18/98 GJ at 42-43.

852. V002-DC-000000052 - 54 (President Clinton's Supplemental Responses to Plaintiff's Second Set of Interrogatories); 1414-DC-00000512 - 17 (same).

853. Lewinsky 8/6/98 GJ at 149.

854. Lewinsky 8/6/98 GJ at 149.

855. V0006-DC-00000009 (WAVES records).

856. Lewinsky 8/6/98 GJ at 150-51. In his grand jury testimony, the President recalled giving her many of these gifts and acknowledged that it was "probably true" that these were more gifts than he had ever given her in a single day. Clinton 8/17/98 GJ at 36.

857. Lewinsky 8/26/98 Depo. at 53.

858. Lewinsky 8/6/98 GJ at 151.

859. Lewinsky 8/6/98 GJ at 151-52.

860. Lewinsky 8/6/98 GJ at 152. In her handwritten statement of February 1, 1998, Ms. Lewinsky wrote: "Ms. L. asked [the President] how he thought the attorneys for Paula Jones found out about her. He thought it was probably 'that woman from the summer . . . with Kathleen Willey' (Linda Tripp) who lead [sic] them to Ms. L or possibly the uniformed agents. He shared Ms. L's concern about the hat pin. He asked Ms. L if she had told anyone that he had given it to her and she replied 'no.'" Lewinsky 2/1/98 Statement at 6.

861. Lewinsky 8/20/98 GJ at 66.

862. Lewinsky 8/6/98 GJ at 152. Ms. Lewinsky acknowledged in the grand jury that she had in fact told others about the hat pin. Lewinsky 8/6/98 GJ at 152.

863. Lewinsky 8/6/98 GJ at 152.

864. Lewinsky 8/6/98 GJ at 152. See also Lewinsky 8/20/98 GJ at 66.

865. Lewinsky 8/6/98 GJ at 168.

866. Clinton 1/17/98 Depo. at 68.

867. Clinton 8/17/98 GJ at 33.

868. Clinton 8/17/98 GJ at 39. He further testified that he did not remember that Ms. Lewinsky's subpoena specifically called for a hat pin. Clinton 8/17/98 GJ at 45.

869. Clinton 8/17/98 GJ at 39.

870. Catherine Davis 3/17/98 GJ at 77-79.

871. Lewinsky 8/6/98 GJ at 154-55.

872. Lewinsky 8/6/98 GJ at 155.

873. Lewinsky 8/6/98 GJ at 155-56.

874. Lewinsky 8/6/98 GJ at 156-58. Ms. Currie could remember only one other occasion in which she had driven to Ms. Lewinsky's Watergate apartment. Currie 5/6/98 GJ at 108.

875. Lewinsky 8/6/98 GJ at 158-59.

876. Lewinsky 8/6/98 GJ at 159.

877. Lewinsky 8/6/98 GJ at 159. See also Lewinsky 8/1/98 Int. at 12.

878. Lewinsky 2/1/98 Statement at 7 (punctuation corrected).

879. Ms. Currie stated, at various times, that the transfer occurred sometime in late December 1997 or early January 1998. Currie 1/24/98 Int. at 3; Currie 1/27/98 GJ at 56-57; Currie 5/6/98 GJ at 103-07.

880. Currie 5/6/98 GJ at 105-06.

881. Currie 5/6/98 GJ at 126.

882. Currie 1/27/98 GJ at 58. In her first grand jury appearance in January, Ms. Currie was asked whether she knew who had been asking the questions about the gifts. She testified: "Sir, no, I don't." Id. In a May grand jury appearance, Ms. Currie responded to a similar question by saying that she understood that Newsweek reporter Michael Isikoff (who had earlier written about Kathleen Willey) was asking about the gifts. Currie 5/6/98 GJ at 107, 114, 120. Ms. Lewinsky testified that she never spoke to Mr. Isikoff. Lewinsky 8/24/98 Int. at 9.

883. Currie 5/6/98 GJ at 107-08. See also Currie 1/27/98 GJ at 57-58.

884. Currie 5/6/98 GJ at 110. When the OIC later obtained the box from Ms. Currie by subpoena, it contained various items that the President had given to Ms. Lewinsky, including (a) a hat pin; (b) a brooch; (c) an official copy of the 1996 State of the Union Address inscribed "To Monica Lewinsky with best wishes, Bill Clinton"; (d) a photograph of the President in the Oval Office with a handwritten note, "To Monica — Thanks for the tie Bill Clinton"; (e) a photograph of the President

and Ms. Lewinsky inscribed "To Monica — Happy Birthday! Bill Clinton 7-23-97";
(f) a sun dress, two t-shirts, and a baseball cap with a Black Dog logo on them; and
(g) a facsimile copy of a Valentine's Day message to "Handsome" that Ms. Lewinsky
placed in the Washington Post in 1996.

885. Currie 5/6/98 GJ at 106-07.

886. Clinton 8/17/98 GJ at 51.

887. Clinton 8/17/98 GJ at 115.

888. Clinton 8/17/98 GJ at 46.

889. Lewinsky 8/6/98 GJ at 186. Ms. Tripp, like Ms. Lewinsky, had been subpoenaed in the Jones case.

890. Lewinsky 8/6/98 GJ at 186-87. Although Mr. Jordan testified that he never
had breakfast with Ms. Lewinsky, See Jordan 3/5/98 GJ at 60, there is strong circumstantial evidence supporting Ms. Lewinsky's testimony that she had breakfast
with Mr. Jordan on December 31. Compare Lewinsky 8/6/98 GJ at 187-89 (describing breakfast) with 916-DC-00000003 (Park Hyatt receipt reflecting breakfast as
described by Ms. Lewinsky).

891. Lewinsky 8/6/98 GJ at 186-89.

892. Lewinsky 8/6/98 GJ at 187.

893. Lewinsky 8/6/98 GJ at 187.

894. Lewinsky 8/6/98 GJ at 188; 8/26/98 Int. at 2; 8/1/98 Int. at 13.

895. Lewinsky 8/1/98 Int. at 13.

896. Lewinsky 8/6/98 GJ at 190.

897. Lewinsky 8/6/98 GJ at 190-91.

898. Lewinsky 8/2/98 Int. at 1.

899. 902-DC-00000232 (Mr. Carter's day-planner); 902-DC-00000037 (Mr.
Carter's bill).

900. Lewinsky 8/6/98 GJ at 192. Mr. Carter agreed that, during one of his meetings with Ms. Lewinsky, he asked her sample questions. Carter 6/18/98 GJ at 110-
12.

901. Lewinsky 8/6/98 GJ at 192-93.

902. Carter 6/18/98 GJ at 67-68; Lewinsky 8/6/98 GJ at 194, 199.

903. Lewinsky 8/6/98 GJ at 195.

904. Lewinsky 8/6/98 GJ at 195; Lewinsky 8/2/98 Int. at 3; Lewinsky 2/1/98
Statement at 9 ("That evening Ms. L placed a phone call to Ms. Currie asking her to

tell the Pres. that she wanted to speak with him before she signed something the next day. He returned Ms. L's call a few hours later.").

905. Lewinsky 8/6/98 GJ at 196.

906. Lewinsky 8/2/98 Int. at 3. See also Lewinsky 2/1/98 Statement at 9 ("The Pres. told Ms. L. not to worry about the affidavit as he had Seen 15 others.").

907. Lewinsky 8/6/98 GJ at 197.

908. Lewinsky 8/6/98 GJ at 197; Lewinsky 2/1/98 Statement at 9 ("Ms. L told him Mr. Carter had asked some sample questions that might be asked of her in the deposition and she didn't know how to answer them.").

909. Clinton 8/17/98 GJ at 126

910. Clinton 8/17/98 GJ at 129.

911. Lewinsky 9/3/98 Int. at 2.

912. Lewinsky 8/6/98 GJ at 198.

913. Lewinsky 8/6/98 GJ at 198.

914. Clinton 8/17/98 GJ at 48-49.

915. Clinton 8/17/98 GJ at 50.

916. Clinton 8/17/98 GJ at 127, 49-50.

917. Lewinsky 8/6/98 GJ at 199-200; Carter 6/18/98 GJ at 70-73. A draft copy of the affidavit, with minor revisions, was found in Ms. Lewinsky's apartment in the course of a consensual search on January 22, 1998.(935)

935. cite

918. Lewinsky 8/6/98 GJ at 200; Lewinsky 2/1/98 Statement at 6 ("After Ms. L received a draft of the affidavit, she called Mr. Jordan to ask that he look it over before she sign it. He instructed her to drop off a copy at his office. They spoke later by phone about the affidavit agreeing to make some changes.").

919. Lewinsky 8/6/98 GJ at 194-95.

920. Lewinsky 8/6/98 GJ at 202.

921. As originally drafted, Paragraph 6 of the affidavit stated: "In the course of my employment at the White House, I met with the President on several occasions. I do not recall ever being alone with the President, although it is possible that while working in the White House Office of Legislative Affairs I may have presented him with a letter for his signature while no one else was present. This would only have lasted a few minutes and would not have been a private meeting, that is, not behind closed doors. 849-DC-00000634 (emphasis added). Ms. Lewinsky deleted the underlined sentence.

922. 849-DC-00000634-35 (emphasis added).

923. Lewinsky 8/6/98 GJ at 202.

924. 849-DC-00000635.

925. Lewinsky 8/6/98 GJ at 202.

926. Jordan 3/5/98 GJ at 11.

927. Jordan 3/5/98 GJ at 11.

928. See Telephone Calls, Table 35. Catalogs of relevant phone calls are included in Appendix G as a Phone Log, Tables 1 through 50.

929. Carter 6/18/98 GJ at 76-77, 92-93.

930. 902-DC-00000030 (Mr. Carter's bill to Ms. Lewinsky).

931. Jordan 5/5/98 GJ at 210, 214.

932. Jordan 5/5/98 GJ at 218-20.

933. 902-DC-00000232 (Mr. Carter's day-planner).

934. Lewinsky 8/6/98 GJ at 204-05. As to the sentence, "I have never had a sexual relationship with the President," she testified that this was not true. She was also asked about the statement that other persons were present on the occasions she met with the President. She termed this paragraph ìmisleading,î explaining: ì[I]t doesnít say the only occasions, but itís misleading in that one reading it would assume that the only occasions on which I saw the President were those listed.î

935. Carter 6/18/98 GJ at 108.

936. Jordan 5/5/98 GJ at 222. See also Jordan 3/3/98 GJ at 192; Jordan 3/5/98 GJ at 11; Jordan 5/28/98 GJ at 62. Ms. Lewinsky testified that she told Mr. Jordan on January 6, that she would be signing an affidavit the next day. On January 13, she showed him a copy. Lewinsky 8/6/98 GJ at 200, 220.

937. See Telephone Calls, Table 36.

938. Jordan 3/5/98 GJ at 24-26.

939. Jordan 5/5/98 GJ at 223-25.

940. Jordan 5/5/98 GJ at 225.

941. Jordan 5/5/98 GJ at 226.

942. Clinton 1/17/98 Depo. at 72.

943. Clinton 8/17/98 GJ at 74.

944. Clinton 8/17/98 GJ at 75.

945. Durnan 3/27/98 Int. at 1.

946. Durnan 3/27/98 Int. at 2.

947. Durnan 3/27/98 Int. at 2.

948. Lewinsky 8/6/98 GJ at 206.

949. Lewinsky 8/6/98 GJ at 207-08.

950. See Telephone Calls, Table 37, Call 6.

951. Jordan 5/5/98 GJ at 230.

952. Jordan 5/5/98 GJ at 231. Asked whether he had ever spoken with Mr. Perelman in the past in the context of a job referral, Mr. Jordan could remember three persons for whom he had made referrals: David Dinkins, the former Mayor of New York City; an attorney at Mr. Jordanís law firm who ìwas good and they actualy stole her away from Akin gump because she was so goodî; and a graduate of the Harvard Business School who was considered for the top position at Marvel Comics. Jordan 3/5/98 GJ at 56-8.

953. Perelman 4/23/98 Depo. at 10.

954. Perelman 4/23/98 Depo. at 11. In his testimony before the House Government and Reform Oversight Committee, Mr. Jordan testified that he helped former Associate Attorney General Webster Hubbell be retained by Revlon by introducing him to Howard Gittes, Vice Chairman and Chief Administrative Officer at MacAndrews & Forbes. Mr. Jordan initially testified that he ìcertainlyî spoke with Mr. Perelman about retaining Mr. Hubbell. He then testified that ìit was entirely possibleî that Mr. Perelman was present on April 6, 1994, when Mr. Jordan accompanied Mr. Hubbell to the New York offices of MacAndrews & Forbes to introduce Mr. Hubbell to Mr. Gittes, General Counsel Barry Schwartz, and Richard Halperin, who was in charge of government relations. Jordan 7/24/97 House of Representatives at 35-37. As stated in the text, Mr. Perelman does not remember Mr. Jordan ever contacting him regarding Mr. Hubbell.

955. Jordan 5/5/98 GJ at 232. Ms. Lewinsky similarly testified that Mr. Jordan called her back that evening and told her "not to worry."(983)

956. Lewinsky 8/6/98 GJ at 209.

957. See Telephone Calls, Table 37. In addition, Mr. Jordan placed a two-minute call to a number at the White House Counsel's office from his limousine at 6:39 p.m.

958. Jordan 5/28/98 GJ at 19.

959. Jordan 5/28/98 GJ at 20-21. Ms. Mills does not recall having any discussions with Mr. Jordan about Ms. Lewinsky prior to January 17, 1998. Indeed, she had no recollection of hearing Ms. Lewinsky's name prior to January 17. Mills 8/11/98 GJ at 10-11.

960. Seidman 4/23/98 Depo. at 37-38.

961. Lewinsky 8/6/98 GJ at 210.

962. Lewinsky 8/6/98 GJ at 210.

963. Jordan 5/28/98 GJ at 30.

964. Jordan 5/28/98 at 39.

965. Jordan 5/28/98 GJ at 59. Mr. Jordan added that the President's response was one of "appreciation, gratitude." Id.

966. 921-DC-00000770-72 (Clerk's minutes of in-camera hearing).

967. Sheldon 4/34/98 Depo. at 22.

968. Lewinsky 8/6/98 GJ at 214.

969. Lewinsky 8/6/98 GJ at 215.

970. 831-DC-00000010. At some point, Ms. Currie and Ms. Lewinsky decided that they would use a code name — Kay — when leaving messages for each other. Currie 7/22/98 GJ at 175; Lewinsky 8/6/98 GJ at 215-17.

971. Bowles 4/2/98 GJ at 78-79. Mr. Bowles placed this conversation with the President at some time between January 4 and January 20. Bowles 4/2/98 GJ at 78. Mr. Podesta recalled that Mr. Bowles passed this request on to him "three or four days before the President's deposition" — that is, January 13 or January 14, though Mr. Podesta did not know who had originated the request. Podesta 6/16/98 GJ at 21-22.

972. Bowles 4/2/98 GJ at 78.

973. Bowles 4/2/98 GJ at 78-79; Podesta 6/16/98 GJ at 24-28; Hilley 2/11/98 Int. at 2; Hilley 5/26/98 GJ at 7-11.

974. Podesta 6/16/98 GJ at 24; Hilley 2/11/98 Int. at 2.

975. Hilley 2/11/98 Int. at 2; Hilley 5/26/98 GJ at 10-11; Hilley 5/19/98 GJ at 74-76. In the grand jury, Mr. Hilley testified: "At this time, I don't recall that piece of the conversation [dealing with Ms. Lewinsky's leaving Legislative Affairs under less than favorable circumstances] with John Podesta." Id. at 76.

976. Lewinsky 8/6/98 GJ at 215. At 2:20 p.m., Ms. Currie paged Ms. Lewinsky again: "Please call me. Kay." 831-DC-00000010. In the grand jury, Ms. Currie stated that she could not remember whether the January 13 page-messages to Ms. Lewinsky involved attempts to notify her of the status of the President's efforts to secure a letter of recommendation for her. Currie GJ 7/22/98 at 147-148.

977. 830-DC-00000007.

978. Clinton 8/17/98 GJ at 111-13.

979. Lewinsky 8/6/98 GJ at 220-21. Mr. Jordan traveled to Florida in the early

afternoon. 1034-DC-00000109 (Mr. Jordan's day-planner). Soon after arriving in Florida, he called Ms. Hernreich's line at the White House. See Telephone Calls, Table 42. Later that evening, he spoke with the President for nearly four minutes. 1064-DC-00000008 (Mr. Jordan's hotel bill). In the grand jury, Mr. Jordan testified that it is "not inconceivable" that they mentioned Ms. Lewinsky. Jordan 5/28/98 GJ at 69.

980. T30 at 61.

981. T30 at 114.

982. T30 at 169-70.

983. Lewinsky 8/6/98 GJ at 223-25; GJ Ex. ML-5.

984. Lewinsky 8/6/98 GJ at 223-37. Ms. Tripp, in contrast, testified that she believed Ms. Lewinsky received assistance in drafting the talking points. Tripp 7/29/98 GJ at 167, 171-172.

985. Currie 5/6/98 GJ at 120-21.

986. Currie 5/6/98 GJ at 130.

987. Akin, Gump records reflect that at some time this day Ms. Currie left a message for Mr. Jordan. The message slip listed the name of the caller as "Betty/Potus." The message was: "Kind of important." V005-DC-00000058.

988. Lewinsky 8/6/98 GJ at 229. Ms. Currie had immediately informed Ms. Lewinsky of Mr. Isikoff's call. 831-DC-00000008 (Ms. Lewinsky's pager records).

989. Jordan 3/5/98 GJ at 71.

990. Jordan 3/5/98 GJ at 71.

991. T22 at 12.

992. T22 at 12-13.

993. Ungvari 3/19/98 GJ at 61.

994. V0002-DC-00000093-116 (President Clinton's Responses to Plaintiff's Second Set of Requests).

995. 1441-DC-00001534-46 (Second Set of Requests From Plaintiff to Defendant Clinton for Production of Documents). Ms. Lewinsky's name was misspelled on the document request as Ms. Lewisky.

996. 921-DC-00000775 - 778.

997. Carter 6/18/98 GJ at 123.

998. 921-DC-00000775. Although the motion (and affidavit) reached the Judge's chambers on January 17, the file stamp date was January 20, 1998.

999. Clinton 1/17/98 Depo. at 1 (849-DC-00000352 et seq.).

1000. Clinton 1/17/98 Depo. at 1-2.

1001. Clinton 1/17/98 Depo. at 10.

1002. Clinton 1/17/98 Depo. at 22-23; 849-DC-00000586 (Clinton Depo. Ex. 1).

1003. Clinton 1/17/98 Depo. at 54.

1004. Clinton 1/17/98 Depo. at 54. In addition, as previously indicated, Mr. Jordan believes he informed President Clinton on January 7 that Ms. Lewinsky had signed an affidavit denying that there had been a sexual relationship. Jordan 5/5/98 GJ at 223-25.

1005. Clinton 1/17/98 Depo. at 53-56.

1006. Clinton 1/17/98 Depo. at 50-51, 58-59.

1007. Clinton 1/17/98 Depo. at 52-53, 59.

1008. Clinton 1/17/98 Depo. at 59.

1009. Clinton 1/17/98 Depo. at 62-64.

1010. Clinton 1/17/98 Depo. at 75-77.

1011. Clinton 1/17/98 Depo. at 75-76.

1012. Clinton 1/17/98 Depo. at 75.

1013. Clinton 1/17/98 Depo. at 68.

1014. Clinton 1/17/98 Depo. at 68-71.

1015. Clinton 1/17/98 Depo. at 72, 79-83.

1016. Clinton 1/17/98 Depo. at 78.

1017. Clinton 1/17/98 Depo. at 212-13.

1018. Podesta 6/16/98 GJ at 62.

1019. Lindsey 2/19/98 GJ at 12-13. Mr. Lindsey refused to reveal the content of these conversations with the President, citing the presidential communication, deliberative process, and attorney-client privileges, both officially and privately, as well as the attorney work product doctrine. Id. at 13.

1020. Lindsey 2/19/98 GJ at 14-15.

1021. See Telephone Table 46, Call 4; Currie 1/27/98 GJ at 65-66; Currie 5/7/98 GJ at 79-85; Currie 7/22/98 GJ at 154. See also Currie 1/24/98 Int. at 5-6 ("CURRIE advised that sometime late that evening, she received a telephone call from CLINTON. CURRIE advised that CLINTON said he and CURRIE needed to talk. CURRIE advised it was too late to do anything that evening, so she and CLINTON agreed to meet at the White House at 5 p.m. the following day, Sunday, January 18, 1998."). Presidential call logs reflect that the President attempted to call Ms. Currie at 7:02 p.m. on January 17, 1998, and that he spoke to her for two minutes at 7:13 p.m. 1248-DC-00000307.

1022. Currie 5/7/98 GJ at 91. Also that evening, the President called Mr. Jordan, who testified that they did not discuss the afternoon deposition. See Telephone Table 46, Call 2; Jordan 5/28/98 GJ at 94-95.

1023. Currie 1/27/98 GJ at 70.

1024. Currie 1/27/98 GJ at 67.

1025. Currie 1/27/98 GJ at 76.

1026. Currie 1/27/98 GJ at 70, 76; 7/22/98 GJ at 6, 22. Presidential call logs reflect that the President called Ms. Currie before their meeting and spoke to her from 1:11 p.m. to 1:14 p.m. on January 18. 1248-DC-00000313.

1027. Currie 1/27/98 GJ at 70.

1028. Currie 1/27/98 GJ at 73 ("[M]y impression was that he was just making statements.").

1029. Currie 1/24/98 Int. at 6-7. The President repeated these statements to Ms. Currie a few days later. See infra.

1030. Currie 1/27/98 GJ at 71-74; 7/22/98 GJ at 6-7, 10-11, 79. See also Clinton 8/17/98 GJ at 55-57. According to Ms. Currie, the way the President phrased the inquiries made them sound like both questions and statements at the same time. Currie 1/24/98 Int. at 6.

1031. Currie 1/27/98 GJ at 74-75. Ms. Currieís testimony that the President wanted her to agree with his statements shifted somewhat between her first grand jury appearance and her last, which occurred five months later. On January 27, 1998, nine days after her conversation with the President, Ms. Currie testified that she understood from the Presidentís questions that he wanted her to agree with him. Currie 1/27/98 GJ at 72-76. By July 22, 1998, however, Ms. Currie claimed that although the President stated ìright?î at the end of the statements, Ms. Currie understood that she could agree or disagree with them. Currie 7/22/98 GJ at 23. Ms. Currie indicated during her first grand jury appearance that her memory about the events was ìgetting worse by the minute.î Currie 1/27/98 GJ at 71. Later, Ms. Currie acknowleged that ìcloser to the event my recollection would be better.î Currie 7/22/98 GJ at 182-183.

1032. Currie 1/27/98 GJ at 71, 75.

1033. Currie 7/22/98 GJ at 65-66. Indeed, she testified that, at some point after

January 18, she heard that Ms. Lewinsky visited the Oval Office on Saturdays, one of her days off. Currie 7/22/98 GJ at 65-66.

1034. Currie 1/27/98 GJ at 32-33; 36-38.

1035. Currie 7/22/98 GJ at 12, 15-6; Currie 1/27/98 GJ at 76.

1036. Currie 7/22/98 GJ at 14. The President, apparently, had a similar understanding of "alone." Before the grand jury, the President explained that "when I said, we were never alone, right . . . I meant that she [Ms. Currie] was always in the Oval Office complex, in that complex, while Monica was there." Clinton 8/17/98 GJ at 132.

Elsewhere in her testimony, Ms. Currie appeared to have a different understanding of "alone." She testified that, on one occasion, because others observed Ms. Lewinsky in the Oval Office complex, Ms. Currie accompanied Ms. Lewinsky into the Oval Office, where the President was working. Ms. Currie explained that she waited in the dining room while Ms. Lewinsky and the President met in the study so "[t]hey would not be alone." Currie 7/22/98 GJ at 130. See also Clinton 8/17/98 GJ at 56 ("I asked her specifically . . . to remain in the dining room, Betty, while I met with Monica in my study."). Ms. Currie testified that she did not want people who had observed Ms. Lewinsky enter the Oval Office to think that she and the President were "alone." Currie 7/22/98 GJ at 132.

1037. Currie 7/22/98 GJ at 79. Ms. Currie testified: "The way the question was phrased to me at the time, I answered, 'Right.' It Seemed to me that was the correct answer for me to give . . . the '[c]ome on to me,' I considered that more of a statement as opposed to a question." Id. at 80.

1038. Currie 1/27/98 GJ at 75.

1039. Currie 1/27/98 GJ at 83.

1040. Currie 1/27/98 GJ at 72-73; 7/22/98 GJ at 7, 10-11. Ms. Currie testified that the President made this statement in a way that did not invite her agreement. Rather, "I would call it a statement, sir." Currie 1/27/98 GJ at 73.

1041. Clinton 8/17/98 GJ at 57.

1042. Clinton 8/17/98 GJ at 132.

1043. Clinton 8/17/98 GJ at 55.

1044. Clinton 8/17/98 GJ at 141.

1045. Clinton 8/17/98 GJ at 55.

1046. Clinton 8/17/98 GJ at 135-36 ("As far as I know, she is unaware of what happened on the, on the occasions when I saw her in 1996 when something

improper happened. And she was unaware of the one time that I recall in 1997 when
something happened.").

1047. Clinton 8/17/98 GJ at 38.

1048. Clinton 8/17/98 GJ at 57-58, 132.

1049. Clinton 8/17/98 GJ at 133.

1050. Clinton 8/17/98 GJ at 133.

1051. Clinton 8/17/98 GJ at 135.

1052. Clinton 8/17/98 GJ at 139. The President referred to a statement he delivered in the beginning of his grand jury appearance: "[B]ecause of privacy considerations affecting my family, myself, and others, and in an effort to preserve the dignity
of the office I hold, this is all I will say about the specifics of these particular matters." Clinton 8/17/98 GJ at 10.

1053. At 5:12 p.m., Ms. Currie paged Ms. Lewinsky, leaving the message:
"Please call Kay at home." At 6:22 p.m., Ms. Currie paged Ms. Lewinsky: "Please
call Kay at home." At 7:06 p.m., Ms. Currie paged Ms. Lewinsky: "Please call Kay
at home." At 8:28 p.m., Ms. Currie paged Ms. Lewinsky: "Call Kay." 831-DC-
00000008 (Ms. Lewinsky's pager records) (Ms. Lewinsky's pager recorded calls in
Pacific time). See also Currie 5/7/98 GJ at 96-97; 7/22/98 GJ at 156, 158.

1054. Currie 5/7/98 GJ at 99-100.

1055. Telephone Calls, Table 47, Call 11. See also Currie 7/22/98 GJ at 161-62.

1056. See Telephone Calls, Table 48. At 7:02 a.m. she paged Ms. Lewinsky, leaving the message: "Please call Kay at home at 8:00 this morning." At 8:08 a.m., Ms.
Currie paged Ms. Lewinsky again. After calling Ms. Lewinskyís home number at
8:29 a.m., Ms. Currie paged Ms. Lewinsky again at 8:33 a.m. Four minutes later,
Ms. Currie paged yet again, leaving the message: iPlease call Kay at hom. Itís a social
call. Thank you.î (Ms. Currie testified that these calls were, in fact, not of a social
nature, Currie 7/22/98 GJ at 161). Receiving no response, Ms. Currie paged Ms.
Lewinsky again at 8:41 a.m. She then placed a one-minute call to the President. Currie 5/7/98 GJ at 104-05; 7/22/98 GJ at 160-62.

1057. Currie 7/22/98 GJ at 162-63. This time, Ms. Currie left a more urgent message: "Please call Kay re: family emergency." 831-DC-00000009 (Ms. Lewinsky's
pager records). See Telephone Calls, Table 48, Call 7.

1058. Currie 7/22/98 GJ at 157-59; 164-66. (1093)

1059. Jordan 6/9/98 GJ at 17. See also Telephone Calls, Table 48 (831-DC-
00000009) (Ms. Lewinsky's pager records).

1060. Jordan 6/9/98 GJ at 38-39.

1061. Carter 6/18/98 GJ at 146.

1062. Jordan 6/9/98 GJ at 54-55.

1063. Schmidt, Baker, and Locy, "Clinton Accused of Urging Aide To Lie," Wash. Post, Jan. 21, 1998, at A1.

1064. Podesta 6/23/98 GJ at 12.

1065. See Telephone Calls, Table 50.

1066. Mr. Bennett was apparently referring to Ms. Lewinsky's affidavit.

1067. Clinton Accused at A1.

1068. Mr. Lindsey, on instructions from the President, See Lindsey 8/28/98 GJ at 23, has invoked the presidential communication privilege, the deliberative process privilege, the governmental attorney-client privilege, and President Clinton's personal attorney-client privilege with regard to conversations with the President and has thus refused to disclose what the President said to him on January 21. Lindsey 2/19/98 GJ at 42. Mr. Lindsey has testified, however, that based on the President's public statements and statements made to others in Lindsey's presence, the President misled him about the nature of his relationship with Ms. Lewinsky. Lindsey 8/28/98 GJ at 93-96, 101.

1069. Currie 5/7/98 GJ at 112-14.

1070. Lindsey 8/28/98 GJ at 90. Mr. Lindsey, citing privileges, refused to testify about the substance of this conversation.

1071. 1034-DC-00000111 (Mr. Jordan's calendar). See also Jordan 3/5/98 GJ at 79 (St. Regis Hotel), 160-61 (New York), 179 (the President's phone call); Jordan 6/9/98 GJ at 76.

1072. See Telephone Calls, Table 50, Call 6. See also Lindsey 8/28/98 GJ at 90. Mr. Lindsey asserted privileges over this conversation as well.

1073. White House Press Conference (Mike McCurry), Jan. 21, 1998.

1074. Lindsey 8/28/98 GJ at 11-12.

1075. Bowles 4/2/98 GJ at 84. See also Podesta 6/16/98 GJ at 85-86.

1076. Ickes 6/10/98 GJ at 73.

1077. Ms. Currie could not recall whether the President called her into the Oval Office to discuss Ms. Lewinsky on Tuesday, January 20, or Wednesday, January 21. Currie 1/27/98 GJ at 80-81.

1078. Currie 1/27/98 GJ at 80-81.

1079. Currie 1/27/98 GJ at 81.

1080. Currie 1/24/98 Int. at 8. The President did not specifically recall this second conversation with Ms. Currie, but did not dispute that it took place: "I do not remember how many times I talked to Betty Currie or when. I don't. I can't possibly remember that. I do remember when I first heard about this story breaking, trying to ascertain what the facts were, trying to ascertain what Betty's perception was." Clinton 8/17/98 GJ at 141-42.

1081. Blumenthal 2/26/98 GJ at 19.

1082. Blumenthal 6/4/98 GJ at 48-49. When later asked how he interpreted the President's statement, "I haven't done anything wrong," Mr. Blumenthal stated, "My understanding was that the accusations against him which appeared in the press that day were false, that he had not done anything wrong. . . . He had not had a sexual relationship with her, and had not sought to obstruct justice or suborn perjury." Blumenthal 6/26/98 at 26.

1083. Blumenthal 6/4/98 GJ at 49. The President said, "I've gone down that road before, I've caused pain for a lot of people and I'm not going to do that again." Blumenthal 6/4/98 GJ at 49. Mr. Blumenthal "understood [this statement] to mean that he had had an adulterous relationship in the past, which is something he made very plain to the American people in his "60 Minutes" interview with the First Lady, which is how he introduced himself to the public . . . . And it's been very well known." Blumenthal 6/25/98 GJ at 32.

1084. Blumenthal 6/4/98 GJ at 49.

1085. Blumenthal 6/4/98 GJ at 50.

1086. Blumenthal 6/4/98 GJ at 49-50; Blumenthal 6/25/98 GJ at 15, 51.

1087. Podesta 6/16/98 GJ at 92.

1088. Podesta 6/16/98 GJ at 92. The President made another misleading statement about his relationship with Ms. Lewinsky to Mr. Podesta a few weeks later. According to Mr. Podesta, "[h]e said to me that after she [Ms. Lewinsky] left [the White House], that when she had come by, she came by to See Betty, and that he — when she was there either Betty was with them — either that she was with Betty when he saw her or that he saw her in the Oval Office with the door open and Betty was around — and Betty was out at her desk."

1089. Clinton 8/17/98 GJ at 101-09.

1090. Clinton 8/17/98/ GJ at 101, 106. The President was asked specifically whether he denied telling Mr. Podesta that he did not have any kind of sex whatsoever, including oral sex, with Ms. Lewinsky. The President responded: "I'm not saying that anybody who had a contrary memory is wrong. I do not remember." Clinton 8/17/98 GJ at 105.

1091. In claiming that this statement was true, the President was apparently relying on the same tense-based distinction he made during the Jones deposition. See Clinton 8/17/98 GJ at 59-61 ("It depends on what the meaning of the word 'is' is. If the — if he — if 'is' means is and never has been, that is not — that is one thing. If it means there is none, that was a completely true statement. . . . Now, if someone had asked me on that day, are you having any kind of sexual relations with Ms. Lewinsky, that is, asked me a question in the present tense, I would have said no. And it would have been completely true.")

1092. Clinton 8/17/98 GJ at 107.

1093. Clinton 8/17/98 GJ at 107.

1094. Broadcast on "All Things Considered" on National Public Radio, 5:07 p.m., Wednesday, January 21, 1998.

1095. "The News Hour with Jim Lehrer," PBS, interview with President Bill Clinton by Jim Lehrer, Wednesday, January 21, 1998. As evidenced by his grand jury testimony, the President is attentive to matters of verb tense. Clinton 8/17/98 GJ at 59.

1096. Televised Remarks by President Clinton at Photo Opportunity at the White House with Palestinian Authority Chairman Yasser Arafat, January 22, 1998, 10:22 a.m.

1097. Roll Call, Inc., January 22, 1998; transcript of press conference.

1098. "All Things Considered," January 21, 1998.

1099. "The News Hour," January 21, 1998.

1100. Televised Remarks By President Clinton at Photo Opportunity at the White House with Palestinian Authority Chairman Yasser Arafat, January 22, 1998, 10:22 a.m.

1101. Roll Call, Inc., January 22, 1998. President Clinton was extended invitations to appear before the grand jury and give his testimony on: January 28, 1998; February 4, 1998; February 9, 1998; February 21, 1998; March 2, 1998; and March 13, 1998. He declined all of these invitations. On July 16, 1998, the grand jury issued the President a subpoena. The President promptly moved for a postponement of two weeks in which to respond. At a hearing on the President's motion, Chief Judge Norma Holloway Johnson stated, "What we need to do is to move forward and move forward expeditiously. . . . [A]pparently the grand jury has determined that [they] need to hear from the [President]." In re Grand Jury Proceedings, Misc. No. 98-267, July 28, 1998, at pp. 27-28. Before Judge Johnson ruled, the President's attorneys negotiated the terms of the President's appearance.

1102. Morris 8/18/98 GJ at 6, 10, 12. Mr. Morris was questioned after the President's grand jury appearance on August 17, 1998; accordingly, the OIC never had an opportunity to question the President about this conversation.

1103. Morris 8/18/98 GJ at 14.

1104. Mr. Morris testified that he interpreted the "something" to be sexual in nature. Morris 8/18/98 GJ at 94.

1105. Morris 8/18/98 GJ at 14.

1106. Morris 8/18/98 GJ at 15.

1107. Morris 8/18/98 GJ at 15-16.

1108. Morris 8/18/98 GJ at 17.

1109. Morris 8/18/98 GJ at 28.

1110. Morris 8/18/98 GJ at 30.

1111. Morris 8/18/98 GJ at 34. Mr. Morris believed that Ms. Lewinsky's credibility was in question based on a claim by a USA Today reporter that there was an occasion when the President and Mr. Morris spoke on the telephone while they each were involved in a sexual encounter. The President was reportedly "having sex" with Ms. Lewinsky while Mr. Morris was allegedly involved with a prostitute at the Jefferson Hotel. Morris 8/18/98 GJ at 32, 34.

1112. Morris 8/18/98 GJ at 35.

1113. Thomason 8/11/98 GJ at 6.

1114. Although Mr. Thomason originally offered to stay with the President for a "couple of days," he stayed at the White House Residence for 34 days. Thomason 8/11/98 GJ at 6, 10. Mr. Thomason testified that while "not particularly an expert in media matters . . . my wife and I Seem to have a feel of what the rest of America is thinking. . . ." Thomason 8/11/98 GJ at 24.

1115. Thomason 8/11/98 GJ at 15-16. Mr. Thomason said he "went on the assumption that [the allegations] were not true," but he never asked the President because he talked to his attorney, Robert Bennett (also the President's personal attorney), who advised him "to make sure you don't ask questions that will get you subpoenaed." Id. at 22, 27. Mr. Thomason also testified he did not ask the President whether the denial was true because "I wanted it to be true and I felt it not to be true." Id. at 32-33.

1116. Thomason 8/11/98 GJ at 15.

1117. Thomason 8/11/98 GJ at 27.

1118. Schmidt and Baker, "Ex-Intern Rejected Immunity Offer in Probe," Wash. Post, Jan. 24, 1998, at A1.

1119. Schmidt and Baker, "Ex-Intern Rejected Immunity Offer," at A1.

1120. Larry King Weekend, Jan. 24, 1998, Transcript No. 98012400V42.

1121. In fact, the President did draw a distinction between "is" and "was." See Clinton 8/17/98 GJ at 59.

1122. Larry King Weekend, Jan. 24, 1998, Transcript No. 98012400V42.

1123. Televised Remarks by President Clinton at the White House Education News Conference, Monday, January 26, 1998, 10:00 a.m. See Chi. Tribune, Jan. 27, 1998, at 1 ("A defiant President Clinton wagged his finger at the cameras and thumped the lectern Monday as he insisted he did not have sex with a young White House intern or ask her to deny it under oath.").

GROUNDS

1. The pseudonym Jane Doe was used during discovery to refer to certain women whose identities were protected from the public.

2. For a discussion of the procedural background to the Jones case, see Appendix, Tab C.

3. Sections 1621 and 1623 of Title 18 (perjury) carry a penalty of imprisonment of not more than five years for knowingly making a false, material statement under oath, including in any ancillary court proceeding. An "ancillary proceeding" includes a deposition in a civil case. United States v. McAfee, 8 F.3d 1010, 1013 (5th Cir. 1993); United States v. Scott, 682 F.2d 695, 698 (8th Cir. 1982). The perjury statutes apply to statements made during civil proceedings. As one United States Court of Appeals recently stated, "we categorically reject any suggestion, implicit or otherwise, that perjury is somehow less serious when made in a civil proceeding. Perjury, regardless of the setting, is a serious offense that results in incalculable harm to the functioning and integrity of the legal system as well as to private individuals." United States v. Holland, 22 F.3d 1040, 1047 (11th Cir. 1994); see also United States v. Wilkinson, 137 F.3d 214, 225 (4th Cir. 1998).

4. Clinton 1/17/98 Depo.; see also Clinton 1/17/98 Depo. at 18.

5. Clinton 1/17/98 Depo. at 19.

6. Written interrogatories are a common discovery device in federal civil cases by which a party serves written questions on the opposing party. The rules require that they be answered under oath and therefore under penalty of perjury. See Fed. R. Civ. P. 33.

7. V002-DC-00000016-32 (Plaintiff's Second Set of Interrogatories, see Interrogatory no. 10). The interrogatory in the text reflects Judge Wright's order, dated December 11, 1997, limiting the scope of the question to cover only women who were state or federal employees at the relevant times.

8. V002-DC-00000052-55 (President Clinton's Supplemental Responses to Plaintiff's Second Set of Interrogatories, see Response to Interrogatory no. 10).

9. Clinton 1/17/98 Depo., Exh. 1.

10. Robert S. Bennett, counsel for President Clinton.

11. Clinton 1/17/98 Depo. at 78 (emphasis added).

12. Id. at 204 (emphasis added). The full text of Ms. Lewinsky's affidavit is set forth in the Doc. Supp. B, Tab 7.

13. White House records reflecting entry and exit are incomplete. For Ms. Lewinsky, there are no records for January 7, 1996, and January 21, 1996.

14. The President's false statements to the grand jury are discussed in Ground II.

15. Lewinsky 8/26/98 Depo. at 6-7.

16. Id. at 7.

17. Id. at 8. Ms. Lewinsky stated that the hallway outside the Oval Office study was more suitable for their encounters than the Oval Office because the hallway had no windows. Lewinsky 8/6/98 GJ at 34-35.

18. Lewinsky 8/26/98 Depo. at 8.

19. Id. at 8, 21. Ms. Lewinsky testified that she had an orgasm. Id. at 8.

20. Id. at 11-12.

21. Id. at 12-13.

22. Id. at 14.

23. Id. at 12-13.

24. Id. at 15-16.

25. Id. at 17. After the sexual encounter, she saw the President masturbate in the bathroom near the sink. Id. at 18.

26. Id. at 18.

27. Id. at 18.

28. Id. at 19. They engaged in oral-anal contact as well. See Lewinsky 8/26/98 Depo. at 18-20.

29. Id. at 21-22. This was shortly after their first phone sex encounter, which occurred on January 16, 1996. Id. at 22; Lewinsky 7/30/98 Int. at 9. Phone sex occurs when one or both parties masturbate while one or both parties talk in a sexually explicit manner on the telephone.

30. Lewinsky 8/26/98 Depo. at 25.

31. Id. at 26. As Ms. Lewinsky departed, she observed the President "manually stimulating" himself in Ms. Hernreich's office. Id. at 27.

32. Id. at 28-32.

33. Id. at 28.

34. Id. at 30-31. Ms. Lewinsky testified that she had an orgasm. Id.

35. Id. at 30-32. They engaged in oral-anal contact as well. See Lewinsky 8/26/98 Depo. at 29-33.

36. Id. at 34-38.

37. Id. at 37-38. The President then put the cigar in his mouth and said to Ms.

Lewinsky: "it tastes good." Lewinsky 7/30/98 Int. at 12-13; see also Lewinsky Depo. at 38.

38. Lewinsky 8/6/98 GJ at 91, 94-97; Lewinsky 8/26/98 Depo. at 40-42.

39. Lewinsky 8/26/98 Depo. at 40-43.

40. Id. at 45-49. They had engaged in phone sex a number of times in the interim, according to Ms. Lewinsky. Lewinsky 7/30/98 Int. at 14-15.

41. Lewinsky 8/26/98 Depo. at 47. On this occasion, the President ejaculated. Id.

42. FBI Lab Report, Lab Nos. 980730002SBO and 980803100SBO, 8/17/98.

43. Lewinsky 8/26/98 Depo. at 49-51.

44. Ms. Lewinsky testified that she had multiple orgasms. Id. at 50.

45. Id. at 50-51; Lewinsky 8/6/98 GJ at 21. On this occasion, the President ejaculated. Lewinsky 8/26/98 Depo. at 50-51.

46. Lewinsky 8/26/98 Depo. at 51-53.

47. Id. at 53. See also Lewinsky 8/6/98 GJ at 35-36.

48. Lewinsky 7/30/98 Int. at 11-16; Lewinsky 8/6/98 GJ at 24. The summary chart of contacts between the President and Ms. Lewinsky, GJ Exhibit ML-7, which is based on information provided by Ms. Lewinsky, lists 17 separate phone sex calls. Id. at 27-28. Ms. Lewinsky also gave the President Vox, a novel about phone sex. Id.

While phone sex may not itself constitute a "sexual relationship," it adds detail to Ms. Lewinsky's testimony and underscores the sexual and intimate nature of the relationship between the President and Ms. Lewinsky.

Ms. Lewinsky also said that the President left a few messages on her home answering machine (although he told her he did not like to leave messages). Ms. Lewinsky provided four microcassettes of four messages to the OIC on July 29, 1998. FBI Receipt for Property Received, dated 7/29/98.

49. FBI Lab Report, Lab No. 9800730002SB0, 8/3/98.

50. FBI Observation Report (White House), 8/3/98.

51. FBI Lab Report, Lab No. 980730002SBO and 980803100SBO, 8/17/98.

52. Id.

53. Catherine Davis 3/17/98 GJ at 9-10. Ms. Catherine Davis talked to Ms. Lewinsky by telephone an average of once a week until April 1997 when Ms. Davis moved to Tokyo; thereafter she and Ms. Lewinsky remained in touch through e-mail. Id. at 14, 27.

54. Id. at 19-20.

55. Id. at 20.

56. Id. at 169.

57. Id. at 37.

58. Erbland 2/12/98 GJ at 9-10. Ms. Erbland testified that she spoke on the phone with Ms. Lewinsky at least once a month. Id. at 18-19.

59. Id. at 24, 30, 31.

60. Id. at 27.

61. Id. at 26 ("She told me that she had given him [oral sex] and that she had had all of her clothes off, but that he only had his shirt off and that she had given him oral sex and they kissed and fondled each other and that they didn't have sex. That was kind of a little bit of a letdown for her."); id. at 29 ("He put his face in her chest. And, you know, just oral sex on her part, you know, to him.").

62. Id. at 29.

63. Id. at 45.

64. Id. at 39 ("They were like phone sex conversations. They would, you know, talk about what they wanted to do to each other sexually.").

65. Ms. Ungvari spoke with Monica Lewinsky on the telephone an average of once a week, and visited her in Washington in October 1995 and March 1996. Ungvari 3/19/98 GJ at 9-11, 14-15.

66. Id. at 18.

67. Id. at 23-24.

68. Id. at 81.

69. Raines 1/29/98 GJ at 11. Ms. Raines and Monica Lewinsky have become "close friend[s]" since Ms. Lewinsky left the White House. Id. at 19.

70. Id. at 35-36, 38.

71. Id. at 30, 43, 48.

72. Id. at 51.

73. Andrew Bleiler 1/28/98 Int. at 3.

74. Id. at 3.

75. Ms. Lewinsky gave this Office permission to interview Dr. Kassorla.

76. Kassorla 8/28/98 Int. at 2.

77. Id. at 2-3. Dr. Kassorla advised Ms. Lewinsky against the relationship, stating that she was an employee having an office romance with a superior and that the relationship would cost Ms. Lewinsky her job. Id. at 2.

78. Tripp 7/2/98 GJ at 104.

79. Id. at 97-105.

80. Finerman 3/18/98 Depo. at 29-33.

81. She testified that the encounter concluded with the President masturbating into a bathroom sink. Id. at 30-31. Ms. Finerman indicated that "it was something I didn't want to talk about," and Ms. Lewinsky "sort of clammed up" thereafter. Id. at 35. See also Lewinsky 8/26/98 Depo. at 18.

82. Finerman 3/18/98 Depo. at 33-35.

83. Young 6/23/98 GJ at 37-38.

84. Estep 8/23/98 Int. at 1. Ms. Estep is a licensed certified social worker; Ms. Lewinsky gave this Office permission to interview her.

85. Id. at 1, 4.

86. Id. at 3. Ms. Estep also thought that Ms. Lewinsky had her "feet in reality." Id.

87. Id. at 2.

88. Id.

89. The President and Ms. Lewinsky had ten sexual encounters that included direct contact with the genitalia of at least one party, and two other encounters that included kissing. On nine of the ten occasions, Ms. Lewinsky performed oral sex on the President. On nine occasions, the President touched and kissed Ms. Lewinsky's bare breasts. On four occasions, the President also touched her genitalia. On one occasion, the President inserted a cigar into her vagina to stimulate her. The President and Ms. Lewinsky also had phone sex on at least fifteen occasions.

90. This denial encompassed touching of Ms. Lewinsky's breasts or genitalia.

91. He provided his responses during his August 17, 1998 grand jury appearance; those responses are separately analyzed in Ground II.

92. Chief Judge Norma Holloway Johnson, United States District Court for the District of Columbia, and Judge Susan Webber Wright, United States District Court for the Eastern District of Arkansas, each has one copy of the videotape, and the Congress may see fit to seek the videotape from either court. The videotape is valuable in facilitating a proper assessment of the facts and evidence presented in this Referral.

93. Clinton 1/17/98 Depo., Exh. 1.

94. Clinton 8/17/98 GJ at 151.

95. Clinton 8/17/98 GJ at 151 (emphasis added).

96. The definition used at the President's deposition also covers acts in which the deponent "cause[d] contact" with the genitalia or anus of "any person." When he

testified to the grand jury, the President said that this aspect of the definition still does not cover his receiving oral sex. The President said that the word "cause" implies "forcing to me" and "forcible abusive behavior." Clinton 8/17/98 GJ at 17. And thus the President said that he did not lie under oath in denying that he "caused" contact with the genitalia of any person because his activity with Ms. Lewinsky did not include any nonconsensual behavior. Id. at 18.

97. She testified that she had orgasms on three of the four occasions. We note that fact because (i) the definition referred to direct contact with the genitalia with the "intent to arouse or gratify" and (ii) the President has denied such contact. Ms. Lewinsky also testified that on one occasion, the President put his hand over her mouth during a sexual encounter to keep her quiet. Lewinsky 7/31/98 Int. at 3.

98. MSL-55-DC-0094; MSL-55-DC-0124.

99. Lewinsky 8/20/98 GJ at 54.

100. Text of President's Address to Nation, reprinted in Washington Post, August 18, 1998, at A5 (emphasis added).

101. Clinton 8/17/98 GJ at 107.

102. Following the President's public admission of an inappropriate relationship, Judge Wright stated sua sponte in an order issued on September 1, 1998: "Although the Court has concerns about the nature of the President's January 17, 1998 deposition testimony given his recent public statements, the Court makes no findings at this time regarding whether the President may be in contempt." Jones v. Clinton, No. LR-C-94-290 (September 1, 1998), Unpublished Order at 7 n.5.

103. Clinton 8/17/98 GJ at 9-10.

104. Id. at 9-10. See also Excerpt from President Clinton's Televised Address to the American People, 8/17/98, reprinted in The Washington Post, at A5 (8/18/98) ("In a deposition in January, I was asked questions about my relationship with Monica Lewinsky. While my answers were legally accurate, I did not volunteer information.").

105. Clinton 8/17/98 GJ at 23-24.

106. Id. at 93.

107. Id. at 110 (emphasis added).

108. Id. at 95-96 (emphasis added).

109. Lewinsky 8/26/98 Depo. at 69.

110. MSL-55-DC-0094; MSL-55-DC-0124.

111. Lewinsky 8/20/98 GJ at 54.

112. Clinton 1/17/98 Depo. at 26 ("If the predicates are met, we have no objection to detail").

113. See, e.g., Ungvari 3/19/98 GJ at 18, 22-24; Erbland 2/12/98 GJ at 23-25.

114. V006-DC-00003737-3744.

115. 827-DC-00000008; 1222-DC-00000156, 1222-DC-0000083-85.

116. Lewinsky 7/30/98 Int. at 6; Lewinsky 8/24/98 Int. at 5.

117. The President contended that he had only one encounter in 1997 with Ms. Lewinsky, whereas she says that there were two. The motive for making a false statement on that issue is less clear, except that perhaps the President wanted to portray the 1997 relationship as an isolated incident.

118. Ms. Jones's attorneys had earlier served President Clinton with a document request that sought documents reflecting "any communications, meetings or visits involving" President Clinton and Ms. Lewinsky. 1414-DC-00001534-46.

119. Throughout the Jones case, Judge Susan Webber Wright ruled that Ms. Jones was entitled to discover information regarding the nature of President Clinton's relationship with government employees, including Monica Lewinsky, a federal employee at the time. See, e.g., 921-DC-00000459-66; 920-DC-00000517-25; 1414-DC-00001006-14; 921-DC-00000736-44; 921-DC-00000751-52; 1414-DC-00001188-92.

120. Clinton 1/17/98 Depo. at 52-53 (emphasis added).

121. Ms. Lewinsky testified that many of her sexual encounters with the President occurred in this windowless hallway. Lewinsky 8/6/96 GJ at 34-36.

122. The President had earlier testified that during the government shutdown in November 1995, Ms. Lewinsky was working as an intern in the Chief of Staff's Office, and had brought the President and others some pizza. Clinton 1/17/98 Depo. at 58.

123. Id. at 58-59 (emphasis added).

124. Id. at 59(emphasis added).

125. Lewinsky 8/6/98 GJ at 20, 52.

126. Lewinsky 8/26/98 Depo. at 22; Lewinsky 8/6/98 GJ at 52-53.

127. Lewinsky 8/6/98 GJ at 76.

128. Id. at 52-53.

129. Id. at 35.

130. Id. at 34-36.

131. Id. at 20.

132. Currie 1/27/98 GJ at 32-33. See also Currie 5/6/98 GJ at 98. The Oval Office area includes the study, dining room, kitchen, bathroom, and hallway connecting the area. See Appendix, Exhibit D (diagram of Oval Office area).

133. Currie 1/27/98 GJ at 34-35 (recalling that after the President's radio address, the President told Ms. Lewinsky he wanted to show her his collection of political buttons and took her into the Oval Office study for 15 to 20 minutes while Ms. Currie waited nearby, in the pantry or the dining room).

134. Currie 1/27/98 GJ at 36-38 (testifying that Ms. Lewinsky came to the White House and met with the President alone for 15 or 20 minutes). See also Currie 5/14/98 GJ at 116.

135. Currie 1/27/98 GJ at 35-36 (testifying that Ms. Lewinsky and the President were in the Oval Office for "[p]erhaps 30 minutes."). Again, Ms. Currie testified that she believes no one else was present. See also Currie 5/6/98 GJ at 103-105.

136. Ferguson 7/17/98 GJ at 23-35 (alone for approximately 45 minutes); Ferguson 7/23/98 GJ at 18-24.

137. Fox 2/17/98 GJ at 30-38 (alone for approximately 40 minutes).

138. Bordley 8/13/98 GJ at 19-30 (alone for approximately 30 to 35 minutes).

139. Garabito 7/30/98 GJ at 25-32.

140. Byrne 7/30/98 GJ at 7-12, 29-32 (alone for 15 to 25 minutes).

141. Muskett 7/21/98 GJ at 9-13, 22-32 (alone on Easter Sunday 1996).

142. The last date that White House records reflect a visit by Ms. Lewinsky is Sunday, December 28, 1997. 827-DC-00000018; V006-DC-00000009.

143. Maes 4/8/98 GJ at 84-89.

144. Clinton 8/17/98 GJ at 9-10 (emphasis added).

145. Id. at 30-33.

146. Id. at 34.

147. Id. at 54.

148. Clinton 1/17/98 Depo. at 58-59.

149. See id. at 52-53, 59.

150. Clinton 8/17/98 GJ at 118; Lewinsky 8/6/98 GJ at 53-55.

151. In criminal law, a feigned lack of memory is sufficient for a perjury conviction. See, e.g., United States v. Chapin, 515 F.2d 1274 (D.C. Cir. 1975); Behrle v. United States, 100 F.2d 174 (D.C. Cir. 1938).

152. Clinton 1/17/98 Depo. at 75 (emphasis added).

153. Clinton 8/17/98 GJ at 36.

154. Lewinsky 8/6/98 GJ at 27-28, 150-51; GJ Exhibit ML-7.

155. FBI Receipt for Property received, 7/29/98.

156. Lewinsky 8/6/98 GJ at 26-28; GJ Exhibit ML-7.

157. Lewinsky 8/6/98 GJ at 151. Ms. Lewinsky's subpoena directed in part: "Please produce each and every gift including, but not limited to, any and all dresses, accessories, and jewelry, and/or hat pins given to you by, or on behalf of, Defendant Clinton." 902-DC-00000135-38.

158. Lewinsky 8/6/98 GJ at 33, 152. See also Lewinsky 2/1/98 Statement at 7. In fact, Ms. Lewinsky had told Ms. Tripp about it. Ms. Lewinsky had also discussed the hat pin and the subpoena's request for the hat pin with Mr. Jordan. Lewinsky 8/6/98 GJ at 132, 140.

159. Currie 5/6/98 GJ at 142 (relating incident where the President asks Ms. Currie about the hat pin he gave to Ms. Lewinsky). After this criminal investigation started, Ms. Currie turned over a box of items — including a hat pin — that had been given to her by Ms. Lewinsky. Ms. Currie understood from Ms. Lewinsky that the box did contain gifts from the President. See Currie 5/6/98 GJ at 107. Ms. Lewinsky testified that the box contained gifts from the President, including the hat pin. Lewinsky 8/6/98 GJ at 154-162.

160. Ms. Lewinsky testified that the President had given her a gold brooch, and she made near-contemporaneous statements to Ms. Erbland, Ms. Raines, Ms. Ungvari, and Ms. Tripp regarding the gift. Lewinsky 8/6/98 GJ at 26-28; GJ Exhibit ML-7; Erbland 2/12/98 GJ at 41; Raines 1/29/98 GJ at 53-55; Ungvari 3/19/98 GJ at 44; Tripp 7/29/98 GJ at 105.

161. Ms. Lewinsky testified that Leaves of Grass was "the most sentimental gift he had given me." Lewinsky GJ, Aug. 6, 1998, at 156.

Ms. Lewinsky made near-contemporaneous statements to her mother, her aunt, and her friends Ms. Davis, Ms. Erbland, and Ms. Raines that the President had given her Leaves of Grass. Davis 3/17/98 GJ at 30-31; Erbland 2/12/98 GJ at 40-41; Finerman 3/18/98 Depo. at 15-16; Marcia Lewis 2/10/98 GJ at 51-52; Marcia Lewis 2/11/98 GJ at 10 ("[S]he liked the book of poetry very much."). Raines 1/29/98 GJ 53-55.

162. Lewinsky 8/6/98 GJ at 27; GJ Exhibit ML-7.

163. Lewinsky 8/26/98 Depo. at 15-16; Lewinsky 8/6/98 GJ at 27; GJ Exhibit ML-7; Finerman Depo. 3/18/98 at 13-17; Ungvari 3/19/98 GJ at 43-44.

164. Clinton 1/17/98 Depo. at 76-77 (emphasis added).

165. Lewinsky 8/6/98 GJ at 27-28, GJ Exhibit ML-7; Lewinsky 7/27/98 Int. at 12-14.

166. Lewinsky 8/6/98 GJ at 235-36.

167. Id. at 27, 150; GJ Exhibit ML-7.

168. V002-DC-00000475 (Letter to OIC, 3/16/98).

169. Lewinsky 8/6/98 GJ at 27; GJ Exhibit ML-7. See also Lewinsky 7/27/98 Int. at 14.

170. Lewinsky 8/6/98 GJ at 185.

171. Letter from David Kendall to OIC, August 3, 1998.

172. V002-DC-00000471. Ms. Lewinsky testified that she bought and gave the President that book in early January 1998, and that when she talked to him on January 5, 1998, he acknowledged that he had received the book. Lewinsky 8/6/98 GJ at 189-192. When testifying before the grand jury, the President acknowledged receiving ìa particularly nice book for Christmas, an antique book on Presidents. She knew that I collected old books and it was a very nice thing.î Clinton 8/17/98 GJ at 36.

173. V002-DC-0000003.

174. Lewinsky 8/6/98 GJ at 27-28, 109; GJ Exhibit ML-7.

175. Id.; Lewinsky 8/6/98 GJ at 26-28; Lewinsky 7/27/98 Int. at 13. The President did not turn over this antique book in response to a subpoena.

176. Lewinsky 8/6/98 GJ at 27-28; GJ Exhibit ML-7. The President did not produce The Notebook in response to a subpoena.

177. Lewinsky 8/6/98 GJ at 27-28, 182-183; GJ Exhibit ML-7. Ms. Lewinsky saw a copy of the book in the President's study in November 1997. Lewinsky 8/6/98 GJ at 183. White House records list Oy Vey and Vox on an October 10, 1997, catalog of books in the West Wing. 1361-DC-00000002 (Catalog of Books in the West Wing Presidential Study as of 10 October 1997). The President did not produce Oy Vey in response to a subpoena.

178. Lewinsky 8/6/98 GJ at 27-28, 183-84; Lewinsky 7/27/98 Int. at 13; GJ Exhibit ML-7. Ms. Lewinsky testified that she had seen the book in the President's study in November 1997. Lewinsky 8/6/98 GJ at 183-84. The President did not produce this book in response the subpoena.

179. Id. at 27-28, 183-84; Lewinsky 7/27/98 Int. at 12-13; GJ Exhibit ML-7.

180. Lewinsky 8/6/98 GJ at 26-28; GJ Exhibit ML-7.

181. These included a Sherlock Holmes game sometime after Christmas 1996; a

golf ball and tees on February 28, 1997; after the President injured his leg in March 1997, a care package filled with whimsical gifts, such as a magnet with the Presidential seal for his metal crutches, a license plate with "Bill" for his wheelchair, and knee pads with the Presidential seal; a Banana Republic casual shirt and a puzzle on golf mysteries on May 24, 1997; the card game "Royalty" in mid-August 1997; shortly before Halloween of 1997, a package filled with Halloween-related items, such as a pumpkin lapel pin, a wooden letter opener with a frog on the handle, and a plastic pumpkin filled with candy; and on December 6, 1997, a Starbucks Santa Monica mug and a Hugs and Kisses box. Lewinsky 8/6/98 GJ at 27-28; GJ Exhibit ML-7; Lewinsky 7/27/97 Int. at 12-15.

182. Clinton 8/17/98 GJ at 47.

183. Id. at 34-36.

184. Id. at 173 (emphasis added). The President testified that "to his knowledge" he has turned over all the gifts that Ms. Lewinsky gave him. Id. at 154-155.

185. Id. at 172-173.

186. Currie 5/6/98 GJ at 88-89; see also id. at 184; Currie 5/14/98 GJ at 78. Courier receipts show that Ms. Lewinsky sent nine packages to Ms. Currie. See 0837-DC-00000001 to 0837-DC-00000027.

187. T1 at 63-64.

188. Currie GJ 5/6/98 at 88-89; see also Currie GJ 5/14/98 at 78.

189. Currie 5/6/98 GJ at 129.

190. Currie 5/14/98 GJ at 145.

191. In his grand jury testimony, the President said that this question at his civil deposition confused him and that he thought that the questioner was asking whether he could list specific gifts he had given her rather than whether he had ever given Ms. Lewinsky a gift. Clinton 8/17/98 GJ at 51-52. Even if that explanation were credited, the President's answer to the hat pin question is inaccurate, particularly because he had discussed it with Ms. Lewinsky on December 28, according to her testimony.

192. Clinton 1/17/98 Depo. at 75.

193. Lewinsky 8/6/98 GJ at 167.

194. Clinton 1/17/98 Depo. at 70-71 (emphasis added).

195. Lewinsky 8/6/98 GJ at 123; Lewinsky 8/26/98 Depo. at 57-58; Lewinsky 2/1/98 Statement at 4.

196. Lewinsky 8/6/98 GJ at 123-24; Lewinsky 2/1/98 Statement at 4 ("When

asked what to do if she was subpoenaed, the Pres. suggested she could sign an affidavit to try to satisfy their inquiry and not be deposed.").

197. Lewinsky 8/6/98 GJ at 123 (emphasis added); Lewinsky 2/1/98 Statement at 4 ("In general, Ms. L. should say she visited the WH to see Ms. Currie and, on occasion when working at the WH, she brought him letters when no one else was around.").

198. Lewinsky 8/6/98 GJ at 123-24.

199. Jordan 5/5/98 GJ at 136, 142, 144-45; Lewinsky 8/6/98 GJ at 133, 135.

200. Lewinsky 8/6/98 GJ at 151-52; Lewinsky 8/20/98 GJ at 65-66; Lewinsky 2/1/98 Statement at 6.

201. Lewinsky 8/6/98 GJ at 152; Lewinsky 8/20/98 GJ at 66.

202. Lewinsky 8/6/98 GJ at 152; Lewinsky 8/20/98 GJ at 66. See also Lewinsky 8/1/98 Int. at 11 (noting that the President said something like "I don't know" or "I'll think about it").

203. Lewinsky 8/6/98 GJ at 154-59. See also Lewinsky 8/1/98 Int. at 11-12.

204. Lewinsky 8/6/98 GJ at 197.

205. Clinton 8/17/98 GJ at 33.

206. Id. at 36-37 (emphasis added).

207. Id. at 39-40 (emphasis added).

208. Clinton 1/17/98 Depo. at 68.

209. Id. (emphasis added).

210. Jordan 5/5/98 GJ at 144; Lewinsky 8/6/98 GJ at 138-39.

211. Clinton 8/17/98 GJ at 36 (emphasis added).

212. Lewinsky 8/6/98 GJ at 149-153, 191-192, 195-198; Lewinsky 8/20/98 GJ at 35-36, 47, 49, 65-66.

213. Clinton 8/17/98 GJ at 106.

214. See 18 U.S.C. ßß 1503, 1512, 1621.

215. Lewinsky 8/6/98 GJ at 121-26.

216. Id. at 126; Lewinsky 8/20/98 GJ at 70.

217. 920-DC-00000013-18.

218. 920-DC-00000018.

219. Lewinsky 8/6/98 GJ at 132.

220. Id. at 132.

221. Id. at 133.

222. Jordan 3/3/98 GJ at 159. Mr. Jordan stated that Ms. Lewinsky was crying both on the telephone earlier that day and then again in his office. Id. at 149-150.

223. Lewinsky 8/6/98 GJ at 149.

224. Id. at 149.

225. Id. At 152. This statement was false. Ms. Lewinsky had ìin factÖtold people about the hat pin.î Id.

226. Id. at 152. In a later grand jury appearance, Ms. Lewinsky again described the conversation, and said "I don't remember his response. I think it was something like, 'I don't know,' or 'Hmm' or — there really was no response." Lewinsky 8/20/98 GJ at 66.

227. Lewinsky 8/26/98 Depo. at 58.

228. Lewinsky 8/6/98 GJ at 166-67 (emphasis added).

229. Id. at 154; Lewinsky 8/20/98 GJ at 71.

230. Lewinsky 8/6/98 GJ at 154-55.

231. Lewinsky 2/1/98 Statement at 7 (emphasis added); see also Lewinsky 8/6/98 GJ at 179; Lewinsky 8/20/98 GJ at 62 ("I was truthful in my [February 1] proffer").

232. Lewinsky 8/6/98 GJ at 155.

233. Id. at 154.

234. Currie 1/27/98 GJ at 57-58.

235. Currie 5/6/98 GJ at 105-06.

236. Id. at 126 (emphasis added).

237. Id. at 108.

238. Lewinsky 8/6/98 GJ at 156-58.

239. Id. at 158.

240. Currie 5/6/98 GJ at 105, 107-08.

241. Lewinsky 8/20/98 GJ at 72-73.

242. Lewinsky 8/6/98 GJ at 158.

243. FBI Receipt for Property Received, 1/23/98; 824-DC-00000001-2 (letter from Karl Metzner, attorney for Betty Currie, dated 1/23/98, to the OIC, listing items in the box).

244. Clinton 8/17/98 GJ at 43-44 (emphasis added). In his grand jury testimony, the President repeated this "whatever you have" language several times. Id. at 45, 46-47, 115.

245. Id. at 51.

246. Id. at 114-15.

247. Id. at 46-47.

248. Id. at 46.

249. Ms. Currie testified that she was taking St. John's Wort to try to remember, but it was not helping. Currie 7/22/98 GJ at 172.

250. Lewinsky 2/1/98 Statement at 7 (emphasis added).

251. Lewinsky 8/6/98 GJ at 154-55; see also Lewinsky 8/20/98 GJ at 70-72.

252. Currie 5/6/98 GJ at 126.

253. Lewinsky 9/3/98 Int. at 2.

254. Id.

255. Id. In addition, under her immunity agreement, Ms. Lewinsky has no apparent motive to shift blame on this issue. In fact, just the opposite. If the truth were that she had called Ms. Currie, she could have said as much, and it would not have affected Ms. Lewinsky's legal rights or obligations at all. Moreover, she stated that does not want to harm the President with her truthful testimony. Lewinsky 8/26/98 Depo. at 69.

256. Currie 5/6/98 GJ at 108.

257. Currie 5/6/98 GJ at 32; see also id. at 44, 45.

258. Clinton 8/17/98 GJ at 106.

259. Clinton 1/17/98 Depo. at 75.

260. Lewinsky 8/20/98 GJ at 5 (Ms. Lewinsky could not visit the President unless Ms. Currie cleared her in); see also Lewinsky 7/31/98 Int. at 4-5 (Currie was "in the loop" when it came to keeping Lewinsky's relationship with the President discreet); Currie GJ 5/6/98 at 14-15, 57-58, 97-98.

261. Lewinsky 8/6/98 GJ at 189-91, 197-98.

262. Id. at 189, 198.

263. Lewinsky 9/3/98 Int. at 2.

264. Lewinsky 8/6/98 GJ at 198.

265. Id.

266. V0002-DC-0000093-116.

267. Clinton 8/17/98 GJ at 127.

268. Id. at 49-50.

269. President Clinton also committed perjury before the grand jury if he was involved in the concealment of the gifts.

270. Lewinsky 8/6/98 GJ at 121-22.

271. Id. at 122-23.

272. Lewinsky 2/1/98 Statement at 4.

273. Lewinsky 8/19/98 Int. at 4-5; see also Lewinsky 8/6/98 GJ at 123.

274. Id. at 124.

275. Id. at 234 (emphasis added).

276. Id. at 145-48.

277. Lewinsky Affidavit, Jan. 7, 1998, ∂ 8 (849-DC-00000634).

278. Ms. Lewinsky spoke to one of her friends, Catherine Allday Davis in early January. Ms. Lewinsky informed her of her situation. Ms. Davis said that "I was very scared for her" and "I didn't want to see her being like Susan McDougal." Catherine Davis 3/17/98 GJ at 80. Ms. Davis said that she did not want Monica "to lie to protect the President." Id. at 173.

279. Lewinsky 2/1/98 Statement at 9; see also Lewinsky 8/19/98 Int. at 4.

280. Jordan 5/5/98 GJ at 223-25.

281. Id. at 223-25.

282. Carter 6/18/98 GJ at 113.

283. Clinton 1/17/98 Depo. at 54.

284. Id. at 54.

285. Id. at 204 (emphasis added).

286. Clinton 8/17/98 GJ at 120. See also id. at 82 ("I was glad she saw a lawyer. I was glad she was doing an affidavit.").

287. Clinton 8/17/98 GJ at 117.

288. Id. at 22 (emphasis added).

289. Id. at 25.

290. Id. at 30.

291. Id. at 59 (emphasis added).

292. Id. at 20.

293. Id. at 61.

294. Id. at 61-62.

295. Id. at 26.

296. Lewinsky 8/6/98 GJ at 53-54 (Q: "When you say that you planned to bring papers, did you ever discuss with the President the fact that you would try to use that as a cover?" ML: "Yes.").

297. Muskett 7/21/98 GJ at 25-26, 83, 89-90; Fox 2/17/98 GJ at 34-35.

298. Householder 8/13/98 GJ at 11; Byrne 7/30/98 GJ at 9, 16, 30, 37; Garabito 7/30/98 GJ at 17. Other Secret Service officers testified that they saw Ms. Lewinsky

in the West Wing carrying paperwork. Moore 7/30/98 GJ at 25-26; Overstreet 8/11/98 GJ at 7; Wilson 7/23/98 GJ at 32.

299. Lewinsky 8/6/98 GJ at 54-55.

300. Id. at 55.

301. Id. at 27-28; GJ Exhibit ML-7. Ms. Lewinsky testified that she met with the President in private after she left her position at the White House on eleven dates in 1997: February 28 (following the radio address), March 29, May 24, July 4, July 14, July 24, August 16, October 11, November 13, December 6, and December 28.

302. See Appendix, Tab E (Table of Recorded Visits).

303. Lewinsky 8/6/98 GJ at 55.

304. Clinton 8/17/98 GJ at 117.

305. Lewinsky 8/6/98 GJ at 123.

306. Id. at 123-24 (emphasis added).

307. Clinton 1/17/98 at 50-51 (emphasis added).

308. Id. at 52-53.

309. Id. at 192-93 (emphasis added).

310. Id. at 197.

311. Clinton 8/17/98 GJ at 119.

312. Id. at 117. According to Ms. Lewinsky, this was the conversation in which the President told her that her name was on the Jones witness list, and in which she and the President discussed her filing an affidavit and the continued use of cover stories. Lewinsky 8/6/98 GJ at 121-23.

313. Clinton 8/17/98 GJ at 118, 119-20 (emphasis added). The President repeated at several other points in his testimony that he did not remember what he said to Ms. Lewinsky in the phone conversation on December 17. See id. at 117 ("I don't remember exactly what I told her that night."); id. at 118-19 ("you are trying to get me to characterize something [the cover stories] that I'm — that I don't know if I said or not").

314. The OIC is aware of no evidence that Mr. Bennett knew that Ms. Lewinsky's affidavit was false at the time of the President's deposition.

315. Lewinsky 8/6/98 GJ at 67-69.

316. 849-DC-00000002-10.

317. Ms. Lewinsky said that on October 6, 1997, she had been told by Linda Tripp that a friend of Tripp's at the National Security Council had reported that

Lewinsky would not be getting a White House job. Ms. Lewinsky said that at that point she finally decided to move to New York. Lewinsky 7/31/98 Int. at 9-10.

318. Id. at 10-11.

319. Id. at 11.

320. Lewinsky 8/13/98 Int. at 2-3.

321. Lewinsky 8/6/98 GJ at 103-04.

322. 968-DC-00003569 (Presidential call log).

323. Bowles 4/2/98 GJ at 67.

324. Id. at 70.

325. Podesta 2/5/98 GJ at 31-33, 35, 40-41.

326. Richardson 4/30/98 Depo. at 28.

327. Lewinsky 7/31/98 Int. at 12. Ms. Lewinsky said that she spoke to President Clinton about the phone call on October 23, during which she suggested to the President that she was interested in some job other than at the United Nations. Id. According to Ms. Lewinsky, the President replied that he just wanted her to have some options. Id.

Ms. Lewinsky said that she spoke to the President again on October 30 about the interview, in which she expressed anxiety about meeting with the Ambassador. Ms. Lewinsky said that the President told her to call Betty Currie after the interview so he would know how the interview went. Id. at 13.

328. Lewinsky 7/31/98 Int. at 14.

329. Lewinsky 8/26/98 Depo. at 67; Lewinsky 7/31/98 Int. at 14.

330. Lewinsky 7/31/98 Int. at 14.

331. Id. at 15. Ms. Lewinsky related this incident to her friend, Catherine Allday Davis, in a near-contemporaneous email. 1037-DC-00000017. See also Catherine Davis 3/17/98 GJ at 124.

332. Lewinsky 7/31/98 Int. at 14-15.

333. V004-DC-00000135 (Akin Gump phone records); Jordan 5/5/98 GJ at 52-55.

334. Lewinsky 8/6/98 GJ at 26-27 and GJ Exhibit ML-7. Ms. Lewinsky stated that just before Thanksgiving, 1997, she called Betty Currie and asked her to contact Vernon Jordan and prod him along in the job search. Lewinsky 8/4/98 Int. at 8. It was Ms. Lewinsky's understanding that Jordan was helping her at the request of the President and Ms. Currie. Id.

335. See Clinton 8/17/98 GJ at 84-85. Under the federal witness tampering statutes, it is a crime to corruptly persuade a witness to alter his testimony. See 18 U.S.C. ßß 1503, 1512.

336. 1178-DC-00000026 (WAVES records).

337. Lewinsky 8/4/98 Int. at 2.

338. Jordan 3/3/98 GJ at 48-49.

339. Id. at 65.

340. 921-DC-000000459-66.

341. Lewinsky 8/6/98 GJ at 121-23.

342. Id. at 121; Lewinsky 8/1/98 Int. at 6, 10.

343. Lewinsky 8/6/98 GJ at 127-28.

344. Id. at 138-41; Lewinsky 2/1/98 Statement at 6; cf. Jordan 3/3/98 GJ at 182-90 (recalls discussion of job search only).

345. V002-DC-000000052 (President Clinton's Supplemental Responses to Plaintiff's Second Set of Interrogatories).

346. Lewinsky 8/6/98 GJ at 149.

347. Lewinsky 8/6/98 GJ at 151-52; Lewinsky 7/27/98 Int. at 7. This was the same meeting where the President and Ms. Lewinsky discussed their concerns over the Lewinsky subpoena and its demand for the production of gifts.

348. Sutphen 5/27/98 Depo. at 39; Lewinsky 7/27/98 Int. at 5.

349. Lewinsky 8/6/98 GJ at 191-98, 205-06.

350. Jordan 5/5/98 GJ at 223-25.

351. Id. at 232; Lewinsky 8/6/98 GJ at 209.

352. Lewinsky 8/6/98 GJ at 208-10.

353. Jordan 5/28/98 GJ at 39 (emphasis added).

354. Ms. Jones's attorney named the "other women" he planned to call at trial:

Mr. Fisher: They would include . . . Monica Lewinsky

Judge Wright: Can you tell me who she is?

Mr. Fisher: Yes, your Honor.

Judge Wright: I never heard of her.

Mr. Fisher: She's the young woman who worked in the White House for a period
of time and was later transferred to a job in the Pentagon.

1414-DC-00001327-28.

355. 1414-DC-00001334-46.

356. Lewinsky 8/6/98 GJ at 214.

357. Bowles 4/2/98 GJ at 78-79.

358. Hilley 5/19/98 GJ at 74; Hilley 5/26/98 GJ at 11.

359. 830-DC-0000007.

360. 921-DC-00000775-78; 1292-DC-000000661-86.

361. The arrangement may not be explicitly spelled out. In this case, for example,
there is no evidence that Ms. Lewinsky received an explicit proposal where someone
said, "I'll give you a job if you lie under oath."

362. In a recorded conversation, Ms. Lewinsky discussed the job assistance various individuals, including Vernon Jordan, gave Webster Hubbell, and she expressed
her concern that someone could similarly consider the assistance she was provided as
improper in some manner: "I think somebody could construe, okay? Somebody
could construe or say, 'Well, they gave her a job to shut her up. They made her
happy.'" T2 at 11.

363. Clinton 1/17/98 Depo. at 68-69 (emphasis added).

364. Id. at 72 (emphasis added). See also id. at 73 ("[m]y understanding was . . .
that she was going to move to New York and that she was looking for some advice
[from Jordan] about what she should do when she got there").

365. Jordan 3/5/98 GJ at 26.

366. Jordan 3/5/98 GJ at 29.

367. 833-DC-0017890 (Pentagon phone records). See also Jordan 3/3/98 GJ at
92-93 (testifying that Ms. Lewinsky called him up and she was "very upset" about
"being served with a subpoena in the Paula Jones case").

368. Jordan 5/5/98 GJ at 142-43.

369. Id. at 133-34. Mr. Jordan had told Ms. Lewinsky to come see him at 5:00
p.m. Lewinsky 8/6/98 GJ at 129. See also Jordan 5/5/98 GJ at 144 (relating why he
wanted to tell the President about Ms. Lewinsky's subpoena).

370. 1178-DC-00000014 (White House phone records); Jordan 5/5/98 GJ at
145.

371. Jordan 5/5/98 GJ at 145-47.

372. Jordan 3/3/98 GJ at 167-69. White House records indicate that Mr. Jordan was scheduled to arrive at 8:00 p.m., and actually arrived at 8:15 p.m. See 1178-DC-00000026 (WAVES record). Mr. Jordan testified, however, that he is certain that he did not arrive at the White House until after 10 p.m. Jordan 5/5/98 GJ at 164.

373. Jordan 3/3/98 GJ at 169.

374. Id. at 172.

375. Jordan 5/5/98 GJ at 221-22.

376. Jordan 3/5/98 GJ at 24-25, 33; Jordan 5/5/98 GJ at 223-26; V004-DC-00000159 (Akin Gump phone records).

377. The affidavit is dated January 7, 1998, so the conversation informing the President that it had been signed could not have occurred any earlier than this date.

378. Jordan 5/5/98 GJ at 224-26.

379. Jordan 3/5/98 GJ at 25. Cf. Jordan 5/5/98 GJ at 225-26 (When President was told Ms. Lewinsky signed affidavit, "[t]here was no elation. There was no celebration.").

380. Jordan 3/5/98 GJ at 26 (emphasis added).

381. Id. at 125.

382. Clinton 8/17/98 GJ at 73-75.

383. Id. at 75-77.

384. That matter is still under criminal investigation by this Office.

385. Under the federal witness tampering and obstruction of justice statutes, it is a crime to attempt to corruptly persuade another person with intent to influence the person's testimony in an official proceeding. See 18 U.S.C. ßß 1503, 1512.

386. Clinton 1/17/98 Depo. at 68.

387. Id. at 70-71.

388. Id. at 72-73, 79.

389. Id. at 80-82.

390. Id. at 212-213.

391. Jones v. Clinton, Order of Judge Susan Webber Wright, January 29, 1998, at 2.

392. Currie 1/24/98 Int. at 8 ("CURRIE advised CLINTON may have mentioned that CURRIE might be asked about LEWINSKY"); Currie 5/6/98 GJ at 118 (Q: "Didn't the President talk to you about Monica's name coming up in those cases [Whitewater or Jones v. Clinton]?" BC: "I have a vague recollection of him saying

that her name may come up. Either he told me, somebody told me, but I don't know how it would come up.").

393. Currie 5/7/98 GJ at 80-81; GJ Exhibit BC 3-10, 1248-DC-00000307 (Presidential Call Log, Jan. 17, 1998). The White House call log indicates that the President called Ms. Currie at 7:02 p.m., they talked at 7:13 p.m., and the call ended at 7:14 p.m.

The President returned to the White House from the deposition at 4:26 p.m. 1248-DC-00000288 (Kearney's logs).

394. Currie 1/27/98 GJ at 65-66. The President confirmed that he called Betty Currie shortly after his deposition, and that he asked her to come in on Sunday, her day off. Clinton 8/17/98 GJ at 148-49.

The next day at 1:11 p.m., the President again called Ms. Currie at home. Currie 5/7/98 GJ at 85. GJ Exhibit BC 3-11, 1248-DC-00000311 (Presidential Call Log, Jan. 18, 1998). Ms. Currie could not recall the content of the second call, stating: "He may have called me on Sunday at 1:00 after church to see what time I can actually come in. I don't know. That's the best I can recollect." Id. at 89.

395. Currie 5/7/98 GJ at 91. See also Clinton 8/17/98 GJ at 149 (acknowledging that Ms. Currie normally would not be in the White House on Sunday).

396. Currie 1/27/98 GJ at 70.

397. Currie 1/24/98 Int. at 6.

398. Currie 1/27/98 GJ at 71, 73-74. At different points in the grand jury testimony, there are minor variations in the wording used or agreed to by Ms. Currie in recounting the President's statements. Compare id. at 71 ("You were always there when Monica was there." (Currie statement)) with id. at 74 (Q: "'You were always there when she was there, right?' Is that the way you remember the President stating it to you?" BC: "That's how I remember him stating it to me.").

399. Id. at 72.

400. Id. at 72. See also Currie 1/24/98 Int. at 6.

401. Ms. Currie interpreted this last comment as simply a statement, not necessarily one for which the President was seeking her agreement. Currie 1/27/98 GJ at 72-73.

402. Currie 1/27/98 GJ at 71 (Q: "Okay. And then you told us that the President

began to ask you a series of questions that were more like statements than questions." BC: "Right.").

403. Id. at 72-76.

404. Id.

405. Currie 1/24/98 Int. at 7.

406. Id. at 6.

407. Currie 1/27/98 GJ at 32-34.

408. Id. at 82-83.

409. Id. at 76.

410. Currie 5/7/98 GJ at 99-100. Ms. Lewinsky called Betty Currie shortly after 10:00 p.m., but told Ms. Currie that she could not talk to her that night. Id. at 101.

411. GJ Exhibit BC 3-12, V006-DC-00002068 (call log). The call lasted approximately one minute.

412. Currie 5/7/98 GJ at 102.

413. 831-DC-00000009 (Lewinsky pager records). As the records reflect, Betty Currie used the name Kay or Kate when paging Monica Lewinsky. Lewinsky 8/6/98 GJ at 215-17; Currie 7/22/98 GJ at 148-49.

414. V006-DC-00002069; V006-DC-00002070 (White House telephone records). Ms. Currie testified that she probably called the President to tell him that she had not yet spoken to Ms. Lewinsky. Ms. Currie does not remember the substance of the conversations with the President for either of the calls that he made to her. Currie 5/7/98 GJ at 106-07. The phone calls from the President were approximately one and two minutes in length. That Monday, January 19, was a holiday, and Ms. Currie was not at work.

415. Currie 1/27/98 GJ at 80-82 (emphasis added).

416. Clinton 8/17/98 GJ at 56-57 (emphasis added). See also id. at 131-32 (Q: "You said that you spoke to her in an attempt to refresh your own recollection about the events involving Monica Lewinsky, is that right?" WJC: "Yes.").

417. Id. at 132-34 (emphasis added).

418. Id. at 134.

419. Id. at 134-35 (emphasis added).

420. Id. at 136-37.

421. The President is referring to the statement he read at the beginning of his grand jury appearance.

422. Id. at 139-40 (emphasis added).

423. Id. at 141-42.

424. Two federal criminal statutes, Sections 1512 and 1503 of Title 18 of the United States Code, prohibit misleading potential witnesses with the intent to influence their grand jury testimony. Section 1512 provides that whoever "corruptly . . . engages in misleading conduct toward another person, with intent to — (1) influence, delay, or prevent the testimony of any person in an official proceeding . . . shall be fined under this title or imprisoned not more than ten years, or both." 18 U.S.C. ß 1512(b). It is no defense to a charge of witness tampering that the official proceeding had not yet begun, nor is it a defense that the testimony sought to be influenced turned out to be inadmissible or subject to a claim of privilege. 18 U.S.C. ß 1512(e).

Section 1503 provides that whoever "corruptly or by threats or force . . . influences, obstructs, or impedes or endeavors to influence, obstruct, or impede the due administration of justice" has committed a felony. 18 U.S.C. ß 1503(a)-(b).

The Governor of Guam was convicted of witness tampering for lying to a potential witness "intending that [the witness] would offer [the Governor's] explanation concerning the [illegally used] funds to the FBI." United States v. Bordallo, 857 F.2d 519, 525 (9th Cir. 1988), amended on other grounds, 872 F.2d 334 (9th Cir.), cert. denied, 493 U.S. 818 (1989).

425. Podesta 2/5/98 GJ at 13. Mr. Podesta has served as Deputy Chief of Staff since January 1997, and previously served as Staff Secretary for the Clinton Administration from 1993 through 1995. Podesta 2/5/98 GJ at 9-10.

426. Podesta 6/16/98 GJ at 84-85.

427. Id. at 85.

428. Id.

429. Id. at 92 (emphasis added).

430. Mr. Podesta dated this conversation as perhaps taking place on January 23, 1998. Podesta 6/16/98 GJ at 88.

431. Id. at 88.

432. Mr. Podesta testified that he was "sensitive about not exchanging information because I knew I was a potential witness." Podesta 6/23/98 GJ at 79.

433. Podesta 6/16/98 GJ at 94; see also Podesta 6/23/98 GJ at 79.

434. See id. at 79 (emphasis added).

435. Podesta 6/23/98 GJ at 77-78.

436. Bowles 4/2/98 GJ at 12. Mr. Bowles has been the Chief of Staff for President Clinton since January 20, 1997. Id.

437. Id. at 83-84 (emphasis added).

438. Id. at 91.

439. Blumenthal 2/26/98 GJ at 4-5.

440. Blumenthal 6/4/98 GJ at 46-53.

441. Blumenthal 6/4/98 GJ at 49 (emphasis added).

442. Blumenthal 6/25/98 GJ at 41.

443. Blumenthal 6/4/98 GJ at 50.

444. Blumenthal 6/25/98 GJ at 27.

445. Blumenthal 6/4/98 GJ at 52 (emphasis added).

446. Blumenthal 6/25/98 GJ at 17. See also Blumenthal 6/25/98 GJ at 26 ("My understanding was that the accusations against him which appeared in the press that day were false, that he had not done anything wrong").

447. Ickes 7/23/98 GJ at 8. Mr. Ickes worked as Deputy Chief of Staff for President Clinton from early 1994 through January 1997. Id.

448. Ickes 6/10/98 GJ at 21-22, 66 (meeting occurred on Monday following the week that the media first reported the Lewinsky story).

449. Ickes 6/10/98 GJ at 73 (emphasis added). See also Ickes 8/5/98 GJ at 88 ("[H]e denied to me that he had had a sexual relationship. I don't know the exact phrase, but the word 'sexual' was there. And he denied any obstruction of justice").

450. Ickes 6/10/98 GJ at 73.

451. Clinton 8/17/98 GJ at 105-109 (emphasis added).

452. Id. at 107.

453. 1512-DC-00000037.

454. Text of President's Address to Nation, reprinted in Washington Post, August 18, 1998, at A5.

455. Morris 8/18/98 GJ at 28.

456. Id. at 30.

457. Id. (emphasis added).

458. Id. at 35.

459. Televised Remarks by President Clinton at the White House Education News Conference, Monday, January 26, 1998, 10:17 a.m.

460. Other than Ms. Lewinsky's status and age, several aspects of the relationship could have raised public concerns.

First, Ms. Lewinsky lost her job at the White House in April 1996 and was transferred to the Pentagon. Under oath, Ms. Lewinsky was asked: "Do you believe that if you hadn't had a sexual relationship with the President that you would have kept your job at the White House?" She answered: "Yes." Lewinsky 8/26/98 Depo. at 60.

Second, Ms. Lewinsky was asked, "Do you believe that your difficulty or inability to return to employment at the White House was because of your sexual relationship with him?" She answered: "Yes. Or the issues that, or that the problems that people perceived that really were based in truth because I had a relationship with the President." Lewinsky 8/26/98 Depo. at 60.

Third, in late 1997, the President saw to it that Ms. Lewinsky received extraordinary job assistance. Such assistance might have been tied to her involvement in the Jones case, as discussed earlier, as well as a benefit to an ex-paramour. If the latter was a factor, then the President's actions discriminated against all of those interns and employees who did not receive the same benefit.

461. NBC News, "Today" Show, interview with Mrs. Clinton by Matt Lauer, Jan. 27, 1998, 1998 WL 5261146.

462. Associated Press, Jan. 27, 1998, 1998 WL 7380187.

463. Nightline, Jan. 26, 1998, 1998 WL 5372969.

464. Associated Press, Jan. 26, 1998.

465. Schmidt and Baker, Ex-Intern Rejected Immunity Offer in Probe, Washington Post, Jan. 24, 1998, at A1.

466. "The NewsHour with Jim Lehrer," PBS, Jan. 21, 1998, 1998 WL 8056086. The President stated later in the interview: "I'll do my best to help them get to the bottom of it."

467. All Things Considered, National Public Radio, Jan. 21, 1998, 1998 WL 3643482.

468. Roll Call Interview, Jan. 21, 1998, 1998 WL 5682372.

469. Lloyd N. Cutler, Legal Opinion of September 28, 1994.

470. Brief for President Clinton, filed June 15, 1998, at 30, In re Lindsey, 148 F.3d 1100 (D.C. Cir. 1998).

471. 418 U.S. 683 (1974).

472. Hernreich 2/25/98 GJ at 5-7.

473. Even though the White House later withdrew the claim, the mere assertion of Executive Privilege as to Ms. Hernreich is important. Such an invocation causes a needless, but substantial, expenditure of litigation resources and delays and impedes the grand jury process. The overuse of Executive Privilege against the United States in the criminal process thus ultimately hinders the faithful execution of the laws — as the Supreme Court unanimously recognized twenty-four years ago in United States v. Nixon.

474. In re Grand Jury Proceeding, 5 F. Supp. 2d 21 (D.D.C. 1998).

475. John F. Harris, Clinton Finds There's No Escape; In Africa, President Side-steps Executive Privilege Questions, Wash. Post, Mar. 25, 1998, at A2.

476. Declaration of Charles F.C. Ruff at ∂ 56 (Mar. 17, 1998).

477. Breuer 8/4/98 GJ at 96-97, 108-09.

478. In re Grand Jury Proceedings, Unpublished Order (under seal), August 11, 1998.

479. Mills 8/11/98 GJ at 53-54.

480. Id. at 53, 54, 64-66, 71-74, 77-78.

481. Clinton 8/17/98 GJ at 167 (emphasis added).

482. Lindsey 8/28/98 GJ at 58. The President's use and withdrawal of Executive Privilege was not new to this Office. In August 1996, the White House invoked Executive Privilege to prevent White House attorneys from producing documents regarding their communications with Hillary Rodham Clinton. After the OIC filed a motion to compel in the United States District Court for the Eastern District of Arkansas, the claim was withdrawn, and the White House relied solely on a claim of government attorney-client privilege, which the United States Court of Appeals for the Eighth Circuit rejected. The public never knew at that time of the President's assertion of Executive Privilege in that case.

In 1997, the President again asserted Executive Privilege — this time to prevent Thomas "Mack" McLarty from testifying fully. The conversations in question related in part to Mr. McLarty's efforts to find employment for Webster Hubbell as Mr. Hubbell was resigning his position as Associate Attorney General. The President withdrew the assertion before the OIC filed a motion to compel.

483. President Clinton's Motion for Continuance, filed July 28, 1998.

484. DeFrank, Prez Vows Cooperation Pledges Complete, Truthful Testimony, N.Y. Daily News, Aug. 1, 1998, at 3.

485. Clinton 8/17/98 GJ at 7.

486. Clinton 8/17/98 GJ at 10.

487. E.g., Clinton 8/17/98 GJ at 12, 102, 109, 110.

488. Text of President's Address to Nation, reprinted in Washington Post, August 18, 1998, at A5 (emphasis added).

489. Breuer 8/4/98 GJ at 96-97, 108-09.

490. In re Grand Jury Proceedings, Unpublished Order (under seal), August 11, 1998.

491. Mills 8/11/98 GJ at 53-54.

492. Id. at 53, 54, 64-66, 71-74, 77-78.

493. Clinton 8/17/98 GJ at 167 (emphasis added).

494. Lindsey 8/28/98 GJ at 58. The President's use and withdrawal of Executive Privilege was not new to this Office. In August 1996, the White House invoked Executive Privilege to prevent White House attorneys from producing documents regarding their communications with Hillary Rodham Clinton. After the OIC filed a motion to compel in the United States District Court for the Eastern District of Arkansas, the claim was withdrawn, and the White House relied solely on a claim of government attorney-client privilege, which the United States Court of Appeals for the Eighth Circuit rejected. The public never knew at that time of the President's assertion of Executive Privilege in that case.

In 1997, the President again asserted Executive Privilege — this time to prevent Thomas "Mack" McLarty from testifying fully. The conversations in question related in part to Mr. McLarty's efforts to find employment for Webster Hubbell as Mr. Hubbell was resigning his position as Associate Attorney General. The President withdrew the assertion before the OIC filed a motion to compel.

495. President Clinton's Motion for Continuance, filed July 28, 1998.

496. DeFrank, Prez Vows Cooperation Pledges Complete, Truthful Testimony, N.Y. Daily News, Aug. 1, 1998, at 3.

497. Clinton 8/17/98 GJ at 7.

498. Clinton 8/17/98 GJ at 10.

499. E.g., Clinton 8/17/98 GJ at 12, 102, 109, 110.

500. Text of President's Address to Nation, reprinted in Washington Post, August 18, 1998, at A5 (emphasis added).

PRELIMINARY MEMORANDUM CONCERNING REFERRAL OF OFFICE OF INDEPENDENT COUNSEL

PRELIMINARY MEMORANDUM CONCERNING REFERRAL OF OFFICE OF INDEPENDENT COUNSEL

David E. Kendall
Nicole K. Seligman
Emmet T. Flood
Max Stier
Glen Donath
Alicia L. Marti
WILLIAMS & CONNOLLY
725 12th Street, N.W.
Washington, DC 20005

Charles F.C. Ruff
Cheryl Mills
Lanny A. Breuer
OFFICE OF THE WHITE
HOUSE COUNSEL
The White House
Washington, DC 20005

September 11, 1998

EXECUTIVE SUMMARY

Summary of Key Points of the President's Case in Anticipation of the Starr Report

1. **The President has acknowledged a serious mistake**—an inappropriate relationship with Monica Lewinsky. He has taken responsibility for his actions, and he has apologized to the country, to his friends, leaders of his party, the cabinet and most importantly, his family.

2. **This private mistake does not amount to an impeachable action.** A relationship outside one's marriage is wrong—and the President admits that. It is not a high crime or misdemeanor. The Constitution specifically states that Congress shall impeach *only* for "treason, bribery or other high crimes and misdemeanors." These words in the Constitution were chosen with great care, and after extensive deliberations.

3. **"High crimes and misdemeanors" had a fixed meaning to the Framers of our Constitution—it meant wrongs committed against our system of government.** The impeachment clause was designed to protect our country against a President who was using his official powers against the nation, against the American people, against our society. It was never designed to allow a political body to force a President from office for a very personal mistake.

4. **Remember—this report is based entirely on allegations obtained by a grand jury**—reams and reams of allegations and purported "evidence" that would never be admitted in court, that has never been seen by the President or his lawyers, and that was not subject to cross-examination or any other traditional safeguards to ensure its credibility.

5. **Grand juries are not designed to search for truth.** They do not and are not intended to ensure credibility, reliability, or simple

fairness. They only exist to accuse. Yet this is the process that the Independent Counsel has chosen to provide the "evidence" to write his report.

6. **The law defines perjury very clearly.** Perjury requires proof that an individual knowingly made a false statement while under oath. Answers to questions that are literally true are *not* perjury. Even if an answer doesn't directly answer the question asked, it is not perjury if it is true—no accused has an obligation to help his accuser. Answers to fundamentally ambiguous questions also can never be perjury. And nobody can be convicted of perjury based on only one other person's testimony.

7. **The President did not commit perjury. Most of the illegal leaks suggesting his testimony was perjurious falsely describe his testimony.** First of all, the President never testified in the Jones deposition that he was not alone with Ms. Lewinsky. The President never testified that his relationship with Ms. Lewinsky was the same as with any other intern. To the contrary, he admitted exchanging gifts with her, knowing about her job search, receiving cards and notes from her, and knowing other details of her personal life that made it plain he had a special relationship with her.

8. **The President has admitted he had an improper sexual relationship with Ms. Lewinsky.** In a civil deposition, he gave narrow answers to ambiguous questions. As a matter of law, those answers could not give rise to a criminal charge of perjury. In the face of the President's admission of his relationship, the disclosure of lurid and salacious allegations can only be intended to humiliate the President and force him from office.

9. **There was no obstruction of justice. We believe *Betty Currie testified* that Ms. Lewinsky asked her to hold the gifts and that the President never talked to her about the gifts.** The President admitted giving and receiving gifts from Ms. Lewinsky when

he was asked about it. The President never asked Ms. Lewinsky to get rid of the gifts and he never asked Ms. Currie to get them. We believe that Ms. Currie's testimony supports the President's.

10. **The President never tried to get Ms. Lewinsky a job after she left the White House in order to influence her testimony in the Paula Jones case.** The President knew Ms. Lewinsky was unhappy in her Pentagon job after she left the White House and did ask the White House personnel office to treat her fairly in her job search. He never instructed anyone to hire her, or even indicated that he very much wanted it to happen. Ms. Lewinsky was never offered a job at the White House after she left—and it's pretty apparent that if the President had ordered it, she would have been.

11. **The President did not facilitate Ms. Lewinsky's interview with Bill Richardson, or her discussions with Vernon Jordan.** Betty Currie asked John Podesta if he could help her with her New York job search which led to an interview with Bill Richardson, and Ms. Currie also put her in touch with her longtime friend, Mr. Jordan. Mr. Jordan has made it clear that this is the case, and, as a private individual, he is free to offer job advice wherever he sees fit.

12. **There was no witness tampering. Betty Currie was not supposed to be a witness in the Paula Jones case.** If she was not called or going to be called, it was impossible for any conversations the President had with her to be witness tampering. The President testified that he did not in any way attempt to influence her recollection.

13. **There is no "talking points" smoking gun.** Numerous illegal leaks painted the mysterious talking points as the proof that the President or his staff attempted to suborn the perjury of Monica Lewinsky or Linda Tripp. The OIC's spokesman said that the "talking points" were the "key" to Starr even being

granted authority to investigate the President's private life. Yet in the end, Ms. Lewinsky has apparently admitted the talking points were written by her alone [or with Ms. Tripp's assistance], and the President was not asked one single question about them in his grand jury appearance.

14. **Invocation of privileges was not an abuse of power.** The President's lawful assertion of privileges in a court of law was only made on the advice of his Counsel, and was in significant measure *validated* by the courts. The legal claims were advanced sparingly and as a last resort after all attempts at compromise by the White House Counsel's office were rejected to protect the core constitutional and institutional interests of this and future presidencies.

15. **Neither the President nor the White House played a role in the Secret Service's lawful efforts to prevent agents from testifying to preserve its protective function.** The President never asked, directed or participated in any decision regarding the protective function privilege. Neither did any White House official. The Treasury and Justice Departments independently decided to respond to the historically unprecedented subpoenas of Secret Service personnel and to pursue the privilege to ensure the protection of this and future presidents.

16. **The President did not abuse his power by permitting White House staff to comment on the investigation.** The President has acknowledged misleading his family, staff and the country about the nature of his relationship with Ms. Lewinsky, and he has apologized and asked for forgiveness. However, this personal failing does not constitute a criminal abuse of power. If allowing aides to repeat misleading statements is a crime, then any number of public officials are guilty of misusing their office for as long as they fail to admit wrong doing in response to any allegation about their activities.

17. **The actions of White House attorneys were completely lawful.** The White House Counsel attorneys provided the President and White House officials with informed, candid advice on issues raised during this investigation that affected the President's official duties. This was especially necessary given the fact that impeachment proceedings against the President were a possible result of the OIC's investigation from Day One. In fact, throughout the investigation, the OIC *relied on* the White House Counsel's office for assistance in gathering information and arranging interviews and grand jury appearances. The Counsel's office's actions were well known to the OIC throughout the investigation and no objection was ever voiced.

This means that the OIC report is left with nothing but the details of a private sexual relationship, told in graphic details with the intent to embarrass. Given the flimsy and unsubstantiated basis for the accusations, there is a complete lack of any credible evidence to initiate an impeachment inquiry concerning the President. And the principal purpose of this investigation, and the OIC's report, is to embarrass the President and titillate the public by producing a document that is little more than an unreliable, one-sided account of sexual behavior.

Where's Whitewater? The OIC's allegations reportedly include *no* suggestion of wrongdoing by the President in any of the areas which Mr. Starr spend four years investigating: Whitewater, the FBI files and the White House travel office. What began as an inquiry into a 24 year old land deal in Arkansas has ended as an inquest into brief, improper personal encounters between the President and Monica Lewinsky. Despite the exhaustive nature of the OIC's investigation into the Whitewater, FBI files and travel office matters, and a constant stream of suggestions of misconduct in the media over a period of years, to this day the OIC has never exonerated the President or the First Lady of wrongdoing.

PRELIMINARY MEMORANDUM CONCERNING REFERRAL OF OFFICE OF INDEPENDENT COUNSEL

This document is intended to be a preliminary response to the Referral submitted by the Office of Independent Counsel to The Congress. Because we were denied the opportunity to review the content, nature or specifics of the allegations made against the President by the Office of Independent Counsel (OIC), we do not pretend to offer a point-by-point refutation of those allegations, or a comprehensive defense of the President.

We commend the House of Representatives for the extraordinary steps it has taken to safeguard the secrecy of the OIC's allegations. Unfortunately, its efforts were thwarted by unnamed sources familiar with the details of the OIC's allegations—sources that could only come from the OIC itself—who saw fit to leak elements of the allegations to the news media.

Based on these illegal leaks, as well as our knowledge of the President's testimony, we offer this document as a summary outline of his side of the case. We will provide you with a specific rebuttal as soon as we have had a chance to review the materials that the OIC has already transmitted to you.

The simple reality of this situation is that the House is being confronted with evidence of a man's efforts to keep an inappropriate relationship private. A personal failure that the President has acknowledged was wrong, for which he apologized, and for which he accepts complete responsibility. A personal failure for which the President has sought forgiveness from members of his family, members of the Cabinet, Members of Congress, and the American people. Such a personal failing does not, however, constitute "treason, bribery and high crimes and misdemeanors" that would justify the impeachment of the President of the United States.

The President himself has described his conduct as wrong. But no amount of gratuitous details about the President's relationship with Ms. Lewinsky, no matter how salacious, can alter the fact that:

1) The President did not commit perjury:

2) The President did not obstruct justice;

3) The President did not tamper with witnesses; and

4) The President did not abuse the power of his office.

Impeachment is a matter of incomparable gravity. Even to discuss it is to discuss overturning the electoral will of the people. For this reason, the Framers made clear, and scholars have long agreed, that the power should be exercised only in the event of such grave harms to the state as "serious assaults on the integrity of the processes of government," or "such crimes as would so stain a president as to make his continuance in office dangerous to public order." Charles L. Black, *Impeachment: A Handbook* 38-39 (1974). We do not believe the OIC can identify any conduct remotely approaching this standard. Instead, from press reports, if true, it appears that the OIC has dangerously overreached to describe in the most dramatic of terms conduct that not only is not criminal but is actually proper and lawful.

The President has confessed to indiscretions with Ms. Lewinsky and accepted responsibility and blame. The allegations concerning obstruction, intimidation, perjury and subornation of perjury that we anticipate from the OIC are extravagant attempts to transform a case involving inappropriate personal behavior into one of public misconduct justifying reversal of the judgment of the electorate of this country.

I. STANDARDS FOR IMPEACHMENT

The Constitution provides that the President shall be removed from office only upon "Impeachment for, and Conviction of, Treason, Bribery, or other high Crimes and Misdemeanors." U.S. Const. Art. II, § 4. Of course, there is no suggestion of treason or bribery

present here. Therefore, the question confronting the House of Representatives is whether the President has committed a "high Crime[]
or Misdemeanor." The House has an obligation to consider the evidence in view of that very high Constitutional threshold. It should
pursue the impeachment process only if there is evidence implicating that high standard.

The House must approach the question with solemnity and with
care, for history teaches that an "impeachable offense" is no ordinary kind of wrongdoing. The Framers included specific provisions
for impeachment in the Constitution itself because they understood
that the most severe political remedy was necessary to remedy the
most serious forms of public wrongdoing. Impeachment is a basic
constitutional safeguard, designed both to correct harms to the system of government itself and to protect the people from ongoing
malfeasance. Nothing less than the gravest executive wrongdoing
can justify impeachment. The Constitution leaves lesser wrongs to
the political process and to public opinion.

Presidential impeachment is thus a matter of incomparable gravity. As Professor Charles Black stated,

> [t]he presidency is a prime symbol of our national unity. The elec-
> tion of the president (with his alternate, the vice-president) is the
> only political act that we perform together as a nation; voting in
> the presidential election is certainly the political choice most signif-
> icant to the American people, and the most closely attended to by
> them. No matter, then, can be of higher political importance than
> our considering whether, in any given instance, this act of choice is
> to be undone, and the chosen president dismissed from office in
> disgrace. Everyone must shrink from this most drastic of measures.

Impeachment: A Handbook 1 (1974). Presidential impeachment
is thus an "awful step." *Ibid.* The Framers knew this. For that reason they framed the constitutional procedure with precision and
specified grounds for impeachment with great care.

The Framers deliberately chose to make "high Crimes and Misdemeanors" the standard of an impeachable offense. They were

familiar with English common law and parliamentary history and they borrowed the expression directly from the English law of impeachment. They did so knowing that the expression was a term of art and they made the choice after deliberate rejection of alternative formulations of the impeachment standard.

The Framers intended the standard to be a high one. They rejected a proposal that the President be impeachable for "maladministration," for, as James Madison pointed out, such a standard would "be equivalent to a tenure during the pleasure of the Senate."[1] The Framers plainly did not intend to permit Congress to debilitate the executive by authorizing impeachment for something short of the most serious harm to the state. In George Mason's apt phrase, impeachment was thought necessary to remedy "[a]ttempts to subvert the Constitution."

In English practice, the term "high crimes and misdemeanors" had been applied to various offenses, the common elements of which were their severity and the fact that the wrongdoing was directed against the state.[2] The English cases included misappropriation of public funds, interfering in elections, accepting bribes, neglect of duty, and various forms of corruption. *Ibid*. These offenses all affected the discharge of public duties by public officials. In short, under the English practice, "the critical element of injury in an impeachable offense was *injury to the state*."[3]

That is why, at the time of the ratification debates, Alexander Hamilton described impeachment as a "method of NATIONAL INQUEST into the conduct of public men." The Federalist No. 65 at 331 (Gary Wills ed. 1982). This "inquest" is perhaps the gravest process known to our Constitution. No act touches more fundamental questions of constitutional government than does the process of Presidential impeachment. No act more directly affects the public interest. No act presents the potential for greater injustice—injustice both to the Chief Executive and to the people who elected him.

For these reasons, the impeachment process must be painstaking and deliberate. It must focus only on such harms as the Framers intended to be redressed by the incomparably severe act of impeachment. And most importantly, it must be understood for what it is—a process of inquiry. That process is itself the exercise of a public trust "of delicacy and magnitude."[4] Accordingly, if the process is begun it is only just that the members engaged in this solemn task withhold judgment until the process is complete and all the facts are known. Our Constitution's most basic values and the requirements of simple justice together demand no less.

The President is sole head of one branch of our government—indeed, in a certain sense the President *is* the Executive Branch. The Constitution provides that "[t]he executive Power shall be vested in a President of the United States of America." U.S. Const. art. II, § 1. The President is the only government official to have been popularly elected by all the American people. When the people elect a President, the popular will is expressed in its most important, most visible and most unmistakable form.[5] The impeachment process, by definition, threatens to undo the popular will. Impeachment presents the prospect of reversing the electoral mandate that brought the executive to office. Conviction upon articles of impeachment actually does so.

For these reasons, impeachment is limited to only certain forms of potential wrongdoing and it is intended to redress only certain kinds of harms. Again, in Hamilton's words:

> the subjects of [the Senate's impeachment] jurisdiction are those offenses which proceed from the misconduct of public men, or in other words from the abuse of violation of some public trust. They are of a nature which may with peculiar propriety be denominated POLITICAL, as they relate chiefly to injuries done to the society itself.

Federalist 65 at 330-31.

The Framers and early commentators on the Constitution are in accord on the question of impeachment's intended consequence. In Justice James Wilson's words, impeachments are "proceedings of a political nature . . . confined to political characters" charging only "political crimes and misdemeanors" and culminating only in "political punishments." J. Wilson, *Works* 426 (R. McCloskey, ed. 1967) And as Justice Story put the matter, "the [impeachment] power partakes of a political character, as it respects injuries to the society in its political character." Joseph Story, *Commentaries on the Constitution* § 744 (1st Ed. 1833).[6] That understanding of the Framers and early commentators reflected the historical understanding of impeachable offenses in England. "'High crimes and misdemeanors' were a category of *political* crimes against the state." Berger, *Impeachment,* at 61 (emphasis in original). Therefore, the Framers "intended that a president be removable from office for the commission of *great offenses against the Constitution.*"[7]

"Impeachment therefore addresses public wrongdoing, whether denominated a "political crime[] against the state,"[8] or "an act of malfeasance or abuse of office,"[9] or a "great offense[s] against the federal government."[10] In short, impeachment is a necessary Constitutional check by a coordinate branch of government upon serious and aggravated abuses of executive power that, given the President's four-year term, might otherwise go unchecked.

Holders of public office are therefore not to be impeached for private conduct, however wrongful. To the contrary, only "serious assaults on the integrity of the processes of government,"[11] and "such crimes as would so stain a president as to make his continuance in office dangerous to public order"[12] should constitute impeachable offenses. Conduct which is not an "offense[] against the government,"[13] or "malfeasance or abuse of office,"[14] and which bears no "functional relationship"[15] to public office, does not constitute grounds for impeachment. Allegations concerning private conduct—private sexual conduct in particular—simply do not implicate high crimes or misdemeanors.

Private misconduct, or even public misconduct short of an offense against the state, is not redressable by impeachment because that solemn process, in Justice Story's words, addresses "offences[] which are committed by public men *in violation of their public trust and duties."* Story, *Commentaries* § 744 (emphasis added). Impeachment is a political act in the sense that its aims are public; it attempts to rein in abuses of the public trust committed by public officeholders in connection with conduct in public office. As one scholar has put it, "[t]he nature of [impeachment] proceedings is dictated by the harms sought to be redressed—"the misconduct of public men" relating to the conduct of their public office—and the ultimate issue to be resolved—whether they have forfeited through that conduct their right to continued public trust."[16]

Impeachment's public character is further evidenced by the fact that, as Justice Story expressed it, the process is conducted "by the representatives of the nation, in their public capacity," and "in the face of the nation." Story, *Commentaries* § 686. Constitutionally, impeachment's public function demands public accountability. Elected officials are no more qualified than ordinary voters to assess the private wrongs of public officeholders. The Constitution's impeachment mechanism does not exist to punish such wrongs.

The public character of impeachable wrongs is also reflected in the fact that the remedy imposed for commission of impeachable acts is a wholly public one. Impeachment results in removal from office and possible disqualification from further office. U.S. Const. art.I, § 3, cl. 7.

To say that impeachment is fundamentally a "political" process, however, is not to say that it is "partisan" in nature. Indeed, the Framers warned against the spirit of partisanship in impeachment proceedings. In Federalist 65, Hamilton wrote that the impeachment process threatened to "agitate the passions of the whole community . . .to divide it into parties . . . [to] connect itself with pre-existing factions [and] to enlist their animosities, partialities, influence and interest." *Id.* at 331. Justice Story warned of the danger that "the decision [to impeach] will be regulated more by the comparative strength of the parties, than by the strength of the proofs." Commentaries § 744. Only substantial evidence of presidential wrongdoing that threatened the processes of government or the public order can justify this grave and ideally bipartisan process.

What is ultimately intended by impeachment's truly "political" nature is the manner of limitation the Constitution allows one elected (political) branch to place on the other elected (political) branch, the Presidency. Impeachment is necessarily a *public* act conducted by public bodies (the Houses of Congress exercising their constitutionally allotted portion of impeachment power) against a public officeholder (here, the President). Exercise of that limiting function is justified only when the people's representatives conclude that the people themselves must be protected from their own elected executive.

Impeachment must therefore be approached with the utmost solemnity. The process must focus on public acts, performed in the President's public capacity, and affecting the public interest. Cognizant of the enormous harm that must follow the bare suggestion of formal impeachment processes, the House should pursue an impeachment inquiry if and only if there is credible evidence of actions constituting fundamental injuries to the governmental process. Indeed, the Committee should consider and approve articles of impeachment *only* for such acts as have, in its judgment, so seriously threatened the integrity of governmental processes as to have made the President's continuation in office a threat to the public order.

Impropriety falling short of that high standard does not meet the constitutional measure. It must be left to the court of public opinion and the judgment of history.

II. THE RELEVANT FACTUAL BACKGROUND

The Monica Lewinsky investigation is the most recent phase of an amorphous, languorous, expensive, and seemingly interminable investigation into the affairs of a small Arkansas real estate firm, Whitewater Development Company, Inc. In January, 1994, Attorney General Reno made an administrative appointment (the Ethics in Government Act of 1978 having expired) of Robert B. Fiske, Jr., to investigate the relationship of the President and Mrs. Clinton to Whitewater, Madison Guaranty Savings & Loan Association, and

Capital Management Services. After the reenactment of the Ethics in Government Act, the Special Division for the Purpose of Appointing Independent Counsels of the Court of Appeals appointed Kenneth W. Starr, a former high official in two Republican administrations, to replace Mr. Fiske on August 5, 1994, and gave him a generally similar grant of investigatory jurisdiction.

During the past four and a half years, the President has cooperated extensively with this investigation. He has given testimony by deposition at the White House to the Independent Counsel on four separate occasions, and on two other occasions, he gave videotaped deposition testimony for Whitewater defendants and was cross-examined by the Independent Counsel. He has submitted written interrogatory answers, produced more than 90,000 pages of documents and other items, and provided information informally in a variety of ways. The OIC subpoenaed from the President, and reviewed, virtually *every* personal financial record and gubernatorial campaign finance record that exists for the period from the mid-1980s to the present, in its endless search to find something to use against the President. This comprehensive and thorough financial review yielded the OIC nothing.

In May 1994, President Clinton was sued civilly by Ms. Paula Jones, who made various claims arising out of an encounter on May 8, 1991, when the President was Governor of Arkansas. Various constitutional questions were litigated, and it was not until the Supreme Court's decision on May 27, 1997[17] that the case proceeded to discovery. The Independent Counsel had no jurisdiction with respect to the *Jones* case, but there were occasional press reports that the OIC was in fact investigating the President's personal life.[18]

III. THE PRESIDENT'S TESTIMONY ABOUT MS. LEWINSKY

In his grand jury testimony on August 17, 1998, the President acknowledged having had an improperly intimate relationship with Ms. Lewinsky. This is enormously difficult for any person to do even in private, much less in public.

It is important to recognize that the improper relationship with Ms. Lewinsky *ended* in early 1997, at the President's behest. It therefore had been over for almost a year at the time of the President's deposition in the *Jones* case. From feelings both of friendship and responsibility, the President remained in touch with Ms. Lewinsky after the improper relationship ended and tried to help her: none of this help was improper or conditioned on her behaving (or testifying) in any particular way.

It is not true that the President had an improper 18-month relationship with Ms. Lewinsky, as several media reports have alleged. In his grand jury deposition, he testified that on certain occasions in early 1996 and once in early 1997, he engaged in improper conduct with Ms. Lewinsky. These encounters did not consist of sexual intercourse, and they did not consist of "sexual relations" as he understood that term to be defined at his *Jones* deposition on January 17, 1998 (explained *infra*), but they did involve inappropriate intimate contact. These inappropriate encounters ended, at the President's insistence, in early 1997, not because of the imminence of discovery, not because of the *Jones* case (which the Supreme Court had not yet decided), but because he knew they were *wrong*. On August 17, 1998, the President expressed regret to the grand jury and, later, to the country, that what began as a friendship came to include this conduct, and he took full responsibility. He has frequently, to different audiences, made similar expressions of regret and apology.

In this investigation, no stone has been left unturned—or (we believe) unthrown. In simple fairness, therefore, it is important to distinguish between what the President has acknowledged and what the OIC merely alleges (on the basis of evidence we have not yet seen).

IV. THE NATURE OF THE OIC'S EVIDENCE

Use of a federal grand jury to compile evidence for possible impeachment proceedings in Congress raises numerous troubling questions regarding the credibility of that evidence. Indeed, given the limited role of a grand jury in our system and the total absence of procedural protections in the process, the Independent Counsel's insistence that his investigation has been a search for "truth" is deeply misleading. In fact, it has been a one-sided effort to present the worst possible version of a limited set of facts.

Section 595(c) requires the OIC to provide the House with "substantial and credible information . . . that may constitute grounds for impeachment." But a grand jury is a totally unsuitable vehicle for generating information that can, without more, be taken as credible beyond challenge. The grand jury's historic role is not to determine the truth but rather to act as an accusatory body. *United States v. Williams*, 504 U.S. 36, 51 (1992). The process excludes contrary views of the information gathered and fails to identify the kinds of exculpatory information that might have been elicited or presented had a targeted individual, and not just the OIC, had an opportunity to cross-examine and the ability to compel responses.

Because it is inherently so one-sided and untested by cross-examination, it normally is not permissible to use grand jury testimony as a basis for anything other than permitting a grand jury to indict or decline to indict. It may constitute nothing more than hearsay, *Costello v. United States*, 350 U.S. 359, 364 (1956), or even multiple hearsay—evidence which would likely be excluded from a trial. Indeed, the information a grand jury gathers is not circumscribed by the Federal Rules of Evidence at all, *see* Fed. R. Evid. 1101(d)(2), nor delimited by the other safeguards of reliability which would be enforced at trial. The testimony a grand jury elicits is not subject to impeachment by interested parties, and such testimony may come from immunized witnesses, from witnesses who fear prosecution, from witnesses prepared by the prosecution, from witnesses with a history of untruthfulness—or from disinterested witnesses. On the record of the grand jury there need be no distinction among these sources, despite the fact that their reliability varies greatly.

In its day-to-day operations, no judge presides over grand jury proceedings. *United States v. Williams*, 504 U.S. 36, 48 (1992). Grand jury witnesses do not have counsel present. Fed. R. Crim P. 6(d). The Double Jeopardy Clause does not prevent a grand jury from returning an indictment after a first grand jury has declined to do so. *Ex Parte United States,* 287 U.S. 241, 250-51 (1932). The exclusionary rule does not apply to grand jury proceedings. *United States v. Calandra,* 414 U.S. 338, 349 (1974). Grand jury witnesses have no right to respond with information, however related, if it is not called for by the prosecution, and targets and subjects of its inquiry have no compulsory process to gather and present their side of the matter. Nor does the target of a grand jury inquiry have any right to offset potentially incriminating information with exculpatory information in his possession. *Williams,* 504 U.S. at 55. In short, the most basic techniques our adversary system of justice employs for testing and assuring the reliability of evidence are completely missing in the grand jury context.

As a consequence, "reliability" simply is not the touchstone of a grand-jury inquiry. The Supreme Court itself has said that "the mere fact that evidence is unreliable is not sufficient to require a dismissal of [an] indictment." *Bank of Nova Scotia v. United States,* 487 U.S. 250, 261 (1988). The same is true of "inadequate or incompetent" evidence. Its presence will not justify dismissal of an indictment. *Calandra,* 414 U.S. at 345; *see also Holt v. United States,* 218 U.S. 245 (1910) (same).

It must therefore be recognized that it is not the grand jury's function to provide information about anything that can be taken as true on its face. Its function is not to get at the ultimate truth. The grand jury's inquisitorial powers serve but one end: to empower a body of citizens to make a threshold decision whether to initiate the search for truth that is the purpose of adversarial proceedings or to decline to indict and thereby forego that search altogether. Only after the grand jury renders that threshold decision does the search for truth really commence because only then are the adversary system's credibility-assessing mechanisms available.

The grand jury secrecy rule, Rule 6(e), Fed. R. Crim. P., is justified—indeed, mandated—by this reality. Grand jury information is to be kept secret largely because it has been generated without the protections of the adversarial system. Unlike information presented

in a trial setting, grand jury information presents an enormous risk
that persons' reputations will be injured or destroyed on the basis of
non-credible or insubstantial assertions. That harm may damage
both witnesses and persons who are subjects of witness testimony.
That is why, when a grand jury elects to indict, grand jury materials
are sealed and withheld from the petit jury ultimately convened to
find the truth and render a verdict.

Accordingly a fair report from the OIC would, *inter alia*, provide
all exculpatory evidence, assess the credibility of witnesses in terms
of bias, reason to falsify, prior inconsistent statements, etc., and
draw reasonable inferences. A fair report would identify shortcom-
ings in the investigation itself, including any excesses, mistakes,
errors in judgment, or impermissible tactics. A fair report would
demonstrate that every possible effort had been made to identify all
possibly exculpatory evidence, and that all such evidence had been
given appropriate weight. And a fair report would address honestly
and answer truthfully the following questions:

1) What were Linda Tripp's motives in seeking out the OIC in
   January, 1998? Did she articulate a fear of being prosecuted in
   Maryland under that State's anti-taping laws? Why did she
   request immunity from prosecution? Why was she given
   immunity?

2) What role did the OIC play in arranging for Ms. Tripp to meet
   with the *Jones* lawyers on Friday, January 16, 1998, the
   evening before the President's deposition? Did anyone from
   the OIC drive Ms. Tripp to this meeting? Did the OIC warn
   Ms. Tripp about the criminal law pertaining to sharing with
   third parties the fruits of illegal tapings or even communicat-
   ing the fact that illegal tapes exist? Has anyone at the OIC
   made any assessment of what impact Ms. Tripp's conduct
   might have on any federal immunity deal Ms. Tripp might
   have obtained from the OIC?

3) What authority did the OIC have to wire Linda Tripp and
   attempt to develop evidence *before* obtaining permission to

expand its jurisdiction from the Attorney General or the Special Division? What prevented the OIC from going directly to the Attorney General upon receiving the tapes from Ms. Tripp? If the primary basis for the expansion of the OIC's jurisdiction was evidence that was obtained in an *ultra vires* manner by the OIC, does that taint other information obtained by the OIC?

4) What assessment has the OIC made of Ms. Tripp's ideological motivations? Was the OIC aware she had submitted an anti-Clinton book proposal to avowed Clinton hater Lucianne Goldberg? Was the OIC aware of Goldberg's role in Ms. Tripp's taping and arrangement for Ms. Lewinsky's use of a messenger service?

5) How many statements on the Tripp-Lewinsky tapes are false or exaggerated? How many statements contradict assertions in the OIC's report?

6) When Ms. Tripp was asked to record Ms. Lewinsky surreptitiously, was this because the OIC was concerned about the legality of Ms. Tripp's previous telephone tapes of Ms. Lewinsky?

7) What was Ms. Tripp's motivation in initiating the surreptitious recording of her conversations with Ms. Lewinsky? Did Tripp steer the taped conversations with Ms. Lewinsky to obtain details about Ms. Lewinsky's sexual activities? Was the taping connected in any way to her relationship with Lucianne Goldberg? If Ms. Tripp began to tape Ms. Lewinsky with an unlawful purpose, did she commit a violation of the federal wiretapping statute (Title III)? If the tapes were obtained in violation of federal law, can the tapes or evidence derived from them be part of any official proceeding in Congress (*see* 18 U.S.C. § 2515)?

8) What, if anything, did the OIC offer the press to keep secret its investigation into Ms. Lewinsky?

9) Why was the OIC in such haste to petition the Attorney General for an expansion of jurisdiction? Precisely what was the Attorney General told about Ms. Tripp's telephone taping of Ms. Lewinsky? Did the "talking points" play any role in the application? What particular alleged crimes did the OIC seek authorization to investigate?

10) Ms. Lewinsky's lawyers, William Ginsburg and Nathaniel Speights, wrote in an essay in *Time* (Feb. 16, 1998) that the OIC informed them on Friday, January 16, 1998, "We've got a deal, and we want to wire her and record some phone calls;" these lawyers also wrote in that essay that "[The OIC] wanted her [Ms. Lewinsky] wired, and they wanted her to record telephone calls with the President of the U.S., Vernon Jordan and others—at their will." What persons did the OIC intend Ms. Lewinsky to record surreptitiously?

11) In a letter from the Independent Counsel to the President's personal counsel, dated February 6, 1998, the Independent Counsel wrote: "From the beginning, I have made the prohibition of leaks a principal priority of the Office. It is a firing offense, as well as one that leads to criminal prosecution." However, Chief Judge Johnson has entered a series of orders finding *prima facie* reason to believe that persons in the OIC violated Rule 6(e), Fed. R. Crim. P., by illegal leaking (for example, "[t]he Court finds that the serious and repetitive nature of disclosures to the media of Rule 6(e) material strongly militates in favor of conducting a show cause hearing" (June 19, 1998, Order, at 5)). Has anyone been fired or disciplined by the OIC for illegal leaking? What steps have been taken to investigate and discipline OIC personnel who have engaged in illegal leaking?

V. LIKELY OIC ALLEGATIONS OF OBSTRUCTION OF JUSTICE, SUBORNATION OF PERJURY, AND INTIMIDATION OF WITNESSES

The OIC obtained jurisdiction on January 16, 1998 to investigate possible obstruction of justice, subornation of perjury, and intimidation of witnesses in the *Jones* case. These crimes are quite specifically defined in the law, and the elements do not always have an obvious meaning. We consider first the definition and then the possible conduct to which these definitions might be applied.

The term "obstruction of justice" usually refers to violations of 18 U.S.C. § 1503, the "Omnibus Obstruction Provision," which prohibits the intimidation and retaliation against grand and petit jurors and judicial officers and contains a catch-all clause making it unlawful to "influence, obstruct, or impede the due administration of justice." It may also refer to 18 U.S.C. § 1512, which proscribes intimidating, threatening, or corruptly persuading, through deceptive conduct, a person in connection with an official proceeding.

For a conviction under § 1503, the government must prove that there was a pending judicial proceeding, that the defendant knew of the proceeding, and that the defendant acted "corruptly" with the specific intent to obstruct or interfere with the proceeding or due administration of justice. *See, e.g., United States v. Bucey,* 876 F.2d 1297, 1314 (7th Cir. 1989); *United States v. Smith,* 729 F. Supp. 1380, 1383-84 (D.D.C. 1990). Thus, if a defendant is unaware of a pending grand jury proceeding, he cannot be said to have obstructed it in violation of § 1503. *See, e.g., United States v. Brown,* 688 F.2d 1391, 1400 (9th Cir. 1992). Perhaps more significant is the "acting corruptly" element of the offense. Some courts have defined this term as acting with "evil and wicked purposes." *See United States v. Banks,* 942 F.2d 1576, 1578 (11th Cir. 1991). Four federal courts of appeals have held that to "act corruptly" under the statute, a defendant must have acted with the specific intent to obstruct justice. *See United States v. Moon,* 718 F.2d 1219, 1236 (2d Cir. 1983); *United States v.*

Bashaw, 982 F.2d 168, 170 (6th Cir. 1992); *United States v. Anderson,* 798 F.2d 919, 928 (7th Cir, 1986); *United States v. Rasheed,* 663 F.2d 843, 847 (9th Cir. 1981). That is, it is not enough to prove that the defendant knew that a result of his actions might be to impede the administration of justice, if that was not his intent.

It is critical to note which actions cannot fall under the ambit of § 1503. First, false statements or testimony alone *cannot* sustain a conviction under § 1503. *See United States v. Thomas,* 916, F.2d 647, 652 (11th Cir. 1990); *United States v. Rankin,* 870 F.2d 109, 111 (3d Cir. 1989). For instance, in *United States v. Wood,* 6 F.3d 692, 697 (10th Cir. 1993), the United States Court of Appeals for the Tenth Circuit found that a defendant's false statements to the Federal Bureau of Investigation during a grand jury investigation did not violate § 1503, because they did not have the natural and probable effect of impeding the due administration of justice. Moreover, § 1503 does *not* apply to a party's concealing or withholding discoverable documents in *civil* litigation. *See, e.g., Richmark v. Timber Falling Consultants,* 730 F. Supp. 1525, 1532 (D. Or. 1990) (because of the remedies afforded by the Federal Rules of Civil Procedure, § 1503 does not cover party discovery in civil cases, and "[t]he parties have not cited and the court has not found any case in which a person was charged with obstruction of justice for concealing or withholding discovery in a civil case").[19] Most cases that have found § 1503 applicable to civil cases do not involve the production or withholding of documents. *See United States v. London,* 714 F.2d 1558 (11th Cir. 1983) (attorney forged court order and attempted to enforce it), *cited in Richmark,* 730 F. Supp. at 1532; *Sneed v. United States,* 298 F. 911 (5th Cir. 1924) (influencing juror in civil case); *cited in Richmark,* 730 F. Supp at 1532. While § 1503 can apply to concealment of subpoenaed documents in a grand jury investigation, the defendant must have knowledge of the pending grand jury investigation, must know that the particular documents are covered by a subpoena, and must willfully conceal or endeavor to conceal them from the grand jury with the specific intent to interfere with its investigation. *See United States v. McComb,* 744 F.2d 555 (7th Cir. 1984).

Section 1512 specifically applies to "witness tampering." However, by its terms, it does not purport to reach all forms of witness tampering, but only tampering by specified means. In order to obtain a conviction under § 1512, the government must prove that a defendant knowingly engaged in intimidation, physical force, threats, misleading conduct, or corrupt persuasion with intent to influence, delay, or prevent testimony or cause any person to withhold objects or documents from an official proceeding. While there is no "pending proceeding" requirement for convictions under § 1512, it is clear that a defendant must be aware of the possibility of a proceeding and his efforts must be aimed specifically at obstructing that proceeding, whether pending or not; § 1512 does not apply to defendants' innocent remarks or other acts unintended to affect a proceeding. *See United States v. Wilson,* 565 F. Supp. 1416, 1431 (S.D.N.Y. 1983).

Moreover, it is important to define the terms "corruptly persuade" and "misleading conduct," as used in § 1512. The statute itself explains that "corruptly persuades" does not include "conduct which would be misleading conduct but for a lack of a state of mind." 18 U.S.C. § 1515(a)(6). It is also clear from the caselaw that "misleading conduct" does not cover scenarios where the defendant urged a witness to give false testimony without resorting to coercive or deceptive conduct. See, *e.g., United States v. Kulczyk,* 931 F.2d 542, 547 (9th Cir. 1991) (no attempt to mislead witnesses knew defendant was asking them to lie); *United States v. King,* 762 F.2d 232, 237 (2d Cir. 1985) (defendant who attempts to persuade witness to lie but not to mislead trier of fact does not violate § 1512).

Subornation of perjury is addressed in 18 U.S.C. § 1622. The elements of subornation are that the defendant must have persuaded another to perjure himself, and the witness must have actually committed perjury. See, *e.g. United States v. Hairston,* 46 F.3d 361, 376 (4th Cir. 1959), *rev'd on other grounds,* 361 U.S. 529 (1960). If actual perjury does not occur, there is simply no subornation. *See id.*

at 376 (reversing conviction for subornation because of conclusion that, in applying *Bronston*, witness did not commit perjury due to his literally truthful testimony). Moreover, § 1622 requires that the defendant know that the testimony of witness will be perjurious—*i.e.*, knowing and willful procurement of false testimony is a key element of subornation of perjury. *See Rosen v. NLRB*, 735 F.2d 564, 575 n.19 (D.C. Cir. 1984) ("a necessary predicate of the charge of subornation of perjury is the suborner's belief that the testimony sought is in fact false").

Based upon illegal OIC leaks and press reports, we believe that the OIC's principal claims of obstruction, intimidation and subornation—the three prongs of the January 1998 expansion of jurisdiction—appear to arise out of:

(1) "TALKING POINTS"

The so-called "talking points"[20] have been widely hailed as the linchpin of any charge of subornation of perjury or obstruction of justice. Not only were they touted as the "smoking gun" of the investigation, they were instrumental in the OIC efforts to secure an expansion of its jurisdictional authority. Charles Bakaly, the OIC spokesman, appearing on Meet the Press, emphasized the critical nature of this document to the expansion of the OIC jurisdiction:

> Tim Russert: . . . How important is it that we find out who is the author of those talking points?

> Charles Bakaly: Well, in the grant of jurisdiction that the special division of the D.C. Circuit Court of Appeals gave to Judge Starr after the request of the Attorney General, *that was the key mandate to look into,* those kinds of issues of subornation of perjury and obstruction of justice.

NBC Meet the Press, July 5, 1998 (emphasis added).

The "talking points" were the basis of thinly veiled smears, groundless speculation, and allegations against President Clinton, White House aides and others close to the President:

"And NBC News has learned more about another critical piece of evidence. A memo first discovered by Newsweek that Linda Tripp claims was given to her by Monica Lewinsky. ° *Sources in Starr's office* and close to Linda Tripp *say they believe the instructions came from the White House.* If true, that could help support a case of obstruction of justice." NBC Nightly News, February 4, 1998.

"Prosecutors suspect the President and his longtime friend, Vernon Jordan, tried to cover up allegations that Mr. Clinton was involved sexually with former White House intern Monica Lewinsky and other women - which is why this document, obtained last night by NBC News, could be a smoking gun. It's called 'Points to Make in Affidavit.' Prosecutors say it might as well be called 'How to Commit Perjury in the Paula Jones Case.'" NBC News at Sunrise, January 22, 1998.

"A three page summary telling Linda R. Tripp how to lie in the Paula Jones sexual misconduct lawsuit remains a key reason why independent counsel Kenneth Starr wants to question top White House aides in the Monica Lewinsky sex-and-lies grand jury investigation. Mr. Starr, according to lawyers and other close to the grand jury probe, wants to know what White House Deputy Counsel Bruce R. Lindsey and senior aide Sidney Blumenthal know about the source of the summary, or 'talking points,' that were given to Mrs. Tripp by Miss Lewinsky, the former White House intern. The summary, which prosecutors are convinced was not written by Miss Lewinsky, could corroborate accusations of a White House attempt to obstruct justice and suborn perjury in the Jones suit, sources said." Washington Times, May 18, 1998.

"Because of Lindsey's earlier discussions with Tripp about the Willey incident, prosecutors appear to be trying to learn whether he had any role in helping Lewinsky prepare the three-page document. Lindsey, who has been summoned to the grand jury twice, has denied any connection to the talking points." Washington Post, March 10, 1998.

"'If the author of the talking points is anywhere near the president,' said Jonathan Turley, law professor at George Washington University in Washington, 'this case will take a dramatic turn against the White House.'" USA Today, July 1, 1998.

"The document has emerged as possible evidence of obstruction of justice as Starr investigates whether Clinton or his associates made attempts to conceal the president's encounters with women." USA Today, June 29, 1998.

"Based largely on two pieces of evidence—those talking points and the secret tapes made by Ms. Tripp of her conversations with Ms. Lewinsky—Mr. Starr is trying to determine whether the President, Mr. Jordan, Ms. Lewinsky or others set about to obstruct justice in the Jones case by lying, concealing evidence and tampering with witnesses. These are the central charges in the case, and the participants' versions appear to diverge." New York Times, March 7, 1998.

"Starr wants to find out if anyone in the White House was involved in preparing the talking points." The Plain Dealer, February 19, 1998.

"The evidence that strikes dread in the White House is a three-page document called 'the talking points. . . . The author of the talking points will most likely be found, is in real danger of going to jail and may not want to go alone for long." William Safire, New York Times, February 12, 1998.

"The memo is a critical piece of evidence to Whitewater independent counsel Kenneth Starr because it could be proof of an effort to induce Tripp to lie under oath. Starr's investigators are exploring whether anyone close to Clinton prepared or knew about the talking points." USA Today, February 6, 1998.

And the "talking points" were regarded throughout the investigation as the critical piece of evidence in any charge of subornation of perjury or obstruction of justice:

"It seems clear that Starr's focus is now on building a case that Clinton or his agents tried to sway the testimony of witnesses in the Jones case. A critical piece of evidence is the 'talking points' memo that Lewinsky gave her friend Linda Tripp, apparently advising Tripp on how to fudge her testimony. *The document is the only known physical evidence of witness tampering,* and its authorship remains one of the great mysteries of the Lewinsky matter." Chicago Tribune, April 3, 1998 (emphasis added).

"The talking points, which seemed intended to coach Ms. Tripp in possible testimony about Mr. Clinton, are central to Mr. Starr's effort to determine whether obstruction of justice occurred." New York Times, July 27, 1998.

"Prosecutors regard the legalistic, three-page talking points—intended to guide Tripp's testimony in the Jones lawsuit—as a key piece of evidence in a possible case of obstruction of justice . . . 'Anyone who wrote a document like that is out of is mind,' one prosecutor said. *'Those talking points are the smoking gun.'*" Pittsburgh Post-Gazette, February 8, 1998 (emphasis added).

"*Leakers from the Starr chamber have implied that the talking points are instructions to lie.* But lawyers routinely give there clients talking points before a grand jury. The Lewinsky case is about something else, spelled S-E-X." Clarence Page, Sun-Sentinel, June 4, 1998 (emphasis added).

"But a three page document known as the 'talking points' may prove to be the most important. . . 'The talking points are the closest thing to a smoking gun in this case. . .' legal scholar Paul Rothstein said Tuesday." USA Today, July 1, 1998.

"The talking points memorandum and the Tripp-Lewinsky tapes form the backbone of the independent counsel's inquiry into whether anyone lied or obstructed justice over Ms. Lewinsky's relationship with President Clinton." New York Times, June 11, 1998.

"The talking points memo, whose authorship is unknown, is of keen interest to Starr." Baltimore Sun, February 26, 1998.

"It is unclear who wrote the talking points and whether they were given to Ms. Tripp on Jan. 14 to encourage her to give false testimony in the Paula Corbin Jones sexual misconduct lawsuit against the President. These are questions of intense interest to the independent counsel Kenneth W. Starr, said lawyers close to his investigation. ° The talking points could be an important piece of physical evidence showing that there were unlawful efforts to encourage false testimony in the Jones case." New York Times, February 19, 1998.

"That suggests one particular piece of evidence will play a huge role: the list of written talking points Lewinsky gave her friend Linda Tripp on how to testify in the Paula Jones sexual harassment case. Who wrote the document is one of the key questions, whoever did could be charged with obstruction of justice." Chicago Tribune, February 15, 1998.

After all of the rumor and speculation regarding a connection between the White House and the "talking points," President Clinton was not asked one single question relating to the talking points during his August 17 deposition. Ms. Lewinsky is reported to have testified that she wrote the document without any assistance other than conversations she had with Linda Tripp. In the venerable tradition of Whitewater allegations, the "talking points" were surfaced as important and damning evidence of wrongdoing, but in the fullness of time and after investigation, have apparently vanished entirely. Only the stigma remains.

(2) Ms. Lewinsky's Transfer of Gifts to Betty Currie

The President frequently gives gifts to and receives gifts from friends and supporters; he gave Ms. Lewinsky the same kind of gifts he has shared with others. He was not concerned about the Jones lawyers' knowledge of the gifts. In the Jones deposition, he acknowledged knowing Ms. Lewinsky, acknowledged seeing her, acknowledged she had given him gifts, and acknowledged he had given her gifts. Moreover, in his grand jury testimony, he acknowledged giving Ms. Lewinsky good-bye gifts on December 28, 1997, shortly before she moved to New York, a date which we believe to be *after* Ms. Currie picked up the box of gifts from Ms. Lewinsky. The gifts simply were not a concern to him.

It is our understanding that Ms. Lewinsky may have testified that she raised with the President a concern about the Jones lawyers' request for gifts from the President and that, shortly thereafter, Ms. Currie appeared at her home stating that she understood Ms. Lewinsky had something for her. Ms. Lewinsky apparently testified that she then provided to Ms. Currie for safekeeping a box containing some of the gifts received from the President.

For Ms. Lewinsky's account to be credible, Ms. Currie must have been asked by the President to contact Ms. Lewinsky for the box. However, her account conflicts directly both with that of the President and with what we believe to be Ms. Currie's testimony. The President told Ms. Lewinsky she would have to produce what she had in response to a request. He did not ever suggest that gifts from him should be disposed of, and he did not ever ask or instruct Ms. Currie to pick up the gifts from Ms. Lewinsky. We believe that Ms. Currie's testimony corroborates this recollection. Ms. Currie has apparently testified that Ms. Lewinsky initiated the contact with her about the box, asking Ms. Currie to come by her apartment building, giving a sealed box to her, and asking her to hold on to it. Ms. Currie has no knowledge that the President ever even knew about the box prior to public disclosures about it, and the President testified that he did not learn about the box until after the OIC investigation became public.

(3) JOB ASSISTANCE TO MS. LEWINSKY

The President made certain efforts to try to assure that Ms. Lewinsky had a fair shot at a job other than her Pentagon position,

388   THE STARR REPORT

where she was not happy, and he generally was aware of other
efforts by his secretary Ms. Currie and his friend Mr. Jordan. These
actions were totally appropriate. At no time did the President ask
that Ms. Lewinsky be accorded specially favorable or unfavorable
treatment because of his relationship with her or for any other reason. These actions began well before Ms. Lewinsky was ever named
a witness in the *Jones* litigation, and they were in no way intended
to influence Ms. Lewinsky to keep secret what was at that time an
already terminated relationship. There is no evidence of any link
whatsoever between the President's actions and possible testimony
by Ms. Lewinsky in the *Jones* case.

In April 1996, Ms. Lewinsky was reassigned from the White
House to the Pentagon. Although the transfer was viewed as a promotion, the President became aware that Ms. Lewinsky was upset
about it, did not see it as a positive change, and feared that the
transfer would be appear to be a demotion or "black mark" on her
resume. To the extent that Ms. Lewinsky was criticized for spending
more time in the West Wing than was required by her responsibilities in the Office of Legislative Affairs, the President felt responsible.

In the summer of 1997, the President spoke to Marsha Scott, the
deputy personnel director at the White House, and inquired about
the possibility of a position being available for Ms. Lewinsky in the
White House. He never ordered Ms. Scott or anyone else to provide
her special treatment or directed that she be given a job at the White
House. He simply wanted to assure that she had been treated fairly
and asked only that Ms. Scott look into the possibility of a position
at the White House for Ms. Lewinsky if it was appropriate. Ms.
Lewinsky was never offered an opportunity to return to the White
House—as a result of that conversation or otherwise.

In the fall of 1997, Ms. Betty Currie spoke to Mr. John Podesta
about finding a job for Ms. Lewinsky in New York, and Mr. Podesta
ultimately spoke to Ambassador Bill Richardson about the matter.
The Ambassador agreed to interview Ms. Lewinsky for a position in
his New York office. The President was not involved in arranging
the Richardson interview. When Ms. Lewinsky indicated to Ms.

Currie that she preferred a job in the private sector, Ms. Currie contacted Mr. Jordan, her long-time friend, to see whether he would be willing to make inquiries regarding a job opportunity for Ms. Lewinsky in the private sector. Mr. Jordan referred her for interviews at American Express and Revlon, and to the advertising agency of Young & Rubicam. As Mr. Jordan said in his January 22, 1998 statement on the matter:

> Throughout my professional career, I have been privileged to assist people with their vocational aspirations. I have done so for two reasons. first, I stand on the shoulders of many individuals who have helped me. Second, I believe "to whom much is given much is required" so I have tried to lend a helping hand.
>
> For many years now . . . I am consulted by individuals, young and old, male and female, black and white, Hispanic and Asian, rich and poor, cabinet members and secretaries, for assistance. And I have met with some success, from paralegals to mailroom clerks, to corporate directors, to CEO's.
>
> I was pleased to be helpful to Ms. Lewinsky whose drive, ambition, and personality were impressive. She was referred by Ms. Betty Currie, a secretary to the president.

Mr. Jordan is a private individual who is free to offer job assistance to whomever he chooses.

Questions have been raised about a connection between the timing of Ms. Lewinsky's affidavit (which was executed January 7 and filed January 16) and the timing of any job offer. There was no connection. Francis Carter, Esq., Ms. Lewinsky's attorney at the time she executed the affidavit, apparently has stated that Ms. Lewinsky never asked him to delay the filing of an affidavit until after she had secured a job in New York and never suggested when the affidavit should be filed. *The Washington Post,* June 19, 1998. Indeed, Mr. Carter has reported that he himself delayed the filing of the affidavit while he attempted to persuade the *Jones* attorneys to withdraw the subpoena to Ms. Lewinsky. *Ibid.*

Indeed, it was totally appropriate for Mr. Jordan to refer Ms. Lewinsky to Francis Carter to represent her in the *Jones* litigation. Mr. Carter is a highly respected lawyer who would owe his duty to Ms. Lewinsky and represent her interests. Assuring a witness has her own counsel in whom she may confide is the surest and most appropriate way to protect the integrity of the process. As Mr. Jordan indicated in his January 22 statement, the referral was "at her request" and Mr. Jordan simply "took her to Mr. Carter's office, introduced them, and returned to my office." Ms. Lewinsky paid Mr. Carter herself. Mr. Carter has said that Mr. Jordan brought Ms. Lewinsky to his office, introduced them, and told him that she had been subpoenaed in the *Jones* case and needed an attorney. The Washington Post, June 19, 1998. According to Mr. Carter, Mr. Jordan did not suggest what should be done or how the matter should be handled, but promptly left. *Ibid.* Mr. Carter has stated, "I never received any kind of information from [Ms. Lewinsky] at any time that contradicted anything that's in that affidavit." *Ibid.*

Finally, in January of 1998, the President asked Mr. Erskine Bowles whether the legislative affairs office where Ms. Lewinsky once had worked would be able to give Ms. Lewinsky a reference that would not be negative. The President understood from Ms. Lewinsky that she thought she could get a good reference from The Department of Defense but hoped for a White House reference that was at least neutral. The President did not instruct anyone to provide such a reference and did not follow up on the inquiry. This innocuous query for an honest reference cannot conceivably be a basis for any charge of wrongdoing.

VI. "ABUSES OF POWER"

From the very beginning, the Lewinsky investigation has been about potential impeachment—a direct attack by the OIC on the constitutional status of the President. It is in that context that the OIC's allegations of abuse of power must be judged.

Any charge the OIC might make that the President has abused the powers of his office through the assertion of privileges—privileges that were asserted at the initiation and recommendation of the Counsel's Office, not by the President himself—is utterly baseless. Indeed, those charges are more a reflection of the OIC's unfettered abuse of his authority and his wholesale abandonment of any prosecutorial judgment in his campaign to prevent the President from consulting with his most senior advisors in confidence. No prosecutor, not even during Watergate, *ever* has contemplated the sort of sweeping intrusion into the President's ability to obtain advice that has been undertaken by the OIC. At bottom, the Independent Counsel believes that, merely because he demands confidential information, the President may not defend himself against impeachment without raising a charge that he is thereby abusing his power.

Before moving to these issues, one other point is worthy of note. It has been suggested in media reports that one of the grounds for impeachment advanced by the OIC is that the President abused his power by denying to his staff, in the days immediately following disclosure of the Lewinsky investigation, that he had engaged in any improper conduct when he knew that they might be called as witnesses before the grand jury and knew that they were making public statements in his defense. If this allegation were not so serious, such a suggestion would be ludicrous.

Implicit in the allegation is the notion that any official, in any branch of the government, who makes a statement about his own conduct, or indeed any other matter, that is not absolutely true is liable for misusing his office for so long as he fails to admit wrongdoing, for the official's staff will inevitable repeat his explanation in any number of forums. It would follow, therefore, according to what appears to be the OIC's reasoning, that no official could mount a defense to impeachment, or to ethics charges, or to a criminal investigation while remaining in office, for anything other than an admission of guilt will be treated as an abuse of his official powers.

1. THE PRESIDENT'S DECISION TO LITIGATE PRIVILEGE ISSUES CANNOT BE COMPARED TO THE ABUSES OF POWER ALLEGED DURING WATERGATE

The Independent Counsel apparently attempts to evoke images of Watergate by charging that the President has abused the powers of his office. This allegation is simply meritless. In the *Federalist Papers,* Alexander Hamilton described abuse of power as the "corrupt use of the office for personal gain or some other improper purpose." Former President Nixon's use of the Central Intelligence Agency (CIA) to thwart a major criminal investigation by the Federal Bureau of Investigation (FBI) of a crime in which he was involved, to take but one example, fits squarely within that definition. President Clinton's lawful assertion of privileges in a court of law and the Counsel's Office conduct of its official duties plainly does not.

There is no comparison between the claimed abuses of power by President Nixon and the public and lawful assertion of privileges during the OIC investigation. Indeed, comparing this White House with President Nixon's diminishes the historical significance of the unprecedented claims of abuse of power by the Nixon administration and attempts to criminalize the proper exercise of presidential prerogatives. The specious nature of the OIC's allegations reveal the OIC's true motive: to create an offense where none exists.

In July 1974, the House Judiciary Committee lodged serious and significant abuse of power charges against President Nixon, alleging that President Nixon, among other things:

Engaged in an elaborate cover-up scheme that included using his secret intelligence operation to pay both for illegal activities and subsequent blackmail money for the cover-up;

Paid hush money to his advisor;

Instructed administration officials on how to commit perjury;

Violated grand jury secrecy rules by obtaining 6(e) material from the Justice Department and passing it on to presidential advisors, who were targets of the investigation;

Attempted to subvert the IRS and CIA;

Authorized illegal intelligence gathering activities;

Directly interfered with the Justice Department's ITT investigation; and,

Pressured the CIA to interfere with the FBI's investigation of the Watergate break-in—a conversation caught on tape.

In contrast, the OIC apparently has made such charges of abuse against President Clinton, however erroneously, for purportedly encouraging the Secret Service to assert privilege claims over their testimony and invoking attorney-client and executive privileges. President Clinton's privilege claims have been open and lawful, and were reviewed and in significant measure *validated* by the courts. Thus, the Nixon investigation and precedent stand in sharp contrast to the OIC's investigation and baseless charges in this matter.

2. THE UNITED STATES SECRET SERVICE'S DECISION TO PURSUE A PROTECTIVE PRIVILEGE WAS THE PROPER EXERCISE OF ITS OWN AUTHORITY AND IN NO WAY AN ABUSE OF POWER BY THE PRESIDENT

The assertion of a protective function privilege by the Secret Service cannot possibly serve as a basis for the OIC's allegations of abuse of power. As a factual matter, the President never asked, directed, or participated in any decision regarding the protective function privilege. Moreover, no one at the White House asked, directed, participated or had any role in such decisions. The Treasury and Justice Departments independently decided to pursue a privilege for the Secret Service to ensure the protection of this and future presidents.

Second, ignoring significant security concerns expressed by the Secret Service, the Independent Counsel sought testimony from agents about *non-criminal* events they may have witnessed as well as *non-criminal* conversations they may have overheard in the course of protecting the President. For the first time in the history of the Independent Counsel statute, the Independent Counsel sought to use the protective service as a source of intelligence for admittedly non-criminal activities of a protectee. In the wake of this unprecedented demand, it was and continues to be the reasoned judgment of career professionals in the Secret Service that the absence of a protective privilege would severely impair agents' ability to fulfill their mission to protect this and future Presidents (as well as other protectees). The Secret Service's position was supported by former presidents and by former agents assigned to protect presidents in both Republican as well as Democratic administrations.

Thus, the Justice and Treasury Departments' assertion of a protective privilege advanced valid concerns about the Secret Service's ability to perform its function. The OIC's suggestion that the assertion of this privilege constituted an abuse of power not only insults the integrity of career law enforcement officials, but that of congressional policy makers too. Indeed, because of the Independent Counsel's unorthodox overreaching, Senator Hatch vowed to seek legislation to enact the type of limited privilege asserted by the Secret Service in response to the Independent Counsel's sweeping actions. Congressional Press Releases, Senator Orrin Hatch, July 17, 1998.

3. THE PRESIDENT'S ASSERTIONS OF EXECUTIVE AND ATTORNEY/CLIENT PRIVILEGE WERE VALID AND NECESSARY

Any charge by the OIC that the President's assertion of privileges constitutes an abuse of power is equally baseless. The White House advanced claims of privilege only sparingly and as a last resort to protect the core constitutional and institutional interests of this and future presidencies. In pursuing his attack on the institution of the Presidency, the OIC took the extreme position that executive privilege was inapplicable and that the governmental attorney-client privilege did not exist in the face of grand jury subpoena. The OIC now seeks to penalize the President for disagreeing with its interpretations of the law, despite the fact that the courts (and the Department of Justice) both also disagreed with the OIC.

A. THE PRESIDENT FOLLOWED THE ADVICE OF WHITE HOUSE COUNSEL REGARDING THE ASSERTION OF OFFICIAL PRIVILEGES

A necessary component of the OIC's abuse of power allegation is that the President initiated the White House's claims of privilege—both executive and attorney-client—with intent to impede the OIC's investigation. The record completely refutes this premise.

The privilege issue initially arose when the OIC served on Bruce Lindsey, Assistant to the President and Deputy Counsel, a subpoena seeking his testimony before the grand jury. Declaration of Charles F.C. Ruff ("Ruff Dec.") ¶ 31. Prior to Mr. Lindsey's appearance, the White House Counsel met with the OIC to discuss privilege issues and to ask the OIC to describe with particularity possible areas of inquiry to determine whether they would encompass privileged information. *Id.* ¶ 32. The OIC declined to discuss this issue, and later stated that it intended to question Mr. Lindsey on areas implicating a wide array of privileges because it believed that executive and attorney-client privileges were inapplicable to information relating to the Lewinsky investigation. *Id.* ¶¶ 32-34. The White House offered, in good faith, to provide the OIC with any factual testimony regarding the Lewinsky investigation. *Id.* ¶¶ 45-50. The OIC rejected this offer. *Id.* ¶ 51.

Instead, the OIC suddenly filed motions to compel the testimony of Mr. Lindsey and other senior staff. *Id.* After careful deliberations, the White House Counsel notified the President of the privilege issue, explained the failed accommodation effort, and recommended that he invoke privilege. As he did in every instance, the President accepted the White House Counsel's recommendation and authorized the Counsel to make the claim of privilege. *Id.* ¶ 56. Thus, the President's decision to claim privilege was never the result of his own initiative, but of his Counsel's advice.

B. THE PRESIDENT'S EXECUTIVE PRIVILEGE ASSERTIONS WERE UPHELD BY THE COURT

To put the OIC's apparent abuse of power charges in context, it is important to recognize that the OIC took the extraordinary position that executive privilege was inapplicable in the face of a grand jury subpoena and that it therefore was entitled to immediate and full disclosure of all strategic and political communication among the President's most senior advisors. This position was squarely at odds with the law of the Supreme Court, and of course, the D.C. Circuit. Executive privilege is constitutionally-based and covers communications relating to the President's official duties and the effective functioning of the executive branch. It ensures that the President receives frank and candid advice and recommendations, which ultimately fosters more informed and effective decision-making.

Here, the President asserted executive privilege over communications that relate to matters that affect the performance of his official duties. *In re Grand Jury Proceedings*, 1998 U.S. Dist. Lexis 7736, *7 (D.D.C. 1998); Ruff Dec. ¶¶ 16-30. Indeed, some of these communications related to the President's decision whether to invoke privilege over other communications. *Id*. ¶¶ 26-28.

Rather than acknowledge the presumptively privileged nature of the information, the OIC maintained that the privilege was inapplicable and that it did not have to demonstrate any need for the information. Chief Judge Johnson rejected the OIC's position holding that the communications were presumptively privileged. *In re Grand Jury Proceedings*, 1998 U.S. Dist. Lexis at *3-10. The Court then required the OIC to make a showing that its need for the information was sufficient to overcome the privilege. *Id*. at * 13-21. Although the Court concluded that the OIC had met its burden, the Court at no time even suggested that the President's assertion of executive privilege was groundless, improper, or made in bad faith. In those circumstances, it cannot seriously be argued that assertion of the privilege was an abuse of power.

C. THE PRESIDENT'S ASSERTION OF THE ATTORNEY-CLIENT PRIVILEGE WAS SOLIDLY GROUNDED IN THE LAW OF THIS CIRCUIT

For centuries, the law has recognized the attorney-client privilege as absolute in protecting the confidentiality of communications between lawyers and their clients. The D.C. Circuit has also recognized that the attorney-client privilege protects confidential communications between government lawyers and officials. *E.g. Mead Data Control, Inc.* v. *Dep't of the Air Force*, 566 F.2d 242 (D.C. Cir. 1977). Courts recognize that a government official, like any other citizen, must be able to provide information to and seek advice from government lawyers without fear of public disclosure. Ultimately, the privilege serves an important governmental function by fostering well-advised and fully-informed decision-making. The possibility that those communications may be disclosed will forfeit the benefits the privilege was intended to protect.

Despite the law in the D.C. Circuit recognizing the attorney-client privilege in the governmental context, the Independent Counsel pushed to breach the bonds of the governmental attorney-client privilege. Unlike his predecessors, who have respected the professional obligation of government attorneys to provide confidential legal advice on official matters, the Independent Counsel has insisted that government attorneys and clients do not have the right to discuss legal issues in confidence. In this context, the White House's assertion of the attorney-client privilege was not only appropriate, but it was an ethical and institutional obligation.

Prior to the D.C. Circuit litigation, the OIC was well aware that the White House fundamentally disagreed with the OIC regarding the applicability and scope of the governmental attorney-client privilege. In the Eighth Circuit, the OIC had attempted to obtain a White House lawyer's notes that reflected confidential communications. *In re Grand Jury Subpoena Duces Tecum*, 112 F.3d 910 (8th Cir. 1997). At the time of that litigation, which the White House resisted and the OIC won, there was no authority rejecting the existence of a governmental attorney-client privilege.

Two years later, the OIC, in the Lewinsky investigation, sought to compel the disclosure of confidential communications between the President and his official lawyers in which legal advice was either being sought by or provided to the President regarding official matters. In view of the law of the D.C. Circuit, which recognized an absolute governmental attorney-client privilege, the White House Counsel recommended, and the President asserted, the privilege.

A recent Supreme Court ruling that rejected the OIC's sweeping attack on the attorney-client privilege provided additional support for the President's position. In *Swidler & Berlin v. United States,* ___U.S.___ (1998); 1998 U.S. Lexis 4214 (1998), the OIC argued that the personal attorney-client privilege should automatically give way to the needs of a criminal investigation. The Court rejected the OIC's position and stated that "there is no case authority for the proposition that the privilege applies differently in criminal and civil cases," *id.* at *7, supporting the principle that the privilege remains absolute in a grand jury context. Accordingly, the President's position on the applicability of the privilege in this context had a substantial basis in the decisions of both this Circuit and the Supreme Court.

Undaunted, the OIC argued that, based upon the non-binding Eighth Circuit opinion, the governmental attorney-client privilege is inapplicable in a grand jury context. 112 F.3d 910 (8th Cir. 1997). From an institutional standpoint, the OIC's position stripped the President of any ability to obtain confidential advice from government lawyers about official matters in the event that the OIC made a referral to Congress for possible impeachment hearings. In an impeachment context, the President is entitled to rely on Counsel's Office lawyers to provide critical legal guidance. Without the ability to receive such confidential advice, he is left without any legal guidance regarding the conduct of his official duties.

The District Court rejected the OIC's position and held that the President had a valid, though qualified, governmental attorney-client privilege. *In re Grand Jury Proceedings,* 1998 U.S. Dist. Lexis at *21-52. Performing a need analysis similar to executive privilege, the Court balanced the President's interests against those of the grand jury and ultimately determined that the grand jury was entitled to the information. Once again, the District Court did not suggest that the privilege claim was spurious or made in bad faith.

On appeal, a divided D.C. Circuit Court of Appeals ruled that the President had an attorney-client privilege with White House Counsel in some contexts, but not this one. *In re: Bruce R. Lindsey,* 1998 U.S. App. Lexis 17066, *7-43 (D.C. Cir. 1998). Judge David Tatel, whose dissenting opinion in the Court of Appeals' decision in *Swidler & Berlin* was adopted by the Supreme Court, dissented here as well. Consistent with his analysis in *Swidler & Berlin,* Judge Tatel found that the Court's opinion did not account for "the unique nature of the Presidency, its unique need for confidential legal advice, or the possible consequences of abrogating the attorney-client privilege for a President's ability to obtain such advice." *Id.* at *54. Judge Tatel's recognition of the validity of the absolute nature of the privilege and the President's need to assert this and belies the notion that the assertion was in any way an abuse of power.

The OIC's apparent argument that the assertions of privilege were for purposes of delay lacks any evidentiary support and, more significantly, overlooks the OIC's own dilatory conduct. After Mr. Lindsey was subpoenaed and *before* he was scheduled to testify, the Office of the President attempted to avoid litigating these issues by reaching an accommodation that would provide the OIC with access to the information to which it was entitled while maintaining the legitimate confidentiality interests of the President. *Id.* ¶¶ 31-32. The OIC rejected those efforts and instead filed its motion to compel. *Id.* ¶51. The OIC has continued to reject any attempt by the White House to compromise, choosing instead to litigate these issues. The Office of the President has sought to avoid any delay by agreeing to expedited briefing schedules involving privilege litigation, and the courts, appreciating the time-sensitivity of the issues, have ruled swiftly on these matters.

In any event, any delay that might have been caused by the White House had no substantive impact on the OIC's investigation. Privilege claims have been advanced as to only a narrow portion of the testimony of three witnesses. The OIC originally filed motions to compel the testimony of two senior staff members and one Counsel's Office lawyer. The litigation only temporarily postponed the testimony of the two senior staffers; in March, they both appeared before the grand and testified fully. The privilege assertions ultimately involved the testimony of only three Counsel's Office lawyers. Each of these individuals has testified at length regarding any facts they may have possessed about whether the President had a relationship with Ms. Lewinsky. The questions as to which they asserted privilege were narrow in scope and irrelevant to the matters being investigated.

Finally, substantial delay in the investigation has been self-inflicted. The OIC has wandered aimlessly down more alleys and byways than any federal prosecutor would appropriately do. The OIC has called current and former White House staffers before the grand jury, and interviewed many others. The OIC has called presidential advisers before the grand jury four, five and six times; sometimes for only one- or two-hour sessions. Some witnesses appeared to testify only to find themselves waiting for hours and then being told to return on another day. The OIC has also insisted on exploring such irrelevant subjects as White House contacts with the press, and has required testimony from attorneys whose primary function was to deal with the OIC. Such actions are highly unusual, if not unprecedented.

4. WHITE HOUSE LAWYERS PLAYED AN APPROPRIATE ROLE IN THE INVESTIGATION

Finally, the open and lawful efforts of the White House lawyers to assist White House staff obtain lawyers, to speak with witnesses and their lawyers, and to provide advice on the ramifications of the investigation also cannot be considered an abuse of power.

As a threshold matter, when there is an official nexus between the duties of the President and an ongoing investigation, which certainly exists here, it is the duty of government attorneys to represent their official client. The specter of impeachment loomed from the day the Lewinsky story broke in the press. Ruff Dec. ¶ 21. Members of the Congress asserted that the investigation, which drew explosive media, public and congressional attention, burdened the President's ability to perform his constitutional and statutory duties. Accordingly, the White House Counsel's Office lawyers, among others, were responsible for providing the President and White House officials with informed, candid advice on the issues raised by the investigation that affected the President's official duties. *Id.* ¶¶ 16-30.

When it suited the OIC's interests, the OIC recognized the appropriateness of, and relied on, the White House Counsel's efforts. From the beginning of this investigation, the OIC sought—and received—the cooperation of the White House lawyers in setting up interviews and grand jury appearances of current and former White House employees. The OIC, however, refused to allow the White House lawyers to represent even the most junior, uninvolved witnesses. Thus, all White House officials, from the most senior to the most junior, were required to obtain private counsel. White House lawyers also provided relevant documents to witnesses' attorneys to ensure complete and accurate testimony, provided privilege instructions and guidance, and followed-up afterwards to discuss an individual's interview or grand jury appearance and any outstanding issues. All of the Counsel's Office activities were well-known to the OIC, and no objection was ever voiced.

Lastly, it was not uncommon for the White House to be faced with inaccurate and spurious stories that seemed to be coming from the OIC or "sources close to the OIC" shortly after a witness testified or was interviewed by the prosecution. Indeed, Judge Johnson examined media reports, and concluded that they contained grand jury material and that there was evidence that the OIC as the source. *In re Grand Jury Proceedings,* Misc. No. 98-55 (D.D.C. June 19, 1998), Mem. Op. at 6. Accordingly, Judge Johnson held that this evidence established a prima facie case that the OIC had violated Rule 6(e) and ordered the OIC to appear to show cause why it should not be held in contempt for Rule 6(e) violations. These leaks created a deluge of press inquiries to the White House; not surprisingly, White House Counsel lawyers were required to gather information and advise senior staff concerning the appropriate response to these inquiries.

VII. ALLEGATIONS OF PERJURY[21]

The OIC cannot make out even a colorable claim of perjury. If answers are truthful or literally truthful but misleading, *there is no perjury* as a matter of law, no matter how misleading the testimony is or is intended to be. The law simply does not require the witness to aid his interrogator. The Referral seeks to punish the President for being unhelpful to those trying to destroy him politically.

A. THE LAW OF PERJURY

Perjury requires proof that a defendant, while under oath, knowingly made a false statement as to material facts.[22] *See, e.g., United States v. Dunnigan*, 507 U.S. 87, 94 (1993). The "knowingly" requirement is a high burden: the government must prove the defendant had a subjective awareness of the falsity of his statement at the time he provided it. *See, e.g., United States v. Dowdy*, 479 F.2d 213, 230 (4th Cir. 1973); *United States v. Markiewicz*, 978 F.2d 786, 811 (2d Cir. 1992). It is beyond debate that false testimony provided as a result of confusion, mistake, faulty memory, carelessness, misunderstanding, mistaken conclusions, unjustified inferences testified to negligently, or even recklessness does *not* satisfy the "knowingly" element. *See, e.g., Dunnigan*, 507 U.S. at 94; *United States v. Dean*, 55 F.3d 640, 659 (D.C. Cir. 1995); *see also* Department of Justice Manual, 1997 Supplement, at 9-69.214.

Moreover, it is of course clear that a statement must be false in order to constitute perjury. It is equally beyond debate that the following types of answers are not capable of being false and are therefore by definition non-perjurious: literally truthful answers that imply facts that are not true, *see, e.g., United States v. Bronston,* 409 U.S. 352, 358 (1973), truthful answers to questions that are not asked, *see, e.g., United States v. Corr,* 543 F.2d 1042, 1049 (2d Cir. 1976), and failures to correct misleading impressions. *See, e.g., United States v. Earp,* 812 F.2d 917, 919 (4th Cir. 1987). The Supreme Court has made abundantly clear that it is not relevant for perjury purposes whether the witness intends his answer to mislead, or indeed intends a "pattern" of answers to mislead, if the answers are truthful or literally truthful.

Thus, in explaining the law of perjury, the Supreme Court and numerous lower federal courts have set forth three clear standards. First, answers to questions under oath that are literally true, but unresponsive to the questions asked, do not, as a matter of law, fall under the scope of the federal perjury statute. That is so even if the witness intends to mislead his questioner by his answer and even if the answer is false by "negative implication." The second clear rule is that answers to questions that are fundamentally ambiguous cannot, as a matter of law, be perjurious. Finally, a perjury conviction under 18 U.S.C. § 1621 cannot rest solely on the testimony of a single witness, and, at the very least as a matter of practice, no reasonable prosecutor would bring any kind of perjury case based on the testimony of one witness without independent corroboration - especially if the witness is immunized, or has *any* question as to credibility or truthfulness. As the Supreme Court has made clear, a perjury case "ought not to rest entirely upon 'an oath against an oath.'" *United States v. Weiler,* 323 U.S. 606, 608-09 (1945).

1. BRONSTON AND "LITERAL TRUTH."

In *United States v. Bronston,* 409 U.S. 352 (1973), the leading case on the law of perjury, the United States Supreme Court addressed "whether a witness may be convicted of perjury for an answer, under oath, that is literally true but not responsive to the question asked and arguably misleading by negative implication." *Id.* at 352. The Court directly answered the question "no." It made absolutely clear that a literally truthful answer cannot constitute perjury, no matter how much the witness intended by his answer to mislead.

Bronston involved testimony taken under oath at a bankruptcy hearing. At the hearing, the sole owner of a bankrupt corporation was asked questions about the existence and location of both his personal assets and the assets of his corporation. The owner testified as follows:

Q: Do you have any bank accounts in Swiss banks, Mr. Bronston?

A: No, sir.

Q: Have you ever?

A: The company had an account there for about six months in Zurich.

Q: Have you any nominees who have bank accounts in Swiss banks?

A: No, sir.

Q: Have you ever?

A: No, sir.

Id. at 354. The government later proved that Bronston did in fact have a personal Swiss bank account that was terminated prior to his testimony. The government prosecuted Bronston "on the theory that in order to mislead his questioner, [Bronston] answered the second question with literal truthfulness but unresponsively addressed his answer to the company's assets and not to his own—thereby implying that he had no personal Swiss bank account at the relevant time." *Id.* at 355.

The Supreme Court unanimously rejected this theory of perjury. It assumed for purposes of its holding that the questions referred to Bronston's personal bank accounts and not his company's assets. Moreover, the Court stated, Bronston's "answer to the crucial question was not responsive," and indeed "an implication in the second answer to the second question [is] that there was never a personal bank account." *Id.* at 358. The Court went so far as to note that Bronston's answers "were not guileless but were shrewdly calculated to evade." *Id.* at 361. However, the Court emphatically held that implications alone do not rise to the level of perjury, and that Bronston therefore could not have committed perjury. "[W]e are not dealing with casual conversation and the statute does not make it a criminal act for a witness to willfully state any material matter that implies any material matter that he does not believe to be true." *Id.* at 357-58. The Court took pains to point out the irrelevance of the witness's intent: "A jury should not be permitted to engage in conjecture whether an unresponsive answer, true and complete on its face, was intended to mislead or divert the examiner." *Id.* at 359.

The Supreme Court in *Bronston* provided several rationales for its holding that literally true, non-responsive answers are by definition non-perjurious, regardless of their implications. First, the Court noted that the burden always rests squarely on the interrogator to ask precise questions, and that a witness is under no obligation to assist the interrogator in that task. The Court "perceive[d] no reason why Congress would intend the drastic sanction of a perjury prosecution to cure a testimonial mishap that could readily have been reached with a single additional question by counsel alert—as every counsel ought to be—to the incongruity of petitioner's unresponsive answer." *Id.* at 359. Moreover, the Court noted that because of the adversarial process, perjury is an extraordinary sanction that is almost always unwarranted, since "a prosecution for perjury is not the sole, or even the primary safeguard against errant testimony." *Id.* at 360. The perjury statute cannot be invoked "simply because a wily witness succeeds in derailing the questioner - so long as the witness speaks the literal truth." *Id.*

Bronston is just one of scores of cases across the federal circuits that make clear that the definition of perjury must be carefully limited because perjury prosecutions are dangerous to the public interest since they "discourage witnesses from appearing or testifying." *Id.* at 359.[23] For instance, in *United States v. Earp*, 812 F.2d 917

(4th Cir. 1987), the defendant, a member of the Ku Klux Klan, had stood guard during the attempted burning of a cross on the lawn of an interracial couple, and further evidence demonstrated that he had personally engaged in other attempts to burn crosses. During questioning before a grand jury, however, he denied ever having burned crosses on anyone's lawn. He was convicted of perjury, but the United States Court of Appeals for the Fourth Circuit reversed his conviction, because "like the witness in *Bronston,* [the defendant's] answers were literally true although his second answer was unresponsive." *Id.* at 919. That is, the defendant had not actually succeeded in his cross-burning attempts, so it was literally true that he had never burned crosses on anyone's lawn. The court noted that "while he no doubt knew full well that he had on that occasion tried to burn a cross, he was not specifically asked either about any attempted cross burnings." *Id.* Literally every federal court of appeals in the nation concurs in this reading of *Bronston.*[24]

2. FUNDAMENTALLY AMBIGUOUS QUESTIONS CANNOT PRODUCE PERJURIOUS ANSWERS.

When a question or a line of questioning is "fundamentally ambiguous," the answers to the questions posed are insufficient as a matter of law to support a perjury conviction." *See, e.g., United States v. Finucan,* 708 F.2d 838, 848 (1st Cir. 1983); *United States v. Lighte,* 782 F.2d 367, 375 (2d Cir. 1986); *United States v. Tonelli,* 577 F.2d 194, 199 (3d Cir. 1978); *United States v. Bell,* 623 F.2d 1132, 1337 (5th Cir. 1980); *United States v. Wall,* 371 F.2d 398, 400 (6th Cir. 1967); *United States v. Williams,* 552 F.2d 226, 229 (8th Cir. 1977). In other words, when there is more than one way of understanding the meaning of a question, and the witness has answered truthfully as to his understanding, he cannot commit perjury. Many courts have emphasized that "defendants may not be assumed into the penitentiary" by "sustain[ing] a perjury charge based on [an] ambiguous line of questioning." *Tonelli,* 577 F.2d at 199.

United States v. Lattimore, 127 F. Supp. 405 (D.D.C. 1955), is the key case dealing with ambiguous questions in the perjury context. In *Lattimore*, a witness was questioned before the Senate Internal Security Subcommittee about his ties to the Communist party. He was asked whether he was a "follower of the Communist line," and whether he had been a "promoter of Communist interests." He answered "no" to both questions, and was subsequently indicted for committing perjury. The United States District Court for the District of Columbia found that the witness could not be indicted on "charges so formless and obscure as those before the Court." *Id.* at 413. The court held that "'follower of the Communist line' is not a phrase with a meaning about which men of ordinary intellect could agree, nor one which could be used with mutual understanding by a questioner and answerer unless it were defined at the time it were sought and offered as testimony." *Id.* at 110. As the court explained further:

> [The phrase] has no universally accepted definition. The Government has defined it in one way and seeks to impute its definition to the defendant. Defendant has declined to adopt it, offering a definition of his own. It would not necessitate great ingenuity to think up definitions differing from those offered either by the Government or defendant. By groundless surmise only could the jury determine which definition defendant had in mind.

Id. at 109.

Many other cases stand for the proposition that a witness cannot commit perjury by answering an inherently ambiguous question. For instance, in *United States v. Wall*, 371 F.2d 398 (6th Cir. 1967), a witness was asked whether she had "been on trips with Mr. X," and she answered "no." The government could prove that in fact the witness, who was from Oklahoma City, had been in Florida with "Mr. X." However, the government could not prove that the witness had traveled from Oklahoma City to Florida with "Mr. X." The court noted (and the government conceded) that the phrase "been on trips" could mean at least two different things: "That a person accompanied somebody else travelling with, or it can mean that they were there at a particular place with a person." The court then stated that "[t]he trouble with this case is that the question upon which the perjury charge was based was inarticulately phrased, and, as admitted by the prosecution, was susceptible of two different meanings. In our opinion, no charge of perjury can be based upon an answer to such a question." *Id.* at 399-400.

Similarly, in *United States v. Tonelli,* 577 F.2d 194 (3d Cir. 1978), the defendant answered negatively a question whether he had "handled any pension fund checks." The government then proved that the defendant had actually handled the transmission of pension fund checks by arranging for others to send, mail, or deliver the checks. The government charged the defendant with perjury. The court held that perjury could not result from the government's ambiguous question. The court explained:

> It is clear that the defendant interpreted the prosecutor's questions about 'handling' to mean 'touching' . . . To sustain a perjury charge based on the ambiguous line of questioning here would require us to assume [defendant] interpreted 'handle' to include more than 'touching.' The record will not allow us to do so and as the Court of Appeals for the Fifth Circuit has observed '[e]specially in perjury cases defendants may not be assumed into the penitentiary.

United States v. Bell, 623 F.2d 1132, 1137 (5th Cir. 1980), is yet another example of this doctrine. In *Bell,* a witness was asked before a grand jury, "Whether personal or business do you have records that are asked for in the subpoena," and the witness answered, "No, sir, I do not." It was later established that the witness's files clearly contained relevant records. Nonetheless, the court held that the question was ambiguous, and therefore incapable of yielding a perjurious answer. The witness interpreted the question to ask whether he had brought the records with him that day, and not whether he had any records anywhere else in the world.[25]

3. A PERJURY CASE MUST NOT BE BASED SOLELY UPON THE TESTIMONY OF A SINGLE WITNESS.

The law is clear that in a perjury prosecution under 18 U.S.C. § 1621, the falsity of a statement alleged to be perjurious cannot be established by the testimony of just one witness. This ancient common law rule, referred to as the "two-witness rule," has survived repeated challenges to its legitimacy, and has been judicially recognized as the standard of proof for perjury prosecutions brought under § 1621. *See, e.g., Weiler v. United States,* 323 U.S. 606, 608-610 (1945) (discussing the history and policy rationales of the two-witness rule); *United States v. Chaplin,* 25 F.3d 1373, 1377-78 (7th Cir. 1994) (two-witness rule applies to perjury prosecutions). The Department of Justice recognizes the applicability of the two-witness rule to perjury prosecutions brought under § 1621. *See* Department of Justice Manual, 1997 Supplement, at 9-69.265.

The crux of the two-witness rule is that "the falsity of a statement alleged to be perjurious must be established either by the testimony of two *independent* witnesses, or by one witness and *independent* corroborating evidence which is inconsistent with the innocence of the accused." Department of Justice Manual, 1997 Supplement, at 9-69.265 (emphasis in original). The second witness must give testimony independent of the first which, if believed, would "prove that what the accused said under oath was false." *Id.; United States v. Maultasch,* 596 F.2d 19, 25 (2d Cir. 1979). Alternatively, the independent corroborating evidence must be inconsistent with the innocence of the accused and "of a quality to assure that a guilty verdict is solidly founded." Department of Justice Manual, 1997 Supplement, at 9-69.265; *United States v. Forrest,* 639 F.2d 1224, 1226 (5th Cir. 1981). It is therefore clear that a perjury conviction under § 1621 cannot lie where there is no *independent* second witness who corroborates the first, or where there is no *independent* evidence that convincingly contradicts the testimony of the accused.

While 18 U.S.C. § 1623 does not incorporate the "two-witness rule," it is nonetheless clear from the case law that perjury prosecutions require a high degree of proof, and that prosecutors should not, as a matter of reason and practicality, even try to bring perjury prosecutions based solely on the testimony of a single witness. In *Weiler v. United States*, 323 U.S. 606, 608-09 (1945), the United States Supreme Court observed that "[t]he special rule which bars conviction for perjury solely upon the evidence of a single witness is deeply rooted in past centuries." The Court further observed that "equally honest witnesses may well have differing recollections of the same event," and hence *a conviction for perjury ought not to rest entirely upon 'an oath against an oath.'* *Id.* at 609 (emphasis added). Indeed, the common law courts in seventeenth-century England *required* the testimony of two witnesses as a precondition to a perjury conviction, when the testimony of a single witness was in almost all other cases sufficient. *See Chaplin*, 25 F.3d at 1377, *citing* Wigmore on Evidence § 2040(a), at 359-60 (Chadbourne rev. 1978). The common law courts actually adopted the two-witness rule from the Court of Star Chamber, which had followed the practice of the ecclesiastical courts of requiring two witnesses in perjury cases. *Id.* The English rationale for the rule is as resonant today as it was in the seventeenth century: "[I]n all other criminal cases the accused could not testify, and thus one oath for the prosecution was in any case something as against nothing; but on a charge of perjury the accused's oath was always in effect evidence and thus, if but one witness was offered, there would be merely . . . an oath against an oath." *Id.* And, as noted above, no perjury case should rest merely upon "an oath against an oath."

B. THE JONES DEPOSITION

Without knowledge of the OIC's specific allegations it is impossible to address why any particular claim of perjury fails although we are confident that no colorable claim of perjury can be made out. However, illegal leaks and speculation make clear that there are certain misperceptions about this testimony that can immediately be laid to rest. For example,

Allegation: The President falsely testified in his *Jones* deposition that he was never alone with Ms. Lewinsky.

Not so. The President acknowledged in his deposition that he met with Ms. Lewinsky on up to five occasions while she worked at the White House. (p. 50). He then referred back to that testimony when asked if he ever was alone with her in the Oval Office (p. 52), and again when asked whether he was alone with her in any room in the White House. (p. 59). The *Jones* lawyers did not follow up and ask the President to describe the nature of any physical contact that may have occurred on these occasions.

Allegation: The President falsely testified in his *Jones* deposition that he never had any improper physical contact of any kind with Ms. Lewinsky.

Not so. The President was asked whether he had "an extramarital sexual affair" with Ms. Lewinsky (p. 78) and responded that he did not. That term was undefined and ambiguous. The President understood the term "sexual affair" to involve a relationship involving sexual intercourse. He had no such relationship with Ms. Lewinsky.

The President also was asked whether he had "sexual relations" with Ms. Lewinsky, "as that term is defined in Deposition Exhibit 1, as modified by the Court." (p. 59). The Court explicitly directed the President's attention to Definition Number 1 on Exhibit 1, which the President had circled.

The President denied he had "sexual relations" with Ms. Lewinsky under this definition. Although the President's counsel, Mr. Bennett, had invited the Jones lawyers to ask specific questions about the President's conduct—"Why don't they ask the President what he did, what he didn't do, and then we can argue in Court later about what it means?" (p. 21)—the Jones lawyers declined to do so, relying instead on the definition. The President was not asked any specific questions at all about his physical contact with Ms. Lewinsky, and in particular he was not pointedly asked whether he had engaged in any of the conduct *outside* the definition provided. The

President's testimony in response to these questions was accurate. He did not have sexual intercourse with Ms. Lewinsky or otherwise engage in sexual conduct covered by the definition, as provided by plaintiff and narrowed by the Court.

The President also testified in the *Jones* deposition that Ms. Lewinsky's affidavit, in which she stated she had never had a "sexual relationship" with the President, was accurate (p. 204). He believed this testimony to be truthful. The term "sexual relationship" was not defined in the affidavit or in the deposition. The definition of the different term "sexual relations" utilized by the Jones lawyers did not apply to that question. The term "sexual relationship," like sexual affair, has no definitive meaning. To the President, that term reasonably requires sexual intercourse as a necessary component of the relationship. Since his relationship with Ms. Lewinsky did not involve intercourse, he truthfully answered that the affidavit was accurate.

> *Allegation:* The President falsely testified in his *Jones* deposition
> that his relationship with Ms. Lewinsky was the same
> as that with any other White House intern.

Not so. The President's answers left no doubt that he had a special relationship with Ms. Lewinsky. He acknowledged knowing how she had gotten her internship at the White House. He acknowledged meeting with her and knowing where she worked after leaving the White House. He acknowledged exchanging small gifts with her. He acknowledged that he knew she was moving to New York and that her mother had moved there. He acknowledged knowing about her job search in New York, and that she had had an interview with (then) U.N. Ambassador Bill Richardson. He acknowledged that Mr. Jordan reported on his meeting with Ms. Lewinsky about her New York job search. He acknowledged receiving cards and notes from her through Ms. Betty Currie. The *Jones* lawyers received affirmative responses to particular questions. Had they opted to ask precise questions on other matters, they would have received truthful responses. They did not do so.

VIII. THE LEWINSKY EXPANSION OF THE WHITEWATER INVESTIGATION

The expansion of the Independent Counsel's jurisdiction to encompass the *Jones* case and Ms. Lewinsky did not occur by accident or easily. The OIC deliberately and purposefully sought this expansion on an emergency basis. Media accounts that the Attorney General herself requested this expansion are highly misleading.

On January 16, 1998, upon the OIC's request, the Special Division of the Court of Appeals for the Purpose of Appointing Independent Counsels expanded the OIC's jurisdiction to allow it to investigate "whether Monica Lewinsky or others suborned perjury, obstructed justice, intimidated witnesses, or otherwise violated federal law . . . in dealing with witnesses, potential witnesses, attorneys, or others concerning the civil case *Jones v. Clinton*." Order, Div. No. 94-1 (Jan. 16, 1998) (Div. for Purpose of Appointing Independent Counsel) (D.C. Cir.). The series of events that led to this expansion of authority raise serious questions as to the motivations and manipulations of the OIC in securing this expanded jurisdiction.

Under the Independent Counsel statute, if the "independent counsel discovers or receives information about possible violations of criminal law by [covered persons], which are not covered by the prosecutorial jurisdiction of the independent counsel, the independent counsel may submit such information to the Attorney General." 28 U.S.C. § 593 (c)(2)(A). The Attorney General is then to conduct a preliminary investigation. 28 U.S.C. § 592. The statute did not give the OIC authority to conduct its own preliminary investigation in order to gather or create evidence to present to the Attorney General to support a request for an expansion of jurisdiction.

According to media reports, Ms. Linda Tripp contacted the OIC on Monday, January 12, 1998. There was no particular logic to this contact, and she could easily have taken her concerns to state or federal authorities. In any event, the OIC arranged for Ms. Tripp to wear an F.B.I. recording device and tape surreptitiously a conversation that she had with Ms. Lewinsky the next day, Tuesday, January 13, 1998 (Ms. Lewinsky had not yet filed an affidavit in the *Jones* case). On Friday, January 16, 1998, at the OIC's request, Ms. Tripp lured Ms. Lewinsky to a meeting, where she was apprehended by OIC agents, who confronted her and attempted to pressure her into doing surreptitious taping herself. She was informed that an immunity agreement was contingent on her *not* contacting her lawyer.[26]

That same day, the Special Division agreed to expand the OIC's authority, based upon the Independent Counsel's earlier application to the Attorney General and on the tapes that the OIC had already created: "In a taped conversation with a cooperating witness, Ms. Lewinsky states that she intends to lie when deposed. In the same conversation, she urges the cooperating witness to lie in her own upcoming deposition. . . . Independent Counsel Starr has requested that this matter be referred to him." (Text of Attorney General's Petition to Special Division, The Associated Press, January 29, 1998.)

The Independent Counsel later suggested that the expansion of authority prior to the taping was unnecessary, as it was already within his jurisdiction. However, the Lewinsky matter had no connection whatsoever to the Whitewater activities, or any other activities, then being investigated by the OIC. In addition, the Attorney General specifically stated in her referral to the Special Division that she was seeking an *expansion* of the Independent Counsel's jurisdiction. Or, as former independent counsel Michael Zeldin pointed out, "If he had jurisdiction to investigate it when he wired her, why did he have to go to court to get it afterward? In some ways, he is talking out of both sides of his mouth. . . . It seems to me arguable that he obtained evidence unlawfully . . . ." Chicago Tribune, January 25, 1998. And former independent counsel Lawrence Walsh declared, "A prosecutor has no business getting into that case [Paula Jones] unless there's something terrible happening. I question Starr's judgment in going into it so hard." Chicago Tribune, January 25, 1998.

Furthermore, the sequence of events suggests that Independent Counsel Starr deliberately delayed requesting the expansion of jurisdiction. Neither Monica Lewinsky nor President Clinton had made any statements under oath in the *Jones* case (at least that had been filed with any court) when Linda Tripp approached the OIC on January 12. The only evidence the OIC possessed at that time were tapes illegally created by Tripp. The OIC itself proceeded to tape the Tuesday, January 13 conversation between Tripp and Lewinsky. Ms. Lewinsky's affidavit was not filed in the *Jones* case until January 16, and the OIC had petitioned the Attorney General the day *before* for an expansion of authority based on the evidence (the Tripp tapes and the OIC's tape) that he had acquired without any authority to do so.

Ms. Tripp remained through the day at the hotel where Ms. Lewinsky was apprehended by the OIC on Friday, January 16, 1998.[27] During that day, Ms. Jones' lawyers repeatedly tried to contact Ms. Tripp for a meeting, but she was unavailable. *Ibid*. Late in the afternoon, when it became clear that Ms. Lewinsky would not cooperate in the surreptitious taping of others, the Jones lawyers received a call arranging a meeting with Ms. Tripp for that night, so she could help them prepare for the President's deposition next day. *Ibid*.[28] It seems probable that Ms. Tripp, who was acting as the OIC's agent under an immunity agreement, must have gotten approval for this briefing from the OIC. Ms. Tripp met with the Jones lawyers at her home in Maryland that night and briefed them on the illegal tapes she had made of Ms. Lewinsky,[29] so they could use the contents of those tapes in their questioning of the President.[30] Ms. Tripp is under investigation in the state of Maryland because she secretly recorded Ms. Lewinsky and then shared the existence and contents of those tapes with the Jones lawyers. It is a crime in that state, punishable by imprisonment up to five years and a fine of up to $10,000, for a person to "wilfully" record a conversation without the consent of both parties or to "wilfully" disclose the contents of such an illegally recorded conversation. Md. Code Ann. § 10-402 (1997).[31]

On January 17, armed with the information obtained from Ms. Tripp, Ms. Jones' attorneys deposed President Clinton in great detail regarding Ms. Lewinsky. At about this time, the OIC sought to prevent press coverage of its attempt to have Ms. Lewinsky cooperate in secret taping.[32]

This entire sequence of events—the OIC's delay in requesting jurisdiction, the OIC's pressure on reporters to withhold public disclosure of the matter,[33] the OIC's unwillingness to permit Ms. Lewinsky to contact her lawyer, and the OIC's dispatch of Ms. Tripp to brief the Jones lawyers about the fruits of her illegal taping the day before they were to depose the President—suggests an intention by the OIC to ensure that the expansion of jurisdiction was kept a secret until the President and Ms. Lewinsky had given testimony under oath and (if Ms. Lewinsky could be so persuaded) she had been enlisted to do surreptitious taping. In other words, rather than taking steps to defer or avoid any possible interference with the *Jones* case, the OIC did everything in its power—and some things outside its authority—to set up a case against the President.

NOTES

1. 2 Max Farrand, *The Records of the Federal Convention of 1787* 550 (Rev. ed. 1966).

2. 1/See Raoul Berger, *Impeachment: The Constitutional Problems*, 67-73 (1973).

3. Michael J. Gerhardt, *The Constitutional Limits to Impeachment and Its Alternatives*, 68 Tex. L. Rev. 1, 82 (1989) (emphasis added).

4. Joseph Story, Commentaries on the Constitution § 745 (1st Ed. 1833); Federalist 65 at 331.

5. Of course that election takes place through the mediating activity of the Electoral College. *See* U.S.Const. art. II, § 1, cl.2-3 and amend. XII.

6. At the time of the Constitution's framing, "[c]ognizable 'high Crimes and Misdemeanors' in England, . . . generally concerned perceived malfeasance—which may or may not be proscribed by common law or statute—that *damaged the state or citizenry in their political rights.*" Julie O'Sullivan, *The Interaction Between Impeachment and the Independent Counsel Statute*, 86 Geo. L.J. 2193, 2210 (1998) (emphasis added) (forthcoming).

7. John R. Labovitz, *Presidential Impeachment* 94 (1978).

8. Berger, *Impeachment* at 61.

9. Ronald D. Rotunda, *An Essay on the Constitutional Parameters of Federal Impeachment*, 76 Ky. L.J. 707, 724 (1987/1988).

10. Gerhardt, 68 Tex. L. Rev. at 85.

11. Charles L. Black, *Impeachment: A Handbook* 38-39 (1974).

12. *Id.*

13. Labovitz at 26.

14. Rotunda at 726.

15. *Id.*

16. Julie O'Sullivan, *The Interaction Between Impeachment and the Independent Counsel Statute*, 86 Geo. L.J. at 2220.

17. *Clinton v. Jones*, ___ U.S. ___, 117 S.Ct. 1636 (1997).

18. *See, e.g.*, "Starr Probes Clinton Personal Life—Whitewater Prosecu-

tors Question Troopers About Women," *The Washington Post* (June 25, 1997), at A1.

19. *Cf. United States v. Lundwall,* 1 F. Supp. 2d 249, 251-54 (S.D.N.Y. 1998) (noting that "[c]ases involving prosecutions for document destruction during civil pre-trial discovery are notably absent from the extensive body of reported § 1503 case law," and that "there are a great many good reasons why federal prosecutors should be reluctant to bring criminal charges relating to conduct in ongoing civil litigation," but concluding that systematic destruction of documents sought during discovery should satisfy § 1503).

20. The term "talking points" refers to a document apparently provided by Ms. Lewinsky to Ms. Tripp in January 1998 regarding possible testimony in the *Jones* case.

21. "Perjury" was not even in the original grant of jurisdiction to the OIC but reportedly is now the crux of the OIC's case.

22. There are two basic federal perjury statutes: 18 U.S.C. § 1621, and 18 U.S.C. § 1623. Section 1621 applies to all material statements or information provided under oath "to a competent tribunal, officer, or person, in any case in which a law of the United States authorizes an oath to be administered." Section 1623, in contrast, applies only to testimony given before a grand jury and other court proceedings. Although there are differences between the two statutes, the four basic elements of each are substantially the same.

23. While *Bronston* involved a perjury conviction under the general perjury statute, 18 U.S.C. § 1621, lower federal courts have uniformly relied on it in reviewing perjury convictions under § 1623(a), which makes it unlawful to make any false material declaration "in any proceeding before or ancillary to any court or grand jury of the United States." *See, e.g., United States v. Porter,* 994 F.2d 470, 474 n. 7 (8th Cir.1993); *United States v. Reveron Martinez,* 836 F.2d 684, 689 (1st Cir.1988); *United States v. Lighte,* 782 F.2d 367, 372 (2d Cir.1986).

24. *See also United States v. Finucan,* 708 F.2d 838, 847 (1st Cir. 1983) (intent to mislead is insufficient to support conviction for perjury); *United States v. Lighte,* 782 F.2d 367, 374 (2d Cir. 1986) (literally true answers by definition non-perjurious even if answers were designed to mislead); *United*

States v. Tonelli, 577 F.2d 194, 198 (3d Cir. 1978) (perjury statute is not to be invoked because a "wily witness succeeds in derailing the questioner"). *United States v. Abroms,* 947 F.2d 1241, 1245 (5th Cir. 1991) (unambiguous and literally true answer is not perjury, even if there was intent to mislead); *United States v. Eddy,* 737 F.2d 564, 569 (6th Cir. 1984) ("An 'intent to mislead' or 'perjury by implication' is insufficient to support a perjury conviction."); *United States v. Williams,* 536 F.2d 1202, 1205 (7th Cir. 1976) (literally true statement cannot form basis of perjury conviction even if there was intent to mislead); *United States v. Robbins,* 997 F.2d 390, 394 (8th Cir. 1993); *United States v. Boone,* 951 F.2d 1526, 1536 (9th Cir. 1991) (literally true statement is not actionable); *United States v. Larranaga,* 787 F.2d 489, 497 (10th Cir. 1986) (no perjury where answer literally truthful and prosecutor's questioning imprecise); *United States v. Shotts,* 145 F.3d 1289, 1297 (11th Cir. 1998) ("An answer to a question may be non-responsive, or may be subject to conflicting interpretations, or may even be false by implication. Nevertheless, if the answer is literally true, it is not perjury."); *United States v. Dean,* 55 F.3d 640, 662 (D.C. Cir. 1995) (perjury charge cannot be based upon evasive answers or even misleading answers so long as such answers are literally true).

25. Many other cases as well hold that ambiguous questions cannot produce perjurious answers. *See, e.g., Lighte,* 782 F.2d at 376 (questions fundamentally ambiguous because of imprecise use of "you," "that," and "again"); *United States v. Farmer,* 137 F.3d 1265, 1270 (10th Cir. 1998) (question "Have you talked to Mr. McMahon, the defendant about your testimony here today?" ambiguous because phrase "here today" could refer to "talked" or to "testimony;" conviction for perjury could not result from the question); *United States v. Ryan,* 828 F.2d 1010, 1015-17 (3d Cir. 1987) (loan application question asking for "Previous Address (last 5 years)" fundamentally ambiguous because unclear whether "address" refers to residence or mailing address, and "previous" could mean any previous address, the most recent previous address, or all previous addresses; based on ambiguity, perjury cannot result from answer to question); *United States v. Markiewicz,* 978 F.2d 786, 809 (2d Cir. 1992) (question "[D]id you receive any money that had been in bingo hall" ambiguous, and incapable of producing perjurious answer, when it did not differentiate

between witness's personal and business capacities). *See also United States v. Manapat,* 928 F.2d 1097, 1099 (11th Cir. 1991); *United States v. Eddy,* 737 F.2d 564, 565-71 (6th Cir. 1984); *United States v. Hilliard,* 31 F.3d 1509 (10th Cir. 1994).

26. *Time,* Feb. 16, 1998, at 49.

27. "Linda Tripp Briefed Jones Team on Tapes," *The Washington Post,* Feb. 14, 1998, at A1.

28. *The Washington Times,* Feb. 15, 1998, at A1, reported:

> "Yesterday, a source close to Mrs. Jones' legal team confirmed that on Jan. 16, the day before Mrs. Jones' lawyers took a deposition from Mr. Clinton, Mrs. Tripp met for two hours with those lawyers at her suburban Maryland home and discussed at length what Miss Lewinsky had said in some 20 hours of secretly recorded conversations. Mrs. Tripp had already given those tapes to Mr. Starr's investigators.
>
> With the information from Mrs. Tripp, the Jones lawyers were able to ask Mr. Clinton in his deposition specific questions about his relationship with and gifts to Miss Lewinsky, according to a person informed about the President's testimony."

29. Under the Maryland electronic surveillance statute, which criminalizes taping without the consent of both parties, it is a violation of the statute simply to disclose that an illegal tape has been made, since the term "Contents", as used in the statute to define what may not be disclosed, is defined to include "any information concerning the identity of the parties to the communication or the *existence,* substance, purport, or meaning of that communication." Md. Code Ann. § 10-401(7) (1997) (emphasis added).

30. There is no doubt that the Jones lawyers believed they had a significant tactical advantage due to their knowledge of the Tripp tapes. They may also have known that Ms. Tripp was an OIC agent. After being asked a highly specific series of questions about Ms. Lewinsky, the President replied, "I don't even know what you're talking about, I don't think," and one of the Jones lawyers, James Fisher, responded, "Sir, I think this will come to light shortly, and you'll understand" (p. 85).

31. Recent news reports indicate that Ms. Tripp was specifically warned at the Radio Shack store where she brought her tape recorder that it was illegal to tape in Maryland without the consent of the other party. *See, e.g.,* "Tripp Was Told of Law at Store," *The Baltimore Sun,* Aug. 28, 1998, at A1.

32. "Pressgate", *Brill's Content,* August 1998, at 128.

33. *See, e.g.,* Stephen Brill, "Pressgate" in Brill's Content (August 1998) at 127 ("Isikoff says that when he talked to Starr deputy Jackie Bennett, Jr., on Thursday [January 15], Bennett begged him to wait until Friday before trying to call Jordan, the White House, or Lewinsky about his story. ... Isikoff says he agreed to hold off in exchange for getting a full report on how the stings had gone.").